Surmounting the Barricades

T0327129

Surmounting the Barricades

Women in the Paris Commune

Carolyn J. Eichner

INDIANA UNIVERSITY PRESS
BLOOMINGTON AND INDIANAPOLIS

This book is a publication of

Indiana University Press
601 North Morton Street
Bloomington, IN 47404–3797 USA

http://iupress.indiana.edu

Telephone orders   800–842–6796
Fax orders   812–855–7931
Orders by e-mail   iuporder@indiana.edu

Library of Congress Cataloging-in-Publication Data

Eichner, Carolyn Jeanne, date
     Surmounting the barricades : women in the Paris Commune /
Carolyn J. Eichner.
         p.   cm.
     Includes bibliographical references and index.
     ISBN 0-253-34442-5 (cloth : alk. paper)—
ISBN 0-253-21705-9 (pbk. : alk. paper)
     1. Paris (France)—History—Commune, 1871.   2. Women
revolutionaries—France—Paris—History—19th century.   I. Title.
DC317.E38 2004
944.081'2—dc22   2004004564

1   2   3   4   5   09   08   07   06   05   04

For my parents
Corrine Bochan Eichner and Norman Eichner

CONTENTS

ACKNOWLEDGMENTS

I first discovered the communardes over fifteen years ago. The revolutionary passion of these women and the beauty of their egalitarian ideals fascinated me as I began my graduate studies. They possessed the will to "surmount the barricades" circumscribing women's lives, whether the economic, political, and social barricades of gender and class, or the literal barricades of a street-fought civil war. This book endeavors to surmount the intellectual and historical barriers not only to understanding feminist socialism as central to the Paris Commune and subsequent fin-de-siècle gender and class politics, but also of the Paris Commune to the history of feminist socialism, and thus more broadly, of feminism.

Over the years of developing this project I have incurred innumerable debts of gratitude. The History Department at Northern Illinois University, where I earned my M.A. in 1988, introduced me to the ideals of historical scholarship and teaching. I am deeply grateful to Harvey Smith, William Beik, Margaret George, and the late Marvin Rosen for their encouragement and guidance, as both mentors and friends. These scholars, by word and example, taught me the power and meaning of history, as well as the extraordinary value of becoming an historian.

UCLA was a fantastic and exciting place to be a graduate student, an experience enriched by a wonderful group of faculty, friends, and colleagues. Among the faculty, I benefited enormously from the knowledge, generosity, and support of Kathryn Norberg, Carole Pateman, Ruth Milkman, Robert Brenner, and John Hatch. Thanks to Barbara Bernstein for her warmth and her help in my navigations through the system. I owe a special debt of gratitude to Edward Berenson for his ongoing mentoring, as well as for his continuing encouragement and friendship. Ed's creative and careful scholarship, and his vivid, flowing prose style, continue to inspire and motivate me.

I have been extremely fortunate in receiving guidance and ongoing support from several thoughtful and generous feminist scholars. I am enormously indebted to Karen Offen, who read and critiqued several chapters of both my dissertation and book manuscript, who shared her unpublished manuscript with me, and who continues to inspire me both by her work and by her truly feminist mentoring and friendship. I have also benefited from a similarly warm relationship with Marilyn Boxer; Marilyn's groundbreaking scholarship on French feminist socialists has deeply influenced my work, and her extensive feedback has helped shaped the best parts of this book. My sincere gratitude goes to Laura Levine Frader for her fine example of feminist labor history and her exceptionally helpful critique of earlier versions of this work; to Rachel Fuchs for her intellectual and personal enthusiasm and support; and to Elinor Accampo for combining feminist critique with theoretical rigor. I would also like to thank Claire Goldberg Moses, Mary Lynn Stewart, and Louise Tilly for their beneficial feedback on portions of this project.

Over the years my work has benefited enormously from many friends and colleagues who have read part or all of the manuscript in its many different stages as it evolved from dissertation to book. My thanks to Holly Brewer, Kirsten Fischer, Sharon Gillerman, Ellen Healy, Sandie Holguìn, Steven Johnston, Shreeram Krishnaswami, Bob Levy, Jim Lichti, James Snyder, and Lori Weintrob. I also want to thank Vikka and Victor Peppard for the translations from the Russian, and Antje Strupp for sharing the photograph of Elisabeth Dmitrieff. My graduate and undergraduate students at the University of South Florida supplied helpful ideas and terrific enthusiasm; Ingrid Laracuente, J. T. McCormick, and Edwin Reynolds deserve special recognition for reading the developing manuscript time and again. My colleagues in the Department of Women's Studies at USF encouraged interdisciplinary approaches while creating a collegial space for feminist discussion and rapport. To Tom Mertes, who met the communardes at the same time that I did, I owe enormous and loving thanks for eternal help, encouragement, and kindness, and I thank him for his careful critiques of my work. I am also profoundly grateful to Philip Minehan for his wonderful friendship, intellectual challenges, superb editing, and creative humor.

A great number of librarians and archivists have helped and guided me over the years. I particularly appreciate the efficient and patient Interlibrary Loan staffs at both UCLA and the University of South Florida. My work literally could not have been done without their assistance. I do, however, expect to see a library wing with my name on it, built from the proceeds of my overdue fines. I also remain grateful to Natalya Fishman, the head of Interlibrary Loan at the Morton Grove Public Library, who went above and beyond the call to obtain books for me, and thereby helped make possible my six months of dissertation writing in Chicago. The staff at the International Institute for Social History in Amsterdam was extremely helpful; I am especially indebted to Mieke Ijzermans, the Information Director at the Institute, not only for repeatedly facilitating my research efforts, but also for her warm hospitality and friendship. In France, many librarians and archivists generously, and often enthusiastically, aided my research. I want to thank the staffs at the Bibliothèque Marguerite Durand, Bibliothèque Historique de la Ville de Paris, Archives de la Prefecture de la Police, Archives Historiques de la Guerre, Bibliothèque Nationale, and the Archives Nationale. Thanks also to L'Association André Léo for providing me with the André Léo photo; to Les Amis de la Commune de Paris for their enthusiasm about my project and their commitment to the Commune; and especially to Alain Dalotel for his scholarly and political inspiration. I appreciate the accommodating and patient archivists who guided me, as a neophyte historian, through the wonderfully rich Schulkind Collection at the University of Sussex in England. Perry Anderson's generous hospitality helped make this early research trip possible.

At the University of South Florida, a generous Research and Creative Scholarship Grant, and a Faculty Development Grant, funded research trips to both Paris and Amsterdam. Earlier travel grants from both the Department of History and the Center for the Study of Women at UCLA facilitated my dissertation research trips. The Center for the Study of Women's Mary Wollstonecraft Award supported additional research for revisions beyond the dissertation.

At Indiana University Press, Marilyn Grobschmidt aggressively pursued the manuscript and supported it through the earliest publication stages. Robert Sloan, Jane Quinet, and Jane Lyle subsequently took great care in shepherding the book to its completion. I could not imagine a more careful and thorough copy editor than Joyce Rappaport. I also want to thank the press's readers who delivered highly thoughtful and constructive critiques of the work. Portions of Chapters 6 and 7 appeared as "'Vive la Commune': Feminism, Socialism, and Revolutionary Revival in the Aftermath of the 1871 Paris Commune," in the *Journal of Women's History* 15, no. 2 (Summer 2003); my thanks to Indiana University Press for permission to reprint this article. An earlier form of Chapter 3, "'To Assure the Reign of Work and Justice': The *Union des femmes* and the Paris Commune of 1871," was published in *Osterreichische Zeitschrift für Geschichtswissenschaften* 9, no. 4 (1998) as well.

This would be a different and far inferior book without the enormous contributions of Kennan Ferguson, for which I have continually threatened to give him co-authorship. Over the past five years he has read every word, every revision, every step of the way, consistently encouraging me to write more critical and theoretical history. Kennan's exceptional mind and superb scholarship inspire me daily, as does his seemingly endless patience and support. His intellectual and loving companionship has deeply enriched my work and my life.

Finally, my family has been incredibly supportive throughout the life of this project. My sister Susan Eichner has continuously provided expert editing and a long-distance "grammar hotline," answering my numerous calls for help with the intricacies of the English language. I appreciate her knowledge and her willingness to share it, and I truly value the long-term role she has played in this book project. My parents, Corrine Bochan Eichner and Norman Eichner, have literally made this work possible. My mother's feminism and social justice activism in the National Council of Jewish

Women, my father's unwavering support of her work, and both parents' decades-long advocacy of progressive causes have provided me with extraordinary influences and role models. A person could not have better parents. I dedicate this book to them with enormous gratitude for a lifetime of love, tolerance, and support.

Surmounting the Barricades

Introduction

On March 18, 1871, a group of Parisian women stepped between armed soldiers and cannons, deploying their words and bodies to block the removal of artillery from their working-class neighborhood. Ordered to fire, the troops instead raised their rifle butts in the air, turned, and arrested their general. Within hours, the general lay dead, the army had pulled out of the city, and the cannons remained in place. This spark ignited the revolutionary civil war known as the Paris Commune, a seventy-two day attempt to establish a radically democratic and social republic. Fired by working women's action, the insurrection developed as a ripe environment for the emergence and elaboration of multiple feminist socialisms. Communardes entered the fight to challenge and change the institutions and power relations that oppressed them.[1] Their radicalization and inspirations arose from an interplay of forces, including feminist and socialist ideals; everyday economic and social marginalizations; gender, class, and religious-based subjugations and resentments; participation in political activism in the preceding years; and the popular legacy of Parisian women's revolutionary tradition. Across the city, insurgent women enacted, inspired, theorized, and led revolution. Communardes formed political clubs and vigilance committees; wrote and edited radical newspapers; established a women's labor association; organized girls' schools; marched in the streets; served as battlefield nurses, cooks, and

1

combatants; and finally fought the invading French national army on the barricades.

During the Commune, Parisian women defied barriers to their political, economic, and military participation, challenging dominant gender ideologies and practices. Communardes seized the revolutionary moment to cross gender and class boundaries that limited their public and private behaviors. Working-class women established political clubs in which they assailed oppressive practices including marriage and confession, and attacked the privilege and wealth of the Catholic Church and the bourgeoisie. The highly educated, primarily bourgeois female leaders critiqued historical limitations on women's access to economic independence and full political participation. From the revolution's inception until its bloody fall, women espoused and enacted a range of feminist socialisms, working to break down existing gender and class hierarchies. In words, ideas, and actions, they struggled to surmount the ideological and physical barricades that circumscribed their lives.

This book illuminates the breadth, depth, and impact of feminist socialisms both within the Paris Commune of 1871 and, in its aftermath, *fin-de-siècle* gender and class politics. The Commune, as a break in established political and social relations, provided a fertile milieu for the birth of multiple competing and complementary feminist socialisms. Liberatory ideals, germinated in the working-class public sphere that emerged in the final years of France's "liberal" Empire, exploded into life as Paris pronounced its independence and freedom. Challenging the accepted peripheralization of the Commune within the history of feminism, this work demonstrates the range and influence of feminist socialisms, both during the insurrection and in the decades following its bloody suppression. It establishes the Commune's central importance in the development and deployment of new conceptions of political, social, and sexual justice, and tells how this experience led female revolutionaries to alter their feminist goals. Re-examining women's radical activism during this period reveals greater depth and complexity within feminist and socialist movements, as well as a richer and more complicated relationship between each movement. This study investigates three distinctly dissimilar revolutionary women leaders, André Léo, Elisabeth Dmitrieff, and Paule Mink, each of who exemplifies a particular strand of communarde feminist socialism. Neither *fin-de-siècle* feminism nor socialism can be fully understood without considering the formative impact of the plurality of communarde feminist socialisms. Historical comprehension of the Commune remains incomplete without a consideration of the integral role and impact of these ideologies and individuals.

Focusing on three revolutionary women and their individual feminist socialisms allows us to view their lives as lenses through which the Commune can be reconstructed and analyzed from feminist perspectives. Léo, Dmitrieff, and Mink established highly visible positions during the uprising, each playing a distinct revolutionary role. These women serve as exemplars of particular feminist socialisms: Léo for literary and journalistic challenges to the often class-based circumscriptions on women's choices and behavior, Dmitrieff for labor organization, and Mink for grass-roots activism and a radical language of insurrection. As thinkers, actors, and leaders, each woman differed in her form of activism and insurgency. Although renowned, influential, and engaged during this time, they and their political activism have been marginalized in the historical retelling of the Commune. Their contributions as theorists and social critics, like those of so many radical women, have been minimized or virtually erased in the historical record. Investigating, reconstructing, and reincorporating their lives and ideas will elucidate the plural contexts that produced both the revolution and these revolutionaries.

The existing historiography presents a limited and incomplete understanding of the extent, diversity, and impact of communarde ideas and actions, and tends to discount their importance within the histories of both feminism and socialism. Mink, Léo, and Dmitrieff typify these revolutionary women in their historiographical invisibility. Among the contemporary accounts of the Commune published in the immediate insurrectionary aftermath, most of the works polarize into two camps: those of the left, which portray the event in a positive, often glorified light; and those of the right, which depict it as a criminal, threatening mob action. The pro-Commune literature either ignores women, or briefly and superficially discusses their roles. The anti-Commune texts depict revolutionary women as wild, evil, and unnatural, most frequently citing them as the *petroleuses,* the mythical women blamed for burning Paris. This dichotomy in the scholarship persisted well into the twentieth century. In 1963, the historian Edith Thomas published her groundbreaking *Les Petroleuses,* appropriating this derogatory term and reinscribing it as a positive, empowered descriptor for "all the women who were involved in the revolutionary movement of 1871."[2] Her text generally serves as a demarcation in both English- and French-language monographs on the Commune: while those published prior to Thomas's study barely mention women,[3] those appearing after it tend to cite her work, although generally in a perfunctory manner.[4]

Initiated in the 1950s and 1960s by Eugene Schulkind, Thomas, and Alain Dalotel (who continues to elaborate his germinal examinations of communarde feminism and revolutionary activism), historical analysis of women in the Commune has recently experienced a resurgence after years of neglect, yet the range and import of radical women's politics, ideology, and revolutionary activism has remained largely unexplored.[5] Within the current literature, works by Gay Gullickson, Martin Johnson, and Kathleen Jones and Françoise Vergès have considered issues of women's representation, citizenship, and politics, respectively.[6] Some studies place the communardes clearly within the history of feminism, but only briefly address the topic in the context of much broader works: Claire Goldberg Moses on nineteenth-

3

century French feminism, Maïté Albistur and Daniel Armogathe on French feminism since the Middle Ages, and more recently, Karen Offen, in her rich work on European feminisms.[7]

Not only does the historiography lack a thorough examination of communarde feminisms, but some scholarship also unequivocally excludes communardes from the ranks of feminists. For example, Laurence Klejman and Florence Rochefort, in *L'Egalité en marche: le féminisme sous la Troisième République,* contend that "it would be wrong to identify women's participation in the [Commune] as feminist. The question of the equality of the sexes was not the order of the day . . . undoubtedly because of the gravity of the situation," attributing a less than dire character to women's subjugation, and disregarding the enormous evidence of communardes' focus on "the equality of the sexes."[8] More recently, Marisa Linton, in her article "Les femmes et la Commune de Paris de 1871" in *Revue historique* (1997), rejects the "feminist" label as essentially anachronistic, arguing that our contemporary conception of feminism would have meant little to the average nineteenth-century working woman.[9] By attributing this singular and fixed meaning to feminism, Linton belies the multiple and historically specific conceptualizations of the term, and with that its enormous analytical and descriptive value.

The word *feminist,* as Karen Offen explains, originated in the French *féminisme.* Emerging from uncertain sources in the 1880s, the term came into wide use in the early 1890s, primarily due to the suffragist Hubertine Auclert, who began self-identifying as a feminist in her newspaper *La Citoyenne.* Communardes were clearly feminists, if feminism is defined—as I define it—as the recognition and condemnation of power inequities between men and women, and the desire and efforts to rectify these relationships. While the term (or any synonym) did not exist before the 1880s, the people, ideas, and actions that fit this definition certainly did. Thus, following Offen, I employ "a careful definition of terms, grounded in historical evidence" in my use of *feminism* for the pre-1880 period.[10]

Like *feminism* and *feminist,* the term *feminist socialism* did not exist during this period. In the absence of any comparable contemporary label, I use *feminist socialisms* to describe the set of ideologies that advocate an end to interwoven inequitable gender and class hierarchies, and a social, political, and economic reconfiguration into a society that does not subscribe to these inequities. Communardes were feminist socialists because their positions brought a gendered critique to a class analysis. Some developed theories of these enmeshed oppressions; some sought to redefine and reconfigure socialist movements and goals to make them integrally feminist; others more informally condemned male and bourgeois power. The label *feminist socialist* reflects these women's (and some men's) understanding of gender and class oppressions as interlinked but not unified: to remedy one would not necessarily result in the other's rectification, thus, the compound nature of the designation.

The problem of categorizing communardes, or more precisely of determining revolutionary women's self-identity, took another form in earlier historical studies of French feminism. Marie-Hélène Zylberberg-Hocquard, in *Féminisme et syndicalisme en France* (1978), argued that "the women of the Commune considered themselves as proletarian combatants, not as female combatants," constructing the two groups as mutually exclusive, and misconstruing most activist women's understanding of themselves during this period.[11] Revolutionary women rose as members of the working class, mostly as artisans rather than proletarians in the Paris of 1871. But their class-based antagonisms emerged from an unequivocal sense of their female-ness and the intertwining set of oppressions this engendered. A second example of an artificial dichotomy between class and gender consciousness, as well as a misreading of communardes' concerns, appeared in Charles Sowerwine's 1982 *Sisters or Citizens? Women and Socialism in France since 1876.* Analyzing Paule Mink, one of the three central communardes in the present study, Sowerwine asserted that "Mink's lack of concern for women's rights was typical of the Communard women." By narrowly defining women's rights as no more than civic rights, Sowerwine denied Mink her feminist activism.[12] Before the Commune, Mink unequivocally claimed full political and legal rights for women. Radicalized by the revolution, she and most other communardes abandoned those goals, focusing instead on social and economic issues. Rights-based goals remained the purview of the mostly bourgeois, republican feminists. Communardes rejected the goal of formal rights as irrelevant within the shifting insurgent context, perceiving themselves on the brink of a new world. They sought, instead, an end to existing gender, class, and religious hierarchies, and a reconceptualization of these socio-economic relations to improve the conditions of women's lives. Sowerwine continued by arguing that "Mink saw herself as a revolutionary, not as a woman," misrepresenting the core of Mink's self-conception as simultaneously and compatibly a woman, a mother, and a revolutionary.[13]

The one woman who has received extensive scholarly attention is the dramatic and iconoclastic anarchist Louise Michel. In a reductionist turn, Michel has, for many, come to be equated with communarde feminist socialism. An absence of attention to other activist women, as well as a romanticization and magnification of her ideas and actions (something she strongly fostered during her life), has led to a diminution in our understanding of the variety and complexities of women's revolutionism and of feminist socialisms that existed during the revolution. Michel undoubtedly played an important role in the Commune and its aftermath, but her role requires contextualization. While she is not central to this study, her participation and significance within the revolution, her relationship with Paule

Mink in the post-Commune years, her feminist anarchist politics, and her ultimate elevation to "legendary" status provide valuable comparative and contextual elements within this larger analysis of feminist socialisms and radicalism. But when historians present one woman as indicative of all female participation, communardes are made to appear as a unitary social, political, and intellectual entity. The assumption that a single person could stand for all, minimizes the importance of revolutionary women and reduces them to a type.

Revolutionary women brought together a range of both feminisms and socialisms, consequently engendering a variety of feminist socialisms. Activists' positions contrasted and complemented each other, reflecting the multiplicities of experiences and perspectives among the insurgent female Parisian population. These women held varied understandings of, desires for, and approaches to socio-economic, political, and cultural change. Feminist socialists shared the belief that they stood on the threshold of the new society, a world ushered in by the Commune and awaiting the sculpting hand of a successful revolution. In the aggregate, this primarily working-class population sought women's emancipation, the abolition of class-based privilege and inequalities, and an end to the power and influence of the Catholic Church. Yet their conceptualizations of each of these goals differed, as did their understandings of how best to attain them. Working-class women's radicalization arose from their familial, economic, political, and social oppressions, denials, and indignities. The politicization of bourgeois communardes emerged from a range of ideological and political influences, and from their particular gendered experiences and perceptions. Revolutionary women's ideologies developed in several strains and along a variety of axes, including dramatic, violent change versus gradual evolution, highly centralized control versus anarchical autonomy, and top-down versus grassroots organization.

The politics, practices, and ideals of Léo, Dmitrieff, and Mink negotiated these tensions. Each represented a particular feminist socialist approach to making revolution. Léo theorized and critiqued civil war and revolution, publishing essays and articles and editing *La Sociale,* an unequivocally pro-Commune newspaper; she embraced an individualist feminism enmeshed with a gradualist, collectivist socialism. Léo believed in teaching and raising the political consciousness of workers and peasants, women and men, leading them to embrace radical change. Elisabeth Dmitrieff organized and led working women, establishing the *Union des femmes pour la défense de Paris et les soins aux blessés,*[14] a centralized association formed to reorder and revalue women's labor, and to defend the revolution; she espoused a feminism interwoven with Marxian and labor-based socialism, and Russian populism. Dmitrieff formed a highly structured citywide organization with top-down authority over its members. And Paule Mink participated in rev-

6

olutionary political clubs, groups that appropriated neighborhood churches as spaces for their anti-clerical, anti-bourgeois meetings. Mink, more than the others, stands as representative of, as well as a leader within, a larger movement: the grass-roots, rhetorically violent, popular insurgency. During the Commune, she advocated a feminism intertwined with an anarchist, decentralized socialism. Although Léo, Dmitrieff, and Mink each espoused different ideologies, they all saw the uprising as an opportunity to forge their desired forms of equality. The experience and its outcomes profoundly changed all three women.

In the aftermath of the Commune, Léo, Dmitrieff, and Mink all struggled to keep the revolutionary flame alive; this, however, had different meaning to each woman, as they followed divergent paths in their evolving political endeavors. Tracing their personal, intellectual, and political experiences from the 1860s through the 1871 uprising, into exile at its fall, and to the end of their lives and the century, the three women's histories constitute a framework in which to investigate the overlapping and disparate strains of feminist socialisms, and thereby to map radical women's activism in this era. Their experiences encompassed the rise of popular radical political action, the fall of France's Second Empire, the revolutionary event of the Commune, the profoundly reactionary backlash following the insurrection, and the emergence of the Third Republic. Shaped by ideologies, events, and structures, these women, in turn, challenged and refashioned their world.

They also fashioned themselves. Influenced by the "new biography," as elaborated by Jo Burr Margadant in her eponymously titled edited volume, my work examines how Léo, Dmitrieff, and Mink each constructed political and public selves within a historical milieu that denied such roles for women.[15] These identities shifted and changed during the course of each woman's public life, reflecting her evolving historical contexts and each individual's understanding of her desires and available options. Thus, for Léo, Dmitrieff, and Mink, the periods before, during, and after the Commune presented differing opportunities and demands for establishing personas. While asserting the relative impermanence of identity, this book emphasizes the grounding of these mobile selves in their material conditions and experiences. The Commune served as an imprimatur on each woman's identity. Léo, Dmitrieff, and Mink lived forever personally, psychically, politically, and/or socially marked as communardes. Their experiences as revolutionary veterans, as well as their individual socio-economic and cultural backgrounds, served as parameters for their outward selves. The insurrectionary event stands central not only to these women's varied experiences, but also to their evolving self-conceptions and emergent ideologies. Revolutionary women created feminist socialisms, but these movements and ideas also created them. Collective biographical methods, therefore, provide tools to investigate the plural strains of feminist socialisms: examining individual women as exemplars and embodiments of the various politics, while simultaneously interrogating the public and personal lives of these women.

Like most feminist socialist female and male socialist leaders, Léo, Dmitrieff, and Mink did not arise from the working class. Born to elite families, they enjoyed educational opportunities and at least a degree of privilege. Nonetheless, these activists deeply engaged themselves with the issues and problems affecting all women and workers. They each perceived and used their class position in different ways, but their privilege undoubtedly shaped their politics. For Léo and Dmitrieff, this perspective manifested itself in their relatively authoritative stances; while rejecting bourgeois elitism, they proffered critiques and solutions to workers who, they both believed, required education, leadership, and guidance toward emancipation. During the uprising they demonstrated their top-down approaches, Léo as the already well-known, male-pseudonymed editor of a revolutionary daily newspaper, and Dmitrieff as the founder and leader of a highly centralized labor and defense organization. Mink, by contrast, embraced the radicalized grass-roots politics emerging within the Commune's working-class political clubs, participating as a firebrand speaker and agitator, but considering herself a spark rather than a guide.

The variety of feminist socialisms emerged, at least in part, due to the disparate histories of their leaders. Birth into elite status did not guarantee ongoing access to privilege. Mink, for example, the French-born daughter of impoverished Polish noble parents, spent most of her adult life in economic need, as a mother, most often single-handedly raising her children. Her lived experience, therefore, gave her particular insight into working women's plight. Dmitrieff, born out of wedlock to a Russian aristocrat and a German nurse, experienced social marginalization but extreme financial privilege. Sympathetic to peasants since her childhood, she nonetheless continued to see them as a group apart. Léo, daughter of a former naval officer and granddaughter of a member of the royal Legion of Honor, grew up in a bourgeois comfort fundamentally different from the lives of the workers and peasants she championed, but whom she viewed as a group apart; a family income provided her some financial security throughout her life.

The idea of communarde feminist socialism as undifferentiated belies feminism's central understanding of the personal as political. Feminist socialists' class backgrounds, familial contexts, economic experiences, political alliances, nationalities, marital states, maternal statuses, educations, and even personalities influenced and shaped their ideological evolutions. Before, during, and after the revolution, feminist socialists embraced a multiplicity of analyses, strategies, and goals. Some women flouted social convention in their marital and childrearing roles, while others subsumed their political interests to those of their husbands. Some working-class male and female Communard political club participants advocated violence against priests and nuns, while the elite communarde leaders asserted a more moderate anti-clericalism. They all sought the reordering of both the gender and class structures, but, at least in part, their particular politics emerged from personal beliefs, experiences, and desires.

The manifestations of anti-clericalism among Communards demonstrated this diversity of positions. Virtually all Communards opposed the power and influence of the Catholic Church; acrimony toward the institution and its representatives was nearly as central as rancor toward the repressive state. Differences in ecclesiastical antagonism, however, existed in kind and degree. The communarde leadership invoked the French revolutionary tradition of opposing the institution and hierarchy of the Church, but not the ideals of faith. For anti-clerical working-class women, the Church represented excessive wealth and a force of unwanted influence and intervention in their lives. Its architecture dominated their neighborhoods, and its representatives and the prevalence and authority of its doctrine pervaded their intimate relationships, families, and communities. Working-class women and men directly expressed their resentments by appropriating churches as meeting places for political clubs, and these gatherings rang with intense anti-clerical rhetoric. In the extreme, some communardes espoused a radical anti-religiosity and, in a break with the French revolutionary legacy, passionately denied the existence of God. Anti-clericalism increasingly grew among France's left wing after the Commune, becoming integral not only to socialism but also eventually to republicanism, and leading, by the 1880s, to a progressively secularized state. For some *fin-de-siècle* feminist socialists, including Mink, only social revolution would truly temporalize the state, and with it, society. Reformist measures would not suffice.

Communarde feminist socialisms constituted a crest in the erratic development of feminist socialisms in nineteenth-century France. They arose from a tradition reaching back to the revolutionary women of 1793, the utopian socialists of the 1830s and 1840s, the female insurgents of 1848, and the re-emerging feminist socialisms of the late, liberalized Second Empire. In the troughs between these times, repressive governments suppressed movements challenging gender, class, state, or Church power. Conscious of their revolutionary heritage as Parisian women, both the rank and file and the leaders among the communardes embraced and repeatedly invoked this tradition, as exemplified by one *clubiste* who spurred women on, reminding them of their duty to the memory of "our grandmothers of '93."[16] Parisian women embraced the palpable tradition of their radical forebears, invoking the shared history of militant uprising to excite and encourage female militancy in 1871.

Most revolutionary women jettisoned political rights-based equality as a goal during the Commune, even many who had embraced it earlier, including Léo and Mink. The predominant tradition in the history of feminism, however, is to define French feminism as existing within the boundaries of bourgeois liberalism. This bourgeois, or republican, feminism also emerged from the French revolutionary legacy, but from a divergent ideology. Republican feminism had developed from the Enlightenment tradition emphasizing civic and individual rights, including suffrage and equality under the law, as exemplified by thinkers such as Condorcet and Olympe de Gouges. Communarde feminists' marginalization within the history of feminism is at least partially attributable to their rejection of individualistic rights-based feminism in favor of primarily social and economic feminism.

Even historians who address the divergences within feminism, such as Joan Scott, conceptualize feminism as a product of liberal individualism. In *Only Paradoxes to Offer: French Feminists and the Rights of Man,* Scott contends that feminism emerged from and is constituent of the contradictions inherent in the language of liberal individualism. To present her assertion schematically, feminists challenged their exclusion from political rights based on the promise of those rights to all autonomous individuals; "individuals," however, were defined as male in opposition to the category female, so women demanded these supposedly universal rights based on their particularity as females. For Scott, feminism thus grounds itself on a paradox.[17] Communarde feminist socialists, however, recognized that individual political rights guaranteed only partial liberty and equality; they understood that only the establishment of social and economic equity, what they termed "the social republic," could create a just society. The majority of these women did not demand political rights, which placed them outside the liberal tradition.

Republican feminists, by contrast, sought women's political equality under a system of political democracy; issues of class and social and economic equity remained external to their concerns. Primarily members of the bourgeoisie, these women saw their emancipation in reform of the law, specifically of the Napoleonic Code. Introduced by its namesake in the first years of the nineteenth century, this Civil Code gave all citizens equal rights under the law, but denied women citizenship. Codifying the Rousseauian dichotomy between public man and private woman, the Code relegated women, particularly married women, to the state of a minor child: the wife owed the husband obedience in return for his protection. The Code, for example, stipulated that married women could not control their own wages, property, or the financial or legal affairs of their children; women automatically took on the nationality of their husbands; they could not live apart from their husbands; woman's adultery could lead her to prison, while a man faced no penalty for the same act, unless undertaken in the marital bed (and then he could only be fined); a husband could legally murder his wife if he caught her with her lover, but if the tables were turned it became a crime; and unmarried women could make no legal claims of paternity. While republican feminists fought to remove the gross inequities in this law code, feminist socialists struggled to eradicate the political forms that engendered and perpetuated such an unjust system.

Recognizing the variety and impact of feminist socialisms emerging within the Commune provides a fuller understanding of the uprising and its aftermath. Theoretically, it demonstrates the complexity of gender, ideology, and action within revolutions. Historiographically, it presents a more accurate picture of the insurrection, its participants, and its context. The rise of the Commune constituted a catalyst for the transformation and generation of plural forms of feminist socialism. The centrality of the Commune in the history of feminist socialism, and thus its importance in the history of feminism, diminishes radically without this understanding. Identifying and analyzing the diversity of feminist socialisms contributes to the richness and complexity of the history of feminism.[18] It also acts as a corrective to the history of socialism. Addressing the role and impact of feminists and feminisms on the era's various socialisms demands a reconceptualization of the movement's development and politics.[19]

As individual activists, Léo, Dmitrieff, and Mink played influential roles in the Commune and its aftermath. Pushing gender and class boundaries, they literally made revolution. And through their radical acts and ideas, they challenged the existing gendered systems. Each individually overcame societal expectations of marriage and childrearing. They all rose to leadership positions, traveled independently, spoke publicly, critiqued and challenged the dominant authorities and societal structures, and attained renown among the communarde population. They earned fame among Communards and socialists, but they also gained infamy among the forces of order and the critics of the uprising. Léo, Dmitrieff, and Mink's biographies are histories of the Commune. Re-examining the event, its antecedents, and its aftermath through the stories of these women's lives illuminates the Commune's status as a true revolution, replete with ideas and endeavors that would fundamentally alter not only class but also gender hierarchies.

The structure of this book reflects the complex relationships between history, biography, politics, ideas, and experience. Divided into three parts, "Before," "During," and "After," it is constructed around the Commune as the central event. The revolution holds a pivotal role in this forty-year era, standing squarely within that history. Contextualizing the uprising locates it as emerging from the developing political and social movements of the immediately previous years; these movements were clearly the seedbed not only of a number of socialisms, but also for many feminisms and anti-clericalisms whose roots took hold within this milieu. Growing from here, they burst forth during the Commune, flowering as multiple varieties of anti-clerical feminist socialisms. Léo, Dmitrieff, and Mink lived these ideologies. Each woman survived revolutionary repression and struggled to keep her feminist socialist vision a vital force through the subsequent decades. As a result of their status as well-known, high-profile activists, they left paper trails of documentary evidence, whether self-produced or generated by critics and observers; the surviving record, which varies by woman in volume and kind, allows the reconstruction and analysis of their ideas, experiences, actions, and identities across nearly four decades.

Part I, "Before," begins with Chapter 1, "The Actors and the Action," which introduces Léo, Dmitrieff, and Mink and retells the story of the Commune from a feminist perspective, interweaving the revolutionary tale with the women's biographical backgrounds. Examining their socio-economic, cultural, familial, and educational histories, the chapter begins to construct multi-dimensional images of each actor's richly evocative experience and her early environment. The three women's personal and early influences and the beginnings of their political activism illuminate the development of their individual ideologies and evolution of their public personas that reached fruition during the Commune. Differences within their backgrounds contributed to the divergent politics and revolutionary visions and identities that each woman ultimately embraced.

Chapter 2, "Politics and Ideas: Staging the Struggle," investigates women's participation in the political opposition and social activism emerging in the late 1860s, in France for Léo and Mink, and in Russia, Switzerland, and England for Dmitrieff. It traces each activist's developing ideologies and forms of expression as she crafted her public self in response to myriad political, intellectual, and personal influences. All three women participated in and worked to influence the International Workingmen's Association, reflecting the organization's diverse ideological membership. Dmitrieff crossed borders to study, to organize workers, and to build a movement to break down barriers of gender, class, and nations. Mink developed a reputation as a feminist socialist and anti-clerical public orator and agitator. Léo, like Mink, actively engaged in the increasingly revolutionary culture developing in Paris, cultivated within the context of a burgeoning working-class public sphere. Léo especially established herself as a successful and respected novelist, journalist, and social critic.

Part II, "During," analyzes the Commune as a unique political and social juncture in which women forged their visions of a just society, seizing the opportunities presented by the larger insurgency. The Commune engendered a range of feminist socialisms that erupted into action in differing, yet mutually supportive ways. They all sought a successful culmination to the social revolution, resulting in an egalitarian society devoid of oppressive gender, class, and religious hierarchies. But, in the insurrectionary process of attaining this goal, they took divergent paths, espoused varied methods, and embraced a range of conceptions of the shape and contours of their ultimate objective. The three female leaders represent three differing types of feminist socialism: the *During* chapters each bear Dmitrieff, Léo, and Mink's names, respectively, but they by no means focus solely on these women. These central chapters demonstrate the richness and diversity of feminist socialisms, and the multiplicity of feminist socialists, vitally present during the uprising. Elaborating critical aspects of these ideologies explicates and differentiates them within the insurrectional milieu.

Chapter 3, "Elisabeth Dmitrieff and the *Union des femmes:* Revolutionizing Women's Labor," examines an organizational approach to feminist socialism, one which established structures and systems to reorder and revalue women's work, and, correspondingly, to assure their access to economic independence. Dmitrieff established the *Union des femmes pour la défense de Paris et les soins aux blessés,* a city-wide women's labor and revolutionary defense association. She planned and implemented the sophisticated program to refigure female labor into producer-owned cooperatives, demonstrating her centralized, top-down feminist socialism. The organization's title reflected the immediate reality of the revolution—if the uprising failed, the opportunity to reorganize women's labor and release women from their disempowered, impoverished work and economic conditions would die with the revolution. Thus, defense became the key to future success and change.

The fourth chapter examines the type of feminist socialism that contested the class and gender-based limitations on women's choices and behavior, as well as the concomitant assumptions and judgments placed on women who transgressed these bounds. "André Léo and the Subversion of Gender: The Battle over Women's Place," explores Léo as exemplary of these contestations: during the Commune she aggressively opposed existing constructions of women's place. Her literary and philosophical approach to creating revolution and critiquing extant gender hierarchies involved theorizing and defending female battlefield roles, challenging the dominant ideologies and images of gender, and championing a fundamentally reconceptualized educational system for girls. Léo viewed revolution as a means to create the space to develop her egalitarian vision, and she led other communardes fighting for the same goals.

Chapter 5, "Paule Mink and the *Clubistes:* Anti-Clericalism and Popular Revolution," investigates the radical working-class approach to insurgency arising from women in political clubs. Mink embodied the type of grass-roots revolutionism embraced by *clubistes* as they verbally, and at times physically, attacked symbols of class, gender, and religious hierarchies. The political culture that emerged from these clubs constituted a popular insurgency deemed threatening not only by the Commune's opponents, but also by the revolution's leaders. This type of feminist socialism lacked the implicit hierarchies and top-down natures of either Dmitrieff or Léo, emphasizing instead egalitarianism and radical democratic action.

Finally, Part III, "After," examines the impact of the uprising and its repression on the three women's lives, reconstructing their subsequent political, intellectual, and personal experiences. Chapter 6, "Dmitrieff and Léo in the Aftermath: Radical Denouement" explores their activism and their environments as each evolved in the post-Commune world, for Dmitrieff in an increasingly repressive Russia, and for Léo in Switzerland, Italy, and then republican France. Each woman initially re-engaged with radical movements, but subsequently slipped out of the limelight, Dmitrieff falling into complete isolation and obscurity in the suppressive Russian context, and Léo gradually withdrawing from organized politics and public involvement, yet never ceasing her intellectual productivity.

Chapter 7, "Mink in the Aftermath: The Red Flag and the Future," investigates Mink's post-Commune life in Switzerland and France. Her feminist socialism, as that of Léo's in this period, engaged with the rise of France's Third Republic, the evolution of anti-clericalisms, and the development of the era's multiple feminisms, socialisms, and feminist socialisms. In contrast to the two other women, Mink continued a life of flamboyant public activism and revolutionary agitation, remaining firmly in the public eye. These *After* chapters examine the Commune's indelible impact on each woman and on the European political landscape, tracing and contextualizing their subsequent ideological and personal evolutions and political actions through the turn of the century and to the ends of their lives.

Part I
Before

1

The Actors
and the Action

Three weeks into the revolution, and one week after France's national army began bombarding Paris, Elisabeth Dmitrieff posted and published a call to the women of the Paris Commune:

> *Citoyennes*, the decisive hour has arrived. It is time that the old world come to an end! We want to be free! And France is not rising alone, all the civilized people have their eyes on Paris . . . *Citoyennes*, all resolved, all united . . . To the gates of Paris, on the barricades, in the neighborhoods, everywhere! We will seize the moment . . . And if the arms and bayonets are all being used by our brothers, we will use paving stones to crush the traitors![1]

Pronouncing the advent of a new world, Dmitrieff summoned women citizens (*citoyennes*) to join in the struggle to bring about its birth. Her proclamation convoked a revolutionary feminist socialist association, the *Union des femmes pour la défense de Paris et les soins aux blessés*, established to organize women to defend Paris and to reorganize women's labor into producer-owned cooperatives. This group exemplified the dual goals of many communardes: to save the revolution while creating the nascent egalitarian society. As the anti-Commune French national (Versailles) troops lay siege to Paris, inside the city walls women and men organized, debated, demonstrated, celebrated, and legislated, struggling over conflicting conceptions of their desired "true" republic, the social republic, the political form through which most Communards intended to build socialism. For insurgent women, however, the male-dominated socialist agendas, focusing almost exclusively on class and religious oppressions, remained sorely deficient in recognizing, theorizing, and addressing gender subjugation. By no means embracing a unified perspective, ideology, or critique, these women espoused a range of revolutionary visions, which they brought to the moment of the Commune. Feminist socialists of this era pried open the social and political fissures created by the uprising, and stepped in to create and promulgate their methods and means to a new world.

The Paris Commune, a seventy-two-day-long revolutionary civil war following the Franco-Prussian war, was a citywide, primarily working-class and socialist insurrection against a French national government widely considered to be reactionary and repressive. As a spontaneous uprising, the Commune allowed the emergence of a broad range of revolutionary approaches. Radical women—from the educated, mostly elite leadership to the working-class rank and file—manifested their ideological and experiential positions in an extensive variety of insurgent actions and organizations. The revolt temporarily overthrew hierarchies of gender, class, and religion, thus generating an intensely violent, viciously retributive repression by France's forces of order. The Commune was crushed at the end of May 1871, as the French army stormed Paris, attacked the peoples' barricades, and slaughtered over 25,000 Parisians.

The Commune, as a short-lived overthrow of the patriarchal status quo, served as an incubator for embryonic feminist socialisms. During the insurrection, feminist socialists played central intellectual and popular roles as journalists, organizers, orators, protesters, nurses, cooks, and fighters. They shaped the face of the Parisian revolution and, subsequently, influenced the idea of women and revolution well into the next century in Europe and beyond. Fully conscious of their revolutionary foremothers' legacies of 1789, 1793, and 1848, communardes bore the mantle of history, refashioning it with contemporary ideological and activist tools.

The story of the Commune has been told many times and in myriad ways. To its detractors, female participants came to symbolize disorder and misrule, deviance and horror, and in many ways personified the insurrection itself.[2] They loomed over subsequent decades, specters of inversion awaiting a cleft in the socio-political order into which they could slip and wreak havoc. This dominant conception of their legacy obscured the realities of communardes' roles and influence for over a century, distorting the historical understanding of the revolutionary event. Re-examining the uprising from a feminist perspective begins to refocus the clouded images.

By investigating the individual histories of three central communarde leaders, Paule Mink, André Léo, and Elisabeth Dmitrieff, we can trace these women's paths to revolutionism. The experiences and influences of their

18

lives—their familial, cultural, intellectual, political, social, and economic milieus—shaped them as thinkers and activists. The Commune provided the formative political moment for each of them. Ultimately these women's stories and that of the Commune emerge as one.

Nearly a year before the proclamation of the Commune, France declared war on Prussia in July 1870, in what André Léo termed "the last act of the imperial drama: the declaration of war, at which point the revolutionary drama began."[3] Less than two months later, in early September, the French army faced a catastrophic defeat at Sedan, during which the Prussians captured Emperor Louis Napoléon on the field of battle.[4] The news of the military disaster reached Paris on September 3. That evening in the city, where years of repression and social unrest had intertwined in an escalating dance, people spilled into the streets, and socialist and republican groups spread word of the next day's mass demonstration.[5] On September 4, France's Second Empire fell. That morning Léo and Louise Michel joined the enormous crowd "first at the *Hôtel de Ville*," where they heard "fiery orations." And then, "all at once, a cry arose: to the *Palais législatif!*"[6] They followed the throng along the Seine. Léo recounted the sense of the scene: "the crowd on the march, filling the breadth of the quai, though uttering no cry . . . striking the ground by the thousands, producing a loud and continuous din, like a mountain torrent crashing onto stones."[7]

Léo evoked the gravity and strength coursing through the crowd, wielding its mass power to assure the Empire's downfall. Michel described people, unsure whether the day would end in violence or peaceful transition, "following the boulevards, speaking somberly amongst themselves: there was anxiety in the air . . . A human sea filled the *Place de la Concorde*."[8] By late afternoon, the Empire was dead, the Republic declared, and a provisional Government of National Defense formed.[9] Victorine Brocher, founder of a cooperative bakery, member of the International, and future communarde, recounted how "thousands . . . repeated with an incomparable ardor and rapture: '*Vive la France! Vive la République!*' These cries rose from everywhere, magically affecting the crowd."[10]

Triumph and excitement rolled through the crowd; the "long and painful birth" of the Republic was complete, wrote Léo, and "finally, our freedom is here."[11] In her memoirs, she related how later that day, "Louise Michel and I . . . our hearts bursting, passed by the great gate of the Tuilleries . . . The Empress had fled that morning—It is now, I said, a beautiful public garden . . . an imperial garden which was going to become the garden of the Nation."[12] Léo and Michel fervently believed, along with many among the Parisian left, that what they considered the "true" Republic, a democratic and social Republic, had arrived. They viewed such social democracy as the ideal state form through which to develop an egalitarian society, as did many of the period's socialists.[13]

But this would not be such a state; factional politics created instead an anti-democratic authoritarian regime. Arthur Arnould, a radical journalist and future member of the Commune government, contended that by "the evening of September 4, Paris, without a doubt, had fallen under the yoke belonging to its cruelest enemies."[14] He spoke of the new Government of National Defense. Louise Michel later asserted that "Paris should have risen in remembrance of its proud and heroic tradition. The city should have cleansed itself by bathing in the blood of the Empire."[15]

Facing recent military disaster and an ongoing war, liberal republicans formed a coalition with the right-wing Orléanist and monarchist factions, hoping to end the war and the threat of social revolt.[16] General Jules Trochu, the first president of the Government of National Defense and head of the French army, exulted that this conservative alliance had successfully "hindered the demagogues from taking the defense of Paris and thus producing an immense social upheaval throughout France."[17] Right and center factions joined forces against the potential of insurgency, and also against the power of France's revolutionary heritage.

In the wake of the Empire's death and the Republic's birth, Karl Marx warned socialists that "any attempt at upsetting the new Government in the present crisis" would be a "desperate folly." Cautioning members of the International Workingmen's Association against the force of historical legacy, he urged that they "not allow themselves to be deluded by the national remembrances of 1792"[18] because, he believed, they were not ready for revolution. But the revolutionary tradition remained potent, and it took many forms. Léo wrote that upon returning home on September 4, the day the Empire fell, she felt "filled with hope that our *patrie,* delivered from the shameful yoke, would put the Prussians to flight, renewing the miracles of '93, and taking the course of revolutionary tradition."[19] At that moment, Léo's conception of following the revolutionary path meant working within the newly proclaimed republic in order to save *la patrie,* "the fatherland." Her view would change dramatically as the undemocratic nature of the republic unfolded. But when Prussia laid siege to Paris on September 18, workers and socialists rallied to the patriotic cause. Victorine Brocher recalled reassuring her mother as the siege began. Brocher invoked the year 1793, professing that "the republicans vanquished the foreigner, [and] we will do the same!"[20]

Paule Mink spent the siege with her older brother, Louis, in Auxerre, writing provocative pieces for the newspaper *La Liberté,* and urging and ultimately leading citizens in the battle to defend their city, even as the municipal government capitulated to the Prussians. She also smuggled documents across Prussian lines with her daughter Wanda; both she and her daughter were shot and wounded. Having paid dearly for her convictions, Mink returned to Paris following France's January 1871 surrender to Prussia, on the Commune's eve.[21] Awarded the *Légion d'honneur* for her actions in defending

France, Mink refused the notable recognition. Stating that she was merely doing her duty, Mink rejected accolades from a government she fundamentally opposed.[22] The war experience likely further radicalized Mink, as she saw the republican government, the Government of National Defense, fail to protect or support its citizens, as the regime feared them more than the external enemy.

Parisians suffered through the deprivation and scarcity of the Prussian siege, generally in inverse proportion to their wealth. The Prussians allowed people in or out of the city, but barred the import of provisions. Shortages spread and prices skyrocketed. Many elites fled the city; others paid exorbitant rates for increasingly rare foodstuffs. At markets, cat replaced rabbit. At restaurants, the wealthy chose menu items including "sweet macaroni with a meat sauce . . . of field mice," "couscous of cat," "brochette of sparrow," and various zoo animals, including elephant, zebra, reindeer, and camel.[23] The government issued stipends to National Guardsmen (among them the majority of able-bodied Parisian workingmen), and subsequently to their wives. The aged, the infirm, and the unwed women received nothing. André Léo termed unmarried working-class women, particularly mothers, "the true martyrs of the siege," as unemployment and starvation rose.[24] Yet working-class Parisians remained committed to the cause of defending France.

Despite the population's willingness to continue its sacrifice in support of the war, the Government of National Defense surrendered to the enemy in January 1871, fearing urban social unrest more than Prussian domination. This sent shock waves of disbelief through the city, which was rocked by the deception. Mink described Parisians left "shuddering with sadness and rage."[25] These sentiments intensified two months later as the newly elected, deeply conservative, heavily monarchist National Assembly passed a series of rather draconian measures that harshly affected Paris's working classes. The Assembly terminated National Guardsmen's pay, lifted the ban on pawnshops selling goods that had been deposited during the siege (often a worker's tools of trade, a family's cooking pots, or a person's only valuable goods), ended the moratorium on rents, introduced measures restricting speech and assembly, and, in an act perceived by many as an abandonment of the city, moved the National Assembly from urban Paris to semi-rural Versailles.[26] The historical antipathy between Paris and the provinces reached a fever pitch.

The city of Paris seethed with discontent and frustration as the Government of National Defense, now led by the profoundly conservative Adolphe Thiers, attempted to subdue the population and restore order. Working-class Parisians reacted against the government's capitulation and escalating repression. On February 20, Léo undertook a mission to the provinces to convince peasants that they and working-class Parisians suffered under a shared yoke of oppression; she hoped to garner their support for a move toward socialism. Days after Léo's departure, and just prior to the Prussians' triumphant ceremonial entry into the capital, Parisian workers dragged cannons across the city, away from the area of Prussian occupation, to the safety of the popular districts. These Parisians mistrusted the Prussians as well as the *capitulard* Adolphe Thiers and the monarchist National Assembly. They believed that the artillery, much of which had been purchased during the war by public subscription, belonged to the National Guard, the people's army. As Mink retrospectively explained, "These cannons were truly the property of the National Guard, and they intended to defend them . . . The government made every effort to try and re-take them, secretly and by surprise if possible, not daring to risk an open struggle with the National Guard."[27]

The question of the ownership and control of the cannons emerged as a hotly contested issue between the national government and the Parisian workers and "their" army, as the government plotted and maneuvered to remove the munitions from their vigilant sentries.[28] In her unpublished memoirs, Léo expressed how "these cannons, now raised up onto the working class buttes, were turned toward the center of the city, toward the city of luxury and palaces, of monarchical plots, of infamous speculators, and of cowardly governments."[29] Workers suddenly controlled the strategically placed cannons perched over the city, focusing them on those who had so recently betrayed them. Ultimately, the government's bungled multi-pronged attack on Paris, in its attempt to reimpose order via military occupation and artillery seizure, served as the revolutionary flashpoint on the working-class buttes of Montmartre. Suffering under increasingly authoritarian measures, and bearing a strong sense of betrayal and mounting resentment, the Parisian population reacted on the morning of March 18.

In the hours before dawn on that day, French national troops entered Paris and covertly climbed the buttes of Montmartre. They intended to retrieve the cannons, and, Mink argued, "they believed, without a doubt, that [this action] would be easy." According to Mink, who was not in Montmartre that morning, "General Vinoy had *forgotten* to bring horses to pull the cannons."[30] Vinoy subsequently dispatched some of his troops to retrieve the horses, leaving the remaining soldiers waiting on the butte. This would prove to be a fatal error.

Word began to spread of the army's stealthy incursion as the early rising neighborhood women left their homes to begin their workday. Alerted to the raid, Louise Michel later recalled,

> "I descended the butte, my rifle under my coat, shouting: Treason! . . . In the rising dawn, the people heard the tocsin; we climbed the butte . . . believing we would die for liberty. We were as risen from the earth. Our deaths would free Paris."[31]

Once atop the hill, rather than finding the raging battle they expected, Michel and her confederates discovered that "between us and the army, the

women had thrown themselves on the cannons and machine-guns; the soldiers stood immobile. When General Lecomte commanded them to fire on
the crowd, a subordinate officer broke ranks and cried: 'Surrender!' The
soldiers obeyed . . . The revolution was made."[32]

Not only "throw[ing] themselves" on the artillery, as in Michel's dramatic
assertion, but the women of Montmartre had also fraternized with the remaining troops while awaiting the return of men and horses. Reminding the
soldiers of their common backgrounds, common experiences, and common
goals, the women declared, "We, our sons, our brothers, are of the army; we
are all children of France, it is not necessary for us to kill each other."[33] When
called on to shoot the National Guard troops that had arrived to defend the
cannon, the Versailles soldiers raised the butts of their guns in the air. With
this, Paris was in revolt. Victorine Brocher recounted the sensation as word
spread to the city below: "The Paris which had desired its liberation seemed
to breathe healthier air; we truly thought that a new era had begun."[34]

Paule Mink immediately immersed herself in constructing this new epoch,
something she had worked toward since her youth. Daughter of a Polish
revolutionary, Mink, born Adèle Paulina Mekarska in 1839 in Claremont-
Ferrand, France, lived a life steeped in the lore of revolution and freedom
fighting. Her father, Jean Népomucène Mekarski, a noble-born military
officer, cousin of the last Polish king, Stanislas II Poniatowski, and nephew
of the Polish general and independence leader Józef Poniatowski, participated in the November 1830 insurrection against Russia's domination of
Poland.[35] More than six thousand insurgents, many of them landed elites,
were exiled to France following the September 1831 suppression of the revolt. Mink's father and mother, Jeanne Blanche Cornelly de la Perrière, the
Polish-born daughter of a family of minor French nobility, were among
them. In Clermont-Ferrand, Mekarski, separated from his wealth, found
work as a tax collection agent; Jeanne Blanche later worked in a pastry shop.
Mekarski became a Saint-Simonian, a member of the utopian socialist group
advocating women's emancipation, and remained strongly allied with the
radical wing of the Polish independence movement.

Raised with a sense of deep connection to a subjugated Poland, and to
the ideas and values of revolution, Mink and both of her brothers became
revolutionaries: she and the younger Jules as Communards, and the older
Louis as one of the radical young intellectuals involved in the ill-fated 1863
Polish insurrection against Russia.[36] Mink identified intensely with her familial revolutionary heritage, referring to herself as a "daughter of a rebel,"[37]
while rejecting and disconnecting herself from her noble lineage. Her relatively privileged youth did provide educations for her and her two brothers;
both Jules and Louis became engineers.[38] Undoubtedly somewhat marginalized as Polish immigrants strongly connected to Poland (despite the chil-

dren's French births), and as social radicals under the Empire, the children grew up on the edges of the dominant culture. Alienated from their class, they enjoyed bourgeois economic comforts, but did not identify with that class either. All three children certainly were affected by and benefited from the cultural capital their parents brought to their French exile. The family carved out a space where independent thought and radical politics flourished. On that terrain, the young Paule developed her ideas and identity as a public opponent of gender, class, and religious oppressions.

Reflecting on her years of activism, in 1889 Mink wrote, "Since my seventeenth year I have struggled against the abuses, the privileges, and the infamies of the Empire and the conservative Republic. I have always fought independently, on my own, without any regimentation."[39] At seventeen, in 1856, Mink disrupted a clerical procession in the streets of Clermont-Ferrand. Her attack on the Catholic clergy in her first independent, public, political act foreshadowed her life-long virulent opposition to the power and hierarchies of the Catholic Church and the French state. It also presaged her decades of dramatic and often singular protest and activism. Mink served a one-week prison sentence for her anti-clerical action.[40] Clearly undeterred from radicalism, the following year she joined an outlawed workers' association, *La Couture*. This transgression brought her an eight-month jail term.[41] Within the next few years Mink migrated to Paris, involving herself in the radical life of the capital city. She established a short-lived working women's mutual aid society, the *Société fraternelle de l'ouvrière*,[42] and in 1866 joined with André Léo, Louise Michel, and the bourgeois feminist Maria Deraismes to form *La Société du droit des femmes*, an organization focusing on education, work, and marriage reform.[43] During these years Mink married a Polish engineer, Bohdanowicz, with whom she had two daughters, Wanda and Anna. The marriage ended before the Empire fell in 1870.[44]

With the liberalization of laws on speech, association, and the press in 1868, Mink established an increasingly high-profile public identity as a feminist and socialist activist, primarily speaking at political meetings and public lectures, but also publishing articles.[45] Familiar with Mink as an orator, the socialist writer and future Communard Gustave Lefrançais commented that

> Among the women who regularly speak at public meetings, one especially notices the *citoyenne* Paule Mink . . . who speaks with tremendous energy. She spiritedly makes fun of her detractors . . . and she doesn't appear, at this point, to have firmly fixed ideas on the diverse positions which divide socialists. But she is indefatigable in her propaganda.[46]

Mink developed a reputation as a flamboyant and engaging speaker, committed to change, but lacking a firm adherence to any particular radical dogma. Her experiences in the era prior to the Commune helped hone her oratorical and critical skills. But it was the revolution itself that would shape and solidify her developing feminist socialist ideology.

Throughout the first day of the insurrection, Versailles troops fraternized with local Parisians and members of the National Guard across the city. By nightfall, two generals lay dead, each shot in Montmartre by both army and National Guard troops, killed in retribution for the military's historic role in suppressing popular movements, and in the case of General Clément Thomas, specifically for his participation in the brutal repressions of 1848. Thiers responded by pulling his troops out of Paris and decamping to Versailles. Fearing a complete collapse of authority and further fraternization, Thiers brought provincial soldiers to join the Versailles army and fight Paris, relying on the traditional rural–urban hostility to retain the troops' allegiance. Meanwhile, the leaders of the Parisian left stepped up to take the reins of the city. Initially seeking an assumed peaceful conciliation with Versailles, they soon recognized that Paris had entered a revolutionary civil war, and it had fallen on them to lead it.

The Central Committee of the National Guard became the interim government, essentially by default, and they immediately concentrated on setting elections for a representative body and gaining official interim recognition from the mayors (of each of Paris's twenty *arrondissements*) to legitimize their position. Concurrently, the followers of Auguste Blanqui, the recently imprisoned revolutionary socialist, pushed the new government to attack the demoralized national troops in retreat. Oddly focused on legalistic matters, the Central Committee instead concentrated on organizing elections for the next week. The vote on March 26 created an independent municipal government of Paris that was overwhelmingly leftist republican and socialist: the Commune. Describing the official inauguration festivities at the Hôtel de Ville two days later, Louise Michel recalled that "The proclamation of the Commune was splendid . . . Their names were announced; an immense cry arose: *Vive la Commune!* The drums beat a salvo, the artillery shook the ground. 'In the name of the people . . . the Commune is proclaimed.'"[47]

The newly elected representatives stood on the steps of the Hôtel de Ville, cloaked in red sashes, beneath the revolutionary red flag and the red-draped statue of Marianne, symbol of the republic. The pseudonymous observer Marforio described communarde women "wearing red scarves in their belts, red ties in their hair, red cockades in their *coiffures*, red petticoats, and red ribbons everywhere."[48] The red of revolution carried the day, representing, at that moment, the triumph of the Left and the working class.

Among those on the dais, the allegorical statue "Marianne" constituted the lone female form.[49] No women officially ran for or won election to the Commune government. From the perspective of most of the newly elected leaders, it was an unquestioned rule that men could and should lead and undertake a revolution without women. The male leaders focused their efforts on establishing a governing body based on traditional republican ideas of representation and male suffrage. They ignored the women's central and political role in instigating the insurrection only days before, and disregarded the significant and visible political and social activism of women during the final years of Empire and the Prussian siege. When six weeks later in a *La Sociale* editorial titled "La Révolution sans la femmes" Léo asked, "Does anyone believe it possible to make a revolution without women?" the men's actions effectively answered a resounding "yes."[50]

Women played integral roles in myriad ways throughout the Commune. They formed political clubs in the tradition of 1793 and 1848, appropriating space in churches, and speaking out against hierarchies of religion, gender, and class; they re-established vigilance committees that had been organized during the Prussian siege, created a citywide labor and defense association, wrote and published newspapers and political tracts, demonstrated in the streets, and fought and nursed on the battlefield. Some espoused feminist and socialist ideologies that had been developed in the Empire's later years, and many working-class women opposed oppressive systems and practices they encountered in their daily work and family lives. Communarde feminists petitioned, appealed to, and criticized the Commune government, but they did not seek to become part of it. These women saw themselves poised on the precipice of social revolution, and believed they were witnessing the birth of a fundamentally restructured socio-economic and political system. The presumed imminence of this new order made superfluous the focus on equal political and individual rights.[51] As Louise Michel contended, "The issue of political rights is dead. Equal education, [and] equal trades, so that prostitution would not be the only lucrative profession open to a woman—that is what is real in our program . . . evolution is ended and now revolution is necessary or the butterfly will die in its cocoon."[52]

Michel's declaration against political rights reflected the intensity of revolutionary polemics, yet its emphasis was consistent with communarde feminisms. They believed that the Commune had definitively overthrown France's reactionary Republic, and had thus relegated most questions of civic and legal inequities to the historical trash heap. Suffrage and electoral politics, in the wake of Louis Napoleon's undemocratic plebiscites, would have borne the taint of Empire and hierarchical manipulation. Rejecting Enlightenment-influenced bourgeois or republican feminism and its relatively abstract rights-based goals, the communardes embraced a range of feminist socialisms, addressing the interlinked oppressions of gender and class. Recognizing that most male socialists intended to retain extant gender hierarchies, these women knew that only through their own aggressive efforts and campaigns would female emancipation be possible. They did not seek positions in the revolutionary government, which they understood to be transitory. They did, however, recognize its authority as well as its potential power, even if the system would be short-lived. Communardes turned to the governmental authority for material assistance, and opposed, challenged, and attempted to influence its decisions, actions, and inaction on many counts. But the female insurgents' faith in the ephemeral nature of this governmental form prevented them from recognizing the potential opportunity to infiltrate the institution, and thus attain a more influential, internal position. Rather, communarde feminist socialists looked beyond immediate formal politics, and labored to influence the philosophy, design, and construction of the newly developing egalitarian society. They saw the insurgency as opening the way for fresh approaches to the organization of life, work, government, and economics. The unique opportunity to contribute to this creation drew women like Elisabeth Dmitrieff to Paris.

Dmitrieff arrived in Paris within a day of the Commune's official proclamation. Leaving London, where she had been attending meetings of the International and studying the British trade unions and workers' movement, she traveled to Paris to join the insurgency. The Commune allowed her to put into practice the plans and theories she had developed in her years of activism in St. Petersburg, Geneva, and London.

Born Elisavieta Loukinitchna Koucheleva on November 1, 1850, in the town of Volok in the northwestern Russian province of Pskov, Dmitrieff was the daughter of Louka Kouchelev, an aristocratic landowner and former army officer, and Natalia-Carolina Dorothea Troskiévitch, a German nurse twenty years his junior.[53] Their five children (Elisavieta was the fourth), all born before the parents married in 1856, grew up fully aware of their "illegitimate" status. This marginalized position was exacerbated because their mother was not Russian, a situation that further pushed the children to the periphery of the provincial Russian aristocracy, among whom they lived. When Kouchelev died in 1859, three years after marrying their mother, his will referred to Elisabeth and her three surviving siblings as merely his "wards," making them recipients of his wealth but not his nobility. Kouchelev sought to protect his noble title from the taint of his own "bastards." Despite this legal status, Elisabeth and her siblings received excellent educations and substantial inheritances.[54]

Dmitrieff's childhood was replete with severe contrasts and contradictions.[55] She lived in great material comfort on a vast estate, surrounded by the deeply impoverished and oppressed peasantry, who were still enserfed during the first decade of her life and who worked the land and served her family. Her father had a reputation as a cruel and severe taskmaster, but he also had a substantial library and an interest in "new ideas." Reflecting a gendered double standard, her brother attended a prestigious school, but the girls' schools barred Dmitrieff and her sister Sophia because of their "illegitimacy." In the eyes of Russia's elite, the mark of bastardy tainted young women more severely; daughters born out of wedlock to a "common" foreign woman would undoubtedly have been considered morally suspect. The siblings had a succession of teachers from across Europe, among them the composer Modest Mussorgsky, and veterans of 1848 who made their living as tutors in exile, including an English woman, "Miss Betsy," and Prussian man named von Madievaïz.[56] Additionally, the Kouchelev family spent each winter in St. Petersburg, exposing the children to urban life during the 1860s, a period of political reform and burgeoning radicalism. Shaped by these experiences and influences, incensed at the conditions and status of the peasantry, Dmitrieff pursued knowledge and radical associations. Conscious of the prejudices toward her and her siblings, and alienated from the mainstream aristocratic community, she sought alternatives to the inequities that surrounded her.

By her teenage years, Dmitrieff had become interested in the revolutionary ideas of Karl Marx, whom she had read in the journal *Rousskoïe Slovo* (The Russian Word), and of Nicholas Chernyshevsky, author of the influential 1863 novel *What Is to Be Done?* that depicted a relatively egalitarian society.[57] These thinkers became the bases for her developing critique of class and gender hierarchies. She participated in St. Petersburg's radical intellectual youth community, but desired more formal education. Because Russia barred women from universities, Dmitrieff determined to continue her studies in Geneva. Following the example of a female character in Chernyshevsky's novel, Dmitrieff entered into a fictitious marriage, a *mariage blanc*, as a means to travel freely under the "legitimacy" of a husband's name. In 1867 she wed Colonel Mikhail Tomanovsky, an agreeable, unwell, older man; and then she and her cooperative husband went their separate ways.[58] Elisabeth Koucheleva Tomanovskaia subsequently left Russia for Geneva. At the age of sixteen, she immersed herself in the intellectual life of the politically charged city. During her three years in Geneva she studied, organized workers, and became a founding member of the Russian emigré section of the First International. Geneva became her revolutionary school, preparing her for her central role in the 1871 Parisian insurrection.

Like Mink, Dmitrieff emerged from the aristocracy, and like Mink, her status and that of her family led to her alienation from that class. In both women's cases, parental choices set their families apart: Mink's parents' revolutionary activities forced them into exile, and Dmitrieff's parents' act of having children out of wedlock created a social stigma (which her father perpetuated). Each woman also had a foreign parent, another factor that contributed to their otherness. Mink followed in her parents' revolutionary footsteps, but added her own gender critique; Dmitrieff sought to eradicate the hierarchies of class, gender, and religion that perpetuated the economic and social privileges that benefited her father (and herself, too, in terms of class), and the prejudices that oppressed her, her mother, and her siblings.

For seventy-two days, the battle for Paris raged militarily and ideologically. Beyond the city walls, the devoted but poorly disciplined and badly armed

National Guard fought the regimented and well-supplied Versailles troops. Within the city, Parisians embarked on building the new society, but differing and often conflicting visions emerged for creating this world. A freshly elected municipal government sat in the Hôtel de Ville, and while they undoubtedly wielded political, economic, and military authority, women, in particular, established alternative venues of power. Concurrent parallel and competing forms of revolution emerged in political clubs, vigilance committees, and labor associations, as well as among writers and speakers and in demonstrations in the streets. Although guns blazed outside the city gates, an air of potential, freedom, and festivity pervaded Parisian life.

The newly constituted Commune government quickly passed a series of measures to ameliorate the conditions of the working class. Their decrees included a moratorium on the sale of goods held in the *Mont-de-Piété*, the national pawnshop; cancellation of all rents due from the period of the Prussian siege; abolition of bakers' night-work; appropriation of abandoned factories by unions and workers' cooperatives; and the separation of Church and State, including the termination of government funding for the Church. On these final points Louise Michel wrote, "One imagines that the bad marriage of the Church and State, which leaves so many cadavers in its wake, could never be separated; only if both are eradicated will either disappear." [59] Michel, as well as most of the men and women of the Commune, sought an end to the power of both the Church and the conservative state. But the Commune government passed measures that were more reformist than revolutionary, and left untouched private property (unless abandoned and potentially productive—and even then, specific legalistic appropriation procedures had to be followed) and capital (the Bank of France remained undisturbed). Nonetheless, those opposing the Commune perceived its actions as deeply radical, and the actual impact on workers' lives was immediate and profound.

Seemingly reformist measures did carry revolutionary implications within them, such as, for example, the Commune's decree assuring pensions to the widows and children of all National Guardsmen, whether or not they were legally married. This act removed juridical distinctions between legally wedded couples and those in free unions; it also, for its purposes, legislated an end to illegitimacy. The Commune government's recognition and legitimization of the *unions libres* effectively subverted the power of both State and Church to sanction conjugal relations. The *unions libres* constituted the prevalent form of marital relationship among working-class Parisians. Many couples were either unable or unwilling to pay the priest's marriage fee, and most within popular communities determined such authorization unnecessary.

While measures such as those benefiting working-class Communards garnered popular support, other acts, including those less democratic and those perceived as reticent, engendered opposition. Just as the Commune government had received strong criticism from the Blanquists for taking a defensive posture rather than attacking Thiers's army at Versailles, so did they face vigorous censure from democratic socialists, including Léo and the International, for suppressing the reactionary press. This debate raged even within the editorial staff of Léo's newspaper, *La Sociale*. An April 7 piece supporting the censorship read, "To say that the press is free is not to confer on citizens the right of all to write without incurring any responsibility."[60] Léo responded, "If we act like our adversaries, how will the world be able to tell us apart?"[61] From her perspective, the Commune, as the social revolution, was abdicating its responsibilities by limiting the freedoms of those under its jurisdiction. Consistently embattled and internally riven, the municipal government struggled between retaining ideals of a social republic and instituting "extraordinary measures" to protect the revolution at virtually any cost. Weeks later, Léo again denounced the Commune authorities when they accused their own Delegate of War, Louis Rossel, of treason, a decision taken in a closed door meeting at the Hôtel de Ville. Convinced of Rossel's innocence, and incensed by the governing body's ongoing insistence on barring the public from its meetings, Léo demanded that "The people who die for this cause have the right to know who serves them and who betrays them. The true democracy does not mistrust the truth."[62] Under rising external pressure and facing mounting military losses, the Commune government turned increasingly upon itself.

André Léo was raised in a more conventional family than either Dmitrieff or Mink. A generation older than the other two women, Léo was born Victoire-Léodile Béra in 1824, in Lusignan, a village in France's Poitou region. She lived a childhood of provincial bourgeois comfort and privilege in a family with a history of public service. Léo's grandfather, Joseph Charles Béra, a member of the royal Legion of Honor, had held the post of procurer general under the Empire, and subsequently that of a deputy during Napoleon's Hundred Days. Her father, Louis Zéphirin Béra, served as a justice of the peace following his earlier career as a naval officer. Léodile's mother, Thalie Belloteau, was the third of Béra's three wives, and the mother of four of his eight children. Léo and her siblings received excellent educations in a rural setting, and came of age in a period of regional economic and population growth.[63]

The building of the railroad from Poitiers to La Rochelle fueled an expansion that brought increased urbanization and some loss of regional distinction to the Lusignan area. Resentful of these disruptive forces, Léo in her writings idealized and romanticized the peasants' lives and their traditional customs. She remembered and interpreted Lusignan's changes in her novel *La Grande illusion des petits bourgeois* (1876), in which she described how the increased industrial production necessary for building the railroad had adversely affected the morality of her fictional village's population.[64] In her work *L'Enfant des Rudère* (1881), she rued the disappearance of traditional peasant clothing both for practical and sentimental purposes. Functionally, the customary short sackcloth skirt did not "drag in the mud of the street, the dust of the field, and the sweat of work," as did the urban and fashionable long skirts that the *paysannes* now wore. She nostalgically lamented the disappearance of

> the most original part of the costume, the coronet, round in the back, triangular in front, with a transparent blue or pink under the muslin, it makes a charming frame, in which the oval of the face appears sweeter, the middle-parted hair looks blacker or blonder, the eyes more sparkling, and the skin whiter. Put the same head under a hat, or simply coiffed without a hat—she will have lost half of her splendor.[65]

Léo romanticized the peasantry as naïfs in danger of losing their picturesque characteristics to the worldly ways of industrialization and urbanization. Evocatively describing the details of village life, customs, and dress, Léo's fiction reflected her affection for and idealization of *paysanne* culture, as well as her desire to record and preserve its rhythms and textures. In her second novel, *Un Mariage scandaleux* (1862), she described a village dance where

> the dance floor was only the well-swept ground of the public square. There were no seats . . . There were wood frames on which, from time to time, several young men sat with young girls on their knees, as is done in the country, and with which no one would find fault; but the girls hardly remained there, preferring to see the dance and especially to be seen, in order to be asked to dance.[66]

Léo portrayed these village youths as engaging in wholesome entertainments. Unsullied by urban life, here the interactions of the sexes remained innocent. Young girls, whose "white tulle or muslin scarves revealed the back of their necks and crossed their chests chastely," inhabited a romanticized form of a vanishing socio-cultural tableau that Léo sought to preserve.[67]

Although she deplored the external imposition of cultural changes on rural life, she later made frequent attempts to politicize and radicalize peasants. Her sentimentalization did not obscure the often dire conditions of rural inhabitants; and she repeatedly returned to this theme in her writing.[68] Recognizing the poverty and oppression within their bucolic milieu, Léo sought to create a socialist-based worker–peasant solidarity.

Information on Léo's early adulthood is incomplete, most notably for the year 1848. On December 12, 1851, however, she and the socialist writer and editor Pierre-Grégoire Champseix received authorization to marry in Lausanne, Switzerland, ten days after Louis Napoleon's coup d'état of December 2.[69] Champseix, seven years her senior, adhered to the utopian socialist ideas of Pierre Leroux, and had edited Leroux's journal *La Revue sociale*, as well as other related publications. Leroux advocated egalitarian cooperative living and supported equality for women, positions that Champseix, as one of his followers, would have embraced. Léo and Champseix most likely met during his short tenure at a local Limoges (near Poitiers) newspaper, *Le Peuple*, prior to his exile. Following the repression of 1848, Champseix lived as a political refugee in Switzerland, teaching high school French in Lausanne.[70] Léo's specific activities prior to this point remain unknown, as do the circumstances of her joining Champseix in Lausanne. We do not know if her bourgeois family approved of her marriage to a socialist political refugee without significant resources.[71] But she chose to leave France and join him. After their marriage they lived in Lausanne, and briefly in Geneva, until the amnesty of August 1860 allowed their return to France.

Léo published her first book, *Une Vieille Fille*, with a Belgian publishing house in 1851.[72] This book and her other early novels exemplify her interest in questions of gender, power, love, and the family. *Une Vieille Fille* also reflects her deep passion for nature and the rural life, as she evokes magnificent images of Swiss mountains, meadows, flora, and sunlight. Her second book, written during their time in Switzerland but not published until 1862, *Un Mariage scandaleux*, critiqued gender relations and class-based marital expectations, advocating unions based on love regardless of the lovers' class positions. She also began *Un Divorce*, serialized in the journal *Le Siècle*, which demonstrated the importance of marriages based on love and equality.[73] During these years she and Champseix lived happily in Paris with their twin sons, André and Léo, born in 1853, whose names she combined as her pseudonym. Intellectually and personally compatible, the two spouses most likely influenced each other's work.

Recognizing the inequity and disharmony of most marriages, particularly when contrasted with her own, and the unhappiness brought about by marriages based more on economics or familial pressure than love, Léo used the novel form to convey her feminist critique. She embraced this didactic approach as a tool to educate and elevate her readers throughout much of her career. *Un Mariage scandaleux* received positive reviews and saw four editions. The critic C. B. Derosne, writing in *Le Constitutionnel*, praised the work as having "pages as beautiful as George Sand's most beautiful: with the same strength . . . and simplicity . . . his [*sic*] novel will hold a place among the finest."[74] Léo established a growing reputation as a respected novelist and defender of women's abilities and rights. In the midst of her mounting success, however, her husband, who had long suffered health problems, became extremely ill and died. Widowed in 1863 at the age of thirty-nine, she continued to write and publish as she raised her children. In 1865 she published *Les Deux Filles de M. Plichon*, undoubtedly in tribute to her husband, an elegy to egalitarian marriage and to married women's intellectual and social independence.[75]

As the decade progressed, Léo wrote and became involved in feminist and socialist organizations and actions.[76] Her path crossed with Mink's in these years prior to the Commune, as both women actively participated in Paris's emerging radical political community. Though they were products

LA PRISE DE PARIS.
(MAI 1871)

La barricade de la place Blanche défendue par des Femmes.

Fig. 1. The Barricade at the *Place Blanche.*
Courtesy of Les Amis de la Commune de Paris.

of extremely different personal and intellectual histories, Léo and Mink developed similar feminist and socialist positions during the late Empire, a period of expanded liberties. Their undertakings and goals overlapped repeatedly, in their involvement in *La Société du droit des femmes,* in the Parisian public meetings, in their efforts toward marriage reform, and in their focus on radicalizing the peasantry. Although they diverged in both their politics and actions, the Commune served as the catalyst that brought their ideas into practice. The uprising opened the fields of ideological possibilities, allowing more highly differentiated and refined positions to flourish. Léo, Mink, and Dmitrieff each brought individual experiences, identities, influences, interests, ideas, and goals into the insurrectional milieu, and there each effectuated her own particular approach to making revolution.

On Sunday, May 21, 1871, Augustine-Malvine Blanchecotte, a generally unsympathetic observer of the Commune, noted,

> It is unbelievable! There is another concert today! Yes, a popular concert
> at the Tuilleries and the Place de la Concorde. The Commune has every-

33

thing: thunder and sunlight! . . . And for tomorrow, they have announced an extraordinary performance at the Opera.[77]

Hours later, Versailles troops smashed through Paris's unguarded Saint-Cloud gate.[78] Parisians awoke Monday morning to fighting in the streets. Although Paris was bombarded and under siege for two months, a current of festivity and optimism had run through the city, its residents exultant in the revolutionary achievement and buoyed by municipally sponsored concerts and spectacles. This elation ended dramatically as Versailles soldiers streamed into Paris, entering through five different gates by dawn, rapidly occupying bourgeois districts, and raging down the new *grandes boulevards,* broad avenues that fulfilled their designers' intentions of facilitating major, rapid troop movements through the city.[79]

Most of the fighting occurred in the working-class quarters. People ripped up paving stones and piled furniture, horse carts, empty casks, books, and sandbags to build barricades and defend their neighborhoods.[80] Louise Michel recalled how

> Red flag at their head, the women . . . had their barricade at the *place Blanche;* Elisabeth Dmitrieff, Madame [Nathalie] Lemel . . . and [Beatrix] Excoffons were there. André Léo was at the Batignolles . . . I was at the barricade barring Clignancourt . . . Blanche Lefebvre came to see me there. I was able to offer her a cup of coffee . . . Blanche and I embraced, and she returned to her barricade.[81]

Protecting their communities carried a cooperative, communal feeling, a last line of defense for manifesting their social ideals. Activist women, fighting women, field cooks, and nurses returned to guard their own districts, as did many National Guardsmen, who, according to Roger Gould, debilitated a coordinated defense against the Versailles army.[82] The sense of community came down to its essence: *la patrie,* Paris, their neighborhoods.

As the fighting began, Elisabeth Dmitrieff issued the *Union des femmes*'s final proclamation, calling the Eleventh *arrondissement* committee to "Gather all the women and the Committee itself and immediately go to the barricades!"[83] Women and men battled side by side, as the *Bulletin communale* condescendingly declared: "Let even the women join their brothers, their fathers, their husbands! Those who have no weapons . . . can haul paving stones up to their rooms and drop them down to crush the invader."[84]

By week's end, the combat became increasingly desperate and Versailles's retribution exceedingly brutal. Louise Michel wrote how "The blood flowed in rivers in every *arrondissement* taken by Versailles. In each place, the soldiers stopped their carnage only when satiated, like wild beasts."[85] And Victorine Brocher recalled seeing "unheard-of, disgusting things. On a pile of dead bodies, there was a poor little girl about eight years old, pretty, with blond curls; a practical joker, no doubt, of this troop of drunken soldiers, had the monstrous idea of lifting the poor little one's skirts up to her neck."[86] The government troops' hatred and dehumanization of Communards played a central role in the viciousness of their attack. Murdering and dumping a child was insufficient; only absolute degradation conveyed the perpetrators' venomous loathing to the survivors in her community. The precise reason for this particular child's killing remains unknown, but, as Gay Gullickson argues, Versailles soldiers shot children suspected of aiding the alleged *pétroleuses,* the women accused of burning Paris.[87] As Alexandre Dumas wrote, "We shall say nothing about their females, out of respect for women—whom these resemble once they are dead."[88]

The toll of the Bloody Week amounted to approximately 25,000 slain Parisians and 877 dead Versailles soldiers.[89] Thiers's army rounded up and marched over 35,000 Communards to prison camps at Versailles; they shot many detainees along the way. The subsequent courts martial convicted 10,000 Communards, 23 of whom were executed, and 4,500 of whom were imprisoned in France. An equal number were deported to prison colonies in New Caledonia. The virulence of Versailles's violent repression of the Commune reflected the enormity of its perceived threat to existing gender, class, and religious hierarchies. As many Communards saw the Commune as the potential source for international social revolution, the Versailles government assumed the responsibility of assuring the bourgeois world that this revolutionary seed would be destroyed.

Mink, Dmitrieff, and Léo all managed to escape Paris during the Commune's final days, each sustaining a particular revolutionary imprint, and each in her own way bearing hopes and objectives for reigniting revolutionary change. Their stories and that of the Commune remain irrevocably intertwined. In the insurrectionary aftermath, as their paths branched apart, the differences between their forms of feminist socialism became increasingly clear.

2
Politics and Ideas

Staging the Struggle

As France's Second Empire waned in the late 1860s, André Léo published a series of articles titled *La Femme et les mœurs: liberté ou monarchie,* "Woman and Morality: Liberty or Monarchy." In a piece called "The Current State of the Question," she explained that

> an awakening is happening, and the struggle finally beginning again between what is usual and what is right, between the ways of the old order and the spirit of the new era. It is necessary to know where we come from and where we are going, because any confusion is fatal in a battle. The religious, moral, and economic independence of woman is . . . the crux of the situation, of which the current word is liberty.[1]

Léo's contention that a just society depended upon female emancipation typifies the sentiments and ideas of activist women during the Empire's *denouement.* Seeing a space to inaugurate social, economic, and cultural change, feminists, including Léo and Paule Mink, articulated and demonstrated the interlinked oppressions of capitalism and patriarchy. Simultaneously, Elisabeth Dmitrieff seized the opportunity during these turbulent years in her native Russia and left the country to work externally for internal, and for international, radicalization and change. Léo's and Mink's endeavors helped to cultivate an increasingly revolutionary culture in Paris, to which all three women would ultimately contribute. During this period they honed their oratorical, critical, and, for Dmitrieff, organizational skills, while delineating their individual objectives and strategies in what Léo termed the "battle" for liberty.

Mink, Léo, and Dmitrieff each focused on female emancipation, creating a central common point among their contrasting formulations of feminist socialism and divergent approaches to its attainment. Prior to the Commune, each of these women developed a distinctive ideology influenced by a multiplicity of socialist, feminist, and revolutionary views and legacies, resulting in three markedly innovative positions. Mink asserted an individualist feminism that emphasized female difference, and a non-collectivist anarchism advocating decentralized authority and a balance between liberty and equality for all men and women. Léo promoted a rights-based feminist socialist collectivism, advancing a society based in individual liberty made just through equality. Finally, Dmitrieff cultivated a feminist Marxian associationism, seeking a centrally controlled, politicized federation of producer-owned cooperatives intended to free working women and men from gender and class-based oppressions.[2] These three women strove to create their visions of a just and egalitarian society. Working to restructure socio-economic relations, they endeavored to eradicate such barriers to liberty, justice, and opportunity. Embracing the legacy of France's revolutionary tradition, Mink, Léo, and Dmitrieff shaped this heritage into contemporary liberatory designs.

Participating in the International Workingman's Association, speaking at public meetings, writing and publishing, organizing workers, and proselytizing to the peasants, these radical women each challenged the era's power relations involving women and the working class. Operating in a mostly male socialist milieu, lecturing before mixed-sex crowds, and traveling alone, they transgressed gender boundaries as they propounded a new kind of feminist social activism. Each held different ideas of how to manifest this feminist socialism, and each took varied, yet overlapping, paths during these years on the eve of the Commune.

All three women belonged to the International—Mink and Léo in Paris, and Dmitrieff in Geneva. The organization (later termed the First International) was founded in London in 1864 to create a common ground for "communication and cooperation between workers of different countries, aspiring to the same goal."[3] André Léo explained this goal as "the emancipation of the workers by the workers themselves—the abolition of the privileges of capital."[4] The International intended to unite all workers and socialists, and to overcome national borders and divisions. It dominated the socialist landscape in this period. Its members ascribed to an array of socialisms and ideological combinations, as exemplified by Mink, Léo, and Dmitrieff. While theoretically open to all socialists and socialisms, the International was nonetheless plagued by internal conflicts, ideological divisions, and sexism. In 1870 the Paris sections of the International established broad organizational parameters, stating that "All sincere socialists have a common aim: to secure the highest possible well-being for all human beings through an equitable distribution of labor and of all it produces. However, they are far from agreeing on the means for attaining this objective."[5]

The official recognition of multiple socialist paths should have allowed activists of opposing views to coexist within the International.[6] In an 1869 letter to the International's weekly paper, *L'Egalité*, of which she was an editorial board member, Léo wrote: "Those who adopt the same goal as us, who search as we do for justice in the equality of social conditions for every human being . . . if we fight them and turn them away because their means are different than ours, it is to hurt ourselves, to combat our own forces, to play our enemy's game."[7] But in reality, these different approaches did not always dwell peacefully; infighting perpetually plagued the organization. Léo's advocacy of accepting various routes to socialism clearly contradicted the authoritarian ideologies of particular members of the International. Following the publication of her letter, the anarchist Mikhail Bakunin charged Léo with being "anti-revolutionary" for endorsing gradualist or reformist socialisms, and removed her from the editorial board of *L'Egalité*.[8]

Feminists particularly challenged the International's open stance and attempted to introduce ideas of women's emancipation into the organization's program. Mink, Léo, and Dmitrieff, among others, constructed their feminisms against presumptions of the era's organized socialisms. In particular, the membership of the Proudhonian-dominated Paris International overtly opposed gender equality. Portraying themselves as defenders of the family, they sought to restrict women's roles to the domestic, private sphere. A French delegation pamphlet, published in 1866 in Brussels (press restrictions prevented its publication in France), contended that "without the family, the woman has no reason for being on earth."[9] The Internationalist authors argued that "If the devotion to public issues, if the preoccupation with collective interests are qualities in a man, they are an aberration in a woman, one which science has long proven lead to inevitable consequences for the child: wilting, rickets, and finally impotence."[10] From the perspective of these Proudhonian Internationalists, a woman who turned her view outward, beyond the *foyer* and into the larger world, doomed her children, most importantly her sons. Whether the issue was sexual, economic, political, or social, the intent is clear: a mother with interests beyond the maternal and domestic would ruin her children's lives.

At the International's Congress in Lausanne, Switzerland in 1867, delegates formed a commission to discuss "the role of man and woman in society," demonstrating the centrality of this issue to their agenda. Lamenting women's historical treatment by men, whom the members nonetheless considered to be women's "natural protectors," they condemned the "errors and prejudices regarding woman and her moral and intellectual faculties which exist in every country in every class of society," errors and prejudices based "on the capital error of assuming the *inferiority of woman*."[11] The commission resulted in two reports. The minority report contended that "work is a sacred right which no one should be denied, and . . . in work alone will women find independence and dignity." But, in sharp contrast, the majority report stated that "we are opposed to women's work in industry . . . women's salary causes men's salary to be lowered . . . because the woman . . . must leave her family without direction . . . because it tends to perpetuate ignorance . . . [and] because . . . it causes the degeneration of the race."[12] This position, calling for women's exclusion from waged labor, continued to dominate the organization's ideology and practice.

In 1869, Léo attacked the International's arguments for female subjugation in her series of articles, *La Femme et les mœurs*.[13] Elisée Reclus, an egalitarian, anarchist member of the International and a future Communard, had informed Léo in a letter that "[Henri] Tolain presented a resolution declaring that women should exclusively devote themselves to their husband and children."[14] Tolain, a founder of the Paris International, espoused deeply misogynist attitudes, blaming women's work for rising prostitution levels and female hysteria.[15] In language reminiscent of the French Revolution, Gondouville, another architect of the International, termed the family "the safeguard of liberty" and protection against "luxury and debauchery." Mathé, a third original member, argued that women's political equality would create a "catastrophe which would set us back several centuries."[16] Their Proudhonian socialist positions reflected complex influences and anxieties. They associated women's economic, social, and political equity with the "decadence" of Empire, and particularly of the pre-Revolutionary *Ancien Régime*, the corruption and degeneration of which they attributed to the "effeminizing" influences of the eighteenth-century salon women. Just as the revolutionaries of the Enlightenment believed that the development of a strong, reasoned, and virile Republic required the eradication of these weak, emotional, and feminine characteristics of the *Ancien Régime*, so, too, did the Proudhonists consider women's social, economic, and political exclusion central to their societal vision.[17] To ensure this exclusion, they strongly accepted and perpetuated the bourgeois ideology of separate spheres, and, in an era of the de-skilling of labor, they feared women's competition for "men's" jobs.

The Proudhonian espousal of this bourgeois conception of gender roles may have reflected not only Proudhon's misogyny, but also his opposition to class-based solidarity. Proudhon advocated a federalist anarchism, involving a government based on "natural" law, to allow the organization of work, but not of politics.[18] He sought working-class, bourgeois, and petite bourgeois cooperation to ensure the inclusion of liberty, and not only equality, in his plan for non-violent social revolution.[19] Decrying the working classes' fervor for equality and what he considered their undervaluation of liberty, he contended that "the people comprehend nothing of municipal, departmental, corporative liberties, of individual guarantees of liberty and domicile."[20] In turn, he praised the bourgeoisie, "who for eighty years have proclaimed . . . all the revolutionary ideas."[21] Harkening back to the French Revolution, he admired the bourgeoisie's enshrinement of liberty and individualism, perceiving it as a counterbalance to the working classes' emphasis on equality.[22] His embrace of the ideology of separate spheres supported an anti-aristocratic, bourgeois ideal that actively promoted male individualism and women's removal from public life. In Proudhon's view, each man would reign freely within the domestic realm, and women would remain separate from the public world, separate from each other, and separate from liberty. The home, thus conceived, embodied a microcosm of both male bourgeois individualism and male individual liberty.

Léo originally wrote her series of articles *La Femme et les mœurs* for the journal *Le Droit des femmes* in 1869, as a rebuttal to Proudhon's *De la justice dans la revolution* (1867), in which he alleged to prove scientifically women's physical, intellectual, and moral inferiority.[23] In *La Femme et les mœurs,* in which she also criticized the chauvinism of male Internationalists, she charged both Proudhon and Michelet with "grossly insulting women," Proudhon in *La Justice dans la Révolution,* and Michelet, "more sweetly, but hardly less insulting," in *l'Amour et la femme.* Here Léo joined two earlier feminist writers in attacking Proudhon: Juliette Lambert, author of *Idées anti-proudhonniennes sur l'amour, la femme et le mariage* (1858) and Jenny d'Héricourt, whose *La Femme affranchie* (1860) also assailed the anti-feminist arguments of Michelet and August Comte. Léo praised both of these women's works, publications which, she conveyed, "had played beautifully against the Proudhonian contradictions, weakening [his] prestige in the world of thinkers, but were read little by the public."[24] Engaging in this hotly contested intellectual debate, Léo questioned the existence of liberty and rights for anyone in a society in which they are denied to women, charging that "Most of the democrats are the last to understand that all rights are interdependent." She contended that on the question of women's liberty, "the revolutionaries become conservatives."[25] In *La Femme et les mœurs,* she wrote:

> These so-called lovers of liberty, if they are unable to take part in the direction of the state, at least they will be able to have a little monarchy for their personal use, each in his own home. When divine right was shattered, it was so that each male (Proudhonian-type) could have a piece of it. Order in the family without hierarchy seems impossible to them—well then, what about in the state?[26]

Accusing Proudhonian men of rejecting monarchy and hierarchy on the state level, while enforcing it—the rule of the father—on their families, Léo further rebuked them for "building a fiction . . . on the pretext used by all despots: order."[27] Referring to the monarchical and imperial states' use of order as justification for repression and reaction, she further implicated Proudhonian men for their appropriation of this despotic rationale. Léo underlined the hypocrisy of the situation in which men defended liberty and individual rights while subjugating half the population to the "free" half, in the petty kingdom of the home.

In the late 1860s, during the liberalized Second Empire, the Proudhonian Internationalists essentially attempted to re-enact the ideological efforts of the 1790s to banish women from public life. The task took on additional urgency as fears of the de-skilling of labor rose among some male socialists and labor unions. By this period in France, only a small number of skilled, male-dominated crafts had become mechanized and broken down into piece work. Skilled trades remained the dominant forms of employment for both male and female workers. Socialist and union men, however, felt constantly threatened by the specter of losing their labor prerogative. Once an artisanal trade became de-skilled or mechanized, employers tended to seek female workers to replace male craftsmen; the women were hired at a significantly reduced wage level.[28] Skilled craftsmen lost not only economic status, but also control of production and of their products. Incomes were diminished, and so were the workers' prestige and pride in their crafts and their positions as artisans.[29] Because employers increasingly hired women for mechanized work, socialist and union men blamed female workers for stealing these newly de-skilled "male" jobs. This provided the incentive for working men to embrace an ideology of separate spheres, which promised to remove females from the labor pool, and thus from job competition. It also promised to "restore" the "natural" order of men in public and women in private life, thus reifying male power in a period of uncertainty and change. A founding member of the Parisian International, Ernest Fribourg, contended that "those who want to make the woman an industrial agent are only shameful communists," reflecting the Proudhonian opposition to what was considered the loss of liberty to the extremes of equality, here specifically in its gendered form.[30] Proudhonian male leaders embraced an ideology with goals severely detrimental to half of their class; they assigned priority to their own gender privilege over economic equity for their sisters, daughters, mothers, and wives. For the Proudhonians, the potential labor crisis gave historical immediacy and further justification to their subjugation of women.[31] When Paule Mink asked a predominantly male, heavily Internationalist public assembly in 1868, "Is a woman's entire life limited to raising children?" the response, to her dismay, was a resounding "Yes! Yes!"[32]

The question of women's work was among the topics addressed by the Workers' Delegations at the 1867 Universal Exposition in Paris. Organized by Frederic LePlay, an engineer, sociologist, and paternalistic social-Catholic reformer appointed by the Emperor Louis-Napoléon Bonaparte (Napoléon III), the Exposition was an enormous spectacle intended to bring the world to Paris and to dazzle the seven million attendees with France's accomplishments, particularly in the area of manufacture.[33] The event brought together representatives of a multitude of trades with the understanding that laborers would be allowed to air their grievances, but also with the intent of encouraging workers' adherence to the Empire and to LePlay's vision of a "social peace." LePlay's efforts at co-opting workers and avoiding class conflict failed, as the subsequent years of unrest clearly demonstrated. Rather, bringing the laborers together actually facilitated the growth of the International.[34] The delegates also formed a three-hundred-and-fifty-member *Commission ouvrière,* a "Workers' Commission," which met "to study the industrial and social questions of particular interest to workers of all professions." The resultant reports, subsequently published under the direction of the Internationalist Eugene Tartaret, declared the meetings "worthy of being cited as the most beautiful demonstration in favor of the right of public assembly." Published just before Louis-Napoléon eased restrictions on speech, the press, and assembly, Tartaret and his advocates understood the chronicle's political potency. Recognizing the value of thoroughly documenting the sessions "to enable them to contribute more completely to the development of ideas of association and solidarity among all the workers, the Commission [chose] to include with the minutes of the meetings all additional information that facilitate[d] their full understanding."[35] In addition to orators' presentations, therefore, the report included letters and supplementary materials that were read at the meetings. Among these was an excerpt entitled *"La Femme"* from Flora Tristan's *L'Union ouvrière* (1843), in which she outlined women's historical marginalization and subjugation; Fribourg again responded that "he did not find these arguments serious."[36]

The *Commission ouvrière* report unequivocally condemned women's wage labor. In the course of two sessions on women and work, held one week apart, a series of male workers and thinkers stepped up to the podium and, in agreement with the polemical writer and educator Jules Simon, declared that when a woman labors outside of her home "there is no longer an interior life, and the spouse is no longer a woman: *she is a worker.*"[37] While some speakers recognized the injustice of women's severely inequitable pay, their solution was to remove women from the work force, rather than support fair wages. Laying blame on the aggrieved women, a locomotive engineer named Durand made the familiar accusation that "going to work in an *atelier* at such a low price often contributes to the diminution of men's salaries."[38]

While the first of the two assemblages drew fewer than one hundred people, including thirty women, the second session attracted nearly four hundred and fifty, with only twenty women.[39] The topic clearly had allure. According to the *procès-verbaux* (the minutes), no woman spoke at either session. Women would finally break their silence when they took the podium the next year at the Parisian public meetings, as social and political restrictions were lifted and cracks began to appear in the power structure. But in

1867 man after man advocated the Proudhonian position, even to the point of emulating his numerical computation of women and men's relative and unequal values.[40] A Monsieur Dupas related a story of a provincial mayor who, in performing a wedding ceremony, proposed the following gendered calculation to the new couple: "Remember that together you will be as strong as ten!" Then he said to the woman: "The husband is one, the wife is zero; if you want to put the zero first, you two together will be weaker than one; if you put the zero after the one, together you two will be strong as ten."[41]

Over the next three years, the Paris International's Proudhonian domination waned as the organization expanded and collectivists gained power. Although Proudhon's influence continued (he had died in 1865), by the eve of the Commune many socialists favored strikes and political action, engagements that Proudhon had opposed as antithetical to individual liberty.[42] This was the faction that the Proudhonist Fribourg termed "communist," as well as "Jacobin" and "nihilist," as he attacked their de-emphasis on individual liberties. Among male Parisian Internationalists, the future Communards Benoît Malon (Léo's partner and future second husband), Léo Frankel, and Eugène Varlin embraced female membership in the organization and subsequently supported the communardes' revolutionary participation. These men had histories and futures as political allies of feminist socialist women: Malon consistently supported Léo's ideas and work; Varlin established the food cooperative *La Marmite* with the future communarde Nathalie Lemel, and was also the sole member of the 1867 *Commission ouvrière* to advocate women's right to work; and Frankel, as a member of the Commune government's Commission of Labor and Exchange, aided and championed Dmitrieff's *Union des femmes*. As advocates of feminists and feminist projects and concepts, they represented a male socialist alternative to the majority of sexist ideologues.[43]

Paule Mink and André Léo had each established themselves as journalists, activists, and orators in the years preceding the Commune, and Léo had confirmed her position as an internationally known socialist critic, journalist, and author, prolifically writing and publishing eight well-received novels by 1869. In 1868, both women participated in a series of widely attended Parisian public meetings, at which they lectured on issues including women's labor and socialism. Léo also reported on the assemblies for the daily political newspaper *L'Opinion nationale*.[44] Although Louis-Napoléon had declared a "liberal empire" in 1859, eight years after his coup d'état and the institution of political repressions, it was only in 1868 that he truly began to liberalize his reign, introducing freedoms of assembly, speech, and the press. The field of debate, discussion, and dissension exploded, as newspapers and public assemblies proliferated, and a popular public sphere began to emerge. Feminists seized the opportunity and reignited a campaign for women's rights unlike anything seen since the revolution of 1848.[45]

During the Second Empire, Louis-Napoléon had created a hierarchical, authoritarian regime that repressed republican and socialist politics. The economic boom of the 1850s, combined with political manipulation, spectacular festivals, military pageantry, the suppression of all opposition, and populist lip service, allowed Louis-Napoléon popular success with the peasantry and the bourgeoisie. Hoping to retain his slipping grasp on power in the 1860s, he introduced political and social reforms that were intended to assert his image as a populist emperor and to shift workers' loyalty away from both the republicans and the International. These efforts, which included half-measures such as the 1864 "right to strike," which did not contain a right to organize or to picket, failed to garner workers' allegiance to Empire, while seriously frightening capitalists. An economic downturn in 1867 compounded Louis-Napoléon's problems, as unemployment and social unrest rose.[46]

Generally considered a time of economic prosperity, the Second Empire brought enormous physical change to Paris, and with it significant social dislocation.[47] The city was essentially rebuilt during the 1850s and 1860s. Dark, narrow, alley-like streets gave way to the broad, expansive boulevards of today's Paris, with avenues built wide enough to prevent the erection of revolutionary barricades, and to allow major troop movement through the city.[48] Newly constructed apartment buildings replaced the older, demolished housing, but the new, high rental prices fell well beyond the means of artisans and laborers.[49]

The old structures had included housing for all socio-economic groups: luxurious ground-level accommodations sat below "middling" apartments, which supported the tiny garrets of the poor. The replacement of these buildings with exclusively high-priced lodgings effectively prevented working-class Parisians from returning to live in the city's central districts. The consequent dislocation involved a shift in Paris's class geography from a vertical division to a series of concentric circles with the bourgeoisie holding the center. At the same time, the working class was pushed out to the periphery.[50] Louis-Napoléon's political and economic power succeeded in altering the city's social space. Artisans and laborers generally still worked in central Paris, but lived in newly incorporated quarters that lacked sufficient water, sewage systems, and housing structures, including Belleville, Montmartre, and La Villette in the north and northeast, and Batignolles and Montparnasse in the south and southeast. These areas held the highest numbers of public meetings in the late 1860s and became the revolutionary cradles of 1871.[51]

The public meetings provided an open environment for expressing grievances and criticisms to an increasingly larger audience. According to Alain Dalotel, Alain Faure, and Jean-Claude Freiermuth, on March 3, 1869, somewhere between ten thousand and fifteen thousand people attended the seven sessions meeting in Paris that evening. The number and frequency of such gatherings fluctuated, and attendance depended upon the particular topic;

interest rose markedly before elections, as in the spring of 1870, when twenty thousand people participated in fourteen different assemblies on May 11, and the next day when twenty-three thousand people filled eighteen conference halls, with at least two times that number being turned away. This meant that in one night nearly seventy thousand Parisians attempted to engage in this popular form of politics. Dalotel, Faure, and Freiermuth asserted that the majority of attendees were workers, and that particularly at forums discussing "The Question of Women's Labor," women comprised up to one-fifth of the audiences. Jacques Rougerie estimated attendance at such lectures at one thousand to fifteen hundred per session. André Léo, in her accounts in *L'Opinion nationale,* reported increasingly packed houses.[52] Examples of other gender-related topics included a September 15, 1868 session on "Marriage and Divorce" that attracted one thousand people, and another on "Marriage or Free-Union, Single or Family" that brought in three thousand participants.[53]

An emergent class-consciousness manifested itself as the meetings progressed. Recognizing common experiences, conditions, interests, and goals, workers began to develop a sense of solidarity and collective power. Correspondingly, a growing number of workers joined the socialist activists by taking the podium and speaking to the crowd. The newspaper *Le Rappel* reported on January 2, 1869, that "An excellent symptom has recently manifested itself in the public meetings neighboring the popular quarters; not only do workers participate, but they have begun to mount the tribune, and several have as much or more success than the usual orators at these meetings."[54]

These gatherings clearly served as a precursor of, and training ground for, the popular political clubs of the Commune. They encouraged not only workers' participation, but also their embrace of leadership positions. In *L'Opinion nationale,* Léo wrote of the meetings' inspirational impact on female laborers, who "came with their husbands, with their brothers, these working women with fingers bruised from toiling all day, listen, learn, search with all the strength of their spirit. Several of them . . . also want to speak."[55] The mass meetings represented the core of the nascent working-class public sphere, a popular, politicized space carved out of a decaying Empire. But while attendance was robust, many male socialists clearly begrudged female speakers their audience. For example, the well-known socialist Gustave Lefrançais sought to denigrate the impact of these women, contending that "All the rhetoric of Mesdames André Léo, Maxime Breuil, Maria Deraismes, and others . . . who have mounted the tribune with their manuscripts . . . generate only mediocre interest. The working public remains cold."[56]

The public meetings had a radical reformist, rather than an overtly revolutionary, tone. To many of the participants, it appeared that progressive change could occur peacefully and gradually. Both Mink and Léo advocated women's suffrage and a rights-based feminist socialism, legal goals that they would abandon during the Commune, but which overlapped in the late

45

1860s with the bourgeois feminism of women like Maria Deraismes. Their focus on class set Mink and Léo distinctly apart from Deraismes, but the climate of the late liberal Empire allowed the public gatherings to provide a forum for a range of positions as well as a variety of voices.

But while freedoms of speech and assembly had been expanded, Imperial limits remained. Following her speech of August 12, 1868, Maxime Breuil, a feminist orator and frequent participant, received two warnings from Paris's Police Commissioner for verbally attacking religion, the army, and the Emperor.[57] Six days later, she again took the podium in favor of women's labor, education, and rights. Undaunted by the warnings, she attributed female oppression and ignorance in part to religious education, in which women remained "within the church walls . . . repeating all day everyday, words without ideas in a language that they do not understand!"[58] Breuil, like Mink and Léo, opposed the reactionary influence of the Catholic Church on women's lives. Attacking "the popes of familial dogma who particularly want women confined within the family," she metaphorically extended her anticlerical language to denigrate all men wishing to subjugate women.[59]

Paule Mink utilized the public meetings to promote her feminist socialism. Speaking on "Liberty: The Condition of Socialism," she exclaimed that

> No one loves and desires equality more than I; but it must have liberty for its corollary, the complete opportunity for individual initiative . . . otherwise, I find equality, practiced alone a shackle to progress . . . I want to be myself, a human being, thinking and active, and not a cog in the great social machine.[60]

In this period prior to the Commune, Mink espoused an anarchist, non-collectivist socialism that included elements of Proudhonian individualism (purged of Proudhonian misogyny), stressing liberty and a removed governmental force. During the Commune, her ideology would lead her to ally with the minority, "moderate" side in the factional schism that developed within the revolutionary government. Although the minority advocated a gradualist approach to socialism, they strongly supported a decentralized governmental structure that, for Mink, took precedent.[61] In "Liberty: the Condition of Socialism" (1869), she had explicitly opposed a "communist" system that "suppresses liberty in favor of equality," while concurrently rejecting the "economists [capitalists], who kill equality with liberty." For Mink, the critical imbalance of these forces, and with them society, would "be resolved when we are able to find the means of reuniting . . . liberty and equality, of developing them together."[62] Politically and personally independent, she bridled at the prospect of limitations to freedom made in the name of ending hierarchies. And she considered capitalism inherently undemocratic. Her vision of socialism rested on an equilibrium between the two polarities. Mink, like Léo, agitated for a radical expansion of the concept of liberty. Both Mink and Léo engaged in this debate, sparked by the ideas of Mill and Proudhon, among others, and made more imperative during the liberalized Empire as questions of rights, duties, and freedoms gained salience within a milieu ripe with possible change.[63] Providing more of a critique than a solution, Mink established parameters in which she hoped this democratic socialism would develop, without clarifying the means by which to attain her goal.

The interrelationship between equality and liberty remained central to Mink's feminism throughout the 1860s. She applied this concept to the issue of women working for wages outside of the home, as well as to questions of women's political and social rights. In one of the public lectures in 1868 on *Travail de femmes,* "Women's Labor," at Paris's Vauxhall, Mink directly repudiated the declaration by Lausanne's International Congress of Workers, which had been reported at an earlier session. The Proudhonian-influenced Lausanne declaration insisted upon women's confinement to the private sphere, thus limiting their liberty in an effort to remove them from the workplace and restore them to their "natural" state. To this end, the Lausanne Congress proposed calling on the government "to close all the *crèches* [day care establishments] . . . women will work at home and will obtain equal rights as promised by the principles of 1789."[64] Mink responded to this suggested manipulation: "You can not invoke your peremptory argument regarding the safety of the family, against women's social, civil, and political emancipation, because, fully accomplishing the duties of wife and mother, women will also be able to practice their social and political duties."[65]

Strongly combating efforts to further circumscribe women's lives, Mink rejected the conception that female emancipation would threaten the well-being of the family. She avowed women's full capabilities in both the private and public worlds, and demanded their rights and freedoms in both. Understanding labor as both personally and economically empowering, Mink called for the removal of gendered barriers to work, arguing, "It is work alone which allows independence, without which dignity is impossible."[66]

Vital to her vision of a balance between liberty and equality was her stand on the right to equal pay. Mink proclaimed: "to equal production, equal remuneration—*voilà:* the true justice."[67] She continued, "Is it not odious that, under the specious pretext that woman has fewer needs than man, she is paid two, three, or even four times less than he?"[68] This claim attacked the era's accepted contention that a man had greater financial needs than a woman, based on the assumption of his having a dependent wife and children—a presumption that most male socialists and working men embraced. Mink underlined the importance of payment for the work performed, not for payment based on the worker's sex. Equal pay for equal work emerged as a key feminist issue during the Commune, advanced not only by Mink, but also figuring prominently in Elisabeth Dmitrieff's plan for the reorganization of women's labor.

To ensure that women attained rights and freedoms, Mink in the late

1860s championed women's full political participation, including suffrage. The radicalizing experience of the Commune would later bring her to abandon this position, but in 1868 her Vauxhall speech exemplified what was then her rights-based democratic feminist socialism, as she stated,

> The true civilization will be that which will have for a goal the satisfaction of each and every person, and not the pleasure of a feeble minority at the expense of the majority. The laws which will be truly good, just, and fertile will be those that, made by all, will provide for the happiness and prosperity of all.[69]

Mink advocated a political and legal route forward to a just society, stating "What we claim, *messieurs*, is our enfranchisement, [our] social, civil, and political enfranchisement."[70] While some bourgeois feminists pressed for women's suffrage, the issue remained peripheral among the majority of French feminists during the late nineteenth century, particularly in comparison to both England and the United States. The experience of the Commune led Mink to abandon this legal and gradual path as insufficient to bring about the fundamental revolutionary change that she would come to see as essential.

While arguing for women's liberty, Mink also defined women's equality as encompassing "the duties of wife and mother."[71] For her, rights rested in the individual, but she was not referring to a universal de-sexed individual. She constructed female freedom in terms of sexual difference, stating that

> Man is the force, woman the resistance; man is the initiative, woman the perseverance . . . Everywhere and always, it is thus . . . "equality in difference." . . . In reclaiming woman's independence, it is not necessary for her to want to become a man . . . it is necessary, above all, to be and remain herself.[72]

Espousing what today could be termed a "difference feminism," Mink conceived of sexual difference as "natural," and of women and men as equals. She emphasized and affirmed an essentialist conceptualization of female versus male, but it was one devoid of hierarchy; hers was an individualist feminism of difference. Mink sought "women's rights as women," stating that "Women have virtues which are their own, and men have qualities particular to themselves."[73] She unambiguously argued for women's independence and individual rights, rights for a sexed female distinctly unlike a man. Mink understood women's liberty as based in their individual rights, but these were rights as both embodied females and as gendered women; women's emancipation would not come at the expense of what Mink understood as her "womanliness."

Mink articulated her class and gender analyses in an 1869 pamphlet entitled *Les Mouches et les araignées*, "The Spiders and the Flies." Dramatically describing the predator and its prey, the spider weaving his web, awaiting his victim, then watching the fly as "breathless, broken, it falls trembling and murdered, without strength and with no more resistance, into the power of its enemy, of its vanquisher, the hideous spider!" Mink informed her readers that

> This fly . . . that it [the spider] kills, this fly that it annihilates, and by whose blood it lives, it is you, peasants and proletarians . . . you, industrial workers; you, trembling young girls or weak oppressed women who do not dare to claim your rights . . . The spiders: these are the lords, the rich financiers, the exploiters, the seducers, the capitalists, the high clergy, the parasites of every sort.[74]

Constructing vivid metaphors of class and gender hierarchies, Mink went on to present multiple pairs of spiders and flies, exemplifying and elaborating on the exploitative nature of their relations. In a piece aimed directly at workers, she proffered a challenge: "If you desire, flies, if you desire you could be invincible. The spiders are strong, but you are more numerous; you flies, you are small . . . but your number is incalculable . . . If you can unite, if you have solidarity . . . then with a vigorous blow, you will be able to . . . break the shackles that enclose and oppress you."[75]

Calling for class consciousness, solidarity, and—ultimately—violence, Mink presented her readers with a potentially liberatory scenario. Consistent with her critique of the oppression of workers and women, and correspondingly, with her advocacy of an individualist, non-authoritarian socialism, Mink suggested the exploited take matters into their own hands. Lacking detail or a particular plan, her provocative pamphlet implied support for violent insurgency. This argument foreshadowed Mink's radicalized post-Commune stance, when she regularly and avidly advocated class war and violent revolution.

Mink considered the Catholic Church central to the perpetuation and enforcement of inequality, and this same anti-clericalism emerged as an important issue in the Parisian public meetings, as exemplified earlier by Maxime Breuil. For most male socialists, this meant economic and political power, but for Mink and other feminists it also meant patriarchy. In a public lecture in 1868 entitled "Marriage and Divorce," Mink expressed a feminist socialist critique of marriage, capitalism, and the Church, arguing that "Marriage has been defended by the theologians . . . Never has the Church supported women. As long as the Church has dominated, woman has been subservient . . . woman has never been protected by the Church, which has always preached the concentration of power and wealth."[76] Mink attacked the Church's support of indissoluble marriage as a primary component of its long-term oppression of women, along with its support of capitalism. She presented a hierarchical dichotomy, with women on the bottom, and power, wealth, and the Church on the top. Within this framework, Mink accused the Church not only of oppressing women, but also of failing in its self-proclaimed paternalistic role as economic and social guardian. These anti-clerical assertions would take dramatic form in the Commune and its aftermath.

Primarily pressing for legalized divorce in this particular lecture, Mink sought to ameliorate women's condition through a diminution or eradication of Church authority, and a recognition of equivalency, but not identity, between the sexes. While understanding the interrelated powers of sex, class, and religion, Mink presented relatively particular and limited solutions, solutions compatible with, but not necessarily constitutive of, socialism. She criticized power relations as she perceived them, paying scant attention to theory and formal organization.

The Parisian public meetings provided Mink a forum for developing the oratorical skills for which she would later become famous. Following the Commune, she honed her style to become increasingly polemical and flamboyant, bringing an aural and visual drama to her much radicalized politics. She would emerge as an engaging, theatrical, and provocative figure.

Like Mink, André Léo was renowned as a social critic, journalist, and speaker in the years preceding the Commune. Fifteen years Mink's senior, Léo had achieved a fame exceeding Mink's during this period. Léo's activism and publications, begun in the 1850s, had expanded and fully flowered during the subsequent decade. The widely recognized author of seven novels, all of which (save one) had gone into multiple printings during the 1860s, Léo also had an international reputation as a feminist.[77] The American feminist newspaper *The Revolution*, edited by Elizabeth Cady Stanton and Susan B. Anthony, translated and published sections of Léo's *La Femme et les mœurs*, in which she evaluated both the newspaper and the American women's rights movement, beginning in September 1869.[78] A year earlier, Léo had written an essay in the Parisian paper *L'Opinion nationale*, lauding *The Revolution* and Stanton and Anthony's ideas and actions. Léo also corresponded with the Chicago women's rights newspaper *The Agitator*.[79] In addition to her international connections, her novels, and her role in the International Workingmen's Association, she also participated in the Parisian public meetings, reported on them for *L'Opinion nationale*, published political tracts, wrote for socialist journals, and organized the *Société du droit des femmes* (Society for Women's Rights), to which Mink also belonged. In person and on the page, Léo and Mink addressed many of the same audiences, similarly providing socialist critiques of society, placing women's emancipation as central to that critique, and attacking the Catholic Church's complicity in the subjection of women. Both women shared a non-revolutionary feminist socialism during the final years of Empire, yet Léo's lacked the essentialism present in Mink's understanding of gender differences. Léo's works, furthermore, reflected a more theoretically and analytically sophisticated framework. Their paths and approaches overlapped and reinforced each other during this period, but they would diverge during the Commune, and subsequently definitively split in its wake.

In the twenty years leading up to the Commune, Léo's individualist feminist socialism undergirded her wide range of work and activism. Exemplified by the words of her 1868 political "Manifesto," she strove to "give woman possession of the rights which belong to her as a human person," based strictly on woman's personhood, not on her particular femaleness.[80] While many of the era's feminists had begun to claim women's rights as individuals, most, like Mink, embraced the idea of "equality in difference," and claimed these rights specifically as female individuals. Léo rejected this conceptualization of sex-based characteristics in terms of this debate, claiming rights and freedoms for women as human beings. Her articulation and expression of these goals evolved over the period, however, reflecting the shifting political climate and the forums and tools available to her.

Léo's commitment to her individualist feminist socialism was demonstrated in her novels, her political journalism, and her anti-clerical, pro-secular education activism. While her work of the late, liberal Empire presented sophisticated arguments claiming women's right to liberty and full equality under the law, her earlier efforts asserted women's right to justice, freedom, and equality in less overtly politicized ways. Léo published only novels between 1851 and 1865.[81] Limited by Imperial censorship and restrictions on speech and the press, she couched her social, economic, and political critiques in fiction. Her well-received novels examined issues initially including gender, class, love, and the embodied female. By mid-decade, she had added education and anti-clericalism to these topics, and finally also addressed women's labor and women's rights. With the increased freedoms of the late 1860s, Léo expanded her forms of expression and activism, and employed a more political and radical language. She continued, however, to publish fiction, clearly seeing a social as well as a creative need for both forms.

In all of her early novels, Léo presented marriage and the family as a microcosm of society. Employing the means available to her, she criticized the multiple manifestations of class and gender inequities that were played out in the private sphere, establishing these as reflections of the larger world. In 1868 she reconceived the domestic metaphor, and in essays in both *L'Opinion nationale* and *La Femme et les mœurs,* accused male socialists of opposing female emancipation in order to maintain "a petty kingdom for their personal use."[82] Léo's early fiction addressed women's lack of independence and their dearth of social and economic power. In *Un Mariage scandaleux* (1862), her second novel, by fashioning a story of a young bourgeoise in love with a youthful workman, Léo demonstrated gender and class-based prejudices and hypocrisies. In the novel, the bourgeoise Lucie's uncle warns her against marrying the worker Michel. He warns his niece as follows: "Have you forgotten how a woman depends upon opinions . . . not only for fortune and rank, but the dignity, honor, and virtue of a woman depend on the man that she marries and his place in the world."[83]

Evoking bourgeois society's constructions of women's impotence and vulnerability, and the social reality of women's subjection, Léo exposed not only the elite hypocrisies of status and propriety, but also the extent of women's dependence on men. Using a personal context, she could unmask and condemn the larger social realities: upon marriage, a woman was subsumed by her husband's legal and social identity; denied educational and earning opportunities, she fell in to his class and economic status by default. Even judgments of her personal qualities, Léo contended, reflected a woman's husband rather than herself.

Léo received rave reviews for *Un Mariage scandaleux*. *L'Independence Belge* avowed that "the author . . . will be a great novelist, and he [sic] will have a beautiful place between Madame Sand and Madame Charles Reybaud."[84] M. Duriez of *Le Siècle* declared that "the rare defects that one finds in this work disappear in the ensemble of qualities which distinguish it."[85] The *Journal des débats* likened her to Balzac, and Charles-Bernard Derosne wrote in *Le Constitutionnel*, likening her to George Sand: "less idealism and lyricism, perhaps; but with a better conceived plan and a more exact observation."[86]

After struggling to find a publisher for several years (eleven years had passed since her first work was issued), Léo became an "overnight sensation." Comparing her favorably to George Sand, critics recognized Léo's more realistic and socially grounded perspective. She had clearly rejected the romantic tradition, as a later critic noted: "she does not believe in impossible things, the man is not a hero and the woman is not an angel."[87] Léo employed the novel form to depict hierarchies and power relations. Using love, romance, and nature, she painted both horrific and pastoral images intended to demonstrate the potency of these forces. She used evocative stories and tableaux to draw in her reader. As Fernanda Gastaldello argues in *André Léo: quel socialisme?* Léo's intent was to "directly implicate the reader" in an emotional way, a manner not possible via political articles and tracts.[88]

In *Une Vieille Fille*, her first book, Léo introduced themes that would remain central to her work: class, gender, and social expectations.[89] She also wrote lovingly of the beauty and restorative calm of the countryside and nature, illustrative of her passion for rural life. This novel tells the story of a lonely young scholar who is befriended by his initially dour and cold landlady Mlle. Dubois, *une vieille fille*, an unmarried older woman (literally "an old girl" or an "old maid") when he comes to live in a bucolic village outside of Lausanne. Albert, the young man, soon becomes engaged to Pauline, Mlle. Dubois's apparently much younger sister, who is beautiful but frivolous, self-absorbed, and flighty. Such characters reappeared in contretemps to the intellectually engaged, questioning, and thoughtful woman throughout Léo's oeuvre. Here, it is the slightly strange older woman, speaking of "reason, literature, and feelings," who truly engages Albert's mind and his imagination.[90]

Both the reader and Albert ultimately discover that the "old girl" (aged forty-five) Mlle. Dubois is really a youngish (aged thirty-five), beautiful woman who has been hiding beneath severe and outdated manners and fashions.

Mlle. Dubois subsequently explains her reasons for undertaking this ruse:

> I was eighteen years old. I was the object of the attentions of a young man who seemed kind . . . One evening I was sitting behind the hedge along the road . . . he came with a friend and stopped near our door; "Are you going to see your sweetheart?" his friend asked, "and when is the wedding?" . . . He replied, "Do you think I am crazy? She hasn't a bit of a fortune. But she is full of kindness and spirit, and in waiting for something better, she amuses me." . . . I then saw the lot the world reserved for poor girls: insults or disdain.[91]

Recognizing this as her future, Mlle. Dubois had chosen to "retire from the world."[92] Léo thus criticized how both class and gender disempowered impoverished young women, while suggesting an extreme approach to attaining a certain kind of freedom. To underline the sex- and age-based limitations placed on young women, Léo created Mlle. Dubois as an eccentric "aged" woman who, because of her years and social marginality as an "old maid," had the freedom to live alone, take in borders, engage in intellectual discussions, and travel freely. Wrapped in layers of unfashionable clothing, the character's apparent lack of sexuality allowed her to operate independently and unthreateningly on the social periphery and without the "protection" of a man.

Léo again addressed the issue of women's freedom from their sexed bodies several years later in *Aline-Ali*. First serialized in *L'Opinion nationale* in 1868, this novel tells the story of Aline, a young woman who disguises herself as a man, Ali, to avoid marriage. *Aline-Ali* depicts the absolute subjection women can face in marriage. Aline's profoundly unhappy sister, Suzanne, relates the shock of her wedding night and the ongoing sexual violence in her marriage: "The wedding night was the most horrible and brutal of awakenings that, because of the perfidy of our education we think will be sublime and poetic . . . Those Christian angels' wings that they attach to our backs, poor girls, they carry you away for prostitution . . . the second day of my marriage I hated my husband."[93]

Léo decried young women's ignorance and naïveté; deprived of knowledge, instructed in religious and deeply gendered fantasy, only minimally involved in selecting their mates, young women entered married life absolutely unprepared. While Léo rejected conceptualizations of women possessing qualities and abilities based on their femaleness, she clearly did not ignore the realities of the embodied woman. She held that rights should not rest on women's particular differences, but neither should laws abuse, denigrate, and take advantage of them.

Léo brutally attacked women's lack of freedom and rights in marriage, from their inability to protect their own bodies, to their powerlessness over their children. In *Aline-Ali,* Léo illustrated the multiple levels of women's oppression in marriage. When the character Suzanne finds some solace in raising her young son, her sadistic and vindictive husband denies her all but the slightest access to the child, and she soon kills herself. The bereaved younger sister Aline, properly engaged to a man her father has chosen, questions "Why? Why abdicate all and put yourself in the hands of another! What excess of confidence!"[94] Just before abandoning her fiancé and disappearing into the male persona Ali (with her bereaved father's complicity), Aline explains: "I have known what sadness, what humiliations a woman can be reduced to by those to whom our laws deliver us, with virtually no control."[95] Written in the late liberal Empire, Léo took advantage of the new freedoms of speech and press, and overtly condemned women's legal and social status. This serialized tale took an overtly political stance, one unavailable during previous years.

In addition to publishing *Aline-Ali, L'Opinion nationale* also served as the vehicle for Léo's political journalism and essays in this period. Reporting on the Parisian public meetings on "Women's Work," she crafted in-depth, engaging, and discerning articles that informed the reader of the previous evening's speakers, arguments, and mood. In writings that editorialized more than reported, she examined and critiqued speakers, relevant ideas, and politics. Léo also utilized *L'Opinion nationale* as her own political platform, publishing three significant pieces: her essay on the American women's movement and its radical newspaper, *The Revolution;* her "Manifesto" claiming women's rights; and a three-part series entitled "The Theories." In the "Manifesto," and particularly in "The Theories," she clearly articulated her individualist, rights-based feminist socialism.[96]

On July 20, 1868, Léo published her "Manifesto" demanding women's rights. She argued that the "American slave . . . has become a citizen. Working men, leagued together to claim their rights, have already glimpsed the day when they will receive just recompense for their labor." But, she emphasized, "no justice and no peace will exist in the world until the gravest of social inequities will be eradicated. This inequity is the servitude of woman, denied by laws and by societies of possessing individual rights."[97]

Propounding women's oppression as the ultimate social injustice, nineteen women signed this "Manifesto," calling for the formation of an association for demanding women's rights. The proclamation asked the basic question, "left in suspense since the day [the Marquis de] Condorcet posed it before the Constituent Assembly . . . Is woman an individual? A human being?" Assuming a positive answer, which even "the most bizarre adversaries would not deny," Léo listed a series of questions that underlined the contradiction between woman's individuality and personhood, and her actual political, legal, economic, and social status. Her topics included these issues:

> Why is she obliged to obey laws that she has neither made nor consented to? Why is she excluded from the right, recognized by all, of choosing her representatives? . . . the rights of the mother are annihilated by those of the

father. A married woman's property rights are sacrificed to those of her husband. Woman's labor, of equal value, is paid half that of man, and often even this work is denied her.

Unambiguously attacking the Napoleonic code of laws, Léo asserted a rights-based feminism, calling for women's and men's equal standing in law, politics, marriage, family, and work. At this historical moment under the Empire, a legally based argument for equal rights for all individuals—which went beyond the purely politically republican to call for the right to work, and for equal pay for that work—constituted a deeply radical claim. The potential threat of violence, in foretelling "no justice and no peace," upped the ante even further.[98]

The "Manifesto" proceeded to present a solution: solidarity, liberty, equality, and fraternity, each reclaimed and redefined for Léo's feminist socialist project. In solidarity, she "invited those who demand social equity, all those who hate injustice, to support our cause, which is theirs, the same that their cause is ours . . . it is one." And then, from a position of power and unity, she appropriated the three central tenets of French republicanism:

> With all and for all, we demand: Liberty, in the religious, civil, political, and moral orders . . . We demand equality. Equality before the law . . . which was once vainly consecrated for all, but then half of humanity was excluded; equality in marriage . . . equality in work . . . We demand fraternity, which must . . . become the general law of relations between men and women.

Radicalizing the rhetoric underlying the French nation, Léo took these terms to what she considered their logical extension. The "Manifesto," which Léo later argued represented Paris's first public discussion of "the question of the rights of women," attracted substantial attention and generated extensive public discussion. Read aloud and debated in Parisian public meetings, it was also reprinted in many journals throughout France, including *Les Etats-Unis d'Europe, Le Siècle, Le Nationale,* and *Le Democratie.*[99] On July 20, two days after its initial publication in Paris, the Lyonnais newspaper *Le Progrès* ran the document.[100] Weeks later, *Le Progrès* published a letter from a group of twenty-two women, thanking the editor for printing the "Manifesto" and announcing in solidarity that "we unite our voices with those of our sisters and we cry out to them: *bon courage* for the realization of your endeavor."[101]

Léo argued and explicated her endeavor in a series of three articles in *L'Opinion nationale,* entitled "The Theories," I, II, and III, in which she constructed a sophisticated argument implicating the opponents of women's individual rights in depressing women's wages, benefiting employers, and divesting "fathers of families" of their jobs.[102] Arguing not only for the importance of theory, but also for its presence and impact in everyday life, she contended that "practice can only exist by virtue of a theory . . . those who practice the most and think the least act by virtue of theories made by others."[103] Léo explained that theory and practice existed in tandem; the abstract and the concrete inter-react and influence each other. Addressing those who complained about an excess of theoretical discussion at the "Women's Labor" public lectures, she explained the importance of discussing the ideas and concepts that shaped women's realities. Léo stated that "it is very legitimate, nearly essential, that before all practical discussions, the rights and the destiny of women have been discussed regarding her work"[104]

For Léo, two opposing theories affected the socialists' debates about women's rights, each regarding the basis of the social order.[105] The first, her position, "applied . . . the new principle of modern society, which bases the social order on the rights of the individual." The opposing stance, which, she explained, emphasized "order" rather than rights, "replaces a unity with three persons: father, mother, child—the family." For them, she contended, the patriarchal family, rather than the individual, formed the basic social unit. Employing inflammatory rhetoric, Léo once again linked the opponents of women's emancipation with the word *order* and its negative and undemocratic connotations. She argued that this theory that valorized the ordered patriarchal family, with its male breadwinner, directly affected not only women's work, but also the terms of all labor. Léo asserted that when women are isolated and subjugated within the family, separated from wage labor and intellectual life, they remain unprepared either to expect or fight for fair treatment. Thus if they do "enter the workshop, it leads to depressed wages." She added, "This social islet, habituated to living on less than necessary, submits to the conditions . . . and accepts the same work [as men], but at half the pay. It is thus that she replaces, to the benefit of the employer, a father of a family."[106] The denial of individual rights to women, manifested in their exclusion from labor and seclusion in the private sphere, thus ultimately serves the capitalist and harms the entire working-class family. And so, she concluded, "it is for the family as well as the individual that it is time, high time, that the woman becomes a free being . . . and that all social ethics . . . embrace the individual being as the model of society."[107]

Supporting her individual rights-based feminist socialism, Léo argued against the theories that claimed women's essential difference and her physical and mental inferiority. Challenging the stereotype of the weak female, she proposed that rather than looking at the "creatures of fantasy who hardly ever exist," socialists should "leave the fiction and just open your eyes."[108] Léo described the exhausting labors that working women were forced to undertake both at home and in the workshop. She pointed out that, in spite of their work demands, women usually survived men and still continued to manage even when they became widowed. She invoked the physically punishing life of rural women, and asked: "Is this not a woman?"[109] Here Léo may be echoing the well-known speech given by Sojourner Truth, the American abolitionist and former slave, who in 1851 described to an audience the myriad physical labors, trials, and degradations she had survived, and then queried "And aren't I a woman?"[110] Both women rejected the myth of women's natural frailty and delicacy, the contention, combined with the theory of women's innate mental incapacity, that underlay the arguments of those who wanted to deny women their rights. Stripping these arguments to the bone, ultimately Léo declared that all of these female faults were either contrived, created by oppression and marginalization, and/or were simple fictions, and therefore "all of these armaments, all of these theses, are inspired by men's fear of losing privilege!"[111]

Turning her attention to American culture and politics, Léo examined the position of women in the United States, which she termed "the most enviable in the world." Writing about the American feminist newspaper *The Revolution,* she explained that "American women possess completely . . . more than the French, the liberty to come and go, and to marry who they wish." But, she continued, "Born in a free country . . . they are not citizens, and they are essentially condemned to be frivolous because they are denied work and an active life."[112] Praising the lack of formality and social restrictions in American women's lives, she looked to them as models of personal independence and emancipation. Yet she argued that in terms of economics and politics, in many respects "The Woman Question is the same in the United States and Europe," for in neither place did women possess rights and full freedoms.[113] Comparing the two societies in *La Femme et les mœurs,* Léo wrote, "There as here the woman is subordinated; there as here her social position depends upon marriage, which renders marriage immoral; there as here insufficient wages forcibly push her into debauchery. There as here, as currently among all of humanity, the woman [is] object and not subject."[114]

In these essays on morality, Léo decried the common oppressions in France and the United States that corrupted individuals and institutions and denied women their subjectivity. She maintained that marriage, the egalitarian potential for which she had argued in her novels *Un Mariage scandaleux, Les Deux Filles de M. Plichon,* and *Un Divorce,* remained an immoral institution because of its compulsory nature: it constituted a precondition for women's social acceptance and economic well-being. For women dependent upon wages, therefore, abysmal pay drove the already marginalized females to prostitution, or, alternatively, to loveless (immoral) marriage. While the existing gendered socio-economic relations subjected all women to unjust and immoral conditions, Léo recognized that the single woman and the working woman in particular faced the extremes of degradation and objectification.

Léo lauded the American women's movement's efforts to alter these conditions as its members traveled throughout their country, "appealing to public opinion, sovereign mistress of all progress." Asserting that the United States had "as much liberty as could exist outside of equality," she recognized that the women's movement benefited from this and built upon it.[115] But liberty without equality, as exemplified in the United Sates, allowed enormous injustices. In *Communisme et propriété,* also published in 1868, Léo

57

explained that "liberty corresponds, in the moral order, to health in the physical order; it is the absence of something bad, it permits all, it gives nothing."[116] Liberty allowed freedoms, "it is the law of our individual expansion," she wrote, but "it is not the social law . . . the social law is justice. And, under another name justice is equality."[117] In contrast to Mink's quest for a balance between liberty and equality, Léo understood the former as the prerequisite for the latter.

Léo praised *The Revolution* and the work of its founders Anthony and Stanton, the originators and leaders of the women's suffrage movement in the United States, for their approach to "the woman question." Calling these women "courageous revolutionaries," she exclaimed that they "feel solidarity with all and claim justice for the worker as well as for the woman, for the black as for the white, [and] they resolutely attack the defects in the social order, which there as here give all privileges to the rich and idle."[118] In the immediate wake of the American Civil War, Léo extolled Stanton and Anthony's condemnation of oppressions based in race and class, as well as gender.[119] She used the term *revolutionaries* to indicate their desire to radically change the social order, but not through violent insurgency. Although the American women's movement had, during these years, begun to focus more specifically on the vote, Léo understood these American feminists to have a larger vision of female emancipation. Declaring an ideological affinity with them, she explained, "This journal, founded and sustained by women, is the only one, to the best of our knowledge, that represents socialism in the United States, a practical, serious socialism."[120]

Léo saw in *The Revolution* an advocacy of non-violent fundamental social, economic, and political change—a gradualist, rights-based feminist socialism. She acclaimed their model for exemplifying a peaceful but truly radical program of assault on extant hierarchies and forms of subjugation. And Stanton and Anthony clearly also saw an international ally in Léo, as *The Revolution* published translated excerpts of *La Femme et les mœurs* in the fall of 1869.[121]

Léo extended her feminist critique to education, attacking the era's instructional philosophy and its practice of educating boys and girls both separately and disparately in order to "respect women's sentiment, and preserve it through ignorance."[122] In a study entitled *The American Colony in Paris in 1867*, she unfavorably compared the French system to the American educational approach; the product of American education, she contended, "is undisputed . . . the superiority of the women to the men in the New World."[123] Léo attributed American women's educational advantage to the Americans' mania for commercial success, which played out particularly among the bourgeoisie. A bourgeois young man had "his own fortune to make," and thus abandoned his studies generally at the age of fourteen, to "throw himself at once into the commercial arena."[124] Here the gendered double standard and enforcement of the ideology of separate spheres actually had a benefit for (privileged) women, for "the young girl pursues her studies, improves herself by teaching, and, married or single, has many hours for study." Léo explained to her readers: "They are the women who study Latin, Algebra, or Geometry, and even undertake the sciences without fear. Look at them and be reassured! The care of their toilettes has not suffered, and the accusation of brusqueness, so often made against learned women, falls to the ground before their luxurious frivolity."[125]

Both appealing to and mocking her French bourgeois readers, Léo presented American-style pedagogy as safe for proper women. Simultaneously, however, Léo criticized the resultant social structure "which makes of woman a queen in chains." Reporting that "the first pride and duty of an American husband is to insure idleness for his wife and sufficient money for her toilette," Léo censured educated women for their unwillingness to take steps to change this situation. "Save an emancipation party formed under the inspiration of Miss Stanton," she wrote, "American women certainly accept their position with fortitude, like spoiled children."[126] Recognizing the paradoxical nature of the American situation, Léo praised women's educational opportunities, but vilified the gendered social relations and values that enabled these possibilities. In a land where commerce trumped ideas, women had relatively greater access to intellectual life because scholarly achievements held less value.[127]

Léo argued for educational equivalency in *La Femme et les mœurs*, decrying these "anti-progressive, anti-civilizing" practices that have "formed man and woman into two completely different beings . . . creating an opposition which exists neither in nature nor in the laws of common sense."[128] She attributed the intellectual and social gulf between men and women to their antithetical formative experiences: in France, boys' education emphasized thought, reason, and logic, while girls' education stressed feeling, piety, and obedience.

This pedagogical critique originated in Léo's strong opposition to the control of the Catholic Church over girls' education. In 1865, under the pseudonym A. M. Duruy, she published an essay in the form of an open letter to France's Minister of Public Instruction, condemning religion in public education. Léo contended that the state and the Catholic Church created a false dichotomy between religion and superstition, where no such differences existed. She queried:

> you and all of the members of today's civilization disapprove of superstition as one of the most terrible agents for the demoralization and destruction of our race . . . you have calculated what superstition has cost the human race in blood, massacres, tears, infamies, inequities . . . why then, *Monsieur le Ministre de l'instruction publique,* why do you teach it to our children?[129]

Maintaining that religion was violent, mean-spirited, and irrational, she argued that it had no place in children's instruction. Léo supported her points with magic, mystical, and superstitious quotations from the Bible.[130] She also accused the educational system of failing in "one of the first cares of education . . . to protect children from bad company," by exposing them to the questionable morality of Abraham, who slept with his servant, and David, who kept concubines and murdered defeated enemies.[131] Clearly intended to provoke, she gave this piece the innocuous title of *Observations d'une mère de famille*, "Observations of a Mother of a Family," employing the moral authority assumed to be embodied in the mother. But her aggressive attack on the Church and its teachings sharply clashed with the "proper" morality usually manifested in this role. As an anti-clerical and intellectual mother of two young boys, Léo chose a deceptively powerful and provocative title that literally anticipated the work's contents.

Her educational critique also dovetailed with her anti-clericalism in two novels, *Les Deux Filles de Monsieur Plichon* and *Jacques Galéron*, published in 1865, the same year as *Observations d'une mère de famille*. *Les Deux Filles* follows more closely the pattern of her earlier pieces, telling a tale of friendship, greed, love, betrayal, and redemption. The two protagonists are friends whose lives take very different paths: Gilbert, representing evil, moves to the city, marries for money, lives a life of deceit, and eventually falls into ruin; while William, symbolizing good, remains in the village, becomes a gentleman farmer, marries for love, and finds great happiness and success. Ultimately William, rooted in nature and egalitarian love, saves his lost friend by bringing him back to the countryside to teach in the village school he and his wife have established in their home. Describing their educational philosophy, William explains, "In our school, boys and girls will be together, as they are in life, because it is absurd to separate those who will come to be most specially united, and because science and truth are the same for all."[132] Condemning the separate and unequal education of boys and girls, and the chasm this disparity creates between the two genders, Léo also attacked religious (non-scientific) instruction.

In *Jacques Galéron*, Léo created another anti-clerical piece. Denouncing the impact of religious pedagogy on young children, she portrayed a conflict between Jacques Galéron, a free-thinking teacher, and the religious education authorities. In this novel, the local priest expresses dissatisfaction with the teacher's secular lessons, criticizing a "little naïve tableaux . . . with a sweet morality" about a mother bird and her nest of young, "because they have not spoken of Jesus or the Virgin Mary."[133] The cleric subsequently gives the young students a book entitled *Christian Thoughts*, which, Galéron reported, "if they understand it at all, their eyes open wide with terror . . . their poor little imaginations carry visions . . . in to their dreams."[134] The children read the following passage: "Become accustomed to taking each action of the day as if you were going to die after having made it . . . In the horror of hell . . . their tears only make the fires burn hotter without consuming them . . . For a moment of pleasure, an eternity of agony."[135] Léo's polemical work attacked this educational approach that frightened young people into submission and conformity, an approach that created the very sort of population that Léo struggled to free with ideas of independence and liberty.

Léo, like Mink, believed that the Church oppressed women by restricting their opportunities for education, marriage, and work. In an anti-clerical article published in the socialist journal *La Cooperation* in 1867, Léo assailed convent-run workshops for both their exploitation of lay women's labor and for their underselling of their competitors, a practice that effectively drove down wages in the competing workshops. Focusing particularly on the provinces, Léo wrote that "what is certain, is that the establishment of a convent of women in a locality will inevitably result in reduced wages for laborers."[136] In both the rural and urban context, she strove to eradicate the Church's economic, social, and intellectual influence on women's lives.

Léo organized to fulfill her aspirations for girls' education. As early as 1866, she and Mink, together with Louise Michel and the bourgeois Maria Deraismes, had formed *La Société du droit des femmes*, "The Society for Women's Rights," which advocated secular primary education for girls, equal access to work, and civil equality for married women.[137] Established during the era of the "liberal empire," which had begun in 1859, but prior to Louis-Napoléon's easing of restrictions on speech, the press, and association in 1868, the *Société* operated in a period of only slight reform. Not only were education and labor relevant to their 1866 agenda, but these women also sought equality under the law.[138] Their goal of civil equality aimed to end women's legal subjugation both within the family and the greater society; it constituted a reformist change within the existing socio-political framework. As a revolutionary event, the Commune would dramatically alter the terms of the debate. The *Société* program reflected not only its temporal context, but also its membership; it developed from the feminist and republican "circle" that met weekly at Léo's home and included bourgeois republican women such as Deraismes.[139] Most feminists during these years were republican in the sense that they perceived the republic as a potentially democratic and egalitarian form of government. However, the definition of a republic, and correspondingly of republicanism, varied widely from radical socialist, to liberal bourgeois, to reactionary.[140]

La Société du droit des femmes reorganized in 1869 as *La Société de la revendication des droits de la femme*. In this second *Société*, Léo participated without Michel, Mink, or Deraismes.[141] The new organization was devoted solely to girls' education as a means of improving women's social condition. It viewed the existing Catholic girls' schools as "merely the training grounds for subjects of the monarchy . . . where initiative, independence, [and] dignity suffocate and perish."[142] This organization emerged from plans for implementing Léo's "Manifesto," articulated at a public meeting where the "Manifesto" adherents announced their intention "to found . . . a primary school without catechism, where the daughters of those who believe in the holiness of rights . . . will not be raised with the hate and scorn of the paternal religion."[143] This profoundly anti-clerical plan clearly belonged to Léo, as she was the only person to sign both the *Société* and the "Manifesto" documents. The Society established a secular instructional plan diametrically opposed to the existing moralistic, conformist, and anti-intellectual program. Writing to fellow Society member and future communarde Maria Verdure, Léo explained that "this conquest of equality which we pursue, and which extends to moral reform, appeared to be best obtained by the reform of girls' education . . . our goal is to form free *citoyennes* in a free country."[144]

The Society members intended that "the authoritarian system of the past be entirely put aside."[145] They saw progressive, secular education as a means to reformulate women's roles, and ultimately, to renew the nation. The Society pledged to "utilize all general methods of propaganda in order to facilitate and hasten the legal recognition of women's rights."[146] Education constituted their primary means to attaining the ultimate goal of individual rights.

During the waning years of Empire in France, Elisabeth Dmitrieff had only begun to develop her own feminist socialism in St. Petersburg, Geneva, London, and finally in Paris. Born November 1, 1850, and thus eleven years younger than Mink, and twenty-six years Léo's junior, Dmitrieff came of age in the 1860s, a period of great political and social ferment in Russia. Dmitrieff became involved in St. Petersburg's young radical intellectual circles. She entered a fictitious marriage to allow her as a "proper" married woman to travel abroad alone, and in 1867, well-educated, schooled in languages, and deeply influenced by Chernyshevsky's vision of an egalitarian society in *What Is To Be Done?* Elisabeth Koucheleva Tomanovskaia left St. Petersburg for Geneva to continue her studies.[147]

Dmitrieff, whose intellectual and political development occurred in milieus distinctly divergent from those of Mink and Léo, conceptualized an ideology reflective of these dissimilar influences. Exposed to the ideas of both Marx and the anarchist Bakunin in Geneva, she allied herself with the Marxists in the Marx–Bakunin struggle for dominance within the Geneva sections of the International (a competition that subsequently expanded to encompass the entire organization). The Geneva International benefited from Switzerland's relatively liberal laws, including their tolerance of associations and their acceptance of political refugees.

Geneva had a substantial Russian community, including Dmitrieff's childhood friend Anna Korvine-Krukovskaya, who, with her future husband Victor Jaclard, would play important roles in the Commune; Nicolas Outine, one of Marx's close associates, who would mentor and later aid Dmitrieff after the Commune; and Ekatérina Bartiénieva and her husband Victor, also future Communards. Dmitrieff was among the founders of the Russian émigré section of the International (the International remained illegal in Russia), a group clearly allied with Marx. Having liquidated large portions of her substantial inheritance before coming to Geneva, she used these funds to support the organization's newspaper, *Narodnoe delo,* "The Cause of the People." Organized in 1869, but only recognized in 1870, the Russian section focused on emancipating their country from Tsarist rule; establishing International sections in Russia to expedite this end; and constructing alliances between Russian and Western workers. Embracing the ideology of Marx, in contrast to the Paris International's Proudhonian line, and facing Russia's particular issues of socio-economic subjugation and oppression, the Russian section lacked the Parisian sections' focus on women's roles and rights.[148] It also lacked its level of misogyny and dissension over gender issues. Women comprised a significant portion of the Russian section's membership, and most of them, and many of the men, were strongly affected by Nicholas Chernyshevsky's extraordinarily influential novel of 1863, *What Is to Be Done?* which created a relatively egalitarian milieu.

In *What Is to Be Done?* Chernyshevsky advocated the radical restructuring of society into working and living cooperatives, based upon the Russian peasant commune as a naturally socialist form. But in stark contrast to the traditional peasant commune, he envisioned female and male participants living emancipated, egalitarian, and independent lives. Typical of young Russian activists in the 1860s, Dmitrieff (at the age of sixteen) had read and embraced Chernyshevsky's ideas. Her advocacy of cooperatives emerged from this experience.[149] Dmitrieff's subsequent exposure to, and espousal of, Marxian tenets led her to develop a Marxian associationism, in which she combined the establishment of cooperatives with a centralized authority. She refocused Chernyshevsky's Russian-based concentration on the peasantry to address the oppressions of urban-based workers in Geneva, London, and then Paris.

Dmitrieff's interaction with the Russian peasantry, her inspiration by the populist movement and ideas of Chernyshevsky, and her influence by Marx resulted in a feminist socialism profoundly different from either Mink's or Léo's. At the time of the Commune, few French socialists could be considered Marxists; in 1871, Marx's work remained relatively obscure in Paris, where he held minimal influence.[150] But Dmitrieff clearly embraced Marxian concepts while rejecting Bakunin's anarchism. In terms of politics, Bakunin rejected the use of political movements as a means to the working class's economic emancipation, because political movements involved the immediate acceptance of the state, and therefore meant a delay of revolution. Dmitrieff, like Marx, embraced and utilized political movements as emancipatory agents.[151] Combining her Marxism with populist and feminist ideas culled from Russian thinkers, Dmitrieff organized worker's cooperatives in Geneva, adapting conceptions of the oppressed Russian peasantry to apply to proletarians within the Swiss context. Correspondingly, she became involved in a working women's association.[152] Her undertakings in Geneva undoubtedly provided her with vital experience when she began organizing women's labor during the Commune.[153]

Shortly after its founding, the Russian section asked Marx to represent them on the International's General Council in London, to which he agreed. Indicative of Dmitrieff's importance within the organization, the section chose her to be their envoy to London. There she apprized Marx of their work, and reported to the General Council.[154]

Dmitrieff arrived at Marx's home in London in December 1870, bearing a letter of introduction from the Russian section, informing him that "Madame Élisa Tomanovskaya" (Dmitrieff's legal married name) was "sincerely and profoundly devoted to the Russian revolutionary cause," and that "We would be happy if, with her as an intermediary, we will be able to get to know you better and if, at the same time, we will be able to better inform you of our section's situation, which she will be able to discuss with you in great detail."[155]

Dmitrieff spent three months in London, attending sessions of the International, studying the London worker's movement and the activities of trade unions, meeting with Marx and his colleagues, and spending time with his daughters, whom she befriended.[156] Exemplary of the warm relations that developed between Dmitrieff and Marx, she had closed a letter to him by suggesting, "Obviously, I do not want to take your time, but if you have several hours free Sunday evening, I am sure that your daughters would be as happy as I would be if you would pass them with us."[157]

Dmitrieff penned this letter in January 1870, when she fell ill with bronchitis within weeks of arriving in London. From her sickbed she replied to Marx's inquiry about her thoughts on Russia's agricultural organization. Discussing the future of Russia's peasant communes, the predominant, communal form of rural land ownership, Dmitrieff wrote,

> its transformation into small individual ownership is, unhappily, more than probable. All government measures . . . have the singular goal of introducing private property, by the means of suppressing collective responsibility. A law passed last year has already abolished [collective ownership] in communes with fewer than forty souls (men's souls, because women, unhappily, do not have souls).[158]

Demonstrating her admiration of the peasant commune as a form of collective ownership and "responsibility," as well as her opposition to private property ownership and women's subjugated status, this letter provides a window into Dmitrieff's feminist socialist thought during this period. By supporting the peasant commune as a brake on Russia's move to private property ownership, Dmitrieff disputed Marx's model of historical progression, which asserted the inevitable evolutionary steps from feudalism to capitalism

64

to socialism. Seeking to convince Marx of the importance of the peasant commune, Dmitrieff posited a Russian exceptionalism, interwoven with an underlying critique of Russian patriarchy. She contended that the basis for collectivist socialism existed at that moment in Russia in the form of the commune. In support of her argument, she offered to send him "a copy of [the newspaper] *Narodnoe delo,* which discusses this question."[159] In this letter to Marx, her ideas reflected more of Chernyshevsky's populism than the recipient's socialism.

The Commune was declared two months later in Paris. Marx and the London General Council determined to send two emissaries to Paris: the first, Auguste Sérailler, left soon after the uprising began; the second, Hermann Jung, was held back by illness. Within days, Dmitrieff took Jung's place, and embarked for Paris, charged to be the eyes and ears of the General Council.[160] She would prove to be much more.

The International clearly provided a contentious yet fairly flexible milieu for developing and expressing a wide range of socialisms. Dmitrieff, Léo, and Mink each came to the organization via different routes, espousing varied ideologies, and advocating diverse paths to their visions of socialism. In the years prior to the Commune, each of these women worked within and beyond the structure of the International, writing, speaking, and agitating for social, economic, and political change. The three women each developed critiques of the dominant hierarchies, and made these analyses public through the various forums and movements that developed during this era. In France, Léo and Mink integrally participated in the political opposition and social activism arising within the context of an emerging working-class public sphere.

In the months encompassing Dmitrieff's stay in London, Paris experienced convulsive change, including the Franco-Prussian War, the fall of the Empire and the founding of the Republic, Prussia's siege of Paris, the capitulation of the French government, and finally the rising of the Commune. Each stage engendered socialists' escalating disenchantment with the republic, as the system's undemocratic and repressive nature became increasingly apparent. Throughout this period, an undercurrent of dissatisfaction and social unrest ran through the city. The people of Paris had maintained hope that the new Republic would be truly democratic. Its failure radicalized them.

As the new decade dawned, the Empire and the Emperor's power and stability continued to wane as their opposition mounted. Léo described the atmosphere as reflected in the popularity of the satirical newspaper *La Lanterne,* which one saw "in everyone's hands: the worker read it walking down the street . . . the *elegante* read it in his car." She continued, saying that "the hatred toward the imperial government, and especially toward the Emperor himself, brought all the classes together in a game . . . which consisted of ridiculing the fool. Orleanists, legitimists, and republicans . . . as if of the same party."[161]

United not only in opposition to the extant regime, these factions would subsequently join together in support of the new Republic. But, once established in the wake of the Empire's fall in September 1870, the new Republic's increasingly authoritarian measures and tight alliances with the monarchists, and its capitulation to Prussia in January 1871, quickly alienated democratic republicans and socialists. Breaking down primarily along class lines, the governmental faction and its bourgeois supporters now united against the socialist and working-class threat. Six months into the life of the new national government, the people of Paris rose against it. Mink, Léo, and Dmitrieff immediately took action, recognizing the opportunity for dramatic social and economic change. Along with thousands of other revolutionary women and men, these three women stepped onto the revolutionary stage, gripping the deeply divided world audience as it anticipated the insurrectionary resolution.

The declaration of the Commune brought enormous hope and excitement to the working classes and socialists of Paris and well beyond. For Mink, Léo, and Dmitrieff, this revolutionary civil war provided the context to shift the theoretical to the practical. Beyond the potential of their idealized republic, the Commune concretized the possibilities of socialism, particularly a socialism informed, and potentially shaped and molded, by their feminisms. The insurgency constituted a forum for political, social, and economic experimentation. At a public meeting in 1869, Mink had declared "Yesterday's Utopia will be tomorrow's reality: let us be Utopians by willing the betterment of the workers, the emancipation of all and the abolition of all castes."[162] And now they faced the opportunity to create this reality, birthing their new forms of feminist socialism.

Part II
During

Fig. 2. Elisabeth Dmitrieff at age 18 in St. Petersburg.

3
Elisabeth Dmitrieff
and the *Union des femmes*

Revolutionizing Women's Labor

On April 11 and 12, 1871, an "Appeal to the Women Citizens of Paris," was posted on walls and published in most of the Commune's newspapers. The announcement proclaimed: "Paris is blockaded! Paris is bombarded! . . . Can you hear the canons roar and the tocsin sound its sacred call? To arms! *La patrie* is in danger!"[1] The entreaty, signed only "a group of *citoyennes*," continued:

> Is it the foreigner who has come to invade France? . . . No, these enemies, these assassins of the people and of liberty are French! This . . . combat to the death, is the final act in the eternal antagonism between right and might, between work and exploitation, between the people and their tyrants! . . . *Citoyennes*, the gauntlet has been thrown, it is necessary to vanquish or to die . . . We must prepare to defend and avenge our brothers.[2]

This dramatic declaration called Parisian women to join in the righteous uprising by participating in the newly founded working women's revolutionary association, the *Union des femmes pour la défense de Paris et les soins aux blessés.* The *Union*'s full name, "The Union of Women for the Defense of Paris and Aid to the Wounded," highlighted its short-term goal of defending Paris against the enemy Versailles troops. But the "Appeal" also decried the exploitation of workers, demanding that "we want work, but to be able to keep the proceeds . . . No more exploiters, no more masters! Labor means well-being for all . . . the Commune will live in work, or die in combat!"[3] Recognizing the immediacy and consequence of the military threat, these women sought to protect the insurgency in its infancy. The revolutionary moment provided the opportunity to redraw the lines of power. For the *Union des femmes,* the short-term defense constituted a necessary prerequisite for the long-term priority of developing women's economic and social equality and independence.[4]

The *Union des femmes* stands as one of the Commune's largest and most clearly delineated and effective organizations.[5] Established by the then-twenty-year-old Elisabeth Dmitrieff within two weeks of the revolution's inception, the association exhibited a sophistication and ideological clarity unique among its contemporaries. Dmitrieff applied her experience and studies that she had undertaken in Russia, Switzerland, and England to analyze the complexity of Parisian working-class women's conditions. The multifaceted agenda of the *Union des femmes* included reordering production relations into producer-owned cooperatives, ending the exploitative employer–laborer relationship, and attempting to eradicate intra-class and inter-gender conflicts regarding women's right to work.[6]

The *Union des femmes* program intended to provide all women with immediate paid work, while initiating a long-term plan toward restructuring and revaluing women's labor. But it did not challenge the gender division of labor. Rather than attempting incursions into male-dominated fields, Dmitrieff and her followers strove to alter the social and economic value of women's work. Focusing on the garment-related trades, which were known as and correspondingly devalued as "women's work," she endeavored to redirect control and economic benefit away from employers into the hands of producer/owner/workers. Dmitrieff intended to re-value these skills by giving women control over their own labor and the products of their production. Along with propaganda and calls for government assistance, these efforts constituted central elements in the plan to valorize women's labor.

Initiating the process, the *Union* issued "definitive resolutions for the formation, in every arrondissement, of committees to organize the movement of women for the defense of Paris."[7] To coordinate the establishment of both the defense and the labor programs, Dmitrieff and the *Union*'s early members appointed a Provisional Central Committee, consisting of Dmitrieff and seven women workers (*ouvrières*): Adélaide Valentin, Noémie Colleville, Sophie Graix, Joséphine Pratt, Céline Delvainquier, Aimée Delvainquier, and a woman known as Marcand or Marquant.[8] Subsequently, a committee of representatives elected from each *arrondissement* replaced this group.[9] The *Union des femmes* developed as a highly structured association, with authority centralized in a top-down, yet democratically elected, set of committees. Dmitrieff held the only unelected, "auxiliary" position in the otherwise representative committee; she was its architect, animator, and overseer.

Dmitrieff had arrived in Paris on either March 28 or 29, sent as an envoy by Karl Marx in his role as General Council of the International.[10] It soon became apparent that Dmitrieff would extend her sojourn. As a precaution upon arriving in Paris, she took the *nom de guerre* Elisabeth Dmitrieff in place of her legal married name, Tomonovskaya. As Dmitrieff was a common Russian surname and the masculine form of her paternal grandmother's maiden name, she correctly assumed that using it would allow her to elude anti-Commune authorities.[11] Her choice of the masculine form *Dmitrieff*, rather than the feminine *Dmitrieva*, stands out as a revolutionary feminist act itself. In assuming a masculine surname, Dmitrieff overtly defied established social truths by rejecting the fixed Russian association between sex and suffix and appropriating a male prerogative. With a false passport supplied by the International, Dmitrieff immediately began investigating the revolutionary situation and its potential opportunities. It was time to put theory in to action.[12]

Upon her arrival in Paris, Dmitrieff met with Benoît Malon, the romantic partner of André Léo and a member of the Commune government, whom she had encountered earlier in Geneva. Having established a connection with the insurrectionary government, Dmitrieff then consulted with activists from the female workers' movement, including the seamstress Marie Leloup, the milliner Blanche Lefebvre, and a woman named Collin, who had no specified profession. After these meetings, she composed the *Appel aux citoyennes de Paris,* the "Appeal to the Women Citizens of Paris."[13]

Dmitrieff formed the *Union des femmes* based upon her particular feminist socialism, a political position she developed from her studies and experiences in St. Petersburg, Geneva, and London. The Commune provided the opportunity to turn theory into praxis. Influenced by both Chernyshevsky and Marx, she shifted the Russian feminist populist advocacy of cooperatives to an urban context, and combined it with a Marxist centralization of authority and coordination of political action. The resulting citywide organization embodied a democratic centralism planned from above. Dmitrieff applied her ideology to the Parisian context, addressing the immediate and long-term needs of working women as she understood them. She investigated the situation through meetings and discussions, including with the labor organizer and activist Nathalie Lemel, who would become a member of the *Union*'s Executive Committee. In her short time in Paris, Dmitrieff assessed the dominant types of female skills and trades, the areas of demand, and available resources. She accordingly planned a centralized federation of cooperatives based upon these factors. The *Union des femmes* nonetheless bore the strong imprint of Dmitrieff's politics and social critique; it was unmistakably her organization.

In *The Paradise of Association* (1996), Martin Johnson questions Dmitrieff's role in founding the *Union des femmes*. Contending that the organization

emerged as the result of several failed marches to Versailles by women supporting the Commune in its earliest days, he misses the strong links between
Dmitrieff's history and the association's structure and goals. The *Union*'s initial *Appel aux citoyennes* did call on Parisian women as "descendants of the
women of the Great Revolution, who . . . marched on Versailles," which, as
Johnson convincingly asserts, appealed to the historical memory of women's
revolutionary participation and harkened back to the October Days' women's
march on Versailles in 1789. This legacy quite possibly contributed to rank
and file women's subsequent adherence to the *Union des femmes*, but it did
not provide the impetus for the group's formation. Johnson overemphasizes
the organization's defense and military component, as well as its connection
to these aborted marches, in describing it as the primary motive for the
Union's establishment.[14]

The surviving *Union des femmes* papers, consisting of administrative statutes,
membership roles, addresses to the government, and plans and proposals
for women's work, indicate that the association's central focus was to reconceptualize and reorder female labor.[15] Although the documents are undoubtedly fragmentary, they show that a consistent structure and set of procedures and goals clearly existed. The administrative documents describe a
tightly coordinated group, assuring a continuous, ready presence of *Union*
members in outposts across the city. Article 1a of the statutes governing the
direction of arrondissement committees states that the *citoyenne* members must
be "ready to serve in the ambulances, at the cooking stoves, or on the barricades!"[16] Defense and military assistance formed an integral aspect of the organization's program, as indicated by its number one position in these statutes,
and by the group's full name, *Union des femmes pour la défense de Paris et les
soins aux blessés*.[17] The insurgency depended upon a fortified defense, which
Dmitrieff believed required women's participation. She wrote to the Commune government's Executive Commission, stating that "it is the duty and
the right of all to fight for the great cause of the people, for the revolution."[18]
But this function did not constitute the association's heart and goal; instead,
bringing women control over their own labor and access to economic independence held primacy of place. Dmitrieff's demands for women's battlefield participation, either in fighting or supportive roles, paralleled Léo's
in reflecting her feminist desire to open once exclusively male arenas to
women. For Dmitrieff, however, these actions also had another specific goal.
The majority of the documents pertain to women's labor and reflect long-
term and substantial objectives. For the duration of the Commune, until
the Versailles troops invaded Paris and citizens took to the barricades, the
agenda of the *Union des femmes* was dominated by issues relevant to the reorganization of women's work and the eradication of economic inequities.

The day after the *Union*'s first meeting, an editorialist of the Communard
newspaper *Le Vengeur* opined, "I have seen three revolutions, and for the first
time I have seen the women involve themselves with resolution . . . It seems

that this revolution is precisely theirs, and that in defending it, they defend their true future."[19] Inspired by the "Appeal to the Women Citizens of Paris," this unnamed commentator and observer of the 1830, 1848, and 1871 insurrections lauded the *Union*'s plans and perceived impetus to actively defend revolutionary Paris. Referring to the gender-based incentives of revolution, the author recognized the organization's feminist motives. To attain the economic and social independence that Dmitrieff sought with her planned labor reorganization, the revolution had to succeed. The *Union des femmes*'s leadership believed that revolutionary triumph would require women's integral participation, both because of the vast demands of defending the besieged city, and in order to influence the nature of the newly emerging society. Although certain male Communards, including Benoît Malon and the Hungarian-born Jewish socialist Léo Frankel (head of the Commune's Commission of Labor and Exchange), sympathized with women's plight, Dmitrieff recognized that without specific and continuous pressure from feminists, gender-related issues would hardly be addressed.[20] The *Union des femmes* published their open "Appeal," and used wall posters and newspapers to advertise all subsequent meetings, with the intent of attracting Parisian women to the association and to the cause. These efforts reflected a well-planned and coordinated undertaking.

At the *Union*'s second meeting on April 13, the Provisional Central Committee, headed by Dmitrieff, expanded and defined its proposed plans and strategies. They presented the revolutionary government with the *Adresse des citoyennes à la Commission Exécutive de la Commune de Paris* ("The Female Citizen's Address to the Executive Commission of the Commune"), outlining the need to fundamentally reconsider and restructure women's work in terms of authority, conditions, hours, and compensation. They requested practical, organizational assistance to attain this end, asking for loans for operational funds and the provision of meeting spaces. The "Address" explained "that a serious revolutionary organization, of a strength capable of giving effective and vigorous aid to the Paris Commune, will only be able to succeed with the aid and cooperation of the government of the Commune."[21] The nascent association conceived of itself as related to, and dependent upon, the insurrectionary municipal government. Dmitrieff conceptualized this relationship as mutual: the Commune assisted the *Union des femmes* in establishing itself, and the *Union des femmes* supported and abetted the Commune in its revolutionary endeavors.

Addressing the fundamental import of women's access to economically viable labor, Dmitrieff couched the *Union des femmes*'s practical requests in a feminist, socialist critique. In the Central Committee's *Adresse des citoyennes*, she argued the following: "The Commune, representative of the great principle proclaiming the annihilation of all privilege, of all inequality, should be simultaneously engaged in taking into account the just demands of the entire population, without distinction of sex, a distinction created and maintained by the need for antagonism on which the privileges of the governing classes rest."[22] Dmitrieff understood class and gender inequity as integrally intertwined: the ruling classes required intergender conflict to maintain their rule. That this rule rested on the "distinction of sex" that was "created and maintained" by the bourgeoisie implied a conception of capitalism and patriarchy as ineluctably interrelated. The Committee did not, however, imply that the end of capitalism would mean the end of gender inequity. In this address, and in other organizational documents of the *Union des femmes*, Dmitrieff via the Central Committee clearly explicated the need for specific actions to reorder women's labor, and thus women's positions in the emerging socio-economic order.

Dmitrieff, like Léo, Mink, Michel, and other communarde feminists, bypassed the relatively abstract goals of political rights, and focused instead on the socio-economic issues that reflected the material reality of most women's lives. In contrast to Léo and Mink, however, she had never advocated a rights-based feminist socialism. During the Commune, feminist socialists worked for the reorganization of labor, equal pay for equal hours of work, mandatory secular education, and the legalization of divorce. These women believed that the revolution had ushered in a new, socialist society, which made questions of suffrage and political liberties irrelevant. Perceiving the Commune as a transitional, embryonic socialist society, they strove for equitable female participation and incorporation in the newly emerging world.[23]

To succeed in this social reconstruction, Dmitrieff promoted the commonality of aims between both sexes, stating that "the triumph of the current struggle, with its goal . . . of complete social renewal to assure the reign of work and justice, has, consequently, equal significance for both female and male citizens."[24] Dmitrieff saw intergender, intraclass conflict as detrimental to all progress. Her concern appeared again in a subsequent letter to the Commune government's Commission of Labor and Exchange, in which she argued that the attainment of "the annihilation of all competition between workers of the two sexes" required the rather progressive conception of "equal pay for an equal number of hours of work."[25] The elevation of female wages to parity with men's could ameliorate the accusation that low-paid women were stealing men's jobs, while allowing women to gain opportunities for economic independence. Accomplishing this would require a complete reconceptualization of the meanings of work for women and men; such a shift directly contradicted the ideology of separate spheres and the era's predominant assumption of the male as breadwinner.

Dmitrieff's strong emphasis on workers' cooperation stemmed from the recent historical experience of laboring women in Paris and the industrializing world. Many male workers accepted and perpetuated a gendered division of labor, which barred women's access to skilled trades and maintained their wages at a fraction of men's. Rather than allying with female laborers to fight against inequitable wages and conditions, working men and male craft unions viewed women as competitors for a shrinking number of positions.[26] Throughout the mid-nineteenth century, the actual de-skilling of labor, as well as exaggerated fears of its potential occurrence, accelerated these anxieties.[27] Mlle. Bosquet, an orator at a Parisian public meeting in 1868, directly confronted this division of labor: "Men do not want to allow us into their work for fear of the competition."[28] Refusing to establish solidarity with female workers, male unions pressed for women's exclusion from the labor force.[29] Dmitrieff, like Léo, considered this practice as playing into the hands of capitalists, facilitating the continued subjugation of the working class, and condemning women to financial dependence or penury. She argued that "the success of the definitive and universal strike of labor against capital" could occur only if an end were put to this male–female rivalry.[30]

The combination of intergender economic competition and the dominant conceptions of "separate spheres" and "women's place" severely circumscribed women's labor options. In mid-nineteenth-century Paris, working women faced limited access to trades. Social attitudes deemed their earnings to be "supplemental," and their wages were kept below subsistence levels. Politicians, policy makers, employers, and male union leaders assumed that every woman either had or should have a male breadwinner supporting her, and therefore did not require a living wage. Rather than being paid for the labor they performed, female workers received wages according to an "understood" need: they were paid based on what they were (*women*), rather than on what they did (*work*).[31]

Organizers of the *Union des femmes* observed that "it is recognized and agreed upon that women have the right to work in the household [*ménage*], but not in the workshop [*atelier*]."[32] While validating unpaid domestic duties as "work," the *Union* also demanded the extension of women's laboring sphere to include waged labor outside of the home. Their statement alluded to the relative acceptability of women's paid labor in the home, generally involving piece work. To rectify an inequitable situation, the Central Committee proclaimed that "Considering that during the past social order women's work was the most exploited of all, its immediate reorganization is thus of the utmost urgency."[33] This reorganization would address the interrelated factors of social attitudes, pay, and acceptable types and locations of work. The *Union des femmes* strove to open the doors of factories, *ateliers*, and homework to women, allowing them choice, control, independence, and respect. Even in the midst of political and social revolution, this was an enormously ambitious project.

Expressions of opposition to women's wage labor had been intrinsic to France's male-dominated labor organizations, as well as to the International, in the years preceding the Commune. The question of the location of labor became paramount. At the International's 1866 Geneva meeting in, five of France's eight delegates issued a document, arguing that from "the physical, moral, and social point of view, the labor of women and children in factories must be energetically condemned in principle as one of the most press-ing causes of the degeneration of the species, and as one of the most power-ful means of demoralization put in place by the capitalist caste."[34] The male delegates blamed women's (and children's) factory work for "the degener-ation of the species," a human crisis that they attributed to a deliberate cap-italist plan. By employing women in factories, capitalists ripped mothers and wives away from their families, causing workers to become dissipated, daunted, and malleable. By accepting waged work, female laborers could thus be considered guilty of complicity in this socio-economic disaster. The del-egates' intense argument reflected their express acceptance of the bourgeois gender ideology that infantilized women, with no distinction existing be-tween the "labor of women and children," where women's natural role rested within the family, and where the flourishing of humankind depended upon women's adherence to this position.

Members of the International did not limit their attacks to women's fac-tory work. In 1868, Henri Tolain, one of the Proudhonist founders of the Paris International, decried the fate of women, and the nation, where women toiled in workshops: "One pities the demoralization . . . Prostitution increases in industrial nations where women enter the *atelier*. A woman's health is ruined, the *atelier* causes hysteria."[35] For Tolain, and most Proud-honian Internationalists, any wage labor outside of the home, whether in a factory or a workshop, endangered both women and society. A report from the International's Lausanne Congress in 1867 stated that "Woman, by her physical and moral nature, is naturally called to the peaceable minutiae of the domestic hearth; this is her department. We do not believe it is useful for society to give her any other charge."[36] Maintaining the propriety of func-tion and of place, Tolain's contention that "the *atelier* caused hysteria" pre-figured the late-nineteenth-century fascination with psychosexual analyses.[37] By entering the workshop, a woman undertook an unnatural, unfeminine role, effectively destroying her innately fragile constitution. Physically and emotionally undone, she would fall prey to the ultimate feminine disorder: hysteria.

Tolain's contention reflected his Proudhonist misogyny, dovetailing with Proudhon's own assertion that "at the workshop, as in the family, she [woman] remains a minor and is not a part of the citizenship."[38] Proudhon professed that "Between woman and man . . . there is no real society. Man and woman are not companions. The differences between the sexes places a wall between them, like that placed between animals . . . Consequently, far from advocating what is called the emancipation of woman, I would be inclined . . . to exclude her from society."[39] In advocating women's "ex-clu[sion] . . . from society," Proudhon argued that women differed funda-mentally from men and, thus, should live in a distinct, separate world. Women's programmatic exclusion from the masculine realm of wage labor, therefore, presented a logical corollary of these ideas.

Debates over waged work generally focused on women stepping out of the private, female sphere and into the workshop and factory. In the pre-Commune era, male critics rarely analyzed the reality of women performing paid labor in their homes as part of the "putting-out" system.[40] As a third locus of labor, the home—clearly within the private sphere—suggested an "ideal" situation where mother and family remained together. Jules Simon, a liberal republican and author of *L'Ouvrière,* an extremely influential study of women's labor, argued for the "superiority, from the point of view of morality, of homework over work in workshops."[41] He contended that

> The father has no need to remain among his family all day . . . But if the mother takes the same road as her husband, leaving the youngest child in a day nursery, sending the oldest to school or an apprenticeship, it is against nature, all suffer: the mother removed from her children, the child deprived of . . . the mother's tenderness, the husband profoundly feeling the abandonment and isolation of all he loves.[42]

Simon did not argue against women earning wages, but rather against their "abandoning" the home and family. In the face of industrially created social degeneration, women's "morality," their adherence to the domestic, private sphere, determined the fate of family and society. For Simon, this domestic factor superseded all other concerns.[43] He proceeded, saying, "If we lament women's entrance into manufacture, it is not that the material conditions are very bad . . . The room where she works, compared to her home, is pleasant; it is well ventilated, clean, and gay. She receives a higher salary . . . What thus is wrong? It is that the woman, once a worker, is no longer a woman."[44] Simon contended that a woman loses her sex by laboring in the public sphere. By prioritizing ideology over economics, Simon revealed that his bourgeois social-reformist view stood distinctly removed from working-class women's experience.

Many Parisian women labored in their homes, but they did so because of economic reality rather than because they accepted bourgeois gender roles. Few working-class women enjoyed such privilege of choice. In 1871, the majority of Paris's female workers labored in garment-related trades. Women frequently produced under the proto-industrial "putting-out system." By "putting-out" a phase of production to people working in their homes, manufacturers minimized overhead, eliminated "down time" via piece work, and effectively maintained a reserve army of labor for the busy season. This system particularly suited garment production because of its extreme seasonality. And while the system did have advantages for working women, as it gave them an element of control over their time and eliminated the problem of finding childcare, the intensive and erratic nature of homework often posed the highest form of exploitation.[45]

During the Second Empire's final years, Léo, Mink, and other feminists had reacted against this and other forms of gender-based discrimination in forums including publishing and public meetings. Julie-Victoire Daubié, the first French woman to earn the baccalaureate degree, published *La femme pauvre au XIXe siècle* (The Poor Woman in the Nineteenth Century) in 1866. Decrying women's lack of economic independence, she compared the nineteenth-century working women's position to that of women during the *ancien regime,* charging that "under the misleading names of liberty and equality woman is held back in deplorable inferiority and excluded from employments that were formerly guaranteed her by both legislation and custom."[46] The Napoleonic Code and the ideology of domesticity, while touted as liberatory for women, instead circumscribed women's rights and freedoms, economic and otherwise. At one of the Parisian public meetings on women's labor in 1868, a woman named Randier confronted the International's antifeminist position, demanding, "Are we to be free, yes or no? . . . The International . . . confines us within the family and declares us inferior to man." She questioned their aims: how could women be included in the International's stated goal of the "complete emancipation of the working class" if they remained "confined," and considered "inferior?"[47] Paule Mink, lecturing at such a public meeting, addressed the interwoven subjugation roles that females faced as both wage laborers and women. She argued:

> In denying women the right to work, you drag her down, you put her under the yoke of man, and you totally surrender her to men's pleasure. In preventing her from becoming a worker, you take her liberty hostage, and consequently, destroy her responsibility . . . she will no longer be a free and intelligent creature, but only a reflection, a detail of her husband.[48]

Mink described women's denigration, dehumanization, and ultimately, dissipation when they are barred from access to economic independence. Impeding a woman's right to work "drag[s] her down" to a position of complete objectification. Her humanity comes into question when, like a beast, she is "put . . . under the yoke of man." Finally, she ceases to exist, becoming "only a reflection, a detail of her husband."[49] Mink portrayed a hideous downward spiral, the result of economic disempowerment leading to social, and ultimately individual, disintegration.

Addressing the question of women's right and need to work, the *Union des femmes* attempted to employ working women displaced by war and economic dislocation. In doing so, Elisabeth Dmitrieff emphasized the importance of focusing on "the crafts essentially practiced by women," in which garment-related trades predominated, including haberdashers, embroiderers, glove makers, bandage rollers, and cotton cloth producers (she also specified book binders, doll makers, umbrella assemblers, glass blowers, and porcelain painters). To utilize this labor force, Dmitrieff asked the Commune government that the Central Committee be charged with "the reorganization and distribution of women's work in Paris, beginning by allowing them [the

Union] to produce military uniforms."[50] Although war and revolution suspended much of Paris's usual production and trade levels, the Parisian National Guard, which was the Commune's army, generated a substantial demand for textile-related goods.

To meet this immediate need, and to develop a long-term, sustainable, self-supporting structure for women's labor, the *Union des femmes* proposed to "assure the product to the producer by establishing free producers' associations, operating various industries to their collective profit . . . [The] formation of these associations, by freeing labor from the yoke of capitalist exploitation, will finally assure workers the control of their own affairs."[51]

To facilitate this process, Dmitrieff requested that the Commune government's Commission of Labor and Exchange "make available, to the federated producers' associations, the sums needed to operate the factories and workshops abandoned by the bourgeoisie."[52] The Commission of Labor and Exchange agreed to finance Dmitrieff's proposal. The *Union des femmes*'s Central Committee immediately commenced developing a detailed structure and strategy to implement the program.

Garment production fell within the realm of women's "traditional" tasks. Working women's various specializations involved skill levels ranging from the production of fine thread cotton cloth and tapestries, to bleaching fabrics and laundering clothes.[53] In their efforts to alter production processes and relations, activist women condemned the conditions associated with this work, but they did not challenge its characterization as feminine. André Léo observed that "Generally, needlework is considered physically easy labor. This is erroneous . . . In a working woman, the circulation of blood is always inactive, the vital warmth very weak, the appetite poor or irregular . . . anemia, illnesses of the chest or stomach, are the frequent results of this exhausting labor . . . performed continuously for 12 to 14 hours."[54]

Paule Mink similarly criticized the existing state of women's labor, terming it "abusive exploitation that turns the worker in general, and the poor woman in particular, into a slave, the serf of modern society, the subject of speculation at pleasure."[55] Thus the traditional, acceptable female labor clearly contradicted prevailing conceptions of the "gentle" tasks of womanhood.[56] The *Union* not only set about ameliorating these circumstances, but also pressed for the social and economic recognition of the value of this work.

The *Union des femmes* perpetuated the French socialist tradition of championing producer-owned cooperatives and workers' associations. This legacy included a mix of revolutionary and reformist socialist proponents: Louis Blanc and Philippe-Joseph-Benjamin Buchez advocated state-assisted cooperation; Pierre-Joseph Proudhon promoted workers' mutualist associations, while opposing strikes or revolutionary upheaval; and, Louis-Auguste Blanqui supported cooperative associations as an ultimate replacement for the state.[57] Since 1830, trade socialists within the labor movement had endeavored to emancipate workers from wage labor by forming producer-owned cooperatives, seeking the collective ownership of the means of production within a federation of trades.[58] Members of the Commune government, including the essentially Proudhonian (although feminist) Benoît Malon and the Blanquist Victor Jaclard, also promoted the cooperatives.[59] Dmitrieff appropriated various influences from these differing, yet overlapping, socialisms. She designed an organization based on a combination of Proudhonian federalism and Chernyshevsky's feminist populism, but with a centralization of authority and a political activism reflective of her Marxian influences.

In developing their socialist program, the *Union des femmes*'s leadership produced a feminist critique of the era's social and labor theories. By appropriating aspects of these positions to form a feminist organization, these communardes rejected the male-centered intent of the theorists and, especially in the case of Proudhon, the specifically anti-female programs they posited. The *Union des femmes*, and particularly Dmitrieff, confronted the contradictions inherent in socialist labor theories that refused to recognize the essential and permanent nature of women's work. They did not, however, address the apparent problems and conflicts in combining various, and often oppositional, socialisms. Proudhon again presents the most obvious example, as the *Union des femmes* adapted his anti-revolutionary, anti-female mutualism to a revolutionary feminist organization.

Organizational documents of the *Union des femmes* indicate a citywide association, its authority centralized in a representative Central Committee and a paid Executive Commission. On April 17, the Provisional Central Committee posted notice of the *Union des femmes*'s "third public meeting, on Friday, April 21"; the notice was signed by Blanche Lefebvre, who would become a member of both the representative Central Committee and the Executive Commission, *femme* Girard, whose first name is not known, and Adélaide Valentin, the only woman who was also on the initial Provisional Committee roster. It invited "all the *citoyennes* devoted to the cause of the people, to join their efforts with those of the committee for the definitive organization of work." The meeting was not intended to seek input into planning and developing their labor program, but the agenda included two items: nominating members to all of the *arrondissement* committees, and an "explanation of the organization's goals."[60] With a plan in place, the *Union*'s leadership sought members for its implementation. Operating with a shifting Provisional Committee, Dmitrieff stood as the one consistent guiding force. Drawing on her studies and her experiences in Geneva and London, she supplied the group with a rather evolved, highly centralized organizational framework.

The representative Central Committee, which was elected to "assume the general direction" of the *Union des femmes*, "received reports from the *arrondissement* committees, gave instructions, [and] met with its respective committees." Considered the "vital link between their *arrondissement*" and the center, they reported daily to the Executive Commission of the Central Committee. Its paid administrative branch, the Executive Commission "does not represent any *arrondissement;* they execute the decisions of the Central Committee."[61] Six out of seven of the Executive Commission members did, however, represent *arrondissements* as members of the Central Committee, indicating their acceptance of two distinct, yet interrelated roles. Only Elisabeth Dmitrieff, an "auxiliary member," was not elected and did not represent an *arrondissement.*[62]

The Executive Commission consisted of Nathalie Lemel, a bookbinder; Blanche Lefebvre, a milliner; Marceline Leloup and Adèle Gauvin, seamstresses; Aline Jacquier, a book stitcher; Jarry, whose first name and vocation are unknown; and Dmitrieff.[63] Although an estimated thousand communardes accepted their proposals and joined the *Union des femmes,*[64] the association's top-down, centralized structure may have alienated other high profile female writers and activists, such as André Léo, Paule Mink, Louise Michel, and Anna Korvine-Krukovskaya Jaclard (who had known Dmitrieff since childhood in Russia). Dmitrieff's youth, inexperience, and recent arrival on the Parisian scene may also have made Léo, Mink, and Michel wary of her or disinterested in her program. Of these women, only Léo participated in the organization, and she did so in a limited capacity, as a 17th *arrondissement* Committee member; both Léo and Anna Jaclard appeared on a Committee list for the 18th *arrondissement,* but no evidence corroborates their participation in this group.[65] Indicative of Dmitrieff's conception of organizational control, she publicly rebuked Léo when Léo's name appeared on a Montmartre Women's Vigilance Committee poster, announcing that

> The Central Committee . . . has decided it necessary to inform all of the *Union* members that the *citoyenne* André Léo, in explaining her reasons for giving her signature to a committee foreign to our union, has declared that she has no connection with the said vigilance committee, and has testified her desire to remain a member of the tenth arrondissement committee of the *Union des femmes.*[66]

Dmitrieff clearly demanded allegiance to the organization, to the point of publicly chastising the widely known and highly respected Léo. This level of control undoubtedly repelled some potential adherents.

Nathalie Lemel, the Executive Commission member, appears to have been excepted from Dmitrieff's monolithic demands. Described by the radical journalist Henri Rochefort as "one of the most beautiful and strongest intellects I have known,"[67] Lemel was trained as a book binder, and she had established a successful food cooperative under the Empire. Unlike Dmitrieff, she had work, union, and strike experience. Lemel probably joined the *Union des femmes* within its first weeks; with her experience in Parisian labor and politics, she undoubtedly provided Dmitrieff with specific information necessary to implement the labor reorganization program. Dmitrieff clearly valued Lemel, the association's second most influential member, sufficiently to

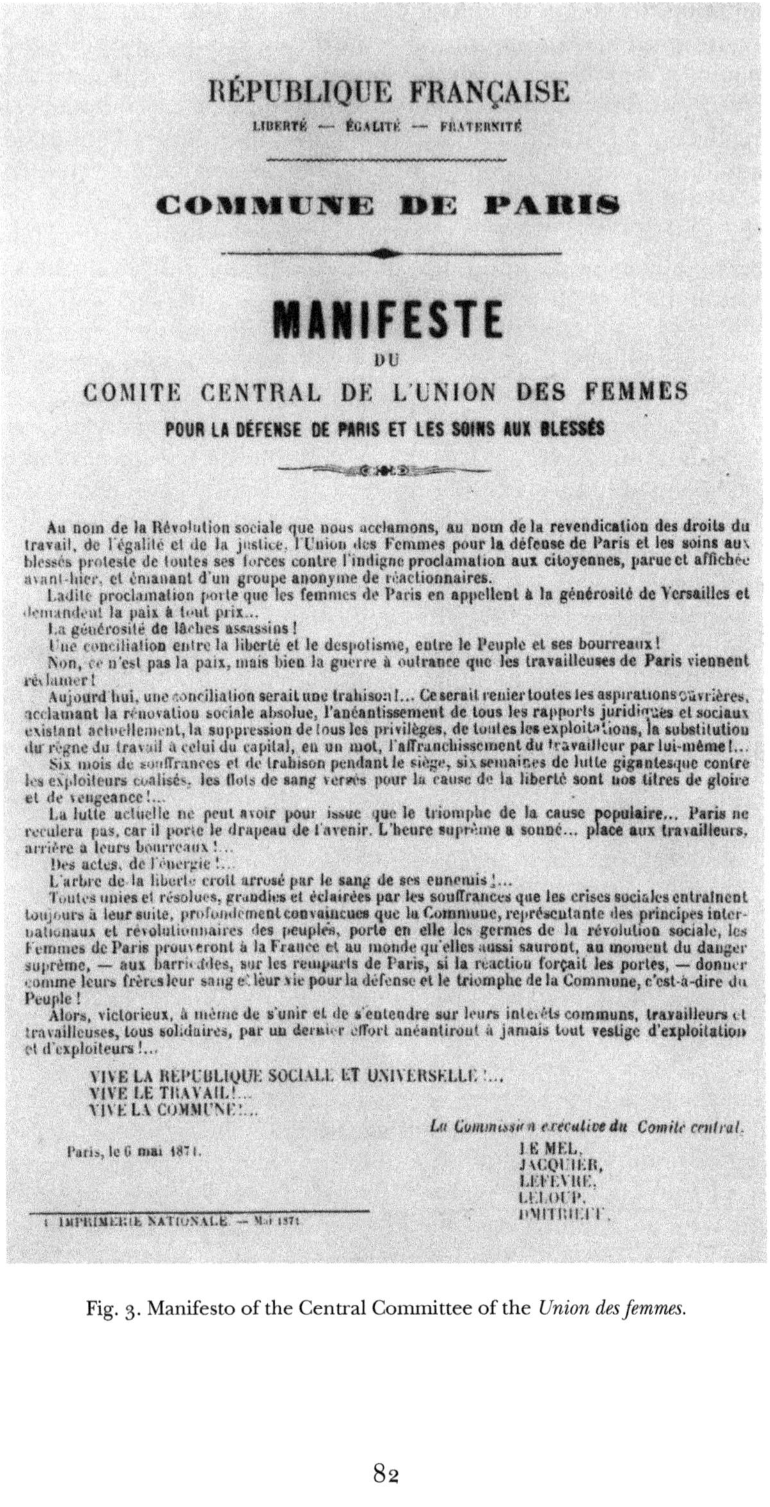

RÉPUBLIQUE FRANÇAISE

LIBERTÉ — ÉGALITÉ — FRATERNITÉ

COMMUNE DE PARIS

MANIFESTE

DU

COMITE CENTRAL DE L'UNION DES FEMMES

POUR LA DÉFENSE DE PARIS ET LES SOINS AUX BLESSÉS

Au nom de la Révolution sociale que nous acclamons, au nom de la revendication des droits du travail, de l'égalité et de la justice, l'Union des Femmes pour la défense de Paris et les soins aux blessés proteste de toutes ses forces contre l'indigne proclamation aux citoyennes, parue et affichée avant-hier, et émanant d'un groupe anonyme de réactionnaires.

Ladite proclamation porte que les femmes de Paris en appellent à la générosité de Versailles et demandent la paix à tout prix...

La générosité de lâches assassins !

Une conciliation entre la liberté et le despotisme, entre le Peuple et ses bourreaux !

Non, ce n'est pas la paix, mais bien la guerre à outrance que les travailleuses de Paris viennent réclamer !

Aujourd'hui, une conciliation serait une trahison !... Ce serait renier toutes les aspirations ouvrières, acclamant la rénovation sociale absolue, l'anéantissement de tous les rapports juridiques et sociaux existant actuellement, la suppression de tous les privilèges, de toutes les exploitations, la substitution du règne du travail à celui du capital, en un mot, l'affranchissement du travailleur par lui-même !...

Six mois de souffrances et de trahison pendant le siège, six semaines de lutte gigantesque contre les exploiteurs coalisés, les flots de sang versés pour la cause de la liberté sont nos titres de gloire et de vengeance !...

La lutte actuelle ne peut avoir pour issue que le triomphe de la cause populaire... Paris ne reculera pas, car il porte le drapeau de l'avenir. L'heure suprême a sonné... place aux travailleurs, arrière à leurs bourreaux !...

Des actes, de l'énergie !...

L'arbre de la liberté croît arrosé par le sang de ses ennemis !...

Toutes unies et résolues, grandies et éclairées par les souffrances que les crises sociales entraînent toujours à leur suite, profondément convaincues que la Commune, représentante des principes internationaux et révolutionnaires des peuples, porte en elle les germes de la révolution sociale, les Femmes de Paris prouveront à la France et au monde qu'elles aussi sauront, au moment du danger suprême, — aux barricades, sur les remparts de Paris, si la réaction forçait les portes, — donner comme leurs frères leur sang et leur vie pour la défense et le triomphe de la Commune, c'est-à-dire du Peuple !

Alors, victorieux, à même de s'unir et de s'entendre sur leurs intérêts communs, travailleurs et travailleuses, tous solidaires, par un dernier effort anéantiront à jamais tout vestige d'exploitation et d'exploiteurs !...

VIVE LA RÉPUBLIQUE SOCIALE ET UNIVERSELLE !...
VIVE LE TRAVAIL !...
VIVE LA COMMUNE !...

La Commission exécutive du Comité central.

Paris, le 6 mai 1871.

LE MEL,
JACQUIER,
LEFÈVRE,
LELOUP,
DMITRIEFF,

IMPRIMERIE NATIONALE. — Mai 1871.

Fig. 3. Manifesto of the Central Committee of the *Union des femmes.*

tolerate her activism in outside organizations, and thus spared her the public chastisement she gave Léo.[68] Lemel had participated in the *Club de l'Ecole de Médecin* during the Prussian Siege, and she was involved in several radical political clubs in addition to the *Union des femmes* during the Commune.[69] An 1873 Ministry of Justice report charged that under the Commune, "the carelessness of her language knew no bounds; one heard her in the clubs at *l'Eglise St. Germain l'Auxerrois* and at *la Trinité*. At *Notre Dame de la Croix*, she preached the most subversive theories."[70]

At *St. Germain l'Auxerrois*, Lemel frequented the *Club des libres penseurs* (Free Thinkers Club);[71] according to the anti-Commune observer Paul Fontoulieu, Lemel advanced her "subversive theories" at a *Club la Trinité* meeting,[72] where she proclaimed to "prolonged bravos" that "we have arrived ... at the supreme moment where it is necessary to know death for the nation [*la patrie*]. No more weakness! No more uncertainty! All to combat! All to duty! We must crush Versailles!"[73]

Lemel devoted herself to the Commune and to the *Union des femmes*, the goals of which she explained as "the defense of Paris and the organization of work."[74] Lemel's questioning at her September, 1872 military trial exemplified the intensity of her revolutionary commitment.[75] The presiding judge, *Lieutenant-colonel* Pierre, asked: "Did you often assist in the Central Committee meetings?" Lemel responded: "Every day." Pierre continued: "You also made the rounds in the *arrondissement* committees each day?" Lemel replied: "Yes."[76]

The daughter of petit-bourgeois café owners, Nathalie Lemel was born Nathalie Duval in Brest in 1826. She received a substantial education, and initially ran a bookstore with her husband, a gilder, in Quimper, until they separated.[77] Edith Thomas summarized Lemel's reasons for leaving her husband as her self-reliance and politics, and his alcohol consumption.[78] After the separation, Nathalie Lemel moved to Paris in 1861, and learned the bookbinding trade to support herself and her three children. She subsequently joined the Bookbinders' Society, where she befriended the Internationalist and future Communard Eugène Varlin. Lemel became involved in organizing workers and actively participated in the bookbinders' strikes in 1864 and 1865.[79]

As exemplified by her central role in the *Union des femmes*, Lemel advocated the reorganization of women's labor into producer-owned cooperatives, she also aimed for a socio-economic and political system based on associationist socialism.[80] She joined the International in 1866, and her agitation and organizational efforts led surveillance police to describe her as "a militant who reads publicly from evil newspapers."[81] Lemel's experiences as a laborer, organizer, and activist led her to take a leadership position in the *Union des femmes*.

Although born into the petite bourgeoisie, Lemel, having learned a skilled trade at age 35, strongly empathized with and identified with the working class.

As a single mother working for wages, she knew gender and class oppression and inequity in a more direct and personal way than other high-profile communardes, with the exception of Mink. As a result, both Lemel's and Mink's radical activism included a "grass roots" component absent from many of their compatriots, including Léo and Dmitrieff.

Shortly after joining the International, Lemel and Eugène Varlin helped form a food cooperative, *la Marmite* ("the pot"). Established in the 6th *arrondissement, la Marmite* served workers inexpensive food and socialist politics.[82] By 1870, three additional locations flourished, fueling the Ministry of Justice's report on Lemel which charged that

> *La Marmite* did not delay in becoming a branch of the International. She [Lemel] combined her functions as *la Marmite* cashier, with those of secretary for a commission intending to federate societies of food distribution, consumption, and production . . . she was more occupied with politics than with supplying food.[83]

Lemel and her fellow organizers did attempt to federate their cooperative restaurant with other mutual assistance societies. Particularly during the Prussian Siege, *la Marmite* played an essential role in feeding poor, hungry Parisians. "Politics" and "supplying food" remained intertwined in striving to circumvent the exploitative market created by hoarders and speculators in the besieged city. According to Louise Michel, "The revolutionary *Marmite,* where during the entire siege Madame Lemel . . . saved I do not know how many people from starving to death, was a veritable *tour de force* of devotion and intelligence."[84]

Organizing bookbinders during the late Empire, and establishing a cooperative restaurant, Lemel attempted to provide workers with the tools of self-determination. She continued her work at *la Marmite* during the Commune, in addition to speaking at political clubs and participating in the coordination and administration of the *Union des femmes.*[85] She did not publish her ideas, and most of her club orations went unrecorded. Like Dmitrieff, she supported producers' associations, but in founding *la Marmite* and attempting to form a federation of food cooperatives, she also made advances for consumers. Lemel bridged the elite intellectual milieu of Dmitrieff and the working-class world of Parisian women, bringing a unique perspective and set of experiences to the Executive Commission of the *Union des femmes.*

Dmitrieff constructed both the Executive Commission and the Central Committee to oversee the implementation of her labor program, the clearly delineated and highly structured "Women's Labor: Organizational Plan." She maintained a close watch and control over the operations of both groups. The Central Committee, with the exception of Dmitrieff and Lemel, consisted of working class women skilled primarily in the "needle trades," with thirteen of its eighteen elected members (there were no representatives from either the 2nd or 15th *arrondissements*) engaged in garment-related work.[86]

The committee functioned as a "powerful coordinator for the organization [of women's labor]," laying the groundwork for a citywide federation of producer-owned cooperatives, built upon the twenty *arrondissement* committees.[87] Once established, the workers' federation would remain a subsidiary of the *Union des femmes*. The plan proposed the creation of eleven-member *Comités d'arrondissements:* "the *arrondissement* committees will each name five members," forming a delegation of one hundred representatives, who would "cooperate in the completion of the federation of working women's associations."[88] This group of one hundred would subsequently divide into five organizational commissions: Drafting Statutes of Federation, Purchasing, Style Selection, Cashiers-Bookkeepers, and Investigating Abandoned Premises. Carefully categorized and cataloged, each commission addressed particular issues relevant to the reorganization of women's wage work; together, the commissions covered the components that the *Union des femmes* deemed necessary to construct a federation of producer-owned cooperatives.[89]

The Commission for Drafting Statutes of Federation ranked first, based upon "the necessity of forming administrative frameworks for each *arrondissement.*" A document entitled "Notes: Women's Labor," explained the rationale and motives behind the final draft of "Women's Labor: Organizational Plan."[90] The "Organizational Plan" directed the drafting commission to "join with the Central Committee to discuss the drafts of the statutes, which will be submitted to the *arrondissement* committees and approved by the General Assembly [of the *Union des femmes*]."[91] This process demonstrated the "democratic centralism" operating in this association. Proposals emanated from above, were vivified by a representative delegation, and finally were ratified by the rank and file. The "Notes," presumably authored by Dmitrieff (although transcribed by another hand), assumed that by the time of the Organizational Plan's issuance, "Certainly, the municipalities will already have directed the most suitable working women to form an administration; it thus only remains to give them the necessary instructions to understand the federated system; in other words, the groups organize and manage themselves, but are all inter-dependent in terms of profits and losses."[92] These "Notes" reflect the faith Dmitrieff had in the organization's duration and influence, and assumed that municipalities would cooperate with the program. The association recognized the local women's ability to establish a functional foundation, but the elaborated plan nonetheless explicitly came from above. The "General Statutes of the Federated Productive Associations of Female Laborers," which the drafting commission issued, clearly illuminated the extent of this prescription.[93]

The "General Statutes" essentially explicated and codified the assertions presented in the above "Notes." Specifically, the ten articles of the "General Statutes" detailed the operating rules and procedures for the federation of producer-owned cooperatives. Echoing the "Notes," Articles Two and Seven of the "General Statutes" decreed as follows: "All female workers' productive associations in Paris are federated together, and are dependent on the *arrondissement* committees of the *Union des femmes* . . . The profits and losses of the collective labor are equally distributed among all the members of the association."[94]

The members of the Commission for Drafting Statutes of Federation accepted the prescribed program. This "democratic centralism" indicated a form of cooperative tutelage by the hierarchy of the *Union des femmes,* particularly by Dmitrieff. While Article Four guaranteed that "each association retains its autonomy for interior administration," Article Nine assured that "the Central Committee of the *Union des femmes* . . . will hold the general direction of women's labor."[95] The Commune presented Dmitrieff with a revolutionary moment, of uncertain duration, to implement her ideas of socialist labor organization.[96] Applying her experiences from Geneva and London, she initiated a federated system intended to meet communardes' immediate needs. Although authority rested in the center, all elected positions, including the Central Committee, were revocable by Union members. No mechanism existed, however, to remove the "auxiliary member." This plan indicates Dmitrieff's perception of communardes: she considered them to be radicalized, ardent, and intrepid, yet frequently unsophisticated and unschooled. An imposed system and structure would immediately harness working women's revolutionary fervor, limiting popular input in favor of rapid organization and development.

Dmitrieff's strong ties to the International undoubtedly precipitated the General Statutes' first article: "All members of the *Union des femmes*'s productive associations are correspondingly members of the International Workingmen's Association, and will be responsible for paying its monthly dues."[97] Although this facet never came to full fruition during the Commune, by bringing a large number of working women into the International Dmitrieff would have somewhat moderated the organization's male-heavy gender balance. Members of the *Union des femmes* would have comprised a significant female and feminist presence in the association. In Dmitrieff's perception of the Commune as the spark to ignite many revolutions, these members would constitute a force to ensure the inclusion of feminist elements.

Dmitrieff intended to take the cooperatives beyond their citywide associations, and into an internationalist milieu. The General Statutes established a framework to "put them in contact with similar associations in France and other countries, in order to facilitate the export and exchange of products." They hoped to surmount national barriers and connect workers of many nations. To this end, Dmitrieff considered maintaining contact with the International in London as central to this project. In a letter to Hermann Jung, the Swiss delegate to the London International, she apprised him of "the great success . . . of the internationalist propaganda I have been conducting, with a view to demonstrating that all countries, including Germany, are on the eve of a social revolution; this propaganda pleases many of the women."[98]

Dmitrieff saw the Commune as a spark to ignite many revolutions. Yet, while agitating locally for international upheaval, Dmitrieff maintained her attention to organizing control of logistical detail. The General Statutes provided that, in the immediate future, "employment agents and traveling saleswomen" would facilitate the proposed intercity and international links between workers' associations. These women would be both economic and political emissaries.[99]

The Purchasing Commission of the *Union des femmes,* the second of the Organizational Plan's subcommittees, aimed to "gather information on the most current merchandise," in order to produce saleable products for "advantageous markets."[100] Composed of five delegates to the Central Committee, it also included members of the Commune government's Commission of Labor and Exchange "who possess special knowledge of fabrics and other raw materials." As requested by Dmitrieff, the Commission of Labor and Exchange would provide financial support; the *Union des femmes* received "a weekly credit for each municipality to immediately initiate the organization of women's labor." In turn, they demanded oversight. No purchases could be made "without previously consulting . . . Labor and Exchange."[101]

The project's success depended upon the monetary assistance and support of the Commune. The *Union des femmes* demanded that the *"citoyennes,* these mothers, lack work and resources, and the Commune . . . will fail in its mandate if it does not immediately find the means to satisfy their legitimate needs."[102] In one of the few examples in which they used the traditional equation of woman as mother, the women imposed a moral imperative on the members of the Commune. As the embodiment of "the new order of equality, solidarity, and liberty," the *citoyennes* held ultimate responsibility for "the completion of the peoples' victory." To this end, the *Union des femmes*'s polemical pronouncement, "The Proposal for the Organization of Women's Labor," proclaimed, "The Commune government bears the strict responsibility, *vis à vis* the workers from whom it comes, of taking all measures necessary to bring about a decisive result."[103]

This "decisive result" clearly included rectifying the "terrible crisis" of working women's lives.[104] Although male suffrage elected the Commune, the *citoyennes* considered the government as representative of, and responsible to, the entire Parisian working class in this transitional, revolutionary moment. Believing that they stood on the threshold of a new, egalitarian socialist society, the *Union des femmes* leaders sought neither female suffrage nor women's representation in the revolutionary government. They understood society to be in the process of fundamental reorganization, and they felt no need for amending or fully engaging in the existing political structure. In the short term, the *Union des femmes* focused on immediate economic need; in the long term, they endeavored to ensure the inclusion of gender equity in the nascent order. Although the association received support from the Commune's Commission of Labor and Exchange, feminist issues remained peripheral to most members of the Commune government.[105] Recognizing the revolutionary government's lack of initiative regarding feminist questions, the *Union des femmes* made specific, tactical demands, and supported these claims with strong ideological and political assertions.

The federation of producer-owned cooperatives received substantial assistance from the Commune's Commission of Labor and Exchange. Led by Léo Frankel, this Commission proposed fundamental labor reform, as did the *Union des femmes* program, but the Commission's reforms were intended for male workers.[106] Dmitrieff and Frankel shared a commonality of interests, presumably reinforcing Labor and Exchange's cooperative stance. The *Union des femmes* accepted the Commission of Labor and Exchange's oversight in turn for their funds and expertise, but they deemed temporary their "tutelage under the Commune." The "Annex to the Project Creating Workshops for Women," addressed the "grave question" of autonomy, maintaining the necessity of a "transitional path" to self-sufficiency. Aware that they must "remain subject to the surveillance of the Labor Commission [which is] responsible for their borrowed funds," the *citoyennes* insisted that once financially stable, they would "take full responsibilities for their undertakings."[107]

The *Union*'s practicality and attention to detail distinctly displayed itself in the Organizational Plan's third commission, the Commission for Style Selection. Once the Purchasing Commission decided on the most marketable products, "the delegates [of Style Selection] must immediately go to shops to acquire information . . . regarding current models and styles within that specialization."[108]

The Commission for Style Selection consisted of two representatives from seven different trades, including sewing-machine operators, and producers of fine thread cloth (*lingerie fine*) and coarse cotton cloth (*grosse lingerie*), children's clothing, layettes, feathers, and flowers. Dmitrieff chose these trades because many communardes had originally trained in these skills. For example, of the 356 women listed on the 7th *arrondissement* rolls, 106, or 30 percent of the members, identified themselves as producers of coarse cotton cloth, and 64, or 19 percent, as fine thread cotton cloth makers; the 71 women of the 10th *arrondissement* included eight producers of coarse cotton cloth and two of fine thread, constituting 14 percent of the total.[109] Dmitrieff explained that

> A considerable number of female workers, forced to leave their original industry because of unemployment, have sought a means of survival in the production of National Guard uniforms . . . However, we must recognize that the Commune will not always have to fill this heavy demand for clothing; this is why it is appropriate to prepare the workers to return to their original industry.[110]

The bourgeois exodus from Paris left many garment workers unemployed; they therefore sought work producing uniforms for the Commune's army, the Parisian National Guard, because such work was available during the

Commune. Looking forward to a peacetime economy, the *Union des femmes* attempted to reorganize and reconstruct these particular vocations based on a combination of practical and optimistic considerations.

Cotton cloth production presented the *Union des femmes* with a particular circumstance involving the issue of anti-clericalism: the convents were "enormous competitors in the production of ordinary and luxury cotton cloth."[111] For decades, French workers had resented the competition of convent-run workshops,[112] as convent *ateliers* consistently depressed the market price for goods by undercutting competitors. Operating with an essentially captive labor force, the convents' production costs remained below those of workshops utilizing wage workers.[113] The *Union des femmes* argued that by "suppressing the convent enterprises, it will be possible to increase salaries [of cotton cloth producers]."[114] Just as in 1867 Léo had accused convents of deflating area wages and prices in her *La Cooperation* article, in 1868 Mink had argued that "One of the major causes of women's excessively low salaries is exploitation by convents, who monopolize certain types of women's work and set the prices ridiculously low, contributing, on a grand scale, to the diminution of salaries."[115] Eliminating these "unfair" rivals would allow wages to rise, once producers received a fair price for their products.

Convent workshops employed lay as well as clerical women, and families frequently consigned daughters to their tutelage. The nuns served in a "protective" capacity over young female employees, maintaining a rather severe form of *in loco parentis*.[116] Jules Simon, a strong opponent of women's work outside of the home, assessed these ateliers:

> It is more than probable that the resident girls are poorly nourished, poorly lodged, poorly cared for when ill . . . thirteen hours a day of work under surveillance, entire Sundays spent in church or school . . . nearly absolute prohibition against communication with the outside, constitutes conditions which frighten the imagination . . . one wonders how this regime differs from that of a prison.[117]

Despite Simon's prejudice against women in any *atelier*, it is clear that these women worked under constant surveillance to ensure their proper behavior, morality, and, especially, productivity. The convent workshops' rigid structures, harsh conditions, and exploitation of young workers, combined with their price-cutting practices, exacerbated anti-clerical sentiments among the working class. During the Commune, working-class women expressed intense hostility toward women in religious orders, as the *citoyenne* Morel proposed at the meeting of the *Club Éloi* on May 19: "I request that we throw all the nuns in the Seine, so we can be done with them."[118]

To communardes, the nuns represented the Church's economic and moral oppression. Yet, a nun was also a woman, who had initially faced the same limited choices as other women. Religious life presented an economically viable, and socially acceptable, alternative to marriage for women across social strata. Communardes' resentment and enmity toward the Church's practices and doctrines were frequently fiercely directed against the religion's female emissaries. While communardes expressed their rhetorical, economic, and sometimes violent wrath toward all levels of the clergy, the nuns, who stood at the bottom of the hierarchy, posed the most visible and proximate threat. Their "cutthroat" economic competition, and moral and physical repression, qualified them as prime targets. Extreme anti-clericalism blinded communardes to the economic pragmatism involved in a poor woman's decision to join the clergy. Most revolutionary women did not blame prostitutes for the social ills of prostitution, but rather sympathized with their plight as "victims" of dire economic circumstances. By contrast, communardes did blame nuns for the social ills of the Church, while disregarding similar causational factors that pressed women into religious life. The prostitute exemplified female victimization, effectively removing the onus of responsibility from these women; the nun, as a conspicuous agent of the despised Church authority, appeared to embody the institution's oppressive power. Communardes' conceptualization of female clerics omitted the reality of nuns' subjugated and repressed existence. The economic, social, and gender oppression suffered by nuns, as females, remained unaddressed. In proposing to abolish convent workshops, the *Union des femmes* intended to develop a strong, lucrative trade in cotton cloth, without the "unfair" competition of the nuns.

Sewing machine operators formed another priority group for the Commission for Style Selection. The Organizational Plan stated that "the sewing machine operators will be able to work in their homes, if the association helps them to own their instrument of labor; they serve in the great division of labor, which in these competitive times, will be able to render sufficient wages."[119] The authors of the plan understood the significant role of the sewing machine in garment production; it could replace hand work for certain facets of an item's production, effectively reducing time and costs. Because sewing machines replaced primarily unskilled tasks, and not fine hand work, their increased use would create additional work for unskilled women, while doing no harm to skilled needleworkers.[120]

The *Union des femmes* selected sewing machine operators as a specialization for long-term development, based upon the intended interrelation of trades. It stated that the proposed producers' association "will be useful to the producers of cotton cloth, children's clothing, and [National Guard] military uniforms; it will be the organization's responsibility to distribute work to them, and to pay them."[121] Taking advantage of this developing technology, sewing machine operators could undertake aspects of production for several trades within the proposed federation of cooperatives. With the financial assistance of the cooperatives, sewing machine operators could own their machines and work in their homes. The *Union des femmes* was not motivated by the bourgeois ideology of domesticity, in terms of women's proper place in the home; rather, practical economic and social factors contributed to this decision. By "own[ing] their instrument of labor," and keeping it in their homes, female sewing machine operators could avoid childcare problems, as well as the time and expense of commuting to an *atelier*. In contrast to exploitative and alienating industrial homework, women would have a degree of control over their hours, conditions, and places of labor as part of a producer-owned cooperative.

Plumes et fleurs, "feathers and flowers," constituted the final trades specified for the Commission for Style Selection. The Organizational plan stated: "Because feathers and flowers are luxury articles, it is important to prepare a new future for this industry."[122] This trade typified the fine handwork performed by Parisian working women. Laboring in highly seasonal occupations, these artisans suffered "considerable periods of unemployment." The Organizational Plan determined that "they will no longer make the merchandise on commission; and the workers' associations, in the long months of unemployment, will be able to manufacture other products."[123] The *Union des femmes* sought to end the agonizing cycle of seasonality, which "in these two professions . . . had the deadliest results."[124] They served a primarily bourgeois clientele, people able to afford the frill and frivolity of crafted feathers and flowers. Retraining these women would allow them access to a consistent, reliable income, and would free them from dependence upon the bourgeois fashion cycle. The *Union des femmes* did not, however, intend to abandon luxury production; although they believed that Paris had inaugurated the new, egalitarian society, the foreign market remained. They expected to compete head-on with capitalist producers.

The Organizational Plan's fourth sub-committee, the Commission of Cashiers-Accountants, was charged with "establishing the levels of prices and wages." They would analyze each style of garment slated for production, as determined by the Commission for Style Selection, "including the value of materials used . . . general expenses involved, and labor costs." In calculating prices, the Cashier-Accountants were to "compare with those of the best-known Parisian shops, so that the competition will not harm the associations."[125]

The *Union des femmes* faced competition from privately owned, capitalist enterprises operating in Paris. The Commune permitted independent businesses to function, as it did the Bank of Paris, as long as they participated in the city's economy and cooperated with the Commune.[126] Relations between these employers and workers remained unaltered. An anonymous *citoyenne* informed the Commission of Labor and Exchange that a "group of women without work, and consequently without bread, are going, at this moment, to seek work with a shameless contractor who will pay them 25 to 35 sous less than the 4 francs the clothing cooperatives pay . . . Is this just? . . . We only ask for our rights, we do not want to be exploited."[127]

Echoing this indignation, another unnamed woman, "an anonymous *citoyenne* from Montmartre," presented Labor and Exchange with a similar example of unequal treatment, querying: "Is what I have come to learn true? Are we under the Empire . . . or under the Commune?"[128] Pressed by Frankel, Malon, and the Commission of Labor and Exchange, the Commune passed a measure on May 12, determining that "purchasing contracts be directly awarded to workers' cooperatives."[129] They did not, however, dispute member Victor Clément's proposal to "forbid changing the terms of existing contracts" with capitalists.[130] This seriously diluted the socialist nature of the Commune's economy, leaving many workers under the exploitative wage system, and newly emerging cooperatives directly rivaling established capitalist enterprises.

The *Union des femmes* consequently attempted to compete with capitalist producers on an uneven playing field. Although subsidized by the Commune government, cooperatives faced labor costs likely to exceed those of capitalist producers. Capitalist production relied on extracting profit from workers' labor; they accomplished this by keeping wages to a minimum. Whether worker-owned cooperatives were willing to pay themselves at depressed rates, or would be able to find alternative means to lower costs, constituted the salient question of the cooperatives' viability.

The *Union des femmes*'s Organizational Plan, inaugurated prior to the Commune's decree on workers' cooperatives, attempted to deal pragmatically with the shifting economic and political/legal milieu. It equipped the Commission of Cashiers-Accountants with a basic financial formula for developing a realistic wage and price structure, instructing them to analyze fixed and variable costs as well as competitors' rates. In creating this Commission, the *Union des femmes* attempted to bridge the gap between a capitalist past, an indeterminate present, and an ideally perceived future.

The Commission for Investigating Abandoned Premises comprised the fifth, and final, subcommittee in the Organizational Plan. The Plan stated that in each *arrondissement* "there will be one or several premises chosen, depending upon the requirements for the distribution, the cutting, and the receipt of manufactured goods."[131] Accordingly, the Commission's objective was "to find abandoned shops which would be usefully employed" by the federation of producer-owned cooperatives. This constituted the final step, the selection of decentralized spaces for production and for sales. In investigating potential sites, the delegates, "accompanied by a ministerial officer, will draft inventories of any furniture, equipment, fixtures, etc., on the premises. A statement of condition will then be drawn up with the aid of the Commission of Labor and Exchange. This statement and the inventories will be deposited in the permanent archives of the Minister of Public Works."[132]

The *Union des femmes* proposed an extremely legalistic expropriation, executed under a ministerial officer's watchful eye. Two delegates of the Commission for Investigating Abandoned Premises, the *citoyennes* Desprez and Ringard, reported that they "continued their investigations into properties," including at least four unattended sites in the 10th *arrondissement*.[133] The police commissioner of the Porte St. Martin Quarter certified that these businesses indeed stood empty, in accordance with *Union des femmes* regulations, and in compliance with the Commune's proclamation on abandoned workshops.[134]

The *Union's* procedures reflected a rather unrevolutionary carefulness and respect for private and personal property; this paralleled the position of the Commune government. The Commune did not abolish private property. On April 16 they decreed that only property "which had been abandoned by people fleeing their civic duty" could be seized, by reason of the owners' "cowardly desertion." The Commune created an investigative commission to "establish the practical conditions for promptly developing *ateliers,* not for the deserters who have abandoned them, but for the workers who might have been employed there."[135] Although the decree ensured property rights to all who demonstrated even nominal cooperation, the appropriation of abandoned workshops constituted a relatively revolutionary measure. At this stage of the insurrection, the Commune refrained from expropriating and redistributing private or public wealth.

In the Commune's final days, the Executive Commission of the Central Committee posted an "Appeal to Women Workers," inviting all female workers "to meet together, today, May 17 . . . to name delegates from each workers' association to form syndicated chambers [*chambres syndicales*], each of which will contribute two delegates to form the Federal Chamber of Working Women."[136] They envisioned citywide cooperation amongst female laborers of every trade. The Executive Commission viewed these "syndicated and federated laborers' associations as organizations of workers, in trade specific sections, forming free productive associations, federated between themselves."[137]

The future of the Federal Chamber of Working Women, finalized at an ensuing meeting on May 21,[138] ended abruptly as the Versailles troops invaded Paris on May 22, leaving unanswered the question of the feasibility of the *Union's* plans. They had struggled to "facilitate the birth of serious and homogenous groups, to preside at their formation, and, while leaving them free and autonomous, give them the spirit of federation."[139] And while they clearly made substantial efforts and progress, the Commune's seventy-two day life allowed little time to develop the projected socio-economic metamorphosis. Dmitrieff's final communication on behalf of the *Union des femmes* came on May 23, as Communard women and men fought in the streets, defending their revolution and their lives. She proclaimed: "Gather all of the women and the Committee members and go immediately to the barricades!"[140] And they did.

Elisabeth Dmitrieff led the *Union des femmes* members until the Commune's final hour. She had conceptualized, introduced, and begun to develop a feminist socialist program to ameliorate working-class women's economic and social subjugation and marginalization, by re-envisioning what comprised women's work, women's appropriate pay, and women's autonomy. With help from an Executive Commission, an elected Central Committee, and the Commune government's Commission of Labor and Exchange, Dmitrieff created and established an ambitious, broad-based, detailed, and tightly structured organization in an extremely short period of time. The *Union des femmes* was the sole women's association to receive aid from the Commune government; no vigilance committee or political club obtained such recognition. The Commune government, while essentially revolutionary, remained relatively conservative and reluctant regarding grass-roots activism, particularly women's. The more flamboyant, extreme, rhetorically violent political clubs received no governmental acknowledgment.[141] And although the Commune's Commission of Labor and Exchange did support the *Union,* they nonetheless demanded a degree of oversight in turn. They clearly held reservations about the radical women's society, not withstanding its adherence to the accepted gender division of labor and its orderly, top-down structure.

The *Union*'s Organizational Plan reflected a revolutionary pragmatism. It attempted to coordinate critical current demands with ideal future aspirations. Operating in a transitional, undefined period, the program combined both revolutionary and reformist components. It called for the fundamental reorganization of production relations, replacing capitalist ownership and wage labor with producer-owned cooperatives. Dmitrieff developed a federated system, combining a highly centralized structure and authority with a degree of local autonomy: essentially, she constructed a labor-based democratic centralism. Yet the *Union* still operated in a capitalist-driven world: production choices, and wage and price levels depended upon market demands and competition. The organization proposed the expropriation of abandoned properties, but, like the Commune government, ultimately respected private capital and property.

Dmitrieff and the *Union des femmes* leaders believed that worker-owned cooperatives could effectively compete with capitalist producers in a somewhat moderated free market. The Commune government's financial and organizational assistance, combined with its agreement to direct all subsequent purchasing contracts to cooperatives, made the federation's potential survival possible. Its viability rested heavily on governmental support. Workers' cooperatives faced competition from exploitative capitalist manufacturers, enterprises that maximized profits by minimizing workers' wages. By carefully selecting and pursuing trades that they determined to be relevant and profitable, the *Union des femmes* may have increased their chances of success. Their survival remained dependent upon the laborer-owners' willingness and ability to draw only limited wages; higher pay would require cost reductions and productivity improvements substantial enough to counterbalance increased labor costs.

The *Union des femmes* presented a feminist socialist critique of capitalist ownership that allowed for the perpetuation of capitalist relations within their emerging socialist society. While seemingly contradictory, their position accorded with that of the Commune government in attempting to introduce socialism while tolerating elements of capitalism. However, the *Union* did unequivocally attack the economic repercussions of the bourgeois ideology of domesticity and separate spheres. The *Union des femmes* considered the recognition of women as full participants within the public, laboring world as essential to their access to economic independence, which was their immediate primary goal; in the long-term, they sought an eradication of capitalist and patriarchal relations. Focusing on the public world of work and its repercussions, they did not address gender relations within the family. Facing the immediate reality of working class women's economic need, and their understanding of the Commune as a developing, evolving society, Dmitrieff and the *Union des femmes* took a pragmatic and transitional stance, while planning for their ideally conceived future.

Dmitrieff believed that a top-down organization, which would harness the anger and frustration of the working class, would prove most effective in the revolutionary milieu. This explains the moderation and order of the *Union des femmes,* particularly in contrast to the grass-roots political clubs explored in the next chapter. Dmitrieff's elite background, and years of studying and organizing, motivated her to design a tightly controlled and centrally overseen association. Like Léo, she trusted working-class women's instincts and capacities, but she saw these women as needing education and guidance, and considered herself the only viable person to lead them. As she wrote to Hermann Jung in late April,

> I am very ill, I have bronchitis and a fever. I work much, we rouse all the women of Paris. I organize public meetings, we have instituted defense committees in every arrondissement . . . and importantly a Central Committee . . . It is necessary that I speak every evening, that I write constantly, and my illness aggravates this . . . I am ill and there is no one to replace me.[142]

Dmitrieff bore this enormous, self-imposed responsibility, even to the detriment of her health. Although she asserted the importance of *arrondissement* committees and particularly the Central Committee, Dmitrieff clearly perceived herself as the *Union des femmes*'s essential motivator and motor. Power ultimately rested in her. Her lamentation that "there is no one to replace me," indicated either her mistrust of other women's competence or their lack of cooperative skills, abilities, or, very likely, time. Dmitrieff had wealth, knowledge, energy, and skill, and her product, the *Union des femmes,* became the largest and most effective organization during the Commune, despite receiving little assistance from older, more experienced activist women. Dmitrieff combined her multiple socialist and feminist influences into a practical socialist feminism, and proceeded to implement it in this dramatic, unique revolutionary context.

Fig. 4. André Léo with her husband
Gregoire Champseix and their twin sons André and Léo.
Courtesy of L'Association André Léo.

4
André Léo and the Subversion of Gender

The Battle over Women's Place

As the Paris Commune erupted on March 18, André Léo was traveling through the provinces, "from Orléans to Limoges," studying rural life and working to educate and radicalize the peasantry.[1] She hoped to help them recognize the commonality of oppressions, and thus commonality of interests that she believed they shared with urban workers. Léo soon returned to Paris to support the revolution. In her unpublished memoirs, she described her departure from Poitiers by train on the night of April 3, relating how a fellow passenger reacted with shock on hearing her destination: "Paris! . . . the violence . . . it is a den of bandits!"[2] Léo wrote that she responded "simply that he was mistaken, that 'I know Paris, and I am returning there with no fear.'"[3]

From its inception, Léo supported the Commune as an all-out war against inequality, injustice, and oppression. She recognized the uprising as an opportunity to implement the social, political, and economic changes she had been advocating for a decade. Léo theorized socio-economic and power relations, presenting a top-down critique intended to educate and guide the population to social renewal. Her acceptance and promotion of violent conflict, while seemingly contradictory to the gradualist, cooperative feminist socialism she embraced, instead allowed the development of her feminist socialist vision. Rather than viewing revolution as a solution itself, she conceived of it as the creation of a space in which to construct and develop transformative change. Total engagement in revolutionary civil war therefore comprised a just and legitimate means to create a context to implement her gradualist socialism, educate the population, and alter and expand women's roles and options.

Léo theorized about the social and political condition of women, the working class, and the peasantry. She particularly analyzed the meaning of femaleness, and the extent of its revolutionary potential. While the revolution would find Dmitrieff organizing from above, and Mink taking a radically democratic grass-roots approach, Léo endeavored to educate and instruct. She held that socio-political change required widespread, informed popular support. But at this historical point, she considered most people of all classes "prejudiced, they almost completely lack serious beliefs . . . Absorbed by material life, egoistic, the struggle of ideas leaves them indifferent."[4] To address this situation under the Commune, she wrote newspaper articles and pamphlets, and worked to establish free, secular education for both girls and boys. These forms of instruction served two purposes for her: to hasten the realization of her desired feminist and socialist goals, and to enlighten the population. Léo felt that she and other "honest and serious individuals of the lettered class," bore a duty to teach and raise the consciousness of those less fortunate.[5]

Three foci exemplify Léo's literary and philosophical approach to revolutionary activism during the Commune: theorizing and defending women's battlefield roles as nurses, cooks, and fighters; contesting the era's dominant ideologies and images of gender; and advocating the reconceptualization and reconstruction of girls' education. Each of these issues stood central to both attaining and fulfilling Léo's ideal of an egalitarian and just world. But she was by no means alone in these endeavors; other communardes also spoke and fought for these goals. As a social critic and leader, Léo stood at the forefront of these efforts, both developing new arguments and positions, and championing other activist women's ideas and undertakings. From her perspective, a society based on her feminist and socialist principles required equal respect, choices, and opportunities for all men and women. Léo continued to press for liberty and equality, but to achieve this, male and female Communards had to win the revolution with both ideas and arms.

Léo advocated an aggressive, broad-based military effort against the Commune's enemy, Adolphe Thiers and the Government of National Defense. She argued that women must be included in all martial capacities, and called for a fundamental reconfiguration of battlefield gender roles and an eradication of sex-based stereotypes, in this, the ultimate "male" arena. The Commune's army, the National Guard, needed to incorporate women, Léo held, if it was to triumph in this revolutionary civil war being fought for the establishment of an egalitarian society. Her memoirs contain a section entitled "Civil War," in which she argued that unlike an international war, which is "made for the profit of kings, in the interest of thievery and pride," a civil war "is the only fruitful, justifiable, and legitimate war, from the perspective of the oppressed."[6] Léo defined civil war as a rightful effort to emend existing inequity and injustice within a nation. While this meant an end to class hierarchies for the Commune government and most male communards, for Léo, and for many revolutionary women, this meant the destruction of both class and gender structures. Therefore, she defined the current conflict which, she reported, Thiers and the other "exploiters of humanity" have "declared a fratricidal war," as a "struggle for liberty, for equality. This war is necessary for the world right now. We are coming to the time when liberty of the spirit and of the word will be respected on the entire earth, when we will no longer have to bear arms."[7] Léo saw the uprising as both just and imperative. It was the opportunity to establish the type of society she had been theorizing and advocating for a decade, a free and equitable society that, she believed, would lead the rest of the globe in its path. "What is civil war?" she asked in her memoirs, "It is the war for ideas and for rights."[8]

Continuing to use the pen as her primary tool of activism, Léo established a newspaper, *La Sociale,* immediately upon her return to Paris from the provinces.[9] She employed this medium to influence revolutionary policy and action, to educate rank-and-file Communards, and to promote feminist socialist proposals. Within a week of commencing publication, on April 12 Léo wrote an editorial, *"Toutes avec tous,"* "All Women with All Men," addressing the issue of women's battlefield participation. She declared that "Democracy has historically been defeated because of women, and it will only triumph with them . . . Women's help is now necessary . . . Let them fully participate in the struggle to which they have already given their hearts. Many desire it, and many are able."[10]

Léo placed women's full revolutionary involvement as central to the Commune's sustenance and ultimate success. She recognized Parisian women's willingness and readiness to act, based at least partially on information emerging from political clubs, and possibly bolstered by the *Union des femmes*'s "Appeal to the Citizens of Paris," which had appeared the day before, posted on walls and published in the Commune government's *Journal officiel.*[11] By full participation, Léo meant access to the battlefield, in both armed and support roles. She did not, however, call for a female presence in the Commune government, which she viewed as transitional. Léo, like Mink, Dmitrieff, Nathalie Lemel, and Louise Michel, did not advocate women's political rights during the revolution, based on an understanding that not only were the present leaders and governing structure temporary, but that all political, economic, and social relations stood open to fundamental change. This did not mean that women should have no political involvement; on the contrary, it was only formal, legal rights that held minimal importance to them in the context of social upheaval. Léo clearly recognized the importance of women's involvement in both defending the uprising and in shaping its ultimate outcome, but she also recognized and warned against the possible impact of an immense female reactionary force. Alleging women's past conservatism, she threatened that their alienation from the current movement, with its enormous transformational possibilities, would once again drive potential allies and supporters to apathy or opposition.

Pursuing this issue several weeks later in a *La Sociale* article entitled "The Revolution Without Women," Léo charged that "one could, from a certain point of view, write our history since '89 under the title 'History of the Inconsistencies of the Revolutionary Party.' The woman question would make up the largest chapter, and it would show how this party had succeeded in pushing half of its troops over to the enemy, troops who had asked to march and fight on the party's side."[12] Although specifically addressed to the Commune's military chief, General Jaroslaw Dombrowski, Léo intended her words as a warning to a much broader audience: the all-male Commune government; the members of the Commune's army, the National Guard; and the leaders of Paris's socialist factions, including the International Workingman's Association. If women were denied incorporation into revolutionary defense and politics, many would turn to their traditional milieu, the Catholic Church, and participate in the reaction against revolution.[13] Léo cited the revolutionary left's historical alienation of women, and their neglect, and often derision, of women's issues and interests as the root of the movements' eighty years of failures. Now she accused the Commune of repeating the same mistake.

In forewarning of women's potential political abandonment of the insurgency, Léo implied a lack of tenacity and commitment on women's part. However, she viewed men in the same way. In her unpublished memoirs, she expressed serious doubt about the logic, focus, and perseverance of the mass of people as political actors. Making no gender distinctions, she contended that

> The crowd loves the grand, recognizes the true, inflames and intoxicates itself . . . with noble thoughts; but it is unable to sustain the effort for long, and it is even less able to tolerate deception. . . . If its idealism is discouraged one time, it will fall back lower, in self-absorption and torpor, with the suddenness of a child who, one moment crying to have the moon, is sound asleep the next. . . . It wants all or nothing.[14]

Léo viewed the mass of people, the crowd, as well intentioned, but having the reliability of a small child, to whom she likened them in this motherly analogy. In this non-gendered aspect of her critique, she theorized both women and men, peasant and worker, as ultimately lacking comprehension and commitment. In foretelling women's regression to the reactionary politics of the Church, however, Léo applied a theory of popular behavior.

Women's alienation would constitute the "deception" sufficient to terminate their revolutionary allegiance. But men, fully incorporated into the revolutionary project, posed no such risk. For Léo, women's lack of commitment and steadfastness emerged not based on essentialist sex-based characteristics, but rather due to their deceived or marginalized position in society; had the tables turned, and men been denied access to full participation, they, then, would have posed the risk.

In addition to denouncing the Commune's military leadership for excluding women, Léo also indicted their military strategy. She charged that they had missed a unique offensive opportunity to attack the city of Versailles, the seat of Thiers's government and the reactionary National Assembly, in the revolution's first days, as the national army retreated from Paris before laying siege. The Commune government chose a defensive posture instead, both to keep Versailles as the aggressor in the eyes of the nation, and because of the National Guard's lack of organization and skillful leadership.[15] Arguing against those who urged negotiation early in the fight, Léo declared: "There is no conciliation that would not be treasonous to the republican cause."[16] To Léo, women's military exclusion only exacerbated the National Guard's weakness, and undercut their ability to stage an all-out armed assault on the enemy. She believed that an aggressive military stance was essential for the precious revolutionary opportunity to succeed and to create the space for the construction of the new society.

In her April *La Sociale* article, "Toutes aves tous," Léo had affirmed the importance of all able-bodied Parisians taking arms, and of men and women forming a unified fighting force. She proclaimed,

> When the daughters, wives, and mothers fight with their sons, husbands, and fathers, Paris will no longer have a passion for liberty, it will have a delirium. And the enemy soldiers . . . will be forced to recognize that what they are facing is not a discordant opponent, but an entire people.[17]

Léo placed women within the familial context, but on a balanced footing with men: daughter for son, wife for husband, mother for father, each person held a specifically and equally gendered role. Women could be incorporated based upon their selves, not upon their either theoretical or actual reproductive and nurturing capacities. She sought a redefinition of the battlefield from a male-only domain, to an intergenerational, intergendered, integrated terrain. Léo exemplified a feminism that represented women as embodied women, as "daughters, wives, and mothers," but also as part of "the entire people," balanced by the "sons, husbands, and fathers," men as embodied men, described in corresponding, comparable terms. Consistent with her pre-Commune politics, she demanded equity for women as human beings, not based upon their specifically female biological, or stereotypical, characteristics, but as complete political and social actors.

In the revolutionary context, Léo reconceptualized her advocacy of women's equal political rights to encompass women's right to the battlefield. Defending the insurrection became a radicalized right to assure a just future. Léo demanded women's full access to this terrain. She held an exceptional position, even among feminists, in arguing for a gender-integrated armed force during the Commune.

Léo had consistently asserted women's right to participate in defense. During the Prussian siege of Paris in 1870, she argued against those who wanted women and children evacuated from the blockaded city, stating that "women . . . are indispensable to the defense."[18] At that point, all able-bodied men were engaged in the military struggle, and, Léo later wrote, "National Guard enrollments were stopped. . . . Paris did not then lack defenders. Alas, they had too many!"[19] But the city suffered terribly, and vehemently arguing against women's removal from the city for their "protection," she proposed that women take over the neglected, but essential, workings of the city—all of the "male" positions left abandoned by the soldiers. Accepting an altered form of a gender division of labor, Léo termed the war *"un grand atelier,"* where "the labor is double: the women will focus on life, the men on death. But all in the service of the nation (*la patrie*)."[20] She avowed women's capacity to do the same work as men, both on and off the battlefield. Her contention, therefore, rested on an existing social split with men on the front and women on the home front, which she neither condoned nor decried. Declaring that "Women are no less courageous than men," Léo asserted women's right to participate in the military ranks, but because the military already had sufficient fighters, women should "reserve their courage for the supreme struggle, for the battle in the streets."[21] The Commune was this supreme battle, where "the safety and success of the Republic is in the balance," and in its final weeks it did become a battle in the streets.[22]

In contrast to Léo's advocacy of a gender-integrated military, the majority of women's vigilance committees and the *Union des femmes* planned and organized for women to join in the revolution's military defense. However, this generally meant only if the battle entered the city. And where suggestions arose to arm women, they were to be organized into female battalions, not integrated into the National Guard.[23] These communardes all understood the battlefield as a principally male realm, but neither a privileged space, nor an exclusively male place.

In the supreme revolutionary moment, Léo and her fellow communardes demanded access to the battlefield, and many simply took it.[24] The vast majority of women's fighting took place during the Commune's final week, the Bloody Week, as the Versailles troops broke through the city's gates. Savage street-fighting ensued.[25] But women did participate militarily prior to the Bloody Week, taking up arms independently, as part of men's National Guard battalions, hunting down deserters in vigilance committees, and as an extension of their roles as *cantinières* (battlefield cooks) and *ambulancières* (nurses). *La Sociale* noted on April 8 that "Louise Michel had fought with a dignified courage worthy of the greatest praise" in battles at Issy and Châtillon, and on April 17 that "several *citoyennes* have been killed or wounded in courageously fighting to defend Paris."[26] But much more typically, communardes readied themselves to repulse an invasion. In the 12th *arrondissement* women formed the *Légion des fédérées* on May 12, organizing and training women to prepare to fight on the barricades if the Versailles troops entered the city, and searching for deserters and other internal enemies of the Commune.[27] A group of *citoyennes*, who called themselves the *Filles du Père Duchêne*, assisted in guarding the city's gates.[28] The *Club des femmes patriotes* formed a women's battalion "to defend Paris, in case of reaction."[29] The *Union des femmes* organized *cantinières* and *ambulancières*, and prepared to dispatch women to the barricades.[30] Louise Michel belonged to both the male and female Montmartre Vigilance Committees, organized to root out deserters and traitors, to aid the wounded, and to eventually defend Paris.[31] And Léo's name appeared on an April 26 notice in *Le Cri du peuple*, along with Krukovskaya Jaclard and Buisard, announcing that "the *citoyennes* of Montmartre" (this may or may not have been separate from the Vigilance Committee) intended "to form *ambulances* to follow troops engaged with the enemy . . . to actively demonstrate their devotion to the Revolution."[32] One week later, *"Le comité des citoyennes du XVII arrondissement,"* including Léo, published an appeal in *Le Cri du peuple*, asking women of their quarter to join them in aiding the wounded on the battlefield, and "finally behind the barricades, if the enemy of the people breaks through our ramparts." They summoned "the courageous and patriotic *citoyennes* to join our committee . . . In this struggle between the past and the future, the injustice against the right, those who consider themselves disinterested are mad, those who remain neutral are guilty."[33] Communardes readied, prepared, and took action, most frequently to provide aid or sustenance on the battlefield. And although the Commune was under siege, and its army was outgunned, out-manned, ill-nourished, and casualty-ridden, women continually faced barriers to their battlefield participation.

On May 1, the Commune's Committee of Public Safety, the powerful, newly established governmental arm holding extra-judicial revolutionary powers, passed a measure barring women from the battlefield. The authoritarian and controversial Committee, supported by the Commune's Blanquist and Jacobin faction, issued this ruling on its first day of existence, exemplifying the depth of sexism amongst male socialist leaders.[34] In reaction, André Léo wrote an exposé of the treatment that nine *ambulancières* received at the hands of the Commune's National Guard troops.[35] She related the reception encountered by "a group of *citoyennes* from the 17th *arrondissement*" attempting to offer aid to the battlefield wounded. The women were sent from place to place over a four-hour period, were denied access to the troops, and were forced to leave areas under fire, where they clearly could have been of help. Léo observed that "throughout the trip to the front lines, we experienced a very marked double sentiment: from the officers and surgeons, without exception, an absence of sympathy, which varied from the curt to the insulting; from the National Guards, a respect, a fraternity, often combined with a sincere emotion."[36]

Léo accused the military's elite males of a class-based gender bias against the communardes. Although the *ambulancières* intended to undertake the acceptably female role of nurse, they did so on their own initiative, in the distinctly male realm of the battlefield. This gender transgression brought them such encounters as with "A young officer . . . who believed he held the right of impertinence, and told the *citoyennes* a crude joke."[37] The women, unescorted by any males, appeared open to disrespect because their actions had crossed the boundaries of permissible female behavior. By contrast, Léo explained that to the mostly working-class National Guardsmen, the rank-and-file soldiers, the communardes represented the egalitarian spirit of revolution: "They feel the right of all in their right."[38] The National Guardsmen demonstrated a regard and appreciation for the women, at one point proclaiming, "*citoyennes,* it is beautiful, it is good that you have come here!"[39] They celebrated the arrival of women supporting the revolutionary cause as nurses: an acceptable, much needed, non-combatant role.

Léo perpetuated the insurgents' gendered functions in this context, explaining that "[the] woman on the field of battle, in the war for justice, is the certainty of faith, the spirit of the city saying to the soldier: I am with you. You are doing well."[40] For Léo, in this instance the "woman on the field of battle" served the traditional purpose of comfort and support both literally, in her capacity as nurse, and metaphorically, as faith and reassurance. Léo willingly employed traditional concepts of womanhood to promote female access to the battlefield, adapting her strategy to further her aims. While not undermining her arguments for women's equal capacities, she played to her audience's sex-based conceptions.

The Commune government's Delegate of War, Louis Rossel, responded to Léo's exposé in a letter published in *La Sociale* May 7; he wrote that he had read her article "with regret," and publicly asked her advice as to how best to utilize this devoted group.[41] Léo suggested "the formation of special ambulances on the ramparts and at the forward posts, ambulances directed . . . by one or two unprejudiced surgeons." She added that the three or four young women who had just passed their exams at the College of Medicine could also serve at these ambulances. These women, she contended, "have had the audacity to force the doors of science; they will lack neither in the service of humanity, nor of the revolution." But Léo was not optimistic about the implementation of her plan. She wrote to Rossel that "What you will be able to do to utilize these devoted republican women, you know better than I, because it depends on your power . . . these women have a strong masculine prejudice against them, and a surgeons' esprit de corps, both separately and in combination."[42]

Fig. 5. Louise Bonenfant, cantinière.
Courtesy of Siege and Commune of Paris collection, Charles Deering McCormick
Library of Special Collections, Northwestern University Library.

This "strong masculine prejudice" had class bias added to that of gender. In contrast to a conception of revolutionary equity, women's battlefield experiences were shaped by hierarchies and stereotypes of both sorts. For the officers, communardes' trespasses onto the battlefield would have been intensified by the connection between an outdated, less professional version of France's army, and the appearance of "unofficial" working-class women on the field of battle. After 1840, the wives of rank-and-file soldiers were barred from traveling with armies as camp followers. In their place, the military hired nuns to act as nurses, and unmarried women, wearing officially assigned uniforms, to serve as cooks.[43] The reappearance of "common," unauthorized women may have represented a regression to the standards and conditions of a less professional force. To the elitist officer corps, leading rather disorganized and inexperienced troops, the presence of these primarily working-class women would have constituted a doubly intolerable affront.

The Commune had drafted all medical men, including advanced students, into the National Guard, thus placing many revolutionary opponents on the battlefield. Many doctors reluctantly participated, or avoided serving if possible, while others heeded the call because of the severe shortage of medical personnel and the high casualties. A doctor's statement that "if there is a stupid way to risk one's life, it is to risk it for such people," typified the condescending and hostile attitude.[44] Some physicians attempted to undermine the Commune through reducing its fighting forces by holding soldiers in hospital beds much longer than necessary, sabotaging weapons and ammunition brought in by the combatants, and citing incorrect numbers of wounded and dead to Commune authorities.[45] The presence of untrained working-class women, particularly those intending to assist doctors, would have generated further anger and resentment among this elite corps.

The grave shortage of doctors made the presence of hostile physicians on the battlefield essentially unavoidable. But in allowing their perpetuation of hierarchy and bias, the Commune undermined its ability to fully utilize skills and commitment of its supporters. Even women who undertook the traditionally female nurturing roles of feeding and nursing the soldiers as *cantinières* and *ambulancières* clashed with the dominant powers. These were women, as Gay Gullickson has explained, who were often caricatured in the press as silly and young, or as motherly. It is little wonder, then, as Gullickson has demonstrated, that the "amazons," the fighting women, tended to be portrayed as threatening, unnatural, or insane.[46]

Working-class women made up the majority of female military participants, most of whom desired to support the Commune actively, perceiving it as the dawn of a new, just society. A minority of female volunteers enrolled to support their husbands or partners by serving as nurses and cooks to the man's battalion. The experience of one of these women, Alix Payen, a young *bourgeoise* and officer's wife, exemplifies how a woman's class position affected her battlefield life.

Alix Milliet Payen, the daughter of bourgeois republican followers of the Utopian socialist Charles Fourier, supported her husband's battalion as an *ambulancière*.[47] In a letter to her mother, Payen described her encampment "in a cemetery . . . When I say encampment, I deceive myself, because we have neither tent nor any coverage. The rain rarely ceases."[48] Payen related the severe lack of supplies and relief, yet she received special treatment as a sergeant's wife and as a *bourgeoise*. She subsequently wrote, "I am always surprised by the attentions I receive. For example, the water for cooking is quite far away, and one carries only what is necessary, but every morning I find a canteen of water for my toilette. Today, as it was cold, Chanoine had warmed my water!"[49] Payen's class undoubtedly affected her battlefield experience. She secured particular privileges based upon the presumed requirements of a bourgeois woman; even under fire, those around her assumed that she needed to maintain the outward characteristics that clearly defined her role. As Léo explained in her 1869 treatise, *La Femme et les mœurs*, bourgeois women were raised to believe that luxury and pleasure constituted their destiny.[50] Although Payen seemed willing to abandon these expectations temporarily, those in her immediate circle did not. In his family history, Payen's brother Jean-Paul Milliet addressed the apparent incongruity of such a woman in this violent and public context. Milliet queried,

> How can a frail young woman, accustomed to the attentive treatment of her family, find herself animated with an unforeseen energy, to be able to confront such dangers? It is that the defense of a just cause provides the enthusiasm which lifts the heart; it is also, and especially, that a reciprocal love transfigures people: the most timid can become heroes.[51]

While "a just cause" can provide motivation for heroic action, Milliet argued that it is "especially" love that enables such transfiguration. Payen seems to have confirmed his analysis, informing her mother, "I dream of being an *ambulancière* in Henri's battalion and of following him everywhere."[52] While her class allowed her certain privileges, it could not spare her from the violence of war; her husband was killed during Bloody Week.[53] She unquestionably met the standards of "true womanhood," by completely sacrificing her well-being, and potentially her life, to remain at her husband's side. Payen undoubtedly trespassed onto the male terrain of the battlefield, but her position both in the company, and in the service of her husband, moderated her transgression. She remained under male authority, and thus, even on the battlefield, retained at least the essence of *bourgeoise* propriety.

By contrast, André Léo struggled to open the battlefield to all communardes, working class and bourgeois. She asserted that "All humans have a preservation instinct, and it is not a man's beard which surmounts this instinct; but, a superior passion. Right now, Parisian women possess this passion."[54] According to Léo, both men and women could overcome their natural opposition to placing themselves in a life-threatening situation, the battlefield, if possessed by "a superior passion." She recognized that women stood excluded based on the contemporary theoretical definition of femaleness, and she demanded a recognition of her antithetical theoretical understanding of women. Consistent with her ideas regarding the equality

of the genders, Léo defined the "preservation instinct" as "human," rejecting the period's dominant gender dichotomies that portrayed women as "naturally" nurturing, submissive, and passive. Rather, she explained, they are
"anxious, enthusiastic, and ardent, their spirits prepared for the vicissitudes
of combat, their eyes more filled with fire than tears, giving themselves entirely (especially working-class women) to the great cause of Paris."[55] Women,
she believed, possessed confidence, strength, and the ability and desire to
combat.

Correspondingly, Elisabeth Dmitrieff and the Central Committee of the
Union des femmes also demanded women's right to defend the revolution violently. The Central Committee issued a Manifesto to protest an appeal by
an anonymous group of *citoyennes,* claiming to represent the women of Paris,
who "appealed to the generosity of Versailles and asked for peace at any
price."[56] Dmitrieff and the Committee responded thus:

> The generosity of cowardly assassins! A conciliation between liberty and des-
> potism, between the People and their executioners! No, it is not peace, but
> all out war that the working women of Paris demand! . . . the rivers of blood
> spilled for the cause of liberty are our titles of glory and of vengeance! . . .
> The women of Paris will prove to France and to the world that they, at the
> supreme moment of danger . . . will give as their brothers their blood and
> their life for the defense and the triumph of the Commune, that is to say
> the People![57]

Members of the *Union des femmes,* like Léo and many communardes, supported women's right to fight to defend the Commune in this "supreme moment of danger." For these female insurrectionaries, and some like-minded
men, military defense was universal, not gender-based. In the Manifesto, undoubtedly written by Dmitrieff, they claimed the right to shed blood and to
give their lives "at the supreme moment of danger," just as Léo demanded
the same right for women in the "supreme struggle."[58] Both women used the
print medium to prepare communardes to defend the revolution, and to
convince the Commune government how necessary this was. Dmitrieff
organized the women, and Léo brought them ideas, analysis, and challenges,
both in support of all-out military assault, by an army of women and "their
brothers."

Defending women's right to battlefield participation was part of Léo's larger
project of critiquing and breaking down the existing, restrictive conceptions
of women's place. Access to the military realm chiseled away at gendered
boundaries. In arguing for women's full revolutionary participation, Léo attacked a sacrosanct male domain, one supported by an ingrained, multi-
faceted, and pervasive web of patriarchal forces.

The gender ideology Léo fought against had deep, penetrating roots, and
transcended the boundary between socialists and capitalists. Critics of the

Commune, and critics of women's behavior during the Commune (comprising mostly overlapping, but also some mutually exclusive groups), frequently attributed communardes' revolutionary activism to moral defect. Many of the era's political, military, and economic elite, struggling to comprehend the meaning and motivation behind female insurgency, found explanatory power in claims of working-class women's "natural" lack of morality, and the conditions of "depravity" in which they lived. These commentators also considered bourgeoise communardes to have abandoned their rightful place and people for a life of debauches. For such critics, observers, and ultimately judges, activist women's public behavior and private relationships flew in the face of decency or propriety, defined in terms of the bourgeois standards of separate spheres of gender activity and expectations of clearly differentiated gender roles.

In her unpublished memoirs, Léo explained how such accusations "have taken on political meaning, under the malevolent pens of adversaries."[59] The quotidian realities of communardes' lives, always objectionable to bourgeois and Catholic authorities, became particularly threatening in the revolutionary context. The predominantly working-class communardes operated in the public, or male, sphere both as wage laborers and as political activists; privately, many did not enter into "legal," or state- and church-sanctioned marriages, but rather maintained *unions libres*, "free unions," with their partners. The Commune provided the space for female insurgents, from both the working class and the bourgeoisie, to step further outside the acceptable confines of female behavior, in myriad ways and to various degrees, as they fought to reconfigure their political and social worlds. Women's participation in political clubs and organizations, their formation of vigilance committees, and their efforts as battlefield nurses, cooks, and warriors briefly expanded their public presence. The introduction of divorce, equally accessible to both women and men, the recognition of *unions libres*, and the *Union des femmes*'s effort to reorganize and reconceptualize women's labor, contributed to the short-lived legitimization of working-class women's conceptions of morality.

In depicting and assessing female revolutionaries, the Commune's male critics transposed the era's predominant associations between female class and sexuality. Rather than presenting the typical portrayal of working-class women as sexualized and available, they characterized them as hideous and threatening.[60] Bourgeois communardes appeared highly eroticized, in contrast to the more common images of the pure, virtually sexless "lady." Revolutionary, class-based conflict shifted the stereotype of working-class women from seductively raw and untamed, to threateningly violent and repulsive. Correspondingly, the insurgent bourgeoise, unfettered by social constraints, became rendered an openly alluring, sexually available woman. She lost the "protection" of bourgeois propriety.

The moment of revolutionary upheaval faced brutal repression and reaction in the aftermath of the Commune. Military courts accused activist women of crimes including "insurrectionary participation,"[61] "complicity in illegal arrest and arbitrary sequestration,"[62] "aiding in the construction of barricades,"[63] and "carrying and using arms in an insurrectionary movement,"[64] but government reports and analyses point to underlying causes of reaction. Clearly, female communardes attacked the bourgeois capitalist state, as did male insurgents, by participating in a revolutionary civil war, but women particularly transgressed bourgeois cultural and social standards by virtue of their gender. Activist women violated gender and class boundaries intended to insure the maintenance of the hierarchical status quo.

In attempting to determine the causal factors and assign blame for these hierarchical breaches, the Versailles authorities attributed much of female activism to what they considered women's dangerous essences: their "natural" irrationality and uncontrolled sexuality. Unrestrained by male authority or bourgeois proscriptions, communardes fell victim to pernicious influences, were easily swayed, and unknowingly wreaked havoc on the bourgeois gender and class orders. According to a Ministry of War report in the Commune's aftermath, none of the female insurgents, with the possible exception of the radical *bourgeoises,* embraced the revolution in any conscious, intelligent, or rational manner. The account propounded various impetuses for female insurgency. Predictably, it blamed "socialist theories, meetings and clubs, [and] immoral and obscene publications," but the document also strongly indicted their "state of concubinage, of demoralization, and of debauchery" as primary causal factors.[65] The military judges viewed women's aggressive, activist, and openly public behavior as both components of, and explanations for, their crimes.

To the authors of the Ministry of War report, female insurgents were "seduced by the theories of socialism developed in the clubs and public meetings since the law of June 6, 1868 . . . [their] laziness, envy, [and] thirst for enjoyments unknown and ardently desired, contributed to their blindness, and they threw themselves, without thinking, into the revolutionary movement which must engulf them."[66] Rooting the source of these insidious ideas in the popular public sphere that emerged following Louis-Napoléon's relaxation of press and speech restrictions, the report posits women as the naïve and impressionable sex, endangered by these freedoms. From this perspective, blind and unthinking selfishness had led women to participate in the Commune. Their revolutionary involvement was likened to sexual enticement. As innocents entering into an ill-advised, illicit love affair, these women were "seduced," seeking to quench their "thirst for enjoyments unknown and ardently desired." Blinded by their desire, "they threw themselves" at the seducer, the Commune, and thus into unavoidable ruin. This assessment reduced activist women to absolutely reactive, unthinking, and weak beings; as such, their immoral and demoralized lives led inevitably to depravity. The report blatantly negated both the appeal of the Commune's ideas and women's abilities to understand and consciously accept or reject them.

Many facets of working-class women's lives and behaviors held this dual criminal–causational status. Publicly, they trespassed onto the male world of work as laborers and into the masculine spheres of politics and the battlefield; privately, many rejected legal, state, and Church-sanctioned marriages, choosing instead *unions libres,* with their partners. Frequently of long duration, these relationships formed the basis for many working-class Parisian families.[67] A communarde, known as *La Matelassière* ("the mattress maker"), announced at a *Club des proletaires* meeting, "I have a sixteen-year-old daughter, and never, as long as I live, will she marry . . . she now lives with someone, and she is very happy without the sacraments of the Church."[68]

Workers' anti-clerical sentiments, and/or their inability or refusal to pay a marriage fee, contributed to the prevalence of *unions libres.* Léo wrote on this issue, arguing that it was "true that the illegal unions are very common, but most of these households have the same regularity as the legal marriages; they raise their children, have the same sense of community, and take the same names of wife, husband, father, and mother."[69] She defended these unions as "more moral than those of the *grand monde,*" stressing their normalcy, consistency, and structure. And while she clearly accepted the legitimacy of these partnerships, she did believe that women had greater economic protection in legal marriage.[70]

When workers did marry, they tended to terminate unhappy relationships by simply separating, thus violating the religious and legal sanctity of matrimony. These rejections of bourgeois morality, as well as the authority of the Catholic Church and the French state, infuriated the political and religious authorities and the elite public.[71] Women in *unions libres* faced moral condemnation for "living in concubinage," a phrase that described their civil state in judicial and police reports and dossiers of communardes.[72] This labeling supplied bourgeois authorities with an "explanation" for female revolutionary activism. The social definition, or labeling, of these women thus served to explicate their behavior.

The case of Sophie Doctrinal Poirier, a seamstress and friend of Léo's, who served as president of the *Comité de vigilance des citoyennes du 18e arrondissement* and founded *Le Club de la Boule Noire* in the 17th *arrondissement,* clearly shows how the governmental authorities used moral judgments to explain women's behavior. Her *Commission des Grâce* (Pardon Commission) dossier, held in the *Archives Nationale,* reports that during the Prussian Siege she organized and operated a cooperative clothing workshop with seventy to eighty women, and that she was "recently living in concubinage with a day laborer, M. Poirier."[73] According to this report, "Her past appears to be beyond reproach. She came to Paris four years ago, and she lost her husband two years later. It was only from this moment that her conduct became irregular."[74] Thus, Poirier's "irregular" behavior stemmed from the "moment" she became a widow; her husband Lamarchand died in 1870, the year of the Siege. For the Versailles government's Ministry of Justice, the absence of a legitimate male authority in her life explained everything: with no husband to control her behavior, or her sexuality, she entered into illicit relations, and undertook improper public and political roles.[75] Her actions, both in terms of her "concubinage," and of her very public organizational and insurrectionary roles, reflected her rejection of bourgeois standards of moral acceptability. Her private transgressions served to exacerbate her political crimes.[76]

Although the Ministry of Justice report described Poirier as a widow, it nonetheless referred to her as "*femme* Lamarchand," or "Mrs. Lamarchand," rather than the more common title of "*veuve*," or "widow." The report also acknowledged that she was "better known under the name of her lover, Poirier." This rather confusing set of labels reflected class differences in the relative values placed on legal marriage and free unions. The official report begins: "Sophie Doctrinal, *femme* Lamarchand, *dite* [called] *femme* Poirier." For the Ministry of Justice, Sophie Doctrinal remained the wife of Lamarchand, even if she considered herself to be something else. For Poirier and many other working-class and activist women, adopting their partner's name indicated their equal acceptance of *unions libres* and legal marriage.[77]

A post-Commune military tribunal, under the 26th Council of War, convicted Sophie Poirier of several actions "in the insurrectional movement in Paris, in 1871," including having "invaded, and violently menaced, an inhabited house."[78] According to the report, "Dr. Barbet's domicile was invaded by the acolytes of *femme* Lamarchand, armed with sabres and revolvers, who summoned him, with injurious force and threats, to aid their stricken comrades."[79] The accusations of home invasion and coercion with threatened violence comprised the legal offenses against the doctor's property and person, but Poirier (Lamarchand) also violated acceptable gender boundaries by leading a group of armed women. A female militant and her "acolytes," brandishing "sabres and revolvers" and physically threatening a medical doctor in his home, dramatically contradicted the proper role of the gentle, maternal sex.

The military court further implicated Poirier for objectionable female behavior by terming the group her "acolytes," thus placing her in an even more menacing, and clearly non-feminine leadership position, and effectively holding her responsible for the other women's actions. The report continued, explaining that the "military authorities believe that the supplicant has exercised a deplorable influence on this part of the feminine population of Paris, which is later found to be disposed to lending its cooperation to the incendiaries."[80] If Poirier's "acolytes," or "this part of the feminine population of Paris," fell victim to her iniquitous sway, were they merely innocent victims of her "immoral influence?" This question presents an interesting insight into the government's ideology of gender. Adhering to conceptions of female "nature" as weak, emotional, and irrational would support the exoneration of this militant group. Poirier's history of establishing and running a cooperative during the Prussian Siege undoubtedly contributed to the court's portrayal of her as a pernicious character. Her official offenses under the Commune indicate that her leadership and organizational roles particularly inflamed her judges, for Poirier's other crimes included "organizing and directing an association of more than twenty persons," "publicly exciting and provoking . . . an assault intended to incite civil war," and "wearing a notorious insignia [the revolutionary cockade]."[81] Her flamboyant trespass into the public, male arena, and her proven and threatening leadership abilities intensified the meaning of her legal transgressions. Her severe sentence, "deportation to a fortified prison," and her subsequently rejected request for a pardon, exemplified the strength of Versailles's intent to reimpose political, social, and gendered order.

As in the case of Poirier, government authorities placed significant emphasis on the idea of women as either weak, powerless creatures, vulnerable to any negative influences, or as immoral, uncontrollable furies, threatening to the decency of other women. The Ministry of War's report on communardes stated that, of the eighty-two *célibataire* arrestees who lived alone,

> we have noticed a score of young girls, whose conduct is certainly not exempt from all reproach, but who merit, nonetheless, not being confused with their co-detainees. Unhappily, they are on the road to vice, and there they will fall one day. Barring a miracle, they are destined to become prostitutes or to eventually form faux-ménages [false families or unions].[82]

This "score of young girls" were regarded as morally superior to their "co-detainees"; apparently, they constituted the exceptions in the report's earlier accusation that "All, or nearly all, are lacking morals."[83] These young communardes faced certain debauch because of their immoral milieu. Clearly, the author saw these women as thoroughly vulnerable to the examples set by their sex and class, influences he considered unavoidably ruinous. Yet, by setting them apart, he created a surprising category: the relatively virtuous communarde. Although the author described them as "certainly not exempt from all reproach," he curiously did distinguish between the groups of female arrestees.

At the time of the February 1872 report, of the 1051 accused communardes, only 33 had faced trial, and of those tried, only 18 received convictions, thus creating the significant possibility of "innocent" detainees. The Ministry of War report's author, Léon Briot, may have assumed the chaste *célibataires* to be among the potential acquittals; although their conduct was lacking, and they faced certain corruption, the value of their presumed sexual purity warranted their distinction from the other, lascivious women.

For the authors of the report, no differentiation existed between the young women's eventual destinies of prostitution or "illicit" unions, either morally or as an ultimate fate. They viewed a union lacking Church and state sanction as presenting a woman with the same lot as prostitution.[84] This attitude typified the irrelevance of bourgeois gender standards to the lives of most working-class women. The contemporary prevalence of *unions libres* underlined this point.[85]

The dominant conceptualizations of gender ascribed women with two contradictory essential natures: the idealized nurturing, caring, pure, and morally superior being, and the demonized dangerous, smoldering, wild and virtually uncontrollable sexual animal. Woman embodied both primal good and primitive evil. Her weak and emotional nature assured that the beast lurking below the surface could emerge, unbridled, at any moment. This perception of female sexuality deeply threatened men, particularly bourgeois men intent on maintaining their gender prerogative.[86] In these terms, woman was emotion and nature incarnate. The apparently conflicting aspects of her character, taken together, comprised "primitive," uncivilized, and irrational behavior. Sweet, maternal, and nurturing conduct, as well as wild, impetuous, and sexual behavior, all constituted instinctive and emotional states. The seemingly discrepant images thus coexisted in their absence of reason. Comparable to a nesting animal, a raging beast, or a docile and endearing pet, woman embodied the antitheses of a rational, civilized being. She was the "anti-man."

Among the bourgeoisie, it fell to the husband to control his wife's sexuality, specifically by preventing her "over-stimulation."[87] Constraints on a bourgeois wife's passions reflected concerns of property and blood, while an unmarried daughter's virginity required vigilant defense, as it defined her viability as a potential, respectable wife.[88] These standards also provided a demarcation between the virtuous, bourgeois woman, and the highly sexualized image of the working-class female, unfettered by the imposition of "proper" behavioral standards. The ultimate fear rested in perceived female power and caprice. An openly sexual woman could upset the existing social hierarchy by bringing men to their knees with her erotic power.[89]

These fears held a particular intensity during the Commune. Bourgeois critics graphically described female dress, weapons, physical appearance, and comportment. Marie Vrecq, *femme* Bediet, "wore a sailor's outfit, and carried a revolver in her belt";[90] Louise Michel "armed with a carbine, wore a National Guard uniform";[91] and Marie Guyard, a rag picker, appeared "always armed with a revolver and wearing a red cockade."[92] These and many other communardes donned military garb to express their active participation in defending the city and the revolution. They appropriated the traditionally male, public role of soldier, wearing uniforms and sashes, and carrying weapons. This was what revolution looked like to these women, and they made it their own.[93]

Marie Guyard, the militant rag picker, took this military role one step farther. According to the anti-Commune observer and critic Paul Fontoulieu, she played an odious role, on May 27, in the bloody drama on the Place de la Roquette, where Monseigneur Surat and other hostages were assassinated. She marched, a red flag in hand, at the head of a sinister cortege, exciting the insurgents to vengeance. She also fired her revolver at the victims. She was condemned to death.[94]

Although Guyard faced a death sentence, the testimony that she "fired her revolver at the victims," did not clarify whether she actually shot anyone. Military dress, militarism, and revolutionary leadership formed her fundamental crimes; she symbolized not only a political or class-related threat, but a specific challenge to the gendered order.

Lodoiska Caweska, described by Fontoulieu as "a very beautiful thirty-year-old Polish woman," was another example of a militant woman. The treasurer of the *Turcos* [Turks] *de la Commune,* she "could be seen, blouse loosened, on horseback, at the head of a battalion of soldiers. Her costume had several picturesque and theatrical components, which seduced the crowd; it was composed of short, Turkish pants, high-buttoned shoes with gold tassels, a vest of crimson velvet decorated with embroidery, a cap with a red cockade, and a blue belt from which hung two pistols."[95] Caweska, "blouse loosened, on horseback," seduced the crowd with her richly textured, deeply colored clothing. She represented the sexual, morally questionable communarde, in contrast to the virtually sexless, ideal bourgeois *dame* ["lady"].

Women's chastity and fidelity constituted essential components in bourgeois conceptions of gender and class. While the elite woman embodied purity based upon a certain "passionlessness," derived from the external forces controlling her ardor, the working-class woman remained sexually available because nothing, or no one, controlled her erotic, carnal nature. The mechanisms for sexually regulating women, including expectations of premarital chastity, marital "moderation," and the relative assurance of legal marriage, remained alien to working-class Parisian culture in this period.[96] Bourgeois respectability existed relative to its opposition; the construct of "lady" relied on the existence of an "other," specifically, a "fallen" woman or a working-class woman. The definition of a proper bourgeois woman rested on what she was not: she was neither "fallen" nor working class.[97] Ironically, working-class women's perceived sexuality disqualified them from "true" womanhood.

As Gay Gullickson has convincingly demonstrated, conservative critics and journalists represented communardes as wild and licentious to elicit horror and fright, and to remove any hint of sympathy in their bourgeois readers.[98] Fontoulieu utilized two different rhetorical methods in presenting the cases of Guyard and Caweska. He portrayed Guyard in blunt, negative terms: "armed with a revolver and wearing a red cockade," she played an "odious role" in a "bloody drama," heading a "sinister cortege." In contrast, Caweska, an exotic *Polonaise,* "seduced the crowd," riding horseback with her "blouse loosened," wearing a "vest of crimson velvet."[99] Caweska's dangerous sensuality contrasted with Guyard's violent aggression, but both sharply clashed with bourgeois conceptions of propriety and women's role.

Fontoulieu's description of Guyard manipulating the crowd, "exciting the insurgents to vengeance," in comparison with his depiction of how Caweska "seduced the crowd," reflected the two women's differing class positions.[100] While Guyard labored as a rag picker, Caweska, according to Edith Thomas, was an occasional journalist, frequent political club participant, and the wife of the doctor Constantin Kawecki, a Commandant in the Parisian National Guard.[101] In contrast to his treatment of the working-class Guyard, Fontoulieu neither insulted nor demeaned the radical Caweska; he fetishized her. His element of relative respect included a definite degree of awe and fear: Caweska represented the unrestrained sexual seductress.

The two women's class differences ensured their exposure to differing influences and images of revolution, and thus they used divergent means to present themselves. Communardes from elite backgrounds primarily donned dramatic and flamboyant costumes, although women of all classes wore red scarves and sashes. This pattern could be attributable to economics, or perhaps to varied conceptions of revolutionary aesthetics. For Caweska, opulent, dramatic, and seductive clothing may have represented a flouting of conventional standards for the proper *bourgeoise*. Her attire and her actions indicated a conscious rejection of the social limitations placed on her gender and class.

Fontoulieu portrayed Caweska's costume as having "several picturesque and theatrical components, which seduced the crowd."[102] By evoking theatrical imagery, he likened her to the era's actresses, women notorious for their overt sexual behavior and their status as courtesans. Fontoulieu carried the connection to the stage farther, describing Caweska as "a very beautiful woman . . . she was the mistress of a former actor of the theater of *la Villette*."[103] Courtesans, such as Emile Zola's actress character Nana, in his eponymously titled novel, were high-priced prostitutes, supported by a clientele described by Alain Corbin, in *Women for Hire*, as including only elite, moneyed men.[104] Wealthy patrons enabled courtesans to live and dress stylishly and extravagantly. Zola described Nana's elevation to the peak of her "art": "Thereupon Nana became a woman of fashion, a beneficiary of male stupidity and lust, an aristocrat in the ranks of her calling."[105] By focusing on Caweska's dress, Fontoulieu reflected the period's common correlation between lavish, dramatic clothing and immorality. Hollis Clayson argues that opulent attire could indicate a disregard for social convention and a rejection of bourgeois precepts.[106] By thus impugning Caweska's morality, Fontoulieu equated the danger of a flamboyant, revolutionary woman, with that of the courtesan: both inverted the dominant gender and class hierarchies. As the courtesan commanded the male bourgeois or aristocrat, so the Communards sought to transpose the existing social order.[107] While Caweska most likely did not seek comparison with courtesans, she did, indeed, challenge the boundaries of female bourgeois acceptability. Fontoulieu's interpretation stemmed, therefore, from Caweska's intended message and self-fashioning. He did not merely impose his image of revolutionary *bourgeoise* on her; she chose her tools and language of rebellion to convey her political message.

Fontoulieu's portrayal of a Polish male Communard, Apollon Kobosko, provides a suggestion of the specifically gendered aspects of his assessments. Born in Warsaw, Kobosko emigrated first to England, and then to Paris, where he worked as a printer, and subsequently served the Commune as a cavalry under-lieutenant. On the evening of April 15, Kobosko attended the political club at the *Eglise Saint-Leu*.[108] Fontoulieu described his impression of the meeting in great detail:

> Thirty or forty *fédérés*, obeying the orders of a foreigner named Kobosko, organized, in the church, an orgy-masquerade as one has never seen, except during the saturnalia of '93; they donned ecclesiastical habits . . . and parodied the divine offices by singing lewd refrains. Kobosko officiated. He gave communion to his worthy acolyte by making the most grotesque gestures . . . After a repast, where one hundred and thirty bottles of wine were consumed, they invited all of the quarter's prostitutes to a ball. At midnight, the doors were tightly closed, and men and women slept jumbled together in the church.[109]

Fontoulieu related a scene of disrespect and debauch that he undoubtedly deplored. He focused primarily on the events, and on Kobosko's participation, but not overtly on his character or personal image. Though Kobosko "organized" the "orgy-masquerade," and "officiated" at the religious parody, making "grotesque gestures," Fontoulieu did not attempt to interpret, characterize, or condemn Kobosko as an individual. He described the Communard's appearance as "a tall man, vigorous . . . one constantly saw him roaming the streets on a richly harnessed horse."[110] Like Caweska, Kobosko appeared on horseback, and yet there the similarities end. Although this represents one of Fontoulieu's most elaborate portrayals of a man, it lacks the strongly gendered tone and language of his description of Caweska.[111] As a depiction of a person leading a shocking act, it missed the opprobrium placed on Guyard for her "odious role" in marching "at the head of a sinister cortege."[112] Although Kobosko directed a blasphemous and profane "orgy-masquerade," his leadership transgressed neither gender nor class lines. As an officer and a man, his actions fell under the purview of wartime activity; Fontoulieu condemned him only within these parameters.

Male elites traditionally viewed working class women as sexually available and appealing, as evidenced in Zola's *Nana*. In Léo's play, *Marianne*, bourgeois men often had working class mistresses, and students commonly "sowed their wild oats" with young *"grisettes,"* single "working girls," before settling down with a "respectable" bourgeois wife.[113] *Marianne* tells the tale of Albert, a provincial young bourgeois, who leaves home and his devoted fiancée Marianne to study medicine in Paris. Having pledged fidelity to Marianne, he nonetheless quickly begins an affair with a working class young woman, Fauvette, who initially knows nothing of his other relationship. When eventually confronted with his duplicity by Fauvette, he admits that Marianne is his fiancée, and informs Fauvette that no respectable man would marry his mistress. In the subsequent scenes, Léo rejects the assumption of this bourgeois male privilege: Fauvette leaves him, and the play ends with Marianne spurning Albert and vowing to marry his roommate, a diligent, honorable medical student who had risen from the working class. Upon hearing the news, Albert's sister, scandalized, sputters *"le fils d'un artisan!"* ("the son of an artisan!"), to which Marianne responds: *"un honnête homme!"* ("an honest man!")[114] Léo's play overtly challenged the acceptability of bourgeois men's sexual procurement and deception of working-class women, and their duplicity toward women of their own class. She wrote against both a stereotype of working class women's sexual availability, and the reality of elite men's tolerated perfidy.

A report in the *Commission des grâce* file of communarde Marguerite Guinder Prévost, who was charged with murdering a bourgeois, contrasted this conception of working women's sexual procurability. The report typified the shift in conflations of female sexuality and class, as anti-communarde critics portrayed working-class women as desexualized, and bourgeois female revolutionaries as highly sexual. The *Commission des grâce*'s testimonial against Prévost, alleging her participation in the execution of a "gentleman," related that she "wore a rifle slung over her shoulder, and two revolvers in her belt . . . after the execution . . . this immodest woman urinated in front of everyone, announcing . . . "I piss with joy!"[115] The report portrayed Prévost as an armed and menacing figure, similar to Fontoulieu's account of the rag picker Guyard; a woman wearing a rifle and two revolvers certainly did not represent sexual availability. The words and images chosen to report her alleged public urination sharply underlined the report's de-eroticization of Prévost. Although described as an "immodest woman," the speaker gave no other indication of her sex.[116] Prévost was in a potentially strongly sexual action and posture, but we hear nothing of her lifting her skirts, squatting down, or exposing herself. The account's significance emerges from what it does not say.

Working-class women's relative crudeness, possibly exciting during social calm, became repulsive and threatening when these women took up arms during the class-based civil war. Bourgeois observers so demonized rank-and-file communardes, that they virtually denied the women's humanity, and with it their sexuality. Correspondingly, male critics also inverted the accepted perceptions of elite women's virtual sexlessness and modesty by portraying bourgeois communardes as seductive and strongly sexual. By abandoning their proper role and comportment, activist *bourgeoises* sacrificed their idealized and rarified image, stripping away the protective layer

Fig. 6. Marguerite Prévost.
Courtesy of Siege and Commune of Paris collection, Charles Deering
McCormick Library of Special Collections, Northwestern University Library.

of purity. Without their assumed male protector/controller, they could be considered sexually available. Even in military attire, so ominous and repulsive on working-class women, bourgeois communardes emerged as alluring and sensuous.

A post-Commune military report described Elisabeth Dmitrieff as "habitually wearing an amazonian dress, a felt hat decorated with red plumes, and a silk scarf of the same color, adorned with gold fringe; she wore this scarf from left to right across her blouse."[117] This dramatic, assertive, and elegant portrait reflected Dmitrieff's distinctive and illusive impression. In describing her "amazonian dress," the author drew Dmitrieff as a strong, fearless warrior. The "amazon," derived from the Latin *a-*, without, and *mazos*, breast, reflects the mythological tale of female warriors who cut off one breast to improve their archery technique.[118] The image of Dmitrieff, wearing her red and gold scarf "from left to right across her blouse," sustained the amazonian/archer allusion. Sexualized by her flamboyant appearance, and yet threateningly de-sexualized by the suggested amazonian willingness to sacrifice a breast to improve combat skills, Dmitrieff presented an ambiguous image as a perilous yet enticing creature.

The Commune provided a context in which women could step out of their delimited roles and begin to redress economic, political, and social injustices and inequities. Nonetheless, in doing so, they faced severe judgments based on not only their gender, but also their class. Critics of the Commune focused intently on female activism, which they explained as the natural result of communardes' rejection of the central pillars of bourgeois and Catholic morality. Rather than recognizing these women as conscious political actors, anti-Commune observers saw them as weak, corrupt, gullible, and without agency. In this milieu, Léo brandished her pen against the dominant conceptions of women's irrationality and inferiority.

In discussing women's apparent morality or immorality, Léo pointed to the reality of women's lives, and focused on the factors that influenced and shaped their options and behaviors. A lack of educational and economic opportunities determined the choices available to women both of the working class and the bourgeoisie. In 1869, Léo had enumerated the factors of women's condition: "By the material dependence . . . removed from nearly all social functions other than the servile, and reduced to an insufficient wage, she is forced either to sell herself in marriage in exchange for an often illusory protection, or to rent herself out in temporary unions . . . she has been made an object."[119] Léo saw education as a way to escape the objectification inherent in loveless marriage and prostitution. Secular schooling could empower and radicalize women, awakening them to alternatives and paths previously unknown or inaccessible, leading them away from the Church and towards a feminist socialism. Léo already operated on the male-dominated terrain of ideas, to which she claimed access for all women. An educated female population, she believed, would press to expand and secure women's economic and social options and independence, thereby enlarging the breadth and depth of women's place. Léo's demands for women's full revolutionary participation emerged not only from her desire to expand female freedom, but also from her understanding that without it, socialism would fail; correspondingly, she considered female instruction necessary for both women's emancipation and revolutionary success. Without an educated female population, the space the Commune allowed for women's autonomy and freedom, while greater than at any other time in this period, remained narrow and perilous in the long term.

Bringing universal, secular education to all females remained central to Léo's feminist socialist work during the Commune. Her educational reform efforts of the previous decade radicalized in this insurrectional milieu.[120] The Catholic Church still controlled education in France, and girls' education, especially, was neither compulsory, uniformly available, nor remotely rigorous.[121] Léo now saw the Church's sway over women as historically detrimental to revolutionary success. She attributed this substantial obstacle both to women's exclusion and alienation from insurgent politics, and to the impact of religious education. She argued that

> The first Revolution awarded [women] the title of *citoyenne* but not the rights. It left them excluded from liberty, from equality. Rejected by the Revolution, women returned to Catholicism, and, under its influence, composed an immense reactionary force . . . which suffocated the Revolution every time it attempted rebirth.[122]

Léo believed the female link to Catholicism was only a default position for women alienated from the political and intellectual realms, and she saw both education and political inclusion as essential to breaking this connection, thus allowing the development of an equitable society. Many communardes clearly rejected this religious legacy in favor of the revolutionary alternative, as evinced by the anti-clericalism expressed in political clubs.[123] For Léo, secular education provided the opportunity to awaken and inspire the mass of people. Just as she continually propagandized in the provinces, wrote accessibly worded newspaper pieces, and published didactic books and a play, she ceaselessly championed public instruction, with the intent of lifting up the working classes and helping them recognize alternatives to accepting their ongoing subjugation.

The separation of the Church from education carried extremely wide support among communardes seeking to end the religious domination over the socialization process. In the anti-clerical language of political clubs, the Montmartre Women's Vigilance Committee addressed a letter to the Commune government, "energetically request[ing] that professional schools and lay orphanages [be] immediately established in place of the schools and orphanages run by the male and female ignoramuses."[124] A palpable resentment existed toward those charged with educating and raising children. Many communardes recognized the importance of access to education, as Louise Michel wrote in her memoirs: "Equal education, equal trades, so that prostitution would not be the only lucrative profession open to a woman—that is what was real in our program."[125] Education could provide not only an avenue to economic independence, but also a means to "facilitate and hasten the . . . recognition of women's rights."[126] However, the Church's patriarchal authority, which influenced both religious and lay schools, resulted in educational programs emphasizing morality, obedience, and piety over any intellectual development or independent thought. A report on Parisian schools in 1870 clearly stated this priority: "The women teachers' . . . knowledge and teaching ability leave something to be desired, but they are morally superior, more tactful, and more devoted [than the male teachers]."[127] Women faced an educational system structured to enforce gender and class hierarchies and to suppress opposition and critical thought.

In the aftermath of the revolution of 1848, Louis-Napoléon's *Falloux* Law had re-established the Church's control over primary education.[128] Lay schools existed, but in far fewer numbers than those run by clerics. This held true particularly for female institutions, as the law required only lay teachers to earn a teaching certificate; nuns merely needed a "letter of obedience" from their supervisors.[129] The preponderance of Church-controlled schools facilitated the state's strong stake in religious education, an interest evidenced by Adolphe Thiers's statement in 1849 that "the parish priest's action must be strong, stronger than ever, because I am counting on him to spread that true philosophy that man is here to suffer."[130] Religious education clearly promoted the reification of the economic and social hierarchies, and the maintenance of order and the status quo.

Working-class and socialist men supported the restructuring of girls' education, but generally for reasons different from the communardes'. For example, the radical *Hébertist* newspaper *Le Père Duchêne,* a resurrection of the 1793 revolutionary paper of the same name, argued for girls' secular education. A popular daily, *Le Père Duchêne* used graphic and colorful language to press its points:

> This is so important! If you knew, *citoyens,* how the revolution depends on women, then you would open your eyes to girls' education, and you would not leave them . . . in ignorance! . . . Ah! In the name of God! The women of Paris are fucking patriotic women! . . . But . . . there are those who are led by the fucking priests, and who swallow the wafers at mass instead of making soup for their husbands! . . . These *citoyennes* have not received a patriotic education![131]

This intensely anti-clerical message posited women's "patriotic education" as an antidote to the influence of the "fucking priests," as well as an assurance of women's adherence to domestic duties. The male editors (Eugène Vermersch, Alphonse Humbert, and Maxime Vuillaume) recognized the importance of female education to revolutionary success.[132] They essentially shifted the concept of Republican Motherhood to what can be termed Revolutionary Motherhood. The Communard *Le Père Duchêne* merely appropriated the Enlightenment idea of Republican Motherhood, of educating girls as future mothers of sons of the republic, and adapted the idea to educate girls as future mothers of sons of the revolution.[133] Like Republican

Motherhood, Revolutionary Motherhood created a civic role for women while keeping them within the private sphere. In stark contrast to communarde women's plans and arguments for female education, the male editors of *Le Père Duchêne* associated women's religious adherence with their neglect of domestic duties and their trespass into the public sphere; because they lacked a "patriotic education," these women "swallow the wafers at mass instead of making soup for their husbands." Appealing to their working-class, heavily male audience in popular, accessible terms, the authors mentioned nothing about women's personal benefits from secular education. Rather, *Le Père Duchêne* contended that secular education would prevent women from playing a counter-revolutionary role, while making them better wives and mothers. "A true *citoyenne* . . . a good mother . . . would despair if she ever saw [her children] become fuckers like Thiers . . . and other riffraff like him."[134]

On March 26, one week after the Commune's declaration, *Education nouvelle,* an educational reform association originally formed during the Prussian siege of Paris, established a committee to present a plan to the Commune government.[135] The delegation, composed of three men and three women, including Maria Verdure, Henriette Garoste, and Louise Lafitte, delivered their strongly anti-clerical proposal on April 1. Calling for the absolute separation of religion and education, they "urgently requested, in the name of the freedom of conscience, in the name of justice,"

> That religious or dogmatic instruction be left entirely to the initiative . . . of the families, and that it be immediately and radically suppressed, for both sexes, in all the schools . . . That houses of education and instruction contain . . . neither religious object nor image.[136]

In addition to completely eradicating religion from the classroom, including banning prayers and any religiously related examination questions, the blueprint presented a proactive pedagogical course: "The quality of education will be determined first of all by integral, rational instruction, which will become the best possible apprenticeship for private, professional, political and social life; . . . the instruction . . . will thus be free and complete for all children of both sexes . . . [it] will be mandatory in the sense that it will become a right within the reach of every child."[137]

The Commune government responded with complete favor, urging the delegates to take steps to initiate these radical reforms.[138] This plan did not separate male and female educational programs or goals. By emphasizing the importance of "rational instruction" to the development of not only private and social, but professional and political life, *Education nouvelle* representatives asserted, and the Commune accepted, an abrogation of basic conceptions of established gender roles. Following in the footsteps of Léo's pre-Commune organization *La Société de la revendication des droits de la femme, Education nouvelle* radically contended that girls and boys required equal educational training to prepare them to operate in all spheres: the private, social world, and the very public professional and political arenas. They erased submission, piety, and morality from the instructional agenda.[139] The Commune government, often inconsistent regarding issues of gender equity, affirmed the redefinition of women's roles in terms of educational opportunities and their corresponding empowerment.

The government subsequently confirmed its stance on May 21, when the Commune's Commission for Education raised and equalized the salaries of male and female teachers. The Commission explained this extraordinary move toward parity by recognizing "that the necessities of life are as numerous and imperative for women as for men, and, as far as education is concerned, women's work is equal to that of men."[140] Although they qualified their statement by inserting the phrase "as far as education is concerned," this stands as one of the Commune government's strongest steps toward eradicating gender inequity. The equation of male and female economic responsibility contradicted not only bourgeois notions of separate spheres, but also the prevailing male working-class and socialist acceptance of gender divisions of labor and focus on the primacy of men's wages. This constituted an enormous, though temporary, leap forward for women in terms of gender ideology, wage labor, and education.

Communardes made various other efforts and gains towards pedagogical restructuring. Marguerite Tinayre, a socialist novelist and teacher, became Paris's first female inspector of schools,[141] Paule Mink started a girls' free school at the Saint-Pierre de Montmartre church,[142] and the Educational Committee of the *Comité des femmes de la rue d'Arras* announced the "establishment of public meetings in every *arrondissement*."[143] Maria Verdure, of *Education nouvelle*, along with Félix and Elie Ducoudray, proposed a plan for day nurseries based on the premise that "education begins with the very first day of life"; their regulations specifically prohibited any "priest or religious representative" from staffing the nurseries.[144] V. Manière, a headmistress, planned an industrial school for girls, which, she argued "would be a great improvement on the needlework school at present managed by nuns."[145] And, on the eve of the Versailles troops' entry into Paris, the Commune government appointed Léo, Anna Korvine-Krukovskaya Jaclard, Marthe-Noémie Reclus, and the *citoyennes* Perrier and Sapia to form a commission "to organize and oversee instruction in girls' schools."[146] The revolutionary moment ended just as Léo, her co-editor Korvine-Krukovskaya Jaclard, and her longtime friend Reclus had begun to turn theory into practice.

Communarde feminism, combined with socialistic ideas of equal education, and intense anti-clericalism, produced revolutionary possibilities for female education. By breaking the Church's grip on girls' instruction, communardes shifted the focus from maintaining gender-based educational limitations and the socio-economic status quo, to allowing intellectual development and a degree of mobility or independence. As Léo had written in the months prior to the Commune, "The partisans of women's equality . . . have come to understand this truth. Their primary objective is the free school, the school of reason and liberty. This will be a girls' school."[147] Opposition to the imposition of Catholic and bourgeois values and structures emanated from the podiums of political clubs, the pages of writers, and the propositions of organizations and individuals. Similarly rejecting the republican and the male socialist conceptualizations of Republican Motherhood, or Revolutionary Motherhood, communardes claimed access to secular education as a woman's right to intellectual development and economic independence. Their class and gender-based assertions rested on an understanding of serious and egalitarian pedagogy as preparation for full ingress into "private, professional, political and social life."[148]

André Léo worked to expand women's sphere, analyzing, theorizing, and advocating the overthrow of existing social forms for equitable ends. Seeking female emancipation, she also recognized that the success of socialism rested both on women's full revolutionary participation and on an educated and engaged female population. Applying arguments and critiques she had developed over a decade of political and didactic writing, Léo served as an intellectual feminist socialist voice during the Commune. She adapted her rights-based feminist socialism within the revolutionary context, abandoning the struggle for legal civic and political rights, and dedicating the idea of rights, in terms of liberty and equality, to full social and revolutionary participation. Her goals remained the same, and the deeply engendered nature of society remained the same. She continued to strive for an end to the continuing gender-based subjugations and discriminations, but now within an altered, insurrectionary milieu. Léo's approach thus involved applying her ideas toward expanding women's access to secular education, and to demanding women's right to defend the revolution in both words and deeds. Building on this base, women would be prepared for integral involvement in developing a new, just and egalitarian society.

Léo's understanding of female potential and abilities stood in stark contrast to that of the dominant ideology, and she seized the revolutionary opportunity to work for the realization of her feminist socialist positions. Léo, like Dmitrieff, undoubtedly had a top-down approach to social change, questioning the focus and tenacity of the working class. But she believed that education could change this situation. She considered free, mandatory, secular schooling essential to overcoming inequalities between both the classes and the genders. Particularly for women, Léo posited education as the key to independence and subjectivity. By expanding women's knowledge, skills, and options, she felt they could begin to dismantle their matrix of objectification. In advocating women's access to the battlefield and full revolutionary participation, Léo also sought the reconceptualization of a particularly male territory, not only to attain the literal entree into the arena, but also to ensure women's right to new domains.

Léo's response to the Commune emerged from her particular approach to feminist socialism, as developed in her writing and activism in the years prior to the uprising. Hers by no means constituted the period's sole feminist revolutionism. By focusing on the intellectual, Léo neglected the potential of popular-driven insurrectionary power, replete with a more grassroots perspective on working-class women's experiences and grievances. Nor did Léo address the methods and benefits of organizing. She assumed that pushing to extend the physical and intellectual arenas open to women would suffice to effect fundamental change, without establishing structures and associations for their implementation. Mink and Dmitrieff did each, respectively, develop feminist socialisms reflective of these other approaches, outlooks, and concerns, creating a web of complementary and contending philosophical and practical positions during the Commune. Responding to the insurrectionary opportunity, each woman applied her particular understanding of how best both to realize her feminist socialist objectives, and to ensure the revolution's success.

Fig. 7. Paule Mink.
Courtesy of Siege and Commune of Paris collection,
Charles Deering McCormick Library of Special Collections,
Northwestern University Library.

5
Paule Mink
and the *Clubistes*

Anti-Clericalism and Popular Revolution

François Bournand, a pro-clerical author and critic, witnessed "out of curiosity" the inaugural meeting of the *Club de la révolution sociale* held in the *Saint-Michel* church, on May 3, in the working-class Parisian neighborhood of Batignolles. He described the scene:

> I have rarely seen such a beastly spectacle . . . the club officers sat around a table directly across from the pulpit. The chairman called again and again for silence.

> The meeting opened. The organ played the *Marseillaise,* and one and all accompanied it in unison; women's shrill voices, men's deep basses, the yelping voices of children: a true charivari![1]

For Bournand, the spectacle of anti-clerical Communard women and men taking over a church, and declaring that now "Instead of dishonest and brutal words, you are going to hear words of truth and emancipation," undoubtedly constituted a world turned upside down.[2] Men, and particularly women, out of their prescribed places in the hierarchies of power, defied the dominant conceptions of religion, class, and gender. This scene also represented somewhat of an inversion for much of the revolutionary elite, the Commune hierarchy, who resisted the bottom-up, oratorically fierce *clubiste* politics. In distinct contrast to Dmitrieff's highly structured *Union des femmes,* these arenas of popular sovereignty—the milieus of Paule Mink—experienced an even greater level of marginalization by the Commune government and the Communard press.[3] This May 3 meeting of the *Club de la révolution sociale* closed with the announcement that "Tomorrow we will discuss a grave and important question, which requires the meditation of all patriots: 'Woman in the Church and Woman in the Revolution.'"[4] For Bournand and other Commune adversaries the fear that these transpositions were not transitory, as a true charivari would be, exacerbated and intensified as the weeks progressed.

In contrast to Léo and Dmitrieff's top-down, more theoretical, intellectually driven approaches, Mink advocated a bottom-up, action-over-organization path to socialism. She supported the grass-roots, rhetorically violent, and intensely anti-clerical communarde. Hers was the type of revolution being made in the political clubs, where declarations of anti-clericalism, class-based hostility, and women's independence rang through the once-hallowed halls of churches, the appropriated spaces where radical meetings were now held. Taken together, the *clubiste*'s positions constituted an attack on the interlinked powers of the patriarchy. The clubs embodied direct democracies, planned and undertaken by rank-and-file communardes. As a participant in at least four clubs, Mink shared a pulpit primarily with working-class women.

Working-class women developed radically politicized positions based on the particular conditions and experiences of their class and gender. Their revolutionary motivations arose from a combination of their economic exploitation and marginalization in the workplace, their subordination in the family, and a palpable revolutionary tradition, resurrected in the crucible of the Commune. They took part in street demonstrations, labor organizations, and vigilance committees; they acted as battlefield cooks, nurses, and sometimes warriors; and they participated in political clubs. These clubs constituted a public arena for laboring women to articulate and coordinate their grievances and goals. The Commune provided a unique political opening for these women to step beyond existing class and gender limitations, and to establish these radical public forums.

Within the clubs, rank-and-file communardes attacked the existence of class and gender inequities and expressed extreme, and often rhetorically violent, anti-clericalism. Working women's antipathy toward the Catholic Church was closely linked to their economic and social discontent. Resentful of the Church's wealth, the employment practices and market influence of its workshops, its control of girls' education, and its intercession in the family, female laborers demonstrated a particular gender- and class-based anti-clericalism. At home, in the workshop, and in the schools, the ecclesiastical authorities influenced their lives in a web of specific ways. A number of *clubistes* opposed not only the Catholic Church and its clergy, but also the very concepts of religion and God. These revolutionary ideas represented a break with France's anti-clerical revolutionary tradition, which had differentiated between the organized Church and the ideals of religion and Christianity and had rejected the Church while maintaining a connection between spirituality and the state. The radically anti-religious club participants expressed a new type of liberatory strategy, one that went beyond striving just to remove the religious institution and its hierarchy. Followers also wished to eradicate the authority of God. Dmitrieff and Léo, while opposing any connection between religion or faith and the state, tended to express their anti-clericalism more moderately.[5]

Mink's position fell closer to that of the more radical *clubistes*. She consistently expressed a virulent anti-clericalism throughout her more than three decades of public life. For example, in arguing in favor of legalized divorce at a Parisian public meeting in 1868, Mink responded to the assertion of marriage as a divine institution by declaiming, "that is why we do not want it [dissoluble marriage], because we do not want God."[6] During the Commune, Mink helped organize the *Club de la victoire* that met at the *Saint-Sulpice* church; she also spoke at the *Club de Notre-Dame de la Croix* in Menilmontant, the *Club de Saint-Nicolas-des-Champs*, and the *Club de la déliverance* at *La Trinité*. In addition to her involvement in political clubs, Mink established a tuition-free girls' school in the church at *Saint-Pierre de Montmartre*, helped organize an ambulance corps, met and strategized with other communardes, and traveled to the provinces to propagandize for the revolution.[7] Historical sources on Mink's undertakings during the insurrection are limited, as her dossier from the *conseils de guerre*, the post-Commune military tribunals, disappeared in 1878.[8] In the absence of this evidence, details about Mink's type of activism leave a documentary void. As Alain Dalotel has pointed out, Communard newspapers rarely printed notices or commented on political club meetings, as they favored instead to publicize the highly structured and organized *Union des femmes*. The government of the Commune also recognized the *Union des femmes*, particularly through its Commission of Labor and Exchange, but mistrusted the clubs' form of radically direct democracy.[9] Thus, Mink's revolutionary footprints have faded, unlike Dmitrieff's organizational paper trail (no matter how fragmentary), or Léo's publications and memoirs. Similarly, the sources for women's political club participation, as for many other endeavors of working-class communardes, are spotty and slanted. As grass-roots, loosely organized, and non-hierarchical political groups, they left no written plans, minutes, or membership rolls; furthermore, their mostly working-class adherents did not write memoirs. In the absence of documentary records of their own words, we must rely on the accounts and commentaries of observers and critics, people such as the Abbé Paul Fontoulieu, who were writing from extremely different political, economic, and gender perspectives. Extant dossiers, limited newspaper articles, and other fragmentary evidence contribute to the reconstruction and critique of the *clubiste* experience.[10]

These political clubs afforded a forum for working-class communarde exposition, oration, and organization, providing their adherents with a public pulpit to challenge hierarchies and promote proposals for economic and social change. The clubs met in neighborhood churches throughout the city. Most met irregularly, and some, such as the *Club des prolétaires,* held meetings at several different churches.[11] In contrast to the *Union des femmes,* political clubs operated with minimal structure or organizational plans. As direct democracies, they held their podiums open to all comers. While some clubs announced a particular speaker, or a central topic or theme for the evening's meeting, others functioned without these sorts of guidelines. Beyond these clubs, working women's means of political expression essentially remained limited to marches and protests. Speaking to groups of women, or groups of men and women in the mixed-sex clubs, communarde *clubistes* expanded their presence within the public sphere. Reminiscent of the Parisian public meetings of the late 1860s, the public forum would have had an empowering effect on individual speakers, and an inspirational impact on female participants. The clubs' adherents discussed and debated activists' ideas, criticisms, and plans, thereby assigning them a certain legitimacy, and facilitating the evolution of working-class women's politicization and political voice.[12]

Involvement in the clubs fostered a sense of solidarity and potency. Within the meetings, *clubistes* articulated their shared experiences and interests, resulting in the identification of general goals and targets for political action and attack. This was more fully articulated in the clubs than in everyday social interaction, and it translated into identifying general goals and targets for political action and attack. The language of an *oratrice* at the *Club de la Trinité,* a club in which Mink participated, captured the essence of communardes' optimism and exaltation: "*Citoyennes* . . . tomorrow you will be in the service of yourselves and not your masters . . . *Prolétaires,* you will be reborn. Frail women, you will nourish yourselves, clothe yourselves, you will become the powerful generators of a strong race."[13]

Activist women sought freedom, strength, and access to economic independence. They considered the barriers that they faced to be religion and the Church, capitalism and the bourgeoisie, and, less frequently but no less virulently, women's oppression and masculine authority. In response, they reacted against these forces in myriad ways, ranging from spewing vitriol to designing concrete action. Many of the clubs had emerged under the Prussian Siege, striving to bring about revolution and follow the club traditions of 1793 and 1848. Women played relatively limited roles in these organizations during the Siege, but this situation changed dramatically with the rise of the Commune. The political clubs carried the legacy of the late Empire's public meetings into a more highly democratized and intensely radicalized milieu.[14] In the heady hours of the Commune, all things seemed within reach.

The female and male Communard critiques of religion and class formed critical elements in their overall assault on the interrelated patriarchal powers of Church and state. Political clubs typically met in churches, undoubtedly sharpening the affront of their often intensely anti-clerical propositions and actions. André Léo's companion and future husband, the Communard Benoît Malon, described the clubs as places "where Catholic priests recently preached respect for authority and resignation to poverty," and where presently "improvisational orators preach . . . the holy revolt of the poor, the exploited, the oppressed, against the exploiters, against the tyrants, and [they] stimulate their passions for the decisive battle . . . it is here where cries of vengeance interrupt the orators."[15]

While Malon and Léo shared *clubistes'* sentiments and supported their ultimate goals, they opposed their radical means. Léo, who only spoke in clubs on one or two occasions, opposed what she perceived as the clubs' extremism, contending that they merely exchanged an uncritical adherence to religion for one to the republic: "they have only changed the catechism," she asserted, "they believe in the Republic with the same feverish devotion, the same mystical blindness, that they had in God and the cross when they were children."[16] Malon, like Léo an advocate of associationist, moderate socialism, critiqued the *clubistes'* political stance as "preserving, with its powerful passion and its theoretical narrowness, the Jacobin ideal, which is nearly banished from workers' societies and from sections of the International."[17] The Jacobin concept of revolutionary violence and insurgency did play a role among some organized Parisian workers and Internationalists.[18] Asserting the virtual obsolescence of Jacobinism, Malon expectantly contended that in time, the people would "correct themselves," and that in liberty they would lose the desire for violence.[19] However, the Jacobin–Blanquist faction dominated the Commune government, in which Malon belonged to the minority, and within the government and the political clubs, many, including Mink, saw violence as a viable vehicle for radical change.

None of the female communarde leaders could be considered Jacobin, although Mink retrospectively became an avid supporter of the Jacobin–Blanquist faction, as she shifted her allegiance to Blanquism in the Commune's aftermath.[20] Despite the leaders' rejections, the Jacobin legacy held a prominent place among rank-and-file communardes: the popular tradition of Jacobinism, the zealous environment of the political clubs, the intense desire for dramatic and rapid change, and the calls for violence combined to create a strongly Jacobin-oriented community of working women.

Communarde *clubistes* did not, nonetheless, label themselves "Jacobin"; most adhered neither to particular factions nor to theories. For these women, such affiliations, seen as central by historians and by the Commune's leadership, remained far subordinate to revolutionary action and organization. Indicative of their position in the economic, social, and political hierarchies, *clubistes* experienced the problems of social and economic marginalization in their daily lives. Working-class female activism rested on the desire to protest and eliminate exploitation and oppression, and occasionally to

Fig. 8. "Nos Bons Curés." Caricature.
*Courtesy of Siege and Commune of Paris collection, Charles Deering McCormick
Library of Special Collections, Northwestern University Library.*

exact retribution. Some of their expressions reflected a rather even-handed desire for economic justice. In the *Club Saint-Ambroise,* the *citoyenne* Thyou argued that the Commune should "force the property owners to give renters three free months," based on the extreme economic hardship under the Siege and the Commune;[21] at the *Club Saint-Sulpice,* a woman proposed that the Commune "close shops of all merchants suspected of *Versaillisme.*"[22] The political clubs provided a context for expressing these desires, frustrations, and resentments; for building solidarity with confederate working women; and for beginning to plan actions to address, and possibly remedy, the conditions of their subjugation.

Reporting on a political club meeting in the Parisian neighborhood of

Montrouge, Marforio, the pseudonymous author of Commune memoirs entitled *Les Echarpes rouges* (The Red Sashes), wrote that an "ugly woman . . . rather old, done up in red . . . opened a large mouth armed with long teeth and said: 'We have enemies: they are the priests. The priest is woman's enemy . . . for him, paternity is a crime, the family nothing! Ah! Criminal and cynical inversion of the laws of nature! The priest is thus a monstrosity . . . *Vive la Commune!* Death to the stinking priests!'"[23] Intense acrimony toward priests, both as individuals and as representatives of the Church hierarchy, pervaded *clubiste* discourse, exemplifying a source of their virulent anti-clericalism. Describing the priest as an unnatural being, far removed from the Catholic intention to cast celibacy as a central feature in suppressing the evils of the body, this unnamed *clubiste* represented the cleric as inimical to women, the family, and the propagation of the species. Ideas of priests as dangerous to the family included accusations of their interference in marriages, and corruption of women and children in both the classroom and the confessional. These deeply gendered and sexually charged conceptions emerged, along with economic and class-based resentments, from the century's contentious and complex history of anti-clericalism.

The vehement anti-clericalism of the Great Revolution, when the state confiscated Church lands and demanded that priests pledge allegiance to France and to a Civil Constitution of the Clergy, and during which two to three thousand ecclesiastics were murdered, cast a shadow over and provided a legacy for the nineteenth century. Over the decades, animosity between the Church and republicans endured, even as the religious and secular doctrines evolved. In the 1790s, Enlightenment republicans rejected the Catholic Church, but retained the idea of a Supreme Being and of faith remaining integral to the state. By mid-century this focus shifted as republicans increasingly viewed religion as a private concern. Simultaneously, Ultramontanism, a politically reactionary, internationalist (as it included loyalty to Rome), and anti-intellectual strain of Catholicism rose to the fore in France. Theocratic in its conception of the role of Jesus on earth, Ultramontane Catholicism clashed directly with republicans' growing liberal individualism and nation-centered ideology.[24]

While clashing with emergent republican intellectual and political currents, the Church enjoyed a close relationship with Louis Napoleon's Second Empire, particularly during the 1850s; both Church and state oppressed and persecuted their republican and socialist opponents, thus exacerbating the existing rift.[25] With the easing of press, speech, and assembly restrictions in the late 1860s, liberal and socialist republicans expressed a deep antipathy toward the Church's ultraconservatism, influence, and power.

Anti-clerical reprobations rang from the pulpits of Parisian public meetings during the years preceding the Commune. Paule Mink, speaking on

"Marriage and Divorce" at a meeting in 1868, cited St. Paul, "in the eyes of whom woman was only an object of scandal and downfall," and argued that the Church had consistently denigrated women.[26] She rejected the conceptualization of marriage as a divine institution, and blamed the religious authorities for advocating the "concentration of power and wealth" at the expense of women's well-being.[27] The Parisian public meetings served as a forum where socialists and working women and men voiced deep resentments towards the Church, antipathies that had built up over decades in terms of the institution's riches, tight government connections, control over education, and economic competition with workers (via convent-run workshops).[28] Orators attacked religion, the clergy, and the concept of God, blaming each for perpetuating class and gender oppression.[29] The discourse of public meetings included violent anti-clerical attacks. A speaker named Brille propounded, "When we have crushed these reptiles called Jesuits, these reptiles who infest everything, their bloody slander serves as their cloak; when they are gone, we will have reconquered our independence."[30] Orators virulently assailed the clergy, as when a participant named Bachellery declared: "I abhor all those who wear the cassock." They also excoriated religion and belief, as the socialist Gilles Laviolette demanded that "we will attack the bases of religion by denying Christ and the Gospels."[31] These public forums reflected a growing willingness to aggressively denounce religion and the clergy as an arm of the French apparatus of oppression.

Born of this political legacy, communarde popular anti-clericalism also had interwoven roots in class- and gender-based resentments. As a class, workers grew increasingly alienated from the Catholic Church, and ultimately religion, as the century progressed. During the earlier part of the century, most non-elites embraced popular religion, comprised of various combinations of traditional, superstitious practices and those sanctioned by the Church. Popular Christianity suffused the radical ideologies of the 1830s and 1840s. The revolutionaries of 1848 opposed the priests and doctrines of the established Church, while simultaneously advocating a "Christian socialism," an egalitarian and democratic ideology centered on a fraternal, and essentially socialist, Jesus Christ.[32] In contrast to the Catholic dogma of waiting for salvation in the afterlife, these leftists believed that Christian socialism could peacefully create a utopian society on Earth, in France, during their lives.[33] A significant number of parish priests sympathized with and supported these movements. But in the increasingly reactionary years immediately following 1848, these "worker-priests" faced censure, and Christian socialism dissipated. Religion and radicalism parted company.[34]

The *clubistes'* resentment of the Church's gender practices emerged from an equally complex history. A substantial upsurge in the number of both lay and clerical women allied with the Church during the nineteenth century has been termed the "feminization" of Catholicism. With the mid-century Catholic resurgence, the Church increasingly appropriated aspects of popular religion, including, particularly, the recognition of miracles and the veneration of the Virgin Mary. Marian devotion exploded with Pope Pius IX's 1854 declaration of the Immaculate Conception as dogma. Miraculous visions of the Virgin proliferated, appearing especially to young women and girls.[35] Explanations for the growing feminization of the Church range from what James McMillan has termed "the enormously condescending view" that the religion's superstition and sentimentality simultaneously repelled men and attracted women, to the more powerful exposition that piety and emotionalism fit within the purview of women's sphere, and that Mary exemplified the ideal, although unattainable, nineteenth-century woman: the mother who remained a virgin.[36] In the years of revolutionary aftermath and reaction, the desire for stability and belief could also have motivated women toward religion. The Church may have served a sociability function, as McMillan suggests, both in terms of meeting with fellow congregants, and in relation to the priest as confessor/advisor. It is this second relationship that elicited extreme anti-clerical opposition.[37] While religious women, and men, viewed the clerical ear as receptive and his word as divine, male and female opponents of the Church saw this as invasive, disruptive, insidious, and dangerous.

Anti-clericals of both sexes considered priests as interlopers in the family and meddlers in marriages. Men felt threatened by the clerics' access to intimate information via the confessional, and deeply resented their influence in private matters, particularly regarding birth control and the monitoring of sexuality.[38] Probing intrusions into the marriage bed, made in the name of enforcing morality, pushed people away from the Church, and fed into a conception of the priest as voyeuristic and licentious.[39]

With the emergence of the Commune, working-class women utilized the clubs to articulate this gendered acrimony. Indicative of the depth of hostility these images generated, a sixteen-year-old communarde named Gabrielle announced at the *Club Saint-Sulpice,*

> We must shoot the priests; they prevent us from doing what we want. Women are harmed by going to confession . . . I therefore urge all women to take hold of all the priests and to burn their ugly mugs off (*brûler la gueule*)! When they are gone, we will be happy. Never fear . . . Go with a good heart . . . I will be the example. To death, to death! That is the cry of my soul! The same for the nuns. Attack these breeders of hell. To death, to death![40]

Few priests were shot and no nuns were murdered, but these gruesome exhortations represented extreme versions of the hatred and resentment many working-class communardes felt toward clerical interventions in their lives.[41] "Prolonged bravos" followed Gabrielle's exhortation, indicating *clubiste* receptiveness to this violent anti-clerical rhetoric. The secrecy of the confessional created a "mysterious" space, in which arose ideas of priestly intercession between husbands and wives, parents and children. The intensity of emotions and force of rhetoric suggest a sense of deep and personal invasion or betrayal. Testifying before a military tribunal after the Commune's fall, Madame Pouissier, a cloth maker, claimed that "on May 26, at six in the evening . . . I saw a cortege of gendarmes and priests pass by, surrounded by a crowd . . . of at least fifteen hundred people," on their way to massacre the priests. Pouissier stated that immediately afterwards she overheard a woman describe the event to a National Guardsman, exclaiming, "That whorish priest, I stuffed my hand into his throat to pull out his tongue, but I couldn't do it!"[42] An undeniably sexual allusion, Pouissier's account is indicative of popular perceptions of priests as both inappropriately sexual and sexually inappropriate. The intent of the attempted violence reflected the implied power of clerical words as a means to seduce and dominate. Whether an accurate account or braggadocio, the symbolism of violently removing the priest's tongue, of tearing away his ability to speak, demonstrated a desire to silence ecclesiastic influence. Muting the priest, and in turn the Church, might protect the vulnerable from clerical abuse, bias, and sway.

For anti-clericals, the familial invasion could culminate in the Church "taking" their children, by leading them to join the clergy.[43] An unnamed communarde *clubiste* of the *Montrouge* neighborhood expressed these fears, insisting that "we must take our children from them . . . we do not have to surrender them to the *prêtraille,* who only teach them shameful vices, vices which impoverish the human body and mind to the benefit of tyranny."[44] Referring to either the vice of celibacy or pedophilia, this orator viewed the clerical vows and influence as dangerous, unnatural, and enervating. Thus weakened by the influence of a cleric, a young person stood ripe for exploitation, be it sexual, spiritual, or economic. Many working-class women perceived government and religious power as deeply intertwined, as expressed by the same *clubiste* above, who asserted that the Church "raised children to become . . . slaves of the monarchists."[45] From this perspective, regardless of the type of ruling government, the power and influence of the clergy persisted. Within the clubs, working-class women dramatically voiced their opposition to this "tyranny," taking advantage of both the democratic forum of the club and the radical potential of the revolution.

During the Commune, working-class women and men's acrimony toward clerical privilege and suspicion regarding the enigma of religious life coalesced in the scandal of *l'église Saint-Laurent.* Feeding on the image of the perversity of priests, an article in the Communard newspaper *Le Cri du peuple* disclosed that the skeletons of fourteen young women had been found buried beneath the church's alter to the Virgin Mary. The highly sensationalized report claimed that the young women, "buried for ten, twelve, or fifteen years at the most . . . had been put to sleep by chloroform, perhaps, and then violated. Their hands and legs were tied, and they were carried here while unconscious."[46] Alleging a relatively recent mass murder, the editors sought to inflame popular anti-clericalism by laying blame on contemporary priests. Continuing the evocation of a sordid and horrifying tale, the journalist envisioned the young women regaining consciousness "tied, sealed, buried alive . . . surrounded by cadavers, before becoming cadavers themselves." And then came the warning to believers:

> mothers of families . . . you who trust the priests with your children's honor and life, you for whom any attack against the clergy is slander or blasphemy, come and see what is in this hideous crypt . . . Here Catholicism is at work. Contemplate it.[47]

Utilizing the excavation as a propaganda tool, the anti-clerical newspaper fanned the flames of popular mistrust and rancor, claiming to expose the true Catholicism. Hundreds of people lined up to see the unearthed victims resting in their crypt beneath *l'église Saint-Laurent.* The accused clergymen embodied the Church's perceived avarice and immorality. Fears of priestly sexual perversion went hand in hand with the belief that celibacy was abnormal, and that one abuse could lead to another. Suspicions of licentiousness and access to women and children, heightened within the highly anti-clerical milieu of the Commune, provided fertile ground for the growth of this frenzied misrepresentation.[48]

The appropriation of *l'église Saint-Laurent* as a site of ecclesiastic indictment stood consistent with the practice of political clubs meeting in churches. The prominent and imposing buildings physically dominated neighborhoods, providing material manifestation of the Church's less visible forms of power. Working-class insurrectionists looted and vandalized convents and churches, releasing years of anger and resentment against the ubiquitous and looming institution: at *Notre-Dame des Victoires,* a woman encouraged the crowd to "leave only absolutely naked walls";[49] and a *cantinière* for the National Guard accepted a soldier's gift of an altar cloth, which she intended to make into handkerchiefs.[50]

Taking over spaces once controlled by a powerful and elite body, working-class communardes frequently extended their purview over their entire *quartier.* At the May 18 meeting of the *Club prolétaires* at the *église Sainte-Marguerite,* a woman named Valentin, "brandishing a saber, with which," according to Fontoulieu, "she was always armed," proclaimed: "Citizens, the scoundrel priests are in our quarter again. It is shameful. When we leave here, we must slit their throats and chop them up like pig meat."[51] The Commune constituted the working class's reclamation of Paris, and just as political clubs claimed churches, so did *clubistes* extend proprietary control over the surrounding neighborhoods. These women conceived of themselves as guardians of their *quartiers,* and the revolutionary moment of the Commune presented the potential for them to rid the areas of priests and all that they represented. Valentin's saber-wielding provocation suggests the level of anger and drama that generated such violently vivid rhetoric.

This rage manifested itself in the extreme with rare cases of physical attacks on ecclesiastics. Revolutionaries arrested l'abbé Mauléon, *curé* (parish priest) of Saint-Séverin, and held him for nearly three months at the fort at Mazas. The seamstress Marie Madrut Ehret faced charges of "complicity in the illegal arrest and arbitrary sequestration" of Mauléon, but the court ultimately decided that she bore no direct responsibility for this act.[52] More seriously, four groups of clerics, a total of twenty-four men, died at the hands of Communards.[53] Following the repression of the Commune, the Sixth Council of War military tribunal accused two women, Marie Cailleux, a day laborer, and Marie Wolf Guyard, a rag picker, of taking part in the May 27 assassinations of four clerics at the *place de la Roquette*. In her testimony, Cailleux asked the court to "have regard for my weakness, my youth, and my ignorance. I repent for what I have done. I will profit from the lesson."[54] The judges responded by declaring her not guilty of assassination, and convicting her only for constructing barricades and taking up arms during an insurrection.[55] In contrast, Wolf Guyard testified that "everything of which I have been accused is false, and I ask your indulgence, please"; she, by contrast, was convicted of assassination and barricade construction.[56]

The differences in these two judgments may reflect how well each woman conformed to dominant gender ideals.[57] Specifically, the *fille* Cailleux "admitted" that her behavior stemmed from her "weakness" and "ignorance"; she appeared chastened and contrite, and essentially submitted herself to her judges. Femme Guyard, while requesting the court's "indulgence," denied its accusations, thereby challenging and refuting the military tribunal's assertions and authority. A rag picker, or scavenger, she had two previous convictions: for vagrancy in 1867, and for theft in 1868.[58] Both women clearly fell short of acceptable bourgeois standards, but twenty-three-year-old Wolf Guyard epitomized the truly marginalized Parisian woman. A well-known *ambulancière* and *clubiste*, active at the *Club Saint-Jacques du haut pas*, Wolf Guyard habitually carried a revolver and wore a red cockade.[59] Accused of shouting "if you don't shoot them, I'll make it my business to,"[60] she represented a virtual "anti-woman" to the military judges: violent, unrepentant, blasphemous, and unrestrained. Her brazenness, combined with her poverty and alienation, could have contributed to the court's decision to condemn her to death (her sentence was later reduced to "forced labor in perpetuity").[61] For Wolf Guyard, attacking the priests likely symbolized revenge against society's oppressive forces as embodied in these clergymen. The insurrectionary milieu allowed this literal attack from below, as working-class women reacted against those they considered to be their subjugators. Wolf Guyard exemplified the once disempowered woman, taking action to better her lot by ridding her world of its oppressors. However, not all women of her class opposed the Church. Raised to venerate and obey ecclesiastical authority and doctrine, others sustained their clerical adherence and belief within an increasingly hostile context.

For devout working women, the sacrilege of anti-clerical clubs holding meetings in churches generated particular offense and outrage. These women remained actively pro-clerical and correspondingly anti-Communard. At the *église Saint Sulpice*, during the Month of Mary celebration in May, a conflict arose between female parishioners and members of the Commune's National Guard (*fédérés*), as the guardsmen made way for a political club by attempting to block the throng of faithful from entering the church. The account, given by François Bournand, author of several pro-clerical works on French ecclesiastics and on Christian art, described the women with "their prayer books under their arms," breaking through the line of guardsmen:

> The *fédérés* and the *clubistes* rushed in behind the women. The women were already mistresses of the terrain and filled all three of the church's naves. The *fédérés* cried 'Vive la Commune!' The women, overexcited to the extreme, responded 'Vive Jesus Christ!' . . . the vast church was not large enough for the huge crowd . . . from which arose an enormous clamor: 'down with the Commune!' The *fédérés* . . . retired.[62]

The women triumphed that evening, but Bournand argued that the success produced domestic conflict between these women and their spouses. He explained that people were "exceedingly upset in the neighborhood. The husbands lectured their wives: 'You are going to compromise us!'"[63] Bournand linked these working-class women with the Church in opposition to their Communard husbands, reiterating a gender-based alliance frequently decried by the left, but here valorized. Bournand described conflict continuing the following evening, but this time the neighborhood men, the husbands, joined the *fédérés* in attempting to eject the women from *Saint Sulpice* in preparation for the club meeting. A growing number of male *clubistes* entered the church, and "pressed up against the praying women, began singing the *Marseillaise*. The women, crammed one against the other, retorted by singing the *Magnificat* and the *Parce Domine* . . . This was in vain, the church was invaded . . . the club was installed."[64]

For Bournand, the battle for *Saint Sulpice* pitted man against woman, husband against wife, male infidel against female believer. These latter represented the "good" working-class women, the loyal adherents of the Church and opponents of the clubs. Unlike Bournand, the anti-Commune writer *l'abbé* Paul Fontoulieu, in his *Les Églises de Paris sous la Commune* (The Churches of Paris Under the Commune), rarely mentioned pro-clerical women, while devoting dozens of pages to female *clubistes*. In his description of the battle over *Saint Sulpice*, gender is never mentioned.[65] Pious working-class women remained virtually invisible to Fontoulieu; his immersion in analyzing the Commune's club life essentially blinded him to the complexity of the working-class female population. By contrast, in Bournand's *Clerge pendant la Commune, 1871* (Clergy During the Commune, 1871), women primarily appeared as pious, and his *clubistes* were almost exclusively male. He saw women within their accepted and traditional religious context. Bournand recognized the existence of female insurgents, but he either rejected or did not comprehend the extent and significance of their roles.

Fontoulieu's examples of pro-clerical women included a group of eighty-three women from *Les Halles,* Paris's central market, who petitioned the Commune's Prefecture of Police, requesting the release of the arrested parish priest of *l'église Saint-Eustache.* The signatories included "*Veuve* (widow) Allemand, poultry pavilion; *Madame* Condat, fish merchant; *Madame* Borda, vendor of small items."[66] He also wrote of a bourgeoise, *Madame* Basset, who, as the *fédérés* cleared *Saint-Philippe du Roule* of the faithful to make way for a political club, "appeared astonished at being expelled in such a way, and asked if under the Commune one did not have the right to pray to God." A *fédéré* allegedly responded that "there is no God, imbecile!"[67] For Fontoulieu, a pious bourgeoise exemplified proper womanhood, and the impudent guardsmen typified the Commune's affront to such righteousness.

A more radical religious reaction involved the "Conspiracy of the Young Women" of the *église Saint-Michel* in Batignolles, in Paris's 17th *arrondissement.* The population of Batignolles, a predominantly working-class area immediately west of Montmartre, ardently supported the Commune, and the *Club Saint-Michel* provided a forum for intense anti-clerical exposition and exhibition.[68] According to Fontoulieu, a group of twelve or thirteen young women, "deeply outraged by the infamies spoken in the club . . . devised a plan for ridding the Batignolles of this group of slanderers . . . by simultaneously blowing up the club and the church!"[69] They filled rubber tubing with gunpowder, and planned to transport the explosives to the church basement for the Sunday, May 14 club meeting. Just prior to the event, the women revealed their plan to a priest, *l'abbé* Bessière, who "fearful of retribution, succeeded, not without difficulty, in convincing them to renounce their plot."[70] Only the first names of the conspirators are known, but their singularity rested in their aggressive action, not in their sentiments. Although we have no statistics regarding working-class women's adherence to the Church during the Commune, a significant number of women clearly remained pious, and these women virulently opposed the clubs' profane use of sacred space. Unremarked on by the press, scarcely mentioned by chroniclers, and irrelevant to the police, religious working-class women emerged as reflections of socialist fears of reaction, such as André Léo's warning against Catholicism's potential influence over women, "composing an immense reactionary force."[71] At the *Club Saint-Ambroise, l'abbé* Delmas reported, "A brave woman, with an honest face and bearing," proclaimed "*Citoyens . . .* and *citoyennes,* I have come to protest against opening a club in a church . . . My mother and father . . . taught me to respect the house of God, and what I

see here is shameful, especially the women, who would do much better remaining with their families."[72] Appropriating the democratic language of
citoyen and *citoyenne*, she nonetheless espoused the bourgeois construct of
women's proper sphere, as well as the authority of religion and the Church.
Escorted to the door, "amidst laughter and ironic jeers . . . but without brutality,"[73] this orator represented those working-class women who continued
to embrace ideas of Catholic and bourgeois hegemony, concepts sufficiently
pervasive to have become conventional morality. The opposition or espousal
of these precepts comprised central points of contention, and served to separate *clubistes* from devout women.

Female *clubistes'* rejection of not only the Church but also the concepts of
God and religion constituted a significant break with French revolutionary
tradition. In 1793, the abolition of the Catholic Church and the expropriation of its property coincided with the introduction of a rational replacement religion: the Cult of the Supreme Being. Although the Jacobins outlawed the old, aristocratically connected formal faith, they maintained the
idea of a higher, mystical power.[74] Again in 1848, French revolutionaries attacked the clergy and the established Church, but in place espoused a populist, egalitarian Christianity.[75] In sharp contrast, communarde *clubistes* not
only violently rejected the clergy, asserting that "every citizen should shoot
them, as one shoots rabid dogs,"[76] but also denied the value of any religion
and the existence of a god. At the *Club Saint-Cristophe*, a woman pronounced:
"You know, citizens, that there are no longer religion, prayers, or God. So,
let's sing the *Marseillaise* . . . the song of good buggers!"[77] Many *clubistes* conceived of "religion, prayers, [and] God" as a whole; their sense of exploitation and hatred was undifferentiated. By 1871, French socialisms held onto
little, if any, of the popular Christianity of earlier decades.[78] The Church, in
a mid-century religious revival, had successfully co-opted popular Catholicism, effectively squeezing out the left.[79]

Female *clubistes* would have had popular knowledge of the revolutionary
tradition of anti-clericalism, but it is doubtful that they recognized their position as radically different from that of their predecessors. Rather, the anti-
clerical sentiments expressed in the public meetings of the late Empire set
a precedent for the expression of working-class communardes' long-term
resentments and increasing alienation toward the Church and for all it stood.
In the revolutionary moment, these experiences combined with the popular legacy of women's revolutionary activism, and resulted in a newly extreme
form of anti-clericalism and anti-religiosity. Popular rhetoric and action
reflected materially based interests and intents, positing the potential for an
egalitarian society completely removed from any religious tradition.[80] Yet
when a mattress maker, at the *Club de la déliverance*, announced, "First of all,
if God exists, and he lets me speak this way, he is a coward," the crowd reacted with widespread murmurs.[81] The absolute public denial, or profound
criticism, of God could still unnerve *clubistes*. No one, however, challenged

or opposed the speaker. While the revolution allowed the expression of virulent anti-religiosity, it required acclimation for some communards, who had been raised with a degree of traditional devotion, to unflinchingly accept such radical, open sacrilege.

God was not, of course, the sole enemy of communarde *clubistes,* but the rejection of religion did develop into the most sensational of their positions. As evinced by the sources, anti-clerical oration and activism, undertaken within an appropriated sacred space, garnered significantly more attention than anti-bourgeois or feminist claims. The Church experienced the most immediate and material attacks of any institution during the Commune, both in terms of loss of property and loss of life. In the aftermath, its proponents rushed to press, publishing professions of ecclesiastical victimhood and excoriating their perceived assailants. To these critics, assumptions of women's "natural" religiosity brought greater focus and outrage to clubwomen's anticlericalism than to their class and gender-based hostilities.

Political clubs did, of course, serve as forums for expressing class-based hostilities. At the *église Saint-Leu,* a prostitute stated that "it is unnecessary to have consideration for the Croesuses of the earth." The next woman at the podium suggested that "all the wealthy be uniformly reduced to a five hundred franc annuity."[82] And during the first meeting of the *Club des citoyennes de Passy,* a 16th *arrondissement* women's club, one-hundred-and-fifty *citoyennes* listened as a female orator proclaimed, "The *bourgeois,* who is our enemy, will be eliminated. Who enriches himself from the sweat of the people? It is the *bourgeois.* Who then builds *chateaux* while the people live in hovels? While the Versailles massacre the people, who refuses to do battle? Again, it is the *bourgeois.*"[83] Unfortunately, we know nothing about the speaker beyond the description of her "red and black outfit."[84] By announcing the impending "elimination" (*supprimer*) or abolition of the bourgeoisie, she strove to inflame the crowd, presenting well-known information in a systematic, provocative manner. The *citoyenne* championed class warfare as a route to an equitable society.

Paule Mink was most likely the orator identified only as "about thirty years old, and now a refugee in Switzerland," who spoke at the *Club de la déliverance* meeting at *l'église La Trinité.* Addressing the all-female group, she contended that "It is the bosses who exploit the worker and enrich themselves from their sweat . . . The workers must join together, they must put their labors in common, and then they will be happy."[85] Mink urged worker solidarity as a means of escaping subjugation by employers, and class consciousness as a way of improving working-class lives. Like Dmitrieff in the *Union des femmes,* Mink propounded the power and value of workers uniting. She continued her class-based critique, declaring, "Another evil of the present society is the rich, who only drink and amuse themselves, without ever troubling themselves. We must get rid of them, along with the priests and nuns. We will only be happy when

Fig. 9. Political club meeting in the church of Saint-Germain l'Auxerrois.
Courtesy of the Department of Special Collections, Charles F. Young Research Library, UCLA.

we have no more bosses, no more rich men, no more priests!"[86] Adding the wealthy and the clerics to the list, Mink presented the triumvirate of oppressors regularly excoriated within the clubs. Typical of her approach, Mink preached the riddance of those with wealth and power. Her words stirred and challenged the crowd, which responded with "applause mixed with laughter and murmurs."[87] She expressed a radical critique of power relations, but had no particular plan to "get rid of" the bosses, rich men, and priests. In contrast to Dmitrieff's top-down method of activism, Mink suggested mobilizing, rather than actually forming an organization. She spoke to inspire and inflame. Her speech epitomized *clubiste* discourse.

Women also aired anger and frustration about the gender hierarchy, particularly in female-only clubs. According to the pseudonymous chronicler Marforio, Mink frequently spent time in *la salle du peuple* of the Hôtel de Ville, meeting with other "distinguished *citoyennes.*" There she prepared notes and speeches for club meetings, lectures intended "to end women's ignorance and humility regarding their enslaved condition," and to ready them "to be independent in the free republic."[88] Women's emancipation played a significant role in *clubiste* discourse. At a meeting on the *boulevard d'Italie*, an *oratrice* explained that

> The master sleeps with a dangerous nonchalance; only the slave maintains an eternal vigilance, always ready, if the hour of vengeance strikes. Man is the master: he is cowardly. Woman is the slave: she is valiant . . . Enough of the old ways, enough of the old errors . . . make way for woman, make way for her talent, her valor . . . all her legitimate ambitions.[89]

Just as with anti-clerical and anti-bourgeois convictions, the experience of the Commune, and the medium of the clubs, provided working-class women a context for attacking the gender hierarchy. *Clubiste* discourse reflected the overlapping and interwoven nature of these patriarchal powers, particularly in terms of marriage and family, milieus shaped by religion and women's limited access to economic independence. At the *Club des libres penseurs*, in *Saint-Germain l'Auxerrois*, a *clubiste* "called for women's complete emancipation"; and a *cantinière* at the same meeting "proposed issuing a resolution in favor of divorce."[90] A woman at a *Saint-Eustache* all-female meeting made a more radical proposal:

> Marriage, *citoyennes*, is the greatest error of ancient humanity. To be married is to be a slave . . . Marriage . . . cannot be tolerated any longer in a free city. It ought to be considered a crime . . . Nobody has the right to sell one's own liberty, and thereby to set a bad example to one's fellow citizens . . . Don't tell me that marriage may be tolerated if you institute divorce. Divorce is only an expedient . . . an Orleanist expedient![91]

The recurrent slave metaphor appeared here linked specifically to the role of wife. For this speaker, entering into the marriage contract equalled selling oneself into slavery. Rhetorically flamboyant and provocative, she termed divorce (seen by many communardes as progressive) to be a monarchist recourse. With this view, she exemplified the often more radical nature of discourse and action found within the clubs.

Louise Michel, an avid *clubiste* and close friend and ally of Mink, propounded working-class solidarity and class war. Described by Fontoulieu as "the most carried-away, the most violent of all," Michel proclaimed at the *Club Saint-Sulpice* meeting of May 17: "The great day has arrived, the decisive day for either the emancipation or the enslavement of the proletariat. But have courage *citoyens*, have strength *citoyennes*, and Paris will be ours; yes, I swear it, Paris will be ours, or Paris will no longer exist! For the people, it is a question of life or death."[92] Michel's impassioned, provocative pronouncement epitomized both her dramatic oratorical skills and the tenor of fiery *clubiste* rhetoric. It also reflected the hour of the proclamation: the final days prior to the Versailles troops' entry into Paris. Michel made an extreme promise of oppositional outcomes, intending to stir her audience's ardor and encourage their continued devotion to the embattled revolutionary cause.

Louise Michel undoubtedly endures as the most celebrated and mythologized communarde. An 18th *arrondissement* Police Commissioner reported, on July 1, 1871, that "the most fanatical individuals regarded her as a God."[93] A Versailles military tribunal accused her of everything from "organizing the famous Central Committee of the *Union des femmes*,"[94] and being "affiliated with the International,"[95] to having an "intimate connection with the members of the Commune," and "knowing all of their plans in advance."[96] None of these assertions were true. Michel contributed to her own notoriety by refusing either to defend herself or be defended at her post-Commune trial. She accepted responsibility for deeds great and small, from "being an accomplice of the Commune," for which she was "honored to be singled out," to burning Paris. On the accusations of incendarism, she stated that "yes, I participated in it. I wanted to block the Versailles invaders with a barrier of flames. I had no accomplices in that. I acted on my own."[97]

While Michel's confessions typified her hyperbolic flair, she clearly exaggerated her role in an effort to shift blame away from her fellow revolutionaries.[98] She saw herself as symbolically representing the people, not as an organizer, but as the embodiment of Paris's working-class women. In contrast to Elisabeth Dmitrieff and André Léo, but comparable to her compatriot Mink, Michel eschewed theory, hierarchy, and organization in favor of vehement emotionalism and flamboyance. Edith Thomas, in *Louise Michel, ou La Velléda de l'anarchie*, explained Michel's iconoclastic behavior as "typical of Louise's 'idealist' character, [as] she did not seem to have understood the importance of [Léo] Frankel and Elisabeth Dmitrieff's directives on the organization of labor."[99] Rather than not understanding the significance of organizing, Michel embraced the power of symbolic speech and action. Michel's brand of politics synchronized perfectly with the clubs. She expounded action and aggression with a theatrical, infectious elegance. Like Mink, with whom she later embarked on propagandistic speaking tours, Michel functioned as a manifestation of radical revolutionism.

Michel viewed politics as theater, the clubs as a stage. She entered into this drama with the utmost seriousness and respect. Michel contended that "there is no heroism; people are simply entranced by events."[100] Manipulating "events" by enticing and exciting revolutionism advanced her political and social agendas, while providing her with the attention she apparently craved. Michel toiled tirelessly during the Commune; as revealed by her own enhanced account she "never really went to bed during that time; I just napped a little whenever there was nothing better to do, and many other people lived the same way. Everybody who wanted deliverance gave himself totally to the cause."[101] Although her lack of sleep was probably overstated, in addition to speaking in the *Club Saint-Sulpice*,[102] Michel frequently presided at the *Club de la révolution,* participated in the *Club de la patrie en danger,*[103] wrote for the newspaper *Le Cri du peuple,* and fought in the 61st Battalion of the National Guard.[104] She also focused substantial energies on the Montmartre Women's Vigilance Committee.[105] Formed to contribute to the defense of the city, this and other vigilance committees initially arose in neighborhoods across Paris during the Prussian Siege. Re-energized or reestablished under the Commune, and frequently populated by *clubistes,* the committees took on a variety of roles. The Montmartre Vigilance Committee, according to one of its members, Béatrix Excoffon, "organized all the aid for the wounded, dispatched nurses into the field . . . [and] sent deputations to funerals to accompany the widows, mothers, and children of those who died for liberty."[106] In addition to these traditional nurturing, female roles, the Vigilance Committees also received and distributed work, sent representatives to political clubs, and hunted down military deserters.[107] They assumed many of the same tasks as the *Union des femmes,* but maintained no connection to the citywide organization. Rather, as Alain Dalotel asserts in "Les femmes dans les clubs rouges 1870–1871," a rivalry existed between the *Union des femmes* and the vigilance committees, particularly from the perspective of the *Union des femmes,* which, as we have seen, required the exclusive allegiance of its members. Dalotel also includes the clubs in this competition, but their difference of focus and less permanent nature and structure make this inclusion questionable. In addition, many vigilance committee members also participated in political clubs. Overlap between the *Union des femmes* and either of these types of organizations was virtually nonexistent.[108]

The Montmartre Vigilance Committee, which was actually two committees, one male and one female, in Michel's words "made the reactionaries tremble."[109] Because they met consecutively in the same place, several women, including Michel, participated in both the men's and women's committees.

The communardes Beatrix Excoffon, Sophie Poirier, and Anna Korvine-Krukovskaya Jaclard participated in the Montmartre Women's Vigilance Committee; none of them belonged to the *Union des femmes*. Excoffon, who had no profession but was the daughter of a clock maker and wife of a printing compositor, also served as vice-president of the *Club de la Boule Noir*, an active political club in the 18th *arrondissement*, in Montmartre, where she "ceaselessly hurled abuse against the priests and nuns."[110] Poirier, a seamstress, had founded the *Club de la Boule Noir*, and was the president of the Vigilance Committee; during the Prussian siege she organized and operated a cooperative clothing workshop, with the assistance of Montmartre's mayor, Georges Clemenceau.[111] Korvine-Krukovskaya Jaclard, the daughter of wealthy Russian aristocrats and childhood friend of Dmitrieff, had become radicalized in the same milieu as Dmitrieff. She subsequently participated in the International in Geneva, worked as a typesetter in Paris, and met and married the young medical student and future Communard Victor Jaclard.[112] During the Commune she co-edited *La Sociale* with Léo, and, according to a police report, she also "attended meetings of the *Boule Noir* . . . one saw her with a red sash around her waist, haranguing the audience and espousing the most extreme positions."[113] But she did not work with the *Union des femmes*. Most of the Montmartre Vigilance Committee members operated primarily within the 18th *arrondissement*, working closely with each other, participating in the *arrondissement*'s political club, the *Boule Noir*, but remaining apart from the quarter's co-existent committee of the *Union des femmes*.[114] The *Union des femmes*'s top-down organizational structure imposed limits on its members' affiliations, and clearly conflicted with the less structured, primarily grassroots clubs and vigilance committees, in spite of the overlap of many of their goals and aims.

A decade after the Commune's repression, and shortly following her return from exile, Paule Mink spoke at a socialist conference in Paris. She contended that

> They believed that the Commune was finished. No! It is more alive than ever . . . After ten years, our slaughterers . . . did not believe . . . that we would return to defend ourselves; we have returned from deportation to fight these infamies and to say to you: It is we who, in 1871, saved the Republic . . . We must have absolute liberty, if they won't give it to us, we will take it. What we want is the democratic republic.[115]

Mink's speech was a reminder to those in power that, for the former Communards, the revolution remained strong, alive, and viable. Demanding absolute liberty and a democratic and social republic, and violently threatening to "take" absolute liberty, she resurrected the ideas and the tone of the Commune's political clubs, the most radical and most democratic aspect of the insurrection. Suppression of the Commune did not mean failure for the project of radical democracy.

Political clubs had emerged as a site for working-class women and men to express their support of insurgency and their opposition to existing religious, class, and gender hierarchies. The urban upheaval provided space for these women to act upon what was often years of frustration and resentment. Emerging as founts of grass-roots activism and bottom-up analysis, *clubistes* demanded radical change for the eradication of a range of inequities. Frequently enunciated in violent, threatening language, *clubiste* discourse ventured beyond the measured rhetoric of the *Union des femmes*, André Léo, and most proclamations of the Commune government. Seeking to stimulate, motivate, and embolden their audience, speakers ranging from Mink to seamstresses to laundresses voiced their anger and ideas from club pulpits. Female *clubistes* had established and experienced popular sovereignty, constituting Paris's first profoundly democratic women's organizations. And as Mink reminded the patrons of the status quo, once the world had been turned upside down, it could never be fully righted again. Unlike the end of a charivari, the participants did not return to their proper places.

Part III

After

6
Dmitrieff and Léo
in the Aftermath

Radical Denouement

As the carnage of Bloody Week neared an end in the final days of May, with Paris in flames and Versailles troops continuing to round up or gun down Communards, Elisabeth Dmitrieff, André Léo, and Paule Mink all successfully avoided both arrest and slaughter. Dmitrieff, wounded on the barricades, and Léo, physically unscathed, each found refuge with friends and political contacts in the city, where they spent weeks awaiting the opportunity to escape France and the danger of Versailles's retribution.[1] Mink managed to stow away onboard a train bound for Switzerland. As it crossed the Swiss border, she leapt out of her hiding place and shouted back at the French border guards: "*Vive la Commune! Vive la Révolution!*"[2]

All three women echoed Mink's cries, in their own ways, for the rest of their lives. Dmitrieff, accompanied by Léo Frankel, the Hungarian-born head of the Commune's Commission of Labor and Exchange, clandestinely crossed France and entered Switzerland in late June. Their fluency in German and their educated, elite bearing enabled them to pose as bourgeois Prussians, and they fled undetected. Within months Dmitrieff returned to Russia, and to several years of attempting to re-establish her revolutionary position. She then joined her husband in his long Siberian exile.[3]

In late July, Léo left her safe haven in the home of Pauline Prins, a sympathetic young schoolteacher. Under a false passport fabricated and smuggled to her by a Geneva-based engraver and Internationalist, Adhémar Schwitzguébel, Léo traveled to Bâle, Switzerland, where Malon awaited her. She immediately organized a lecture tour, and began speaking and writing of her revolutionary experiences and observations. Léo would soon abandon the podium, but she would wield the pen to promote her feminist socialism for the rest of her life.[4]

Mink spent the next thirty years traveling, speaking, and agitating, keeping the memory and the spark of the Commune alive, working for feminism, socialism, and the re-ignition of revolution. In the insurrectionary aftermath, Mink radically altered her ideological stance, rejected her Commune-era support of an anarchistic, grass-roots approach to socialism, and instead advocated centrally planned, radical, violent insurgency. Mink now considered social revolution to be the necessary precondition for all forms of equity. She thus subordinated her feminism and anti-clericalism, but by no means did she abandon either of these positions.

The experience of the Commune had an indelible impact on its participants, the French nation, and the European (and American) political climates for the next decade and beyond. Historians often refer to the years immediately following the Commune as a period of little socialist, labor, or feminist activism in France.[5] The French national government's brutal repression of the Commune and severe retaliation against its participants left the majority of insurrectionists dead, exiled, or in prison. As in the cases of Dmitrieff, Mink, and Léo, a significant number of female and male revolutionaries, particularly those with money or international socialist connections, did succeed in escaping France. Many former communardes continued their political and social activism throughout the 1870s from exile in Switzerland, England, or Italy, and much of their activities focused on France.[6] The surviving French socialists remained politically engaged with France, but they did so from afar. Of those arrested, convicted, and deported to penal colonies in the South Pacific, including Louise Michel and Nathalie Lemel, many resumed their militancy when they returned to the metropole at decade's end.[7]

The revolutionary experience affected and shaped Dmitrieff, Léo, and Mink's lives in momentous, yet differing ways. All three communardes remained committed to social and political activism in the insurrection's aftermath, but consistent with their dissimilar undertakings and experiences during the uprising, each woman took a unique path in her continued radical activism. In the much-changed post-Commune world, they operated in new contexts, with new constraints, trying to make sense, both personally and politically, of the recent events and their implications. All three women survived to see the turn of the twentieth century. They lived through the repression and reaction of the 1870s, a decade in which Léo and Mink experienced exile, while Dmitrieff returned to rebuild her life in Russia. In the 1880s and '90s, Léo and Mink came home to a republican France, while

Dmitrieff endured Siberian exile. Both Léo and Dmitrieff faded from the public eye during these years, yet each continued to struggle for her cause. Mink held on to the limelight, forging a public and political persona as she pressed to revive revolution.

Dmitrieff and Léo both experienced the Commune as the apex of their activist careers. Léo, at age forty-seven, had a decade of literary and political success behind her, while Dmitrieff, at twenty, had embarked on her work and study only three years earlier. The repercussions of the insurrection resulted in each woman's gradual withdrawal from organized feminist and socialist politics to her own extent and for disparate reasons. By the end of their lives, both women's fame had evaporated.

Dmitrieff's post-Commune experience was one of alienation and frustration, leading ultimately to her complete disappearance as a political actor. She returned to Russia depressed and shaken by the Commune's brutal defeat. Attempting to re-enter radical political life, Dmitrieff found a much changed Russian milieu, one into which her feminist socialism did not fit. Both the deep personal impact of the revolution and the inhospitable political climate circumscribed her ability to replicate the exceptional organizational efforts of the *Union des femmes*. Her marriage to a man with a criminal history, involved in marginally revolutionary, marginally extortionist activities, ultimately led her to follow him into exile in Siberia. Over the decades, Dmitrieff remained unable to reconnect with either the feminism or socialism to which she had been devoted.

Dmitrieff immediately dropped her pseudonym, Elisabeth Dmitrieff, at the Commune's end, and resumed using her legal name, Elisabeth Tomonovskaya. She effectively erased "Dmitrieff's" existence. Military commission reports dated May, August, and October 1872, more than one year after Dmitrieff's escape and the Commune's fall, reflect the authorities' frustration in attempting to locate and arrest this revolutionary leader. The May document relates that "It has not been possible to discover what Dmitrieff did before March 18, as research undertaken by the police has been fruitless."[8] Following a catalogue of her activities during the Commune, the report concludes with the legal charges entered against her in absentia: "Incitement of civil war by encouraging citizens or inhabitants to arm themselves," and "Provoking the assembly of insurgents by distributing orders or proclamations." The document also attests that "according to information furnished by the Prefecture of Police, her true name is Dimitriew."[9] In August, the same military investigator, M. Maruies, requested information on "Elisabeth Dmitrieff" from the Prefect of Police.[10] Two months later the Prefect of Police responded first by clarifying her name as "Dimitriew, not Dmitrieff" and reporting that "We have not been able to find her in Paris, despite numerous and thorough searches."[11] Based on their erroneous information, they could not even determine her name, whether she was single, married, or widowed, or where she lived during the Commune.[12] Condemned in absentia on October 26 to "deportation to a walled fortress," Dmitrieff successfully eluded French and subsequently Swiss and Russian authorities.[13] She arrived in Geneva in late June 1871, and returned to Russia that October under her legal identity of Elisabeth Tomanovskaya.

Although Dmitrieff temporarily reunited with her comrades in the Geneva International during her months there, she began perceptibly removing herself from this organization. Dmitrieff did not participate politically while in Geneva, in contrast to both Mink and Léo, who each immediately began speaking and writing about their Commune experience. Instead, she spent her time recuperating in a community that clearly felt paternalistic toward this twenty-year-old woman, but about whom she may have had increasingly mixed feelings. On July 1, Hermann Jung wrote to Marx that he had just been informed by telegram that "Elisa T." had arrived safely in Geneva. Several days later, Jung received a letter from Henri Perret, Secretary General of the *Federation romande* (one of the two Swiss divisions) of the International, announcing "Good news: our dear sister Elisa is saved; she was able to leave Paris in spite of many obstacles, under bullets and shells. It is a miracle . . . she is with us in Geneva, and we will protect her with the greatest solicitude . . . She will write to you."[14] She did not write to Jung or Marx. Little of Dmitrieff's correspondence exists, and it seems likely that she wrote relatively few letters in general. She clearly felt resentment toward Jung, Marx and the other London Internationalists who chose not to come to Paris and defend the Commune, as the historian Yvonne Singer-Lecocq suggests. In late April Dmitrieff had written to Jung, querying "How can you remain there doing nothing, when Paris is about to perish?"[15] Originally, Jung had planned to join Dmitrieff in Paris. As we saw in her letter to him stating "I am ill and there is no one to replace me," she had undoubtedly felt overwhelmed and isolated in Paris, despite her *Union des femmes* contacts and her connections with other Internationalists such as Malon and Frankel, of whom she wrote "I see little of them . . . we are too busy."[16] Her anger and frustration at the revolutionary rout combined with a sense of disappointment and abandonment. She refused Frankel's offer to travel with him to London, and remained in Geneva, maintaining a very quiet, low profile.[17]

On July 23, Perret wrote Jung once again, explaining that "Our dear Elisa is threatened with arrest, but we are watching over her."[18] The revolutionary refugees had been living fairly openly in Geneva until the Swiss authorities, prompted by the French government, arrested the former Communard Eugène Razoua, sending panic through the exiles' ranks. Simultaneously, the French Ministry of Foreign Affairs, under Jules Favre, pressed the Swiss government to extradite all Communards as common criminals. They used diplomatic channels to request Frankel's extradition on July 1, and on July 12 they asked for "a woman named Elise," clearly Dmitrieff. Jules Favre argued that "The abominable work of the scoundrels [Communards] . . . can-

not be confused with a political act. It is made up of a series of crimes pun-
ished by all civilized people."[19] Rather than dignifying the insurgency as political, and thus embodying a potential moral legitimacy, as well as qualify-
ing the participants for political asylum, France's forces of order defined the
primarily working-class and socialist uprising as the perpetration of the "criminal class." Yet, in spite of France's extensive diplomatic efforts, the Swiss released Razoua, and they honored the traditional right of asylum and refused
to extradite former Communards.[20]

In late October, Marx received a telegram informing him that Dmitrieff
had left Geneva; she was on her way home to Russia, in what Woodford Mc-
Clellan has termed "a state of extreme emotional depression."[21] Dmitrieff
clearly sought retreat. She spent time with her family in St. Petersburg, recuperating, and successfully maintaining her anonymity, while French, Swiss,
and Russian authorities continued in vain to search for her.[22] Dmitrieff returned to a St. Petersburg of reaction, in which the liberal intellectual circles of the 1860s had given way to increasing conservatism and repression.
Following an attempt on his life in 1866, Tsar Alexander II had begun to
move away from the reformist ideas of his early reign, fearing student
protest, social unrest, and revolution. The reactionary climate intensified into
the 1870s. The notorious Third Section, the imperial Russian secret police,
became increasingly powerful, charged with ferreting out radicals, including former Communards. Within Russian revolutionary circles, the Narodnik movement dominated the scene, focusing intensely on "going to the
people," going out and living among the peasants to educate and attempt
to radicalize them. The "woman question" had essentially disappeared from
the radical agenda, along with other revolutionary personal and individualistic goals of the 1860s, including labor, education, and gender relations.
Dmitrieff therefore found herself in a hostile climate, with a government aggressively looking to arrest former Communards, in an activist milieu unsympathetic to her feminist socialism.[23]

After several months of respite, Dmitrieff began reconnecting with the
radical world. Although she did not embrace the Narodnik ideology, she
maintained links with their newspaper *Narodnoe delo* (The Cause of the
People).[24] She and her friend and fellow former-communarde Ekatérina Bartiénieva, considered joining a Narodniki commune outside Moscow, but ultimately rejected the idea.[25] She sought a re-entry into the revolutionary
world, but struggled to find her ideological niche. In 1872, she met Ivan
Mikhaïlovitch Davidovsky, the overseer of her legal husband's estate, and a
young revolutionary with a shadowy past and questionable connections.[26]
This meeting altered the course of her life.

Dmitrieff fell in love with Davidovsky. Over the next few years they had
two children and eventually married. She came to accept Davidovsky's revolutionary methodology, further distancing her from her feminist and socialist roots. Well educated and of noble birth, Davidovsky became involved

in a series of conspiratorial plots, a path distinctly divergent from Dmitrieff's highly centralized, labor-based revolutionary approach. In particular, he participated in "The Jacks of Hearts," an infamous, mysterious group of young men of privilege, which allegedly "appropriated" money from the wealthy via blackmail, swindling, or any other means. Dmitrieff rejected the multiple accusations against Davidovsky, and in spite of friends' strong warnings, remained with him. In early 1872 she became involved in a conspiracy, most likely planned by Davidovsky, to agitate military officers to rise against the Tsar. She approached her childhood friend Alexei Kurapotkin (not to be confused with the revolutionary Peter Kropotkin), the future general and Tsartist government official, then studying at the military academy in St. Petersburg. He later described the encounter in his memoirs:

> Elisabeth told me unambiguously that she intended to attract me to her revolutionary organization. It seemed that she was also charged with recruiting other officers. For this to succeed, she counted on her beauty and eloquence, both very powerful resources. Lisa's beauty fully blossomed, and her oratorical skills, acquired in Geneva, would be absolutely irresistible to our officers.[27]

Dmitrieff pursued this plan, but it is probable that Kurapotkin projected his own interpretation of Dmitrieff's methods of persuasion, in assuming that she overtly intended to use her physical beauty on a par with her rhetorical skills. From the perspective of a military man, a beautiful revolutionary woman, even one he recognized as highly skilled, had to be using her appearance and sexuality as a tool. Words and ideas could not possibly suffice. She returned to meet Kurapotkin several times, once questioning him as to which government and military buildings could be most easily taken in an insurrection. Loyal to the Tsar, he refused to supply her with this information.[28] Clearly influenced by Davidovsky, Dmitrieff turned to a new revolutionary path. In a period of searching and questioning in her life, in the aftermath of the traumatic and cataclysmic Commune experience, she chose to personally and politically ally herself with this controversial man.

In attempting to explain Dmitrieff's ideological shift, one of her biographers, Singer-Lecocq, portrays Dmitrieff as romantically, and childishly, swept away by Davidovsky, and thus rather blindly following his lead. Singer-Lecocq describes Dmitrieff's perspective as follows: "She loves, she is fascinated, her judgment has lost the cold calm of Geneva and Paris. Papa Marx is far away. The revolution has suddenly taken the handsome face of this boy who speaks of conspiracies, who affirms that change will come from the masses, but by maneuvering the key milieus, those of high ranking officers."[29] Singer-Lecocq, in an otherwise generally well-researched work, occasionally describes Dmitrieff's thoughts and motivations with no documentary evidence. Here she romanticizes and infantilizes her subject. Dmitrieff chose to follow Davidovsky and his revolutionary approach; to attribute her behavior solely to romantic emotion denies her agency, and disregards her history and prior radical study, action, and leadership. Although fomenting governmental overthrow within the upper military echelons does constitute a definite ideological alteration from her earlier politics, Dmitrieff never, as Singer-Lecocq suggests in the above quotation, saw socialism as arising purely from the masses. As evinced during the Commune, Dmitrieff espoused a centralized, top-down approach to revolutionary socialism; she organized and led working-class women. The Commune's failure likely brought Dmitrieff closer to a more aggressive, potentially more rapid route to socialism, as it did Mink. Dmitrieff's disappointment with her International compatriots certainly extended to the working classes. And, consistent with the era's predominant Russian radicalism, but in sharp contrast to her earlier activism, she likely accepted that feminism, and other issues deemed personal and secondary, would be dealt with after the revolution.

Dmitrieff's first husband, the colonel Mikhaïl Nicolaïevich Tomanovsky, with whom she shared a *mariage blanc,* died in 1873 after a long illness. Having spent her considerable inheritance on years of revolutionary agitation, Dmitrieff had returned to Russia penniless; with Tomanovsky's death, she once again received a substantial bequest. Within three years, according to Singer-Lecocq, Davidovsky would spend it all on various plots and conspiracies, revolutionary and otherwise. By 1874, Dmitrieff gave up her project of propagandizing among military officers, and, while still politically committed, did not embark on an alternate radical undertaking. That year she gave birth to her first daughter, Irina, and the next year brought Vera; caring for two young children overlapped with her absence from radical activism until late 1876, when Davidovsky's arrest on murder charges led her to seek assistance from her old comrades.[30]

Davidovsky stood accused of killing a magistrate charged with investigating the "Jacks of Hearts." He and the organization's other members also faced charges of fraud, embezzlement, and additional financial crimes. Journalists sensationalized the offenses and the offenders, and once the trial began, crowds thronged to view the proceedings.

Upon Davidovsky's arrest, Dmitrieff took action. Recognizing his need for a highly skilled lawyer, and their inability to pay for one, she turned to her old network of Internationalist confederates. Although Davidovsky faced criminal charges, Dmitrieff contended that his activities were actually revolutionary, and that his indictments were a governmental ruse. She set in motion a chain of communication and action, seeking an attorney to unmask these machinations and to free her partner. Initially she contacted her friends and compatriots Ekatérina Bartiénieva and her husband Victor Bartieniev in St. Petersburg; they wrote to the Russian revolutionary and Internationalist Nicholas Outine, then in exile in Liège, who conveyed the information to Marx on December 17, 1876. Dmitrieff had written Outine in 1872, asking his advice and opinion about Davidovsky shortly after they met; Outine had strongly urged her to stay away from the "scoundrel." Now Outine, addressing Marx as "Dear father," explained Dmitrieff's circumstances.

> You will be surprised and pained by the contents of this letter. It regards our dear Elisa and her grievous story . . . her husband is in prison, accused of belonging to an association, not political, but of swindlers and embezzlers . . . Elisa ardently loves her husband and assured me that if he is condemned, she will follow him to Siberia . . . She is in great need. And she is a "daughter of our regiment!"[31]

Either Outine did not know or chose not to tell Marx of Davidovsky's murder charge. The letter also indicates that apparently Outine took Davidovsky's charges at face value, not conveying to Marx that Dmitrieff considered her husband's arrest as essentially political. Nonetheless, based on his regard for her, Outine informed Marx that Dmitrieff sought three thousand rubles for a lawyer. He continued:

> Should we or should we not aid our "poor lost child"? I think we must help her, and if I thought otherwise, I would not deign to call myself your son . . . I am able to send a thousand francs . . . Olga [Levachova] will follow my example . . . but this is not enough. Can you speak to Engels about this? . . . If anyone has a right to our assistance, it is without a doubt Elisa . . . did she not spend her fortune for our cause?[32]

Marx immediately made inquiries and found a lawyer to accept the case without pay. The correspondence sent in all of these efforts reflected an exceptional regard for Dmitrieff and her revolutionary history. While clearly tinged with paternalism, as in Outine's reference to her as their "poor lost child," these men felt a strong obligation toward her as a comrade, as a "daughter of the regiment." Dmitrieff's age and gender undoubtedly shaped these Internationalists' attitudes, but her work for and devotion to the cause established relationships to which she could turn, nearly six years after returning to Russia, and in spite of her husband's reputation.

Dmitrieff legally married Davidovsky on his temporary release to house arrest in 1877, knowing that only a wife could accompany a man into exile. Ever since the Decembrist uprising of 1825, a tradition had emerged for wives of the gentry and aristocracy to join their husbands in deportation. Dmitrieff and Davidovsky, revolutionary children of nobility, followed in kind. Davidovsky was found guilty on all charges, permanently stripped of his civic rights, and exiled to Siberia. Dmitrieff, her two children, and her mother-in-law, along with other *Dobrovolni* (volunteers), made the arduous journey to Siberia several months later.[33]

In Atchinsk, Siberia, Dmitrieff and Davidovsky opened a pastry shop, and attempted to meet the many political prisoners in the area. But her husband had been convicted as a "common criminal," and the political deportees shunned them. The "Jacks of Hearts" had gained infamy, and most of the populist political prisoners rejected the organization's end-justify-means methods. Many of these exiles had experienced and subsequently abandoned this cynical approach which had been advocated by the revolutionary Nechaev, who garnered a substantial, but short-lived, following of women and men in the late 1860s. Asserting the acceptability of literally anything that furthered revolution, Nechaev went as far as to supply police with moderate activists' names, so that they would be arrested and thus radicalized by their hatred of the regime.[34] This created a subsequent radical climate in which methods such as those of the "Jacks of Hearts" garnered substantial suspicion, including questions as to the extent of the organization's political, rather than financial, motivations. Simultaneously, Dmitrieff had no way of proving her insurrectionary past or her involvement in the Commune.[35] Correspondence to convicts and their families was censored and she carried no evidentiary documentation. If she had written Marx or any of her former compatriots, her identity would have been discovered and she would have faced prosecution. Unaware of Dmitrieff's history, the political exiles boycotted their pastry shop, the locals rarely purchased such luxuries, and the enterprise failed.

In April 1879, the French government granted Dmitrieff a pardon, as part of a wave of pardons issued the year before the general amnesty for former Communards. The news never reached her. If it had, she would have possessed proof of her revolutionary role, but such proof may also have identified her to Russian authorities. In 1881, the assassination of Tsar Alexander II introduced a new period of intensified repression. Later that year, the revolutionary Mikhail Sajine, Dmitrieff's former compatriot in both Geneva and the Commune, was temporarily held in a prison in Krasnoïarsk, a nearby city. Dmitrieff repeatedly, but vainly, tried to contact Sajine, with the hope that he could prove her radical past. Clearly putting herself at risk of discovery and arrest, these actions reflect the depth of her alienation, marginalization, and desperation. She continually attempted to engage with the political exile community throughout the 1880s, but remained distrusted, ostracized, and isolated.[36]

By the 1890s, Dmitrieff reacted to her political and social isolation by turning to religion. She began attending church regularly and brought icons into her home. Increasingly fascinated by astronomy, she passed the decade embracing the Orthodox faith and tutoring the local gentry's children in languages and the stars.

By the century's end, Dmitrieff's relationship with her husband worsened as well. She had repeatedly written to governmental authorities seeking a pardon for him, to no avail. Davidovsky had found a degree of success in the mining industry, which was curtailed by yet another scandal.[37] She left him between 1900 and 1902, and took her daughters to Moscow, where they supported themselves doing needlework in their home.

Dmitrieff's final years and her death remain a mystery. Both Braibant and Singer-Lecocq trace her and her daughters at various addresses in Moscow,

Braibant through 1916, and Singer-Lecocq through 1917, at which point they all disappear.[38] The Russian historian Knizhnik-Vetrov, who devoted decades to researching Dmitrieff, gave 1918 as the year of her death. No evidence exists as to whether she played a role in the revolution of 1905, or, if she still was living in 1917.

Dmitrieff, and her feminist socialism, disappeared from revolutionary history. Her absolute success at guarding her identity ultimately served to erase her access to that selfhood. As a Russian, as a young woman, as an aristocrat, and as the wife of an infamous "common criminal," her fellow radicals-in-exile could not imagine, or accept, her as a former communarde leader. The external definitions of her self effectively led to the denial of both her radical past and her potential for contemporary recognition and acceptance. Faced with this critical alienation, she turned away from activism and to religion. In an 1871 *Union des femmes* document, Dmitrieff warned that revolutionary women, if exposed to "continuous privations" would return "to a passive state."[39] Her years of social and political ostracism, and repeated denials of her identity, pushed Dmitrieff to a point where she released her political self, and looked instead to less concrete, less earthly pursuits. Both faith and the stars stood outside the bounds of her control. She made no effort to influence or reorder either one.

In the years following the Commune, André Léo's life and politics took an increasingly inward direction. Beginning with her very public efforts to place blame for the Commune's fall and brutal repression, she soon became disillusioned with traveling and lecturing, and refocused her energies on internal socialist politics for the duration of her exile in the 1870s. Léo decided that the most efficacious approach to political, economic, and social change lay in influencing the direction of the International, which she saw as laden with transformative potential. She, and her companion Benoît Malon, deeply immersed themselves in the organization's internal battles, until they finally split from the group near the decade's end. Shortly thereafter their relationship ended, and in 1880 Léo returned to Paris, and to a private life of journalism and political fiction. There she continued her long-term advocacy of a gradualist approach to a moderate, non-authoritarian socialism. No longer involved in party politics, and no longer considered a threat by the French authorities, she passed her final decades in relative obscurity.

After the Commune's fall, Léo escaped France and reached Bâle, Switzerland by train in late July, traveling on her International-supplied false passport. Malon had arrived several days earlier. Léo and Malon had each found separate refuge, and only now, after two months, were they reunited. Within days they traveled to Neuchâtel, joining other Commune refugees and members of the International. The group went on to Geneva, but Léo remained behind, immediately planning and undertaking a series of public lectures, intent on telling the world of France's brutal repression of the Commune.[40] In a letter from Chaux-de-Fonds on the Swiss–French border, the site of the first lecture, Léo wrote to her friends Elise Grimm, a teacher and activist, and Mathilde Roederer, a member of the International:

> Yes, I am here in Switzerland, but without my children. I was able to hide for two months, to deny the Versailles executioners my health and liberty. What scenes! My dear girls, what horrors! The sole thought of . . . denouncing them to the human conscience consoles me as a survivor when so many were martyred. I will begin to tell the tale here, tomorrow. I will then carry the story to Geneva, to England, to everywhere that I will be heard.[41]

Expressing enormous anger, Léo proceeded to denounce Versailles's atrocities in speeches, conferences, and journals. She carried a sense of obligation, clearly feeling guilt for having survived such a brutal massacre. Writing again to Roederer several weeks later, she reconfirmed her understanding of the centrality of peasants to political progress, stating that she "would like to propagandize where it will be the most useful: in the countryside."[42] As witnesses, she and other surviving communardes, including Mink, vowed to preserve and to disseminate the memory of the national army's savagery, and to turn popular opinion virulently against the perpetrators.

Within a year, however, Léo essentially ceased lecturing for the rest of her life. Thwarted by her perceived lack of impact, and questioning the usefulness of speaking to popular audiences, she shifted her energies. Léo turned her focus away from memorializing the Commune and retreated from public forums. Instead, she redirected her efforts toward examining the theory and practice of socialism. Aiming her arguments toward the existing socialist community, Léo wrote and edited journals, and became deeply involved in the International's internal ideological struggles. She once again relied on her intellect and her pen to promote her vision, analyzing, critiquing, and interpreting events and ideas. Consistent with her belief that the intellectual elite bore a duty to enlighten the masses, Léo focused on influencing those elites. She stepped out of the public eye, but maintained a strong literary and intellectual presence in the socialist world.[43]

Léo spoke by invitation on September 27, 1871, at the fifth anniversary meeting of the *Ligue de la paix et de la liberté* (the League of Peace and Liberty), an important post-Commune conference in Lausanne, Switzerland, which Mink and other former Communards also addressed.[44] This would be the final major speech of her life. During these months, according to the Internationalist James Guillaume, Léo "sought every opportunity to express her outraged protest against the atrocities committed by the men of Versailles."[45] She used this pulpit to pillory not only the "false republicans" of Versailles, but also her hosts, the liberal bourgeois members of the League of

Peace and Liberty, and especially the Commune government's Blanquist–Jacobin majority faction. Accusing the liberal and socialist political communities of an unwillingness to self-reflect and to accept their share of blame for the Commune's defeat, Léo was eventually forced off the stage before completing the delivery of her speech. In her critique, later published under the title *La Guerre sociale* ("The Social War"), Léo told her audience of the Commune's Bloody Week

> They made an immense human abattoir! I have seen days of blood . . . And as long as I live, wherever I can be heard, I will testify against this monstrous incarnation of egoism, of hypocrisy, and of ferocity, which the vulgar imbecile accepts under the name of the *party of order* . . . who can know the number of dead in a slaughter without end, in a massacre without judgment, which was essentially ruled by drunken soldiers and the political furor of officers? Ask the families who search in vain for a father, a brother, a missing son.[46]

Léo's bitter denunciation of Versailles's attack on Paris evoked the incendiary power of the class-based vitriol underlying the revolution, and in particular, the insidiousness of its influence over the "vulgar imbecile" and the "drunken soldier." The "imbecile" may have believed the devastation served class interests, as did the military "officers" to whom she referred. But for Léo, the deeply misguided soldier, brought in from the provinces and fed bile and hatred toward Parisians, remained blinded and deceived regarding a commonality of interests with the urban workers. Once again, she recognized the pivotal role of rural education and radicalization. Socialists needed to actively counter the propaganda Versailles disgorged, as the misinformation actively "incited France against Paris," demonizing the city as a place where "infants are thrown in the Seine; the aged are nailed to walls."[47] Honoring her vow to testify as a witness to this bloodbath, she also took significant steps to try to assure it would never be repeated. Her speech to the League of Peace and Liberty went well beyond retelling the horrendous tale; she analyzed its underlying causes and suggested means to create a just social peace.

From the podium, Léo specifically addressed her audience's role in the events. She lauded their organization as republicans, for opposing the "monarchical war" between France and Prussia, but censured them for their blindness to the ongoing class war, the "social war" of her speech's title. She stressed that "there is another war, which you have not thought of, and which has surpassed the others in ravages and frenzy. I speak of the civil war. It has existed in France since 1848; but many obstinately refuse to see it."[48] Condemning the League members for choosing not to recognize the damage caused by capitalism, and to not acknowledge the ongoing class war, she implicitly described the behavior of the League of Peace and Liberty as warlike in their acceptance or support of economic inequities. She continued: "The major point dividing the liberal democrats and the socialists is the question of capital . . . it is a question of liberty and equality."[49] Returning to a point she had long argued, Léo denounced the bourgeois League members for championing peace and liberty, but not equality.[50] "It is not possible," she declared, "to have equality without liberty, or liberty without equality. One absolutely implies the other. Hollow out one of the two terms, and you will find the other at its core."[51] Allowing the perpetuation of capitalist relations precluded the development of actual equality. Taking sharp aim at her audience, she thus asserted that a society based on class stratification and one based on liberty remained mutually exclusive. She thus directly attacked the liberal bourgeois ideology of the League of Peace and Liberty.

Léo continued her lecture in this mode. Turning to the administration and direction of the Commune, she confronted divisions among socialists and within the revolutionary government. Consistent with her opposition to anti-democratic, authoritarian socialism, she denounced the Commune government's Blanquist–Jacobin majority for discounting the minority's temporizing efforts. Labeling Blanqui "the most detestable of politicians," Léo declared that "More than anyone, I have deplored, I have cursed the blindness of these men—I speak of the majority—whose stupid ineptitude has lost the most beautiful cause."[52] Disappointed and frustrated by the Blanquist majority's anti-democratic decisions and actions during the uprising, she blamed them for the Commune's fall. The majority in the Commune government also faced accusations of terror from both revolutionary supporters and critics. Léo defended them against these indictments. In the process, however, she underlined the ineffectiveness of the Blanquist–Jacobin majority. Addressing charges that made analogies between them and the Jacobin Terror, she asserted that "all the threats, all the parody of [17]93 . . . only existed in words, phrases, decrees. It was a pose."[53] By attacking her socialist political opponents through revelations of their moderation and their "secret repugnance . . . of terror," Léo sought to vindicate socialism and the Commune, demonstrating that "true democracy," and thus for her true socialism, "is human."[54]

Intensifying her defense and redefinition of French socialism, Léo proceeded to relativize the Jacobin Terror of 1793 by comparing it with the Versailles government's repression of the Commune. Léo asked, "[What] was this red terror of the past century. . . in comparison to the tricolor terrors, of which the terror of [18]71 is the most horrible . . . What month of [17]93 equaled this bloody week, when 12,000 cadavers . . . littered Parisian soil?"[55] Comparing the guillotine of the "red terror" to the machine guns of the bourgeois "tricolor terror," Léo attempted to minimize the violence of the socialists' revolutionary legacy while vilifying the recently installed reactionary republican government and its bourgeois supporters. She dramatically clarified and contextualized the concept of "terror," emphasizing the random and rabid nature of the rampant repression of 1871. In this piece, delivered immediately after the fall of the Commune, Léo seriously underestimated the number of dead in "the terror of '71."[56] The Terror of 1793 killed about 20,000 people (2,627 in Paris, and roughly 17,000 in the rest of France) over eighteen months, while approximately 25,000 Parisians died in one week at the hands of France's National Army.[57]

Further distancing socialism from any perceived negatives, Léo finally tightened its definition dramatically, declaring that "the revolution of March 18 [the Commune] was not in the hands of socialism . . . but . . . in the hands of Jacobinism, of bourgeois Jacobinism, by its majority . . . The minority, worker and socialist . . . protested nearly constantly, but never successfully influenced affairs."[58] Léo thus defined the Commune's majority Blanquist/Jacobins as bourgeois. In labeling them "bourgeois," as were the original Jacobins of 1793, with its nineteenth-century associations of elitism and exploitation, she endeavored to strip the majority group of the moral "socialist" label. By defining the minority as "worker and socialist," she anointed them the true inheritors of the socialist mantle in the Commune's wake. Her placement of Jacobinism outside socialism implicitly resurrected the narrow, class-based definition of the 1793 Jacobin. It also asserted, in this speech, in this specific context, the Jacobins' relegation to the status of her mostly liberal, capitalist audience—clearly apart from the realm of socialism. In *La Guerre sociale*, she wove an intricately accusatory pattern of Blanquist–Jacobin weakness and culpability, ultimately revealing them tucked within the enemy fabric.

Toward the conclusion of her talk, Léo stressed the responsibilities of intellectuals and democrats to establish a just and peaceful world. This emphasis provided a window onto the direction her activism would soon take as she shifted her focus to party politics and moved away from larger public political actions. Léo called for the unity of "all democratic factions," socialist and republican, something she recognized as facing tremendous ideological and political hurdles.[59] Reiterating the illiberty of the oppressed, Léo again challenged her audience to recognize that the socio-economic system that they embraced ultimately perpetrated war on the majority of its participants. Having accused the League of Peace and Liberty of domestic warlike behavior, she then pressed them to unify to found a socialist order.[60]

These criticisms were not well received. Infuriated and outraged, the audience had loudly interrupted her talk several times, and the chair, Eytel, struggled to maintain order. Finally, he halted Léo's presentation and barred her from continuing, claiming she was not addressing the topic.[61] In the published version of her lecture, Léo addressed the issue of her silencing:

> I was invited to participate in the Congress of Peace and Liberty by one of the committee members, with the guarantee of absolute *and complete liberty of discussion,* and not me alone, but *my friends in the International and the Commune.* By inviting the banished, I believed they sincerely desired to know and illuminate the truth.[62]

Léo used the League's podium to present a larger critique of the socio-economic conflicts that had led to the recent civil war. She also presented her analysis of why the insurrection had ended in brutal failure. But her liberal republican hosts were not prepared for her charges of complicity. In the transcript's conclusion, Léo expressed outrage at the organization's rationale for terminating her speech: "What does the Congress of Peace mean by the word "war"? . . . The social war would not be considered a war! But it is more bitter and more cruel!"[63] She also continued her critique of the liberal bourgeoisie and their role in perpetuating this social war:

> It is a great and cruel mistake of the liberal bourgeoisie, to believe that by closing their eyes to facts so enormous and grave, they will be able to escape the consequences and retain their influence and valor . . . The bourgeoisie have the pen, the word, the influence. They could be the medium and the mouthpiece for the demands of the people bloodied, oppressed, vanquished . . . I came to this conference with hope; I leave profoundly saddened.[64]

Clearly disappointed in the League's members and the conference's outcome, she responded to her silencing by publishing the full text of her lecture with a critical addendum addressing the experience. Léo had optimistically interpreted her invitation to speak as an overture by this liberal bourgeois international organization, whose *raison d'être* was to form something of a "United States of Europe," to try to understand the type of social conflict that engendered the Commune. An article in the socialist newspaper *Liberté Belge* described Léo as "the sole orator to broach, without reticence, the social problem."[65] Exemplifying the socialist–liberal republican split, this paper lauded Léo's focus on the social, the issue for which the League removed her from the podium.

Léo's speech garnered her praise from the socialist community. Extolling both the speaker and the speech, the *Liberté Belge* journalist queried

> Is it not a strange thing to see a woman who is certainly neither adventurer, nor virago, a generous, indignant woman, to take, in the face of Europe, in the full triumph of reaction, in the milieu of a hostile public, the defense of the vanquished? What are the official leaders of the French republican party doing during these times? Where were they? Invited to participate in the Congress, *messieurs* Louis Blanc, Quinet, and the others recused themselves.[66]

The League had invited socialists and republicans to speak at the conference, to provide their individual, and their party's, insight and interpretation of the Commune and its aftermath, but the republican leaders declined to participate. The journalist berated the French republican leaders as frightened and ineffectual, both in this particular instance and in the larger contemporary context. He set off these accusations by rhetorically asking if it was not "strange" for a decent woman to have bravely taken the podium in defense of the defeated, a duty he contended to be the shirked responsibility of "official" male leaders.[67]

In Léo's long discourse, she had discussed nothing about women—neither about revolutionary participation, nor about emancipation. She spoke as a socialist, making no reference to her own sex, providing no qualifications about her right and ability to speak before an all-male group, presenting political and social analysis and criticism. The three foci of her talk—the Commune's repression, the revolutionary government's mistakes, and the inequities and inherent conflicts in capitalism—all were ripe for the type of gender analysis Léo frequently undertook. Nonetheless, she chose to ignore gendered questions. In assessing her intended topics and her audience, Léo may have considered that the League's potential non-receptivity to her class analysis would only be intensified if she introduced feminist issues. Léo's work up to this point, particularly in her journalism and memoirs, while consistently informed by her feminist analysis, did often address political, social, and economic concerns without referring to gender, including issues regarding the peasantry and internal politics in both the Commune and the International. She focused on the more structural or formalized aspects of the insurrection's failure when addressing the League's congress. Léo shaped her discourse to her audience, while simultaneously critiquing their ideology and politics.

Believing she had been afforded a unique opportunity to make headway toward social peace, she faced deep disappointment and frustration at her suppression. As she withdrew from public speaking, Léo subsequently immersed herself in the internal politics of the International, moving away from the larger political forum. Her initial intent to travel and lecture widely in the Commune's wake foundered; she could retell the tale of Versailles's repression of the revolution, but from her perspective, these milieus provided no ground for building socialism. She focused instead on influencing socialist theorists and activists. Léo, along with three other Communard exiles, founded the newspaper *La Révolution sociale*, which first appeared on October 26, 1871. She was responsible, according to James Guillaume, "for making *La Révolution sociale* an organ championing the principals of autonomy and liberty against the projects of Marx and his coterie"; at her impetus, it became the paper of the opposition, Bakuninist faction.[68] Remaining adversarial to Bakunin's anarchism, Léo nonetheless firmly allied herself to this federalist bloc based on her strong antipathy toward Marx and centralized socialism.

Arriving in Switzerland in 1871, the Commune veterans found themselves in the midst of an ossifying split within the Swiss International, reflective of the division within the larger organization. The two factions were the anarchist-influenced, Bakuninist *Fédération jurassienne*, directed by James Guillaume, and the politically centralized, essentially Marxist *Fédération romande,* supported by the London General Council. The two groups developed an increasing animosity, fueled by attempts to garner the allegiance of the Commune exiles.[69] Bakunin sought a collectivist anarchism, involving the replacement of all central authority with a localized federation of communes. To attain this goal, he planned a network of secret societies to overthrow the government. While Léo had consistently advocated decentralized authority, she now held a more democratic, open model for change. Léo retained her ideological convictions, and although she argued with Bakunin as in the past, she supported his power struggle against Marx, whom she despised. Léo's vehement opposition to centralized socialism segued from her enmity toward the Blanquist–Jacobin Communards, to their ideological successors, the London-based Blanquist–Marxist faction of the International. She became an important figure in the Geneva-based context of this conflict.

Writing from Geneva on October 21, Léo informed her young friend Mathilde Roederer, "Yes, there is dissension in the International, as elsewhere in the world. There are the Germans, following Marx, who advocate centralization, despotism, and false unity . . . There could be a break. It would be unfortunate. But the great currents affecting the world at this hour are felt here as elsewhere."[70] Viewing the internal conflicts as repercussions of larger political questions, Léo also understood the impact of the International on these "great currents." This realization motivated her allegiance to the organization and her zeal in opposing the Marx-backed faction. Her partisanship ran to the depth where she could accept an organizational split.

Léo's letter also reflects the shaken condition of the post-Commune world, the effects of which resoundingly reverberated throughout Europe and the International. Writing to Roederer one month later, she followed up with intensified rancor: "We are conducting a campaign against the resolutions of the London Conference, which are monolithic and authoritarian, and against Karl Marx, the evil genius, the Bismarck of the International. I am the one who gave him that moniker. You will have seen all of this if you are receiving *La Révolution sociale.*"[71] These personal letters clearly demonstrate an antipathy toward Marx and Marxian socialism, made much more public in her articles in *La Révolution sociale.* She worked devotedly to wrest control of the International from them, and to establish the organization as a powerful force for democratic socialism in this period of instability and reaction.

Responding to the London General Council's expulsions of opposing Internationalists, and to their attempts to establish and enforce a political line within all of the organization's sections, Léo wielded her pen and her editorial authority against this faction. She particularly vilified Marx. In a published dialogue between an expelled Internationalist and an interviewer (Léo) in *La Révolution sociale* on November 2, she responded to the banished man's reports of censure, exclaiming, "Is it Bismarck who reigns in the London Council? . . . And I had believed that the International was the most democratic society of which one could dream."[72] She subsequently analogized Marx to the Pope, referring to "the last papal bull," the "infallibility of the Supreme Council," and the "threat of excommunication," finally charging that "Karl Marx crowned himself pontiff of the International Association."[73] Léo linked Marx with the kind of authoritarian leadership that she asserted France had suffered under "since the beginning of the century," a form of rule that "constructed false unity, reduced independent initiative," and placed "all the force, all the power, in the capacity of one single will." Rejecting these politics, she asserted the decentralized, municipal authority of the Commune as the desired model:

> The new unity is not uniformity, but its opposite; it is the expansion of all initiatives, of all liberties . . . it is the autonomy of the citizen, realized by the autonomy of the first social group, the Commune . . . It is the second act of the Great Revolution . . . And the International Association is the natural agent of this project.[74]

For Léo, the International clearly constituted the primary battlefield in the fight for a just society, and she believed that Marxist centralization threatened its potential to generate the new Commune. She had pilloried the Commune government's majority faction, so here she defined the Commune as the federated, collectivist, non-authoritarian socialist society she envisioned and strove for. The International provided the vehicle to its attainment. Léo's zeal for publicly communicating her ideas to a range of readers and audiences had become progressively party-oriented and focused. The intensity of her passion and devotion to building her type of socialism, and her goal of defeating Marx, who she perceived as the greatest threat to its fruition, explains her desire to devote herself to internal International politics. The public forums of speeches and conferences held little appeal. The crafted argument and the written word embodied real power for her.

Léo seriously strove to develop the International into a strongly working-class socialist party, which she believed required a substantial program of education and propaganda. In her unpublished memoirs, she explained how the "politics of the past . . . shamefully and criminally exploited the passions and credulity of the masses."[75] She continued: "Unhappily, thanks to the intellectual darkness into which the majority of humanity remains plunged, and to the false and superficial instruction received by the rest, shrewdness succeeds there more than the truth."[76] Reiterating her earlier perceptions of the mass of the working class and the peasantry as unconscious and falsely informed historical actors, Léo emphasized the importance of bringing the International's socialist program to the masses in a top-down educational effort. She fervently believed that education and heightened awareness would uplift and empower the people. Her socialism of "realism and action" required an enlightened and class-conscious populous to create a "serious, skillful . . . and generous politics . . . a politics of the present and of the future," with "human hope put to the service of progress."[77] Léo's advocacy of a decentralized, federated socialism therefore rested upon the prerequisite preparation of the people. She had faith in their potential. For her, a gradualist socialist approach would enable those she termed "the honest and serious individuals of the lettered class"[78] to collaborate with the urban and rural laborers and peasants to develop a political program. Based upon the International's extant policies, programs, and power struggles, the extent of workers' actual contributions unavoidably comes into question.

In 1873, Léo married her companion and political ally of at least five years, the Communard veteran Benoît Malon.[79] Seventeen years his senior, the forty-nine-year old Léo was acutely aware of the unconventional nature of their relationship. In a letter to Mathilde Roederer, Léo exhibited both hesitancy and excitement in informing her friend of the union. She wrote:

> In spite of this white hair . . . I have been loved, and I have loved. I have been loved with a profound, naïve, enthusiastic love . . . My reason and my conscience have struggled for a long time. I have ceded to something fatal and irresistible. Then I suffered again for a long time, from the terrible discord between my sentiment and reason.[80]

Léo, who did not hesitate to break intellectual and social taboos regarding women's public speaking, publishing, and political participation, felt deeply conflicted about the age difference between her and Malon. "The world," she wrote, "would have already separated us if it had been possible."[81] Léo asked Roederer to share the information with their friend Elise Grimm, but otherwise to keep it in confidence, as Léo had yet to tell her sons. "I pray you," she continued, "to respond to me in all frankness. I want your complete sentiment."[82] Clearly apprehensive even of her young friends' reaction, Léo felt she had crossed an enormous social barrier.

Léo had long advocated legal marriage in theory. While she supported the non-sanctioned option of *unions libres,* the type of conjugality often preferred by the working class, she regarded legal wedlock to be the potentially preferable state. Léo considered marriage economically more secure for women, because of the difficulty a single woman had supporting herself.[83] But the marriage she championed stood leagues away from the typical legal union. In her 1862 novel *Un Divorce* (originally serialized in the socialist newspaper *Le Siècle*), she decried men's befouling of the institution: "Men have made a debauchery of love . . . So, in these unfortunate conditions, crime and shame reign in marriage . . . the most solemn and grave act becomes the game of their pride and their cupidity."[84]

In this novel, rather than advocate divorce (only legalized in 1884) as the answer to women's freedom from bad marriages, she looked at the further destruction such a separation would bring. She portrayed a family torn apart, with a child who essentially dies of sorrow as a result.[85] Instead, Léo argues for a reconceptualization of matrimony as a union of free and equal beings based on love. She exemplified this theory in another early novel, *Les Deux Filles de M. Plichon.* The protagonist and hero William writes to his friend, describing his relationship with his wife: "We remain distinct and independent, as much as love permits . . . our thought has maintained its liberty . . . She is the delight and charm of my life; but also a free and clear-sighted being . . . whose judgment is more precious to me than that of any other, whose esteem is more necessary than her love."[86]

Léo propounded a reordering of familial gender relations along autonomous and egalitarian lines, with each partner retaining individuality, and involving mutual care and respect. Published four years prior to John Stuart Mill's *The Subjection of Women,* Léo promoted the possibility of marriage similar to Mill's ideal that "there exists that best kind of equality, similarity of powers and capacities with reciprocal superiority in them—so that each can have the luxury of looking up to the other."[87] Earlier in the century, Saint Simonian feminists had challenged the structure of marriage and family. Other French feminists, including the socialist Flora Tristan and the republican Juliette Adam, had advocated divorce, and Jeanne Deroin and Pauline Roland had challenged the extant marital hierarchy.[88] But Léo's ideas of a legal union of equals, both an intellectual and a romantic companionship, constituted, when published in 1862, a radical departure from typical marital expectations both among the working class and the bourgeoisie. Published the year in which her first husband, Grégoire Champseix, died, the work was most likely an homage to him and to their egalitarian and happy relationship.

In her second, novel, the 1862 *Un Mariage scandaleux,* which was lauded by a contemporary critic as "one of the most remarkable works we have seen emerge in recent years," Léo had told the tale of Lucie, a young bourgeoise who overcomes tremendous familial and social opposition to her romance and eventual marriage to a working-class man.[89] Eleven years before her union with Malon, Léo had asserted the right of women to marry outside the strictures of social convention. The novel focused on class, and particularly how a woman's class position depended upon that of a man—whether her father, husband, or even brother. But she also celebrated love and choice, and proselytized that these should lie at the heart of wedlock.

Léo dealt with the question of women's age in her first novel, *Une Vieille Fille* (1851). The character Mlle. Dubois, masquerading as an "old maid" to be able to live peacefully on her own, falls in love with a young male boarder, and he with her. Léo demonstrated how once Mlle. Dubois revealed herself to be thirty-five, rather than forty-five, she became the subject of malicious gossip centering not just on her sex, but her age, as her sister callously reported: "They say that Monsieur Albert is your lover, and that you two have an arrangement in which you each give the other what each of you lack: you receive love, he bread."[90] At thirty-five, nearly a decade Albert's senior, Mlle.

Dubois now fell within the realm of the still somewhat sexual, but remained inappropriately, and to the critical outside world, undesirably old. Léo attacked the era's sexist and ageist assumptions, giving her hero the power to test Albert's love and loyalty, and to establish the terms of their fairytale happy ending. Léo believed in the power of love over the forces of hierarchy and inequity; this was not a purely romanticized love, but a passion of thoughts, ideas, and feelings between equals that would reoccur in her subsequent works, and that uncannily presaged her future relationship with Malon. In *Une Vielle Fille,* such a love triumphed over age, social expectations, and (initially) poverty. The novel closes with a glimpse five years into the future. Sitting in the garden of their lovely home in Nice, the older of the couple's two children finds his mother's first gray hair, much to her distress. But Albert quickly declares, "Let your hair whiten, my love; together we are as old as our love and as young as our affection."[91]

For her post-Commune self, however, Léo experienced an ongoing dissonance over her marital decision. While she happily transgressed public gender and class boundaries, and advocated the reconstitution of gender-based family relations, the issue of her physical self, her "grey hairs," her possibly menopausal body, constituted a particularly daunting personal barrier for her to overcome. She viewed this contravention as personally unacceptable.

Indeed, Léo blamed this barrier when she terminated her relationship with Malon in 1878, a decade after its inception. In letters to Elise Grimm and Mathilde Roederer, she explained that "my union with Benoît Malon . . . has been broken for a long time, but now we are about to separate in fact."[92] Expressing her ongoing care and friendship toward him, she explained to Mathilde that "a union as disproportionate in age has no right to be eternal."[93] She elaborated to Elise: "I have always felt that one could, that one should, brave prejudices, but not the natural laws . . . I have always said that this union would not be eternal, that one day I would give him his liberty, not chain him to my old age, and allow him the possibility of the joy of a complete family, which I am unable to give him."[94]

Léo clearly felt that she and Malon had violated the laws of nature in attempting to bridge their seventeen-year difference. This, for her, differed qualitatively from breaking class-based taboos, constructs she considered antithetical to nature. Her resultant pessimism in the marriage's ability to succeed was clear as she reminded Elise of her earlier hesitations: "You know, dear child, with what remorse and sadness that I contracted this union. But when the affection is great and profound, it is difficult to have another desire other than that of the man you love—especially when a thousand dangers menace him, and it is possible to be useful to him."[95] Malon had convinced Léo to marry him, in the wake of the Commune, in exile, under police surveillance, in a deeply tenuous situation. Her sense of her usefulness to him—intellectually and emotionally—allowed her to surmount her strong hesitations. But she remained acutely aware of the instability of both the relationship and their larger lives. Concluding her letter to Mathilde, she stated that Malon, "only thirty-eight years old, could still establish a normal life."[96] Referring to the abnormality of their age disparity, Léo also implied the issue of a thirty-eight-year-old man's wife's inability to bear children. At the crux, she saw herself as a burden to him, denying him his "normal" right to paternity. Again, she wrote, "Having been unable to give him a complete family, menaced by the ravages of time, so rapid at a certain age, I have always wanted to protect his liberty."[97] At fifty-four years old, after two marriages, two children, and two decades of writing and activism, she viewed herself as a victim of time.

Léo emphasized normalcy and liberty, two factors at least somewhat absent in the couple's émigré existence. During their five-year marriage, Léo and Malon had moved from city to city across Switzerland and Italy, living and working in places including Geneva, Como, Milan, and Lugano, making a living by their writing, while persistently under police observation. Léo continued to focus her efforts on socialist journalism and party politics. In Geneva, they both wrote for *La Revolution sociale*. Beginning in 1873 they lived in Milan under the name Béra, Léo's maiden name. In January 1876, Malon was arrested, held for three days, and then expelled from Italy. He established himself in Lugano, where Léo joined him that March. Late the next year they founded *Le Socialisme progressive*. Simultaneously, they broke with Bakunin and the Jura Federation of the International, including Guillaume, with whom both Léo and Malon had been so closely allied. This split was over the issue of anarchism, which both Léo and Malon overtly opposed.[98]

The break with Bakunin seemed relatively inevitable, as, even while supporting his faction of the International, Léo continued to oppose him on ideological matters, as she had since prior to the Commune. Her alliance with the Bakuninists emerged essentially from the perspective that "the enemy of my enemy is my friend." Bakunin, too, detested Marx. Additionally, Léo felt a strong allegiance to the International, with which she wanted to remain involved. When she and the other émigrés arrived in Switzerland, they landed in the center of an intensifying internal division; to remain in the organization, they had to choose sides.

Ideologically, Léo rejected Bakunin's conspiratorial anarchism, as well as his belief in the viability of completely abolishing the state. Simultaneously, and in keeping with her long years of moderate, collectivist socialism, Léo asserted the right of every person to own property, which, in her conception, would be worked cooperatively. Echoing Locke, she contended that "it is by the suffering and poverty which result from its [property's] absence, that the people finally understand that this natural right was the first right of all!"[99] The question of private property remained a point of contention among socialists of the era. As exemplified by her Bakuninist confederation,

Léo formed political alliances, but she consistently retained her ideological independence.

While still in exile, Léo published a "fairytale" titled *La Commune de Malenpis: conte* (a tale), which marked her post-Commune return to using fiction as a means for social change. Although no longer speaking publicly, she used the fairytale to popularize her feminist socialism. *Malenpis* told the story of a perfect city, where "school was free, and the male and female teachers were well paid and so numerous that each child received a good education."[100] This anti-war, anti-monarchist tale leads up to the final socialist lesson, concluding that "After all that had passed, after having seen kings and princes with their bad morals, thievery, and war, there is now no one who does not believe that true riches are in work, and that happiness and truth can only exist in liberty."[101] This didactic, often humorous fable reflected Léo's ongoing efforts to instruct and lead with both fiction and theory. She wrote this story in 1874 while living with Malon in Milan. Presenting the possibility of a society learning from the evil and destruction of undemocratic leaders, she put forth *La Commune de Malenpis* as exemplary and worthy of emulation. In contrast to the Commune of Paris, in which work and liberty fell under the onslaught of undemocratic leaders, *Malenpis* presented a hopeful inversion of outcomes.

In 1880, nine years after the fall of the Commune, the French government declared a general amnesty for all exiled and imprisoned Commune veterans. The move reflected the increasing strength of the republicans, after a decade of power struggle with the monarchists. This amnesty, which Dmitrieff was granted but never notified of, allowed Léo, Mink, and many other socialist exiles to return to France. And it was a France which that year had finally made July 14 (Bastille Day) a national holiday, symbolically marking the triumph of the republic over the monarchy. The next year, 1881, individual rights and freedoms, including of association, speech, and the press, would finally be guaranteed under law.[102] Returning to Paris in 1880, Léo settled into a private life. Although she continued to publish novels and write political articles, she disappeared from the public eye. The year 1880 also marked the termination of her file in Paris' Prefecture of Police. Both during and after the exile years, under reactionary governments including those of Thiers and the monarchist Marshal MacMahon, and through the more democratic republic of Jules Ferry, the Parisian police persisted in carrying out espionage against revolutionary veterans, both in France and abroad. The extent and duration of the espionage depended upon the degree of threat the police believed the subject posed. Police reports included quoted, "verbatim" accounts of political speeches and meetings, analyses of the women's words and influence, descriptions of their appearance, and critiques of their personal and public behaviors. The officers and informants writing these reports reflected the desires of the police hierarchy to remain apprized of every detail of these "dangerous" women's lives. The results of their efforts provide a rich historical resource reflecting the power of communardes' legacies as a threat to the established order, and the role of the police as guardians of that order.

When the Swiss government refused to extradite Communards in the revolutionary aftermath, Paris reacted by maintaining police surveillance of the former insurgents without regard for national borders. Two years following the Commune's fall, the Minister of the Interior, the duc de Broglie, under whose authority the police fell, wrote to the president of the Republic, MacMahon, outlining the role and significance of police espionage: "A country must have a good police force, informing the government in a complete and timely fashion, indicating the perils to which the society is exposed, without diminishing or exaggerating their gravity, and allowing the central authority to take just, repressive measures when necessary."[103]

In peacetime, in the insurrectionary wake, the police spies were intended as a front line against political threats and social unrest. An extensive espionage network carried out surveillance on hundreds of former revolutionaries and suspected activists, relaying information from the substantial to the extraordinarily mundane, from the substantiated to the surmised. The communardes' police dossiers reflected the efforts of agents striving to protect France from the societal perils embodied in these feminist and socialist women.

The Paris police represented France's forces of order. Reeling with the memory of the Commune's dramatic social upheaval, those deeply invested in the status quo—the members of the national government, the military, the Church, and the bourgeoisie—relied on the police to ensure the maintenance of order. And as demonstrated by France's national troops during the Bloody Week, they sought order at any cost. The role of the police spies at this time involved monitoring and reporting the words, actions, and associations of all revolutionary veterans. Communardes posed a triple menace in this context, as they threatened class, gender, and religious hierarchies.

The Paris Police had monitored Léo's whereabouts, writing, activism, and personal behavior throughout the 1870s. Reports vary from a few brief lines in August 1872, relating that Léo was in Locarno, Italy, planning the next congress of the International with Bakunin, to multi-paged, detailed summaries of her life and work.[104] For example, a January 1873 communiqué briefly outlined her personal life, listed the seven political novels she had published and the newspapers she had edited, and discussed her role in the Commune and its immediate aftermath. A report written seven months later noted that "we do not know where she is at the moment," indicative of the less than precise system that had allowed her, Dmitrieff, Mink, and many others to escape France.[105] In terms of her personal life, an April 1872 document, typical of several others, suggested that she had probably joined Malon in Neuchâtel, and that "She has, they say, very intimate relations with him."[106] In May 1878, an informer wrote "Malon is in Lugano with André Léo, who inspires and virtually directs his journal,"[107] and later that year, "André Léo has separated from Malon."[108] In their attempt to piece together the life and work of an emigrée wanted by the state, the police spies in many ways found evidence that fit the crime. As a revolutionary woman, social activist, and a writer, Léo transgressed numerous boundaries of proper womanhood. Her personal relationships, both sexual and intellectual, provided the lenses through which the police could view her public behavior. It made sense that a woman flouting personal propriety would also disregard established public, civic, and political structures.

The Paris Prefecture of Police stopped monitoring Léo once she returned to Paris in 1880. By that time, she had not lectured publicly in almost a decade, she had focused most of her efforts on internal socialist conflicts, she published in narrowly focused political journals, and her novelistic production had slowed significantly. In dramatic contrast to Paule Mink, whose enormous police dossier testifies to surveillance until she died, Léo had ceased to pose a significant threat to the forces of order.

In 1879, Léo had written to a friend, "I carry all the weight of fifty-five years on myself: fatigue, sadness, lost illusions."[109] Politically and personally disappointed and frustrated, she nonetheless persevered with her work on her return to Paris, but increasingly isolated herself. Following her break with the International's Jura Federation in Geneva, Léo never again allied herself with a socialist, or a feminist, faction. She remained committed to her social and political ideals, and her feminist socialist vision, continuing her two-pronged (fiction and non-fiction, literary and intellectual) tack. During the final two decades of her life, she wrote two serialized novels for the socialist paper *Le Siècle* in the early 1880s, and published several more novels and a political treatise in the 1890s, addressing feminist and socialist topics including education, marriage, child rearing, and justice.[110] She also faced personal tragedy: in 1885 one of her sons, Léo, passed away at the age of thirty-two, and eight years later, his twin followed him to an early death.[111] Benoît Malon died two years before Léo as well.[112]

To France's forces of order, Léo, as an intellectual, party politician, and novelist, had no real tangible impact on either the working class or the government. From their perspective, her ideas had no effective means to reach a significant target, or they lacked the power to influence a consequential group, or they were intrinsically unthreatening to the existing order. This once perilous revolutionary woman had seemingly become benign. Unlike Mink, who spoke publicly, frequently, and flamboyantly, Léo kept an extremely low public profile. She advocated no violence or appropriation of private property. Particularly with the emergence of mainstream reformist socialism late in the century, Léo's politics appeared increasingly less radical.

Léo remained known within the European socialist community, but ceased participation in socialist party politics.[113] Her popularity dwindled over the decades, since its peak under the late Empire and during the Commune. When she died without heirs in 1900, consistent with her lifelong work for a collectivist socialism, she left "a small annuity" for "the first community in France to attempt a collectivist system by purchasing land communally and working together to share its fruits."[114] Léo was buried in the Champseix family plot, but her grave bore no name.[115]

7
Mink in the Aftermath

The Red Flag and the Future

On May Day, 1901, a police informant observed Paule Mink's funeral procession as it wound through the streets of Paris. He reported: "At the moment the cortege left the mortuary, cries of *'Vive la sociale! Vive la Commune! Vive l'Internationale!'* rose from the crowd. These cries arose again and again along the route."[1] Thousands of mourners attended her funeral, filling the streets, and over six hundred police, five hundred foot soldiers, and one hundred cavalry patrolled the procession route. Thirty years after the fall of the Commune, Mink's interment reflected the significant role that the veterans, the ideas, and the mythology of the Commune played in the decades following the revolution. It also indicated the enormity of her renown. Mink's legendary status as a communarde who remained passionately devoted to the cause, and her theatrical approach to feminist socialist politics—combining popular lectures and party activism with her vivid personality and frequently public personal life—had brought her fame (or from the police perspective, infamy). The report of her burial, one of a series of extraordinarily detailed, virtually minute-by-minute accounts of the day's events, concluded at least thirty years of police surveillance of Mink. (She was most likely under observation prior to 1871, but the fires of the Commune destroyed the Prefecture of Police and virtually all of its records.) The trajectory of her life presents a dramatic contrast to that of both Dmitrieff and Léo.

Paule Mink escaped France and arrived in Geneva with her daughter Wanda within two months of the Commune's demise, sometime before July 10, 1871. James Guillaume reported seeing her that day at a meeting of Communard exiles. The revolutionary veterans intended to establish a section of the International specifically focused on France, to counter the Versailles Government of National Defense's massive anti-Communard propaganda, but the plan never coalesced.[2] Although Mink remained connected to the emigrée Internationalists in Geneva, she did not became as deeply involved as Léo did in the organization's politics. She did, however, speak at the League of Peace and Liberty conference, taking the podium on September 28, 1871, the day after Léo. Declaring herself a socialist, Mink discussed the International, which "she praised to the skies," declaring it "the force of the future."[3] She went on to propose two motions: first, to support the right of labor association and an end to persecutions of the International, and second, to denounce the Versailles government for massacring Parisians. The first passed, but the second measure failed in the face of the same opposition Léo had encountered from the primarily bourgeois League members. Many of them refused to place complete blame on Versailles, demanding, instead, a statement protesting all of the "crimes" committed in Paris.[4] Contrary to Mink and to Léo, they wanted the revolutionaries to share the burden of guilt.

Mink's socialism sharply diverged from other feminist socialisms in the wake of the Commune's loss. Although Mink and Léo had clearly taken differing paths toward feminism and socialism before and during the Commune, both women had opposed any centralized, authoritarian approach. Within a year, Mink radically altered her ideological stance, rejecting the idea that socialism would best be brought about via a grass-roots, anarchist approach. In its place, she embraced the advocacy of centrally planned, violent revolution. For Mink, social revolution became the primary goal. She believed that only revolution would create the circumstances in which gender and religious oppressions and persecutions could finally be eradicated. So she focused her efforts on agitating for a socialist uprising, but she also continued to advocate feminism and anti-clericalism in her speeches. While Mink understood that her feminist and secular goals could not be attained under the existing socio-political system, she still recognized the importance of keeping these issues central to the debate. And she also saw in them a means of inciting the population to revolt.

Both Mink and Léo constructed analyses of the Commune's defeat and suppression, each assigning blame to opposing sides within the revolutionary government. Mink's newly conceptualized socialist authoritarianism led her to celebrate the Blanquist majority. She retrospectively condemned the minority faction for attempting to moderate the majority's extra-governmental revolutionary measures, such as confiscating property, appropriating funds, and limiting rights and freedoms during the insurrection, acts that she now believed could have enabled the Commune's triumph. Léo, as we have seen, embraced the antithetical stance. Consistent with her opposition to anti-democratic, authoritarian socialism, she denounced the Blanquist majority for disregarding the minority's temporizing efforts.

As much as Léo decried Blanquist authoritarianism, Mink came to celebrate it in the aftermath of the Commune. Newly advocating a conspiratorial, highly centralized revolutionism, Mink tirelessly devoted herself to resurrecting and reforming the Commune—to bringing about violent social revolution in order to rebuild *la république sociale*, the true republic, free from class, gender, and religious oppressions. The following March 18, at a meeting celebrating the first anniversary of the uprising, Mink attacked the revolutionary government's minority, moderate faction, charging that the Commune "lacked the courage to deliver a great blow because of its lack of logic. It impeded the movement . . . it deliberated when it should have fought."[5] Completing her speech with a "toast to the new Commune," she blamed the failure of 1871 on the minority faction's caution and moderation. Apparently, the experience of the Commune government's inaction and confusion, the brutality of the bourgeoisie's defense of the status quo, and the frustration of the revolutionary loss, led Mink to re-evaluate her political stance. Rejecting her previous anarchistic, individualist position, she now championed direct and authoritative action, an approach well suited to her dramatic and flamboyant sense of self. She became an avid supporter of centralized, conspiratorial Blanquist socialism.

Mink's turn to Blanquism did not entail a rejection of her feminism, nor did it involve a separation from the International. She strove to make her feminism and socialism central to the organization. Although Mink radically shifted her socialist affiliation in the Commune's aftermath, she remained a loyal member and advocate, as well as critic, of the International. Adamant that socialism's ultimate success required the inclusion of women, immediately following the Commune Mink admonished the International for having "forgotten women," pronouncing their actions "a great wrong, and it is perhaps because of denying justice to women that the International has not prospered more rapidly."[6] Mink understood women's continued oppression and marginalization as seriously impeding the socialist agenda. She contended that by "denying justice to women," the International had hampered its own progress and, with it, the advancement toward socio-economic and political change.

While a vocal critic of the International, Mink simultaneously strove to revive the organization, and resuscitate socialism, by incorporating women into its membership, thereby creating a base of support for an egalitarian agenda. Writing for the International's Geneva-based newspaper *L'Egalité* in the wake of the Commune, Mink encouraged women that "the future belongs to us, but you must give everything to aid our triumph . . . bring your enthusiasm to the social revolution . . . embrace a noble cause!"[7] She appealed to both women and men as citizens, touting the International as the post-Commune route to emancipation:

> *Citoyens et citoyennes!* It is in the name of women that I speak, in the name of women to whom the International has given the rights and duties equal to those of men . . . only socialism will be able to emancipate women materially and morally, as it will be able to emancipate all those who suffer.[8]

Placing socialism as the key to women's emancipation, Mink demonstrated the logic behind her giving greater priority to socialism over feminism: she understood the former to be a necessary prerequisite to the latter. Consistent with her feminism of difference, Mink employed a maternalist argument and appealed to women to "come to us, not for the present alone, but especially for the future of your children, come to us so that your children can have a better life than you."[9] Within the International, women held the same rights as men. By bringing more women into the association, Mink hoped to shape its membership and agenda, and to develop it into the catalyst for a free and fair future.[10]

As her ideological position solidified, she remained peripatetic. During her decade in exile, Mink concentrated her feminist socialist activism on traveling to cities and towns, agitating and advocating social revolution. She posed a controversial, dynamic, popular figure, speaking publicly to groups of men and women, working to incite social unrest.

Mink's public lectures served an additional purpose: they provided a source of much needed funds.[11] She struggled financially not only throughout her decade in Swiss exile, but also for the rest of her life, relying on giving French lessons, doing millinery and other needlework, and occasionally asking friends and colleagues for financial assistance. Her estranged husband, Bohdanowicz, sent money infrequently. She had been raising her daughter, Wanda, eight years old in 1872, on her own through the tumultuous years. While still in exile, she had two more daughters, Mignon and Héna, with the painter and socialist activist Noro, with whom she had been romantically allied since the Commune.[12] Mink maintained a close relationship with her brother and fellow Communard, Jules Mekarski, but he, too, was a political exile in dire financial straits.[13]

In addition to giving public lectures, Mink participated in the formation of *La Société des proscrits de Genève,* "The Geneva Society of the Banished," an organization of Commune exiles separate from the International, but not in conflict with it. This group focused on, among other things, smuggling politically incendiary literature and arms into France. According to a police report on March 30, 1872, Mink wanted to head the *Société,* which intended to establish subsidiary branches in many countries. The police informant scoffed at this possibility, writing "Paule Mink giving orders to all the European countries! We think that this plan is too vast to be directed by a woman."[14]

Mink, described in the report as "very ambitious," lost the directorship election at the following meeting.[15] Apparently her comrades held views similar to those of the government's spy.

She subsequently traveled to Porrentruy, a small Swiss town near the French border, and in alliance with the *Société*, established a base for smuggling "prohibited publications, munitions, and other objects . . . to be used in the revolutionary cause."[16] Mink slipped in and out of France during the first half of 1872, setting up a highly effective smuggling ring. Explaining the flow of contraband into the country, a Parisian police spy wrote to his superior that "the day when a [revolutionary] movement begins, the arms will come from Porrentruy."[17] Denied leadership of this exile association most likely because of her sex, and sent off to a small provincial town to undertake her work, Mink nonetheless devoted herself to coordinating these subversive efforts. Her dedication to the cause of reigniting social conflict, her skill at establishing the conspiratorial operation, and her bravery in clandestinely crossing the international border repeatedly, resulted in a successful smuggling operation that clearly threatened France's forces of order.

Paule Mink holds the dubious honor of having a police dossier far larger than any other communarde, with the exception of the legendary Louise Michel. In the 1872 documents, there are pages of information and accusations about her whereabouts and her smuggling, including reports asserting that her lover, Noro, aided her in spreading illegal propaganda throughout France. On March 16, an informant wrote that "Norot [*sic*] and Mme. Mink will be going to France . . . to establish a new contraband route to bring their literature to Lyons and the Midi."[18] Subsequent missives track their travels and actions, reflecting the government's fear of Mink's ideas being disseminated not only in Paris, but also across the provinces. During the same period, police spies also suspected her in a possible "conspiracy against the life of Thiers."[19] And when she joined the staff of *L'Esperance* (The Hope), a women's journal, an agent described the periodical as "up to this point moderate, but now Mme. Mink is involved."[20] Police informants reported on Mink at times almost daily during these months, considering her to be "an enormous influence," and clearly a serious threat.[21]

Part of the police agents' reporting duties involved efforts to portray their subjects physically. Laden with moral, corporeal, and political judgments, their representations reflected the antagonism of the spies for the espied. In response to a request for a photograph of Mink, an informant wrote his superior that he was unable to find one and was sending a description in its place. He then listed her characteristics as including a "pale and thin face marked with several freckles; sickly appearance; black hair; long nose slightly turned up; large mouth . . . [and] right shoulder higher than the left."[22] Even when attempting to create the most literal description possible, the informant used only negative terms, omitting any hint of attractiveness or femininity from his subject. In another example, an agent depicted Mink as having a "medium nose, rather large mouth . . . deathly complexion . . . very bad teeth . . . neglected hygiene," a depiction going well beyond the descriptive.[23] Léo, too, was subjected to these denigrating portrayals: a detailed report relating her activities and interactions concluded with an extended physical description of her, quoted from the September 1871 issue of an anti-Commune newspaper, *La Liberté.* The quotation the police agent chose reflects his fascination with the appearance of the female insurgents, as though presenting the messenger as repugnant would guarantee the repulsiveness of the message. Léo is depicted as a "fat gossip, brunette, pimply, red faced, [with a] bulging forehead, grey and watery eyes, hoarse voice. One could easily take her for a tobacco merchant on the rue St. Martin."[24]

The contrast could not be more stark between the dry and factual tone used to describe her work, and the embellished "portrait" that describes her physical attributes. While an extreme example, this pattern remains consistent throughout the surveillance documents. Police spies typically reported women's actions and undertakings in a straightforward, journalistic manner, but used significant editorial license for their occasional physical descriptions. Such derogatory portraits reflected the disdain the police agents felt for the lives and ideas of these women who not only challenged, but also actively worked to subvert the dominant class and gender hierarchies. The fear of revolutionary women upending the social order remained palpable in the years following the Commune.

The gendered quality of the reports appears clearly in documents describing both men and women. For example, in a June 20, 1872, statement depicting Mink as "slightly deformed, she leans a little to the side . . . large mouth, very strong lower lip, large, square-tipped nose; ugly—she is missing front teeth," the informant went on to present her brother Jules Mekarski as having "very long, brown hair, brown eyes . . . a full, short beard . . . straight nose . . . nervous constitution, he speaks very rapidly."[25] His physical portrayal lacks the denigrating terms and tone of his sister's. Rather, Mekarski is demeaned in being described as "nervous," clearly an unmasculine characteristic. Aggressive towards and disdainful of both his subjects, the informant used an insulting physical description to besmirch the woman, while making a character attack on the man. From this perspective, typical of the era's dominant way of thinking, a woman's worth rested in her body, while a man's lay in his constitution.

Surprisingly, but indicative of Mink's rhetorical talent, this police agent qualified his depiction of her, explaining that "this woman, endowed with a defective physique, completely metamorphoses when she speaks; her face lights up, and her eyes sparkle."[26] Even according to this hostile observer, Mink shone when she took the podium. Her ability to enchant even such an antagonistic observer with her oratorical skills testifies to her power and to the extent of the threat she posed. This gift, in the hands of a radical, female, political agitator, intensified her menace enormously.

Mink returned to France in 1880, as did many other Communard exiles, allowed repatriation following the government's issuance of the General Amnesty. She had made several clandestine trips in and out of Paris at decade's end, no longer smuggling, but slipping in to appear at socialist functions. The General Amnesty was not issued until July 1880, yet in January of that year, Mink spoke at a *"soirée litteraire, historique et musicale"* organized by the *Société du journal le proletaire* to benefit the orphans of the Commune.[27] Back in Geneva by March, she subsequently made her "official" departure for Paris, traveling via London, traversing the provinces and lecturing on feminism, socialism, and anti-clericalism, on topics including "Marriage and Divorce," "The History of Women in Society," "Capital and Labor," "Socialism and Revolution," and "Jesuits and Clericals."[28]

In distinct contrast to Léo's return to a private, literary life, and continued advocacy for a gradual move to a democratic, collectivist socialism, and to Dmitrieff's disappearance from the political realm, Mink traveled tirelessly, agitating for social revolution. Younger and more public than Léo, and experiencing completely different circumstances than Dmitrieff, Mink survived economically, intellectually, and psychically by remaining in the public eye. Speaking on the topic *"Liberté, Egalité,"* at a conference organized by *L'Union des femmes socialistes* shortly after her arrival in Paris, she declared that "The Versaillais have fooled themselves into believing that the Commune is dead; they don't realize that Paris is revolutionary . . . soon I hope the entire world will be revolutionary."[29] Although both Mink and Léo survived thirty years after the Commune's fall, Léo's politics—both her ideas and her means of communicating and enacting them—led France's forces of order to dismiss her as non-threatening, and thus to terminate their surveillance of her in 1880. Mink's politics, her more violent and radical ideas, and her popular, dramatic methods of communicating and enacting them, led the police to rule her a visible, public risk to gender, class, civic, and religious hierarchies.

Mink played on her appeal as a former communarde in her lecture tours. Whether speaking alone, with fellow socialists such as Jules Guesde, or with other Commune veterans, especially Louise Michel, she often drew crowds in Paris and the provinces.[30] A police report described her series of provincial conferences, which she undertook in 1880, as a "mission to revolutionize and to win the socialist cause . . . in every city where she brought her socialist conferences, she retold the history of the Commune, and she contacted local revolutionary groups or worked to organize new ones where there were none."[31]

She, like Léo, remained a strong advocate of rural radicalization, but she physically brought an insurrectionary message to people in towns across the country. Speaking at a socialist meeting in Paris in 1880, Mink asserted the importance of assuring that "the provinces march with Paris" in order to bring about "the day, so desired, of the *révolution sociale*."[32]

Mink and Louise Michel met with warmly enthusiastic public embraces and accolades as they traveled France, either separately or together, speaking in cities and towns. Although Michel had become an anarchist during her exile, the same period during which Mink had abandoned her anarchism, Michel and Mink shared several positions, including a devotion to agitation, an opposition to rights-based feminism, and a taste for the theatrical. In December 1880, Mink wrote to Michel following two evenings of speeches, "Oh, that you were here . . . in Elbeuf with me! What enthusiasm, what profound emotions!" She described the scene of the night of her first lecture when Mink asked that the tricolor flag, France's flag, be removed; she considered it to be a symbol of repression. Her hosts rolled up the standard so that only the red portion showed, and on the next night "the hall was decorated . . . with three superb red flags," the flags of revolution. She continued, "When I was here in '69, eleven years ago, nothing was organized . . . and [now] my dear Elbeuvien friends say to me . . . 'we organized because of what you said, and while we were once a group of five we are now one hundred.' They all came to . . . thank me. My friend, is this not a magnificent result, and is the provincial propaganda not an excellent thing?"[33]

While Léo had established renown as an author and journalist prior to the Commune, both Mink and Michel had begun to develop strong reputations as orators before and during the revolution. Mink's exile and Michel's deportation each served to enrich their respective standings. Describing the meetings she had just attended, Mink told Michel, "They love you here, dear friend, they venerate you here as everywhere, and they would very much like to see you."[34] They were not alone in this sentiment.

When Michel had returned from exile in New Caledonia only the month before, she received a staggering reception as she debarked from the train in Paris, on November 9, 1880. Between six and eight thousand people welcomed her at the Gare Saint-Lazare, shouting *"Vive Louise Michel! Vive la Commune! Vive la révolution sociale!"*[35] Brochures had been printed in advance; and thousands joined in singing "La Marseillaise." Michel's participation on the battlefield and in the clubs during the Commune, heightened by her performance before the Versailles military tribunal when she essentially claimed personal responsibility for much of the revolution, had elevated her to legendary status. The next twenty-four years of her life continued in a now much-documented, dramatic vein.

Following her arrest for carrying the black flag of anarchism at the head of an enormous demonstration by unemployed workers in 1883, the judge questioned Michel: "I see that you have been convicted before. Do you take part in every protest? Do you think that demonstrating for the unemployed will bring them work?" And she responded, "Yes, I am at every demonstration because I am always with the poor. No, I did not think that protesting

Fig. 10. Marie Ferré, Louise Michel, and Paule Mink.
*Courtesy of Siege and Commune of Paris collection, Charles Deering McCormick
Library of Special Collections, Northwestern University Library.*

would change their fortune. I thought that the crowd would be swept away by cannons, I went there as my duty."[36]

Once again Michel claimed culpability far beyond her actions. She performed the role of revolutionary angel, watching over and guiding the downtrodden and oppressed. The combination of her political commitment and her flair for the sensational brought her much attention: following this trial the poet Paul Verlaine honored her with a poem, as Victor Hugo had following the Commune.[37] On January 20, 1888, Michel, while giving a lecture, was shot in her left temple by a deeply offended audience member; the bullet did not penetrate her skull, and she recovered fully.[38] This attack, however, catapulted her even further into French martyrology, building upon Verlaine's likening her to Joan of Arc in his tribute poem.

Michel ultimately came to stand for the Commune. An iconoclastic revolutionary devoted to the cause of women and workers, a prodigious writer who eschewed theory, and a fervent activist who disregarded organizing, her image and story effectively occluded the multi-faceted reality of women's Commune participation, and with it the rich variety of feminist socialisms that emerged from the uprising. This legendary Michel emerged as a combination of the real woman's self-fashioning, and the interpretation, appropriation, and manipulation by admirers, critics, and observers. She was labeled the "Red Virgin," an epithet used by both left and right, which, as Gay Gullickson points out, Michel came to embody.[39] Her entire being became devoted to the political cause. Unmarried, childless, physically plain, and recklessly brave, the "Red Virgin" was safely sexless to the men of the left, socialists who disdained women's entry into public life. The right embraced the desexed image to underscore her deviance and perversion of femininity.

Both Michel and Mink strode flamboyantly through the post-Commune decades, leaving scandal and adulation in their wakes. But Michel enormously eclipsed Mink in the historical memory. Michel wrote voluminously, particularly compared to Mink's thin paper trail, which certainly contributed to historians' focus on the former.[40] And while both women lived public lives, Mink's world involved men, marriages, separations, and children. She lacked the purity of a revolutionary icon. As a single mother for much of her life, Mink perpetually struggled to make ends meet, using time and energy on financial worry and labor, on relationships and childcare. She could not give all to the cause; she did not become the cause. Mink's was a messier revolutionary existence.

Mink conceptualized *la révolution sociale* as the rebirth of the Commune. Even as she shifted from anarchism to a more centralized and conspiratorial socialism, she remained wedded to the values and efficacy of insurrectional violence. In her lectures, Mink affirmed the need for class war and repeatedly invoked the heritage of France's violent revolutionary past to inflame conflict. Consistent with the Blanquist emphasis on historical precedent and revolutionary tradition, Mink used the rhetoric and images of insurgency in general, and of the Great Revolution and the Commune in particular, as models and inspiration to perpetuate the radical tradition.[41] Ridiculing those who believed that "the next revolution could be made without shooting guns," she asked: "will it be sufficient to present yourselves at the Palais Bourbon, armed with economic theories, to chase away the Deputies?"[42] Continuing this theme at a public lecture two days later, she argued that "a prompt, energetic solution is necessary, which will conclude with the suppression of the execrable bourgeoisie."[43] Mink labored to incite a working-class uprising; for her, all significant social, economic, and political changes depended on the revolutionary institution of socialism.

Following the insurrection, Mink's relatively balanced pre-Commune foci on socialism, feminism, and anti-clericalism became subordinated to her overarching goal of reigniting social revolution. In a telegram sent to a Parisian socialist meeting on March 18, 1882, the eleventh anniversary of the Commune's nascence, Mink wrote "Revolutionary Parisian citizens—Our hearts are with you, count on us for the *révolution sociale*, which alone can emancipate the working people."[44] Rejecting the usefulness of a gradualist socialism, and publicly arguing that "the word revolution is not evolution,"[45] she took fellow socialists to task. The radicalizing experience of the Commune consolidated her class, gender, and religious critiques—she saw violent socialist revolution as the necessary precursor to fundamental change. But in working to bring about a socialist revolution, Mink continued to expend considerable energy addressing religious and gender issues. She saw propagandizing women's emancipation and anti-clericalism as a means of agitating the population to revolutionary ends.

Mink played a key role in the November 1880 socialist conference at Le Havre. While she formally represented *chambres syndicales* (workers' associations) from Valence and Tarare, her real work came as the conference split into what became a long-term division between the revolutionaries, the Marxist-influenced group led by Jules Guesde, and the Proudhonian-influenced reformists, including Léo's former husband Benoît Malon.[46] Historian Marilyn Boxer has shown the centrality of "the woman question" to defining the differences between these factions, as well as Mink's substantial influence in developing the Guesdist position.[47] The reformists' declaration reflected their Proudhonian perspective, as they asserted women's place in the home, affirmed a strict gender division of labor, and called for women's political rights to be "limited . . . for an educative period." By contrast, the Guesdists proclaimed support for "civil, political, and economic" equality between the sexes, which, they explained, "will be sanctioned only with the social revolution." The Guesdists encouraged women in the mean time to organize with men, and to "demand their rights by revolution, peaceful if possible, violent if the bourgeoisie forces them."[48] As Boxer explains, the

Guesdists took an undefined feminist stand, but did not need to act on it, as they argued that women's emancipation relied on the social revolution. According to Boxer, this rhetoric reflected Mink's influence on the conference, as well as her paradoxical attempts to combine her socialism and feminism.[49]

Mink remained allied with Guesde and his party for a decade, pushing them to integrate the feminist issues she continued to advocate. But on the reformist side, the feminist Clémence Kéva, an associate of the suffragist Hubertine Auclert, had unsuccessfully proposed that the Proudhonian-influenced group support women's full economic and political rights. Alienated by the sexism of the reformist socialists and by the radical revolutionism of the Guesdists, both Kéva and Auclert subsequently abandoned organized socialism and focused solely on feminism.[50] Mink continued working to weave them together.

In addition to her efforts to link feminism and socialism, Mink promoted unity among revolutionary factions, working to expedite the coming of the revolution. And while she allied herself with Guesde, she retained her adherence to the more violent, more historically based Blanquism. In one of her most noted and threatening speeches, Mink enthusiastically responded to the March 1881 assassination of Tsar Alexander II, exemplifying her celebration of direct revolutionary action over theoretical debate. Celebrating the act, Mink declared, "As a revolutionary, as a Pole, I cry out Bravo! Teach the people to rid themselves of their tyrants, to annihilate the despots: Thus you will make the Social Revolution."[51]

While consistent with her advocacy of violent social revolution, here Mink espouses an anarchist approach to instigating governmental overthrow by one violent action. In a proclamation supporting the Russian Nihilists who killed the Tsar, Mink applauded their "propaganda by the deed." On behalf of the four hundred "revolutionary socialists of Toulon," who approved this missive by acclimation at a tenth anniversary celebration of the Commune, she wrote:

> We send you felicitations for the great act of justice that you have accomplished in ridding the earth of the odious monster named Alexander II . . . [Thank] you for your courage . . . for the heroic example you have given us . . . Propaganda by the deed as extolled and practiced by our venerated master Blanqui has begun to be understood.[52]

Mink praised the Nihilists for their action, and for their hope to spark a larger conflict with this act. She invoked Blanqui, who had died two months before, and referred to his valorizing of willpower and courage as essential components in sparking revolution. Blanqui also held that war made lines of conflict clearer, and thus allowed the revolutionary struggle to progress.[53] In implying Blanqui's approval of their deed, particularly only months after his death and his enormous, highly politicized funeral, Mink intended the highest of honors.[54] Writing to Louise Michel, she explained the message to the Nihilists, saying, "we have promised to follow them and to destroy the tyrants."[55]

Not only did she commend the act, but she also absolutely supported one of the actors: Jessa Helfmann, one of the six young Russian Nihilists (two were women) charged with the Tsar's assassination. Mink organized a large demonstration in her honor in Marseille on May 10. Announcing this action, Mink wrote in the Blanquist newspaper *L'Intransigeant* that she "supported the protest in favor of Jessa Helfmann as a woman, mother, and revolutionary."[56] Here Mink appropriated the era's dominant ideas of woman and mother, applying them to Helfmann as one who embraces and celebrates a female assassin—but an assassin who has killed a tyrant, an act she hoped would bring about social revolution. Thus both she and Helfmann remained within Mink's conception of the female realm: Helfmann selflessly undertaking an act to benefit her people, and Mink supporting her efforts in the hope of bringing about the revolution and thus a better future. Ultimately, Helfmann was the only defendant to escape execution, because she was pregnant.[57] Ironically, the Russian state's idea of motherhood protected this regicide, defended by Mink in protest and in the press for her maternal selflessness, from execution; the mother murdered the Tsar, known as "The Little Father," to save the children.

The Marseille police issued an arrest warrant for Mink following the pro-Helfmann rally, but Mink managed to remain free in the weeks before her trial. She made an unannounced appearance at a meeting in Lyon on May 23, hosted by Louise Michel and Edouard Vaillant, the editor of the Blanquist newspaper *Ni Dieu ni maître* (Neither God nor Master); the meeting was organized to raise funds for a statue of the recently deceased Blanqui. Though under a widely publicized arrest warrant, Mink surprised the audience of twelve hundred, and bearing a red flag trimmed in mourning black, dramatically took the podium. She spoke for an hour and a half on issues including the Commune, the Bloody Week, the illegal revolutionary red flag, the Nihilists, Jessa Helfmann, and Léon Gambetta, the republican leader and former member of the Government of National Defense.[58] According to an informant's report, Mink focused particularly on Jessa Helfmann, and submitted a proposition stating that for the triumph of the social revolution, "Monsieur Gambetta should be sacrificed just like Alexander II." According to the police agent, she "publicly defied the public prosecutor" in appearing despite her warrant. Another report expressed amazement at her audacity: "I find it extraordinary that Paule Mink has lectured in Lyon without worry."[59] Mink's participation and her incendiary rhetoric blatantly and publicly defied the state's authority to silence her.[60]

Mink fully intended to appear at her trial, but she refused to submit to prior preventative imprisonment, as she explained in a letter published by the socialist newspaper *Le Citoyen*. Staying with friends to avoid arrest, she complained that her home had been ransacked by the police. Armed with an arrest warrant, but not a search warrant, when the authorities found her home empty, they illegally entered and tore through her belongings. Mink publicly protested this action, recognizing the specifically gendered treatment she was receiving at the hands of the police. She argued that "I am a woman, I am single, this is why the police can act with such offhandedness toward me; if this is happening now . . . what will they do if I am condemned?"[61] Conscious of her vulnerability, she declared her refusal to be victimized. Mink continued to live her life in the public, relying on the podium or the press to make her cause, or her grievance, known. Her actions absolutely transgressed accepted behavior standards for women, intensifying her affront to authorities. In her letter to *Le Citoyen*, she began with an appeal: "I count on you, as on all the socialist press, to let the public know how I have been treated by the agents of the court of Marseilles."[62] Not merely rejecting physical and political circumscription, she introduced her personal experience into the public. She breached the boundaries of gendered propriety, while simultaneously threatening the established order. These trespasses, combined with her ongoing resistance against attempts to intimidate or silence her, further enraged the forces of order.

At her trial, Mink faced charges of provoking a crime, insulting a foreign leader, carrying a red flag (a "traitorous emblem"), and using "seditious cries" for shouting *"Vive la Révolution Sociale."* Defending herself, she explained that "several years ago the cry *Vive la République* was considered to be seditious. Today it no longer is. Soon, neither will *Vive la Révolution Sociale.*"[63] Mink was convicted, but received only a one-month sentence. In his decision, the judge wrote that he "recognizes her as extremely fanatical," and "doubts that her intellectual faculties are well balanced." He determined that her situation constituted special circumstances necessitating an abbreviated prison term.[64] Mink's public, insurrectionary actions, and her overt support of political terrorism, appeared to be so removed from acceptable female behavior that the magistrate declared her mentally unstable. The judge invoked a psychiatric dichotomy of the era: mentally healthy equilibrium versus unhealthy destabilization, or lack of balance.[65] From his perspective, Mink's "extremely fanatical" conduct provided evidence to support a judgment of instability.

Mink reacted with outrage, and addressed the Minister of Justice accordingly: "This is a grave injury which was made carelessly and without any justification. I am prepared to accept responsibility for my actions and to submit to the punishment determined by the tribunal, but I cannot support an insult which is an attack on my dignity, nearly to my respectability."[66] Mink defined her dignity and respectability rather differently than the dominant bourgeois conceptions. As a political activist, she relied on her mental faculties, and others' perceptions of these faculties, not only to strive for her ideological and practical goals, but also to earn a living. Her letter to the Minister of Justice continued: "I am a writer, teacher, and lecturer, and it hinders my ability to earn my living, and that of my three children, whom I solely support, to invent an unknown derangement in my intellectual faculties."[67] She asked for an investigation into her mental state, and declared her willingness to be examined by a *médecin alieniste,* a psychiatrist, with the intent of clearing her name.

Simultaneously, she turned to her friends and comrades to defend her. Mink wrote to Louise Michel, asking her to "take my cause in hand. This outrageous slander must be reduced to silence. I trust you for this, my friend, as for everything."[68] And her friends did come to her defense. The Swiss socialist and labor organizer J. Delhomme, in a letter published in the Grenoble newspaper *L'Excommunié,* professed that "Four months ago, the *citoyenne* Mink dined at my home, and I had the pleasure, over four hours, of conversing with her about the social question . . . The magistrate of Marseilles wants to pass her off as a crazy woman; we adamantly protest against this infamy."[69] Testifying to her stability in an intellectual, social setting, Delhomme sought to demonstrate the absurdity of the magistrate's determination. In another example, an open letter to Mink from the Paris-based Revolutionary Collectivist Social Studies Group, printed in *Le Citoyen,* took a more emotional, politicized tone. Fervently defending Mink, the group proclaimed that they

> are able to proudly attest that the ardor that you demonstrate in the struggle against our oppressors, is only due to the generosity of your humanitarian sentiments, which are far from being a weakness of your mental faculties, but rather a convincing proof of your firmness, of your just and right spirit, and of an energy perfectly in harmony with the indefatigable devotion that you give to the cause of the proletariat, who you love more than all the world.[70]

The publicity and public support did nothing to hurt Mink's image. On the contrary, testimonials to her intelligence, steadfastness, and political devotion only added to her visibility and her renown.

Mink's friends and comrades also aided her three children during her imprisonment, further reflecting her integral role in this supportive community. She was plunged into dire economic straits by her financially tenuous situation, imprisonment, and her concomitant inability to earn money. In response, Louise Michel presented a benefit lecture to a group of free thinkers in Paris, donating proceeds to Mink and her children; the *chambres syndicale* of Grenoble collected money on their behalf; and the Paris *Alliance Révolutionaire* organized a meeting to raise funds for the family, reacting to a "desperate" letter from Mink's sixteen-year-old daughter Wanda.[71] On her many speaking tours, Mink had held fundraisers for a wide range of causes and people, and now socialists in France and Switzerland responded in kind. As she traveled, she clearly related to impoverished workers and peasants, and they to her. Her tireless devotion to the cause, her indefatigable traveling and lecturing, and her high profile persona brought Mink and her children attention and compassion in their time of crisis.[72]

In the Marseille court's decision against Mink, the magistrate explained that his administration "had decided to use indulgence toward her, because of her conduct in 1870."[73] Referring to her heroic bravery during the Prussian siege, the judge had spared her deportation, but, he threatened, if she would again "trouble the public order," she would be "expelled from French territory."[74] Although Mink had been born in Clerment-Ferrand, France, of Polish parents, her first husband was a Pole, and this legally made her a "foreigner." Upon release from prison, she responded to the deportation threat by writing to the Minister of the Interior, announcing that in France, "women do not exist before the law. They have only the nationality of their husband. I am thus going to marry a Frenchman, to finally have all the rights of a Frenchwoman, and to be able to continue with more courage, with more energy than ever, to struggle for the people's rights . . . we will see if you will be able to expel me then."[75]

And marry a Frenchman she did—the forty-one-year-old Mink wedded the young worker and fellow Blanquist, the thirty-one-year-old Maxime Négro.[76] Commenting on the magistrate's statement that "My administration has decided to use indulgence," an article in *Le Pays* maintained that Mink responded, "My socialism has decided to use marriage."[77] And another journalist, snarkily noting their age disparity (and adding six years to Mink's age), assured his readers that Négro was "in love with the orator not for her youth and beauty—she is forty-seven—but for the social theories she professes." He sarcastically continued, wishing them *"bonne chance,"* and the hope that "Paule Mink never becomes a *négrophobe.*"[78]

One of the witnesses to Mink and Négro's wedding was Benoît Malon, Léo's former husband.[79] Léo could never accept the wide age disparity between herself and Malon, her junior by seventeen years, yet Mink appeared unperturbed with the ten years difference between herself and her husband. While Léo and Malon's age gap exceeded Mink and Négro's by seven years, the latter's union could not be termed conventional, either in terms of their respective ages or of their much publicized reasons for marrying. Mink, far more than either Léo or Dmitrieff, flouted bourgeois convention, and frequently enjoyed the notoriety it brought.

Consistent with this flamboyant individuality, Mink and Négro named both of their sons in memory and veneration of Blanqui, and in honor of the radical, revolutionary tradition: Lucifer Blanqui Vercingétorix was born in 1882, but lived less than two months, and Spartacus Blanqui Révolution was born two years later. The municipality refused to officially record these names, citing the law limiting children's names to those from either the Catholic calendar or Roman history (although clearly not all of it). Mink wrote in protest that "in these times of free thought and of the Republic, this law should long ago have been abrogated."[80]

By the early 1880s, republicanism had become an increasingly powerful and entrenched movement in France, and with it came republican anti-clericalism. Although left and moderate republican lawmakers worked consistently to secularize the state, Mink argued that socialist revolution provided the only reliable path to freedom from the dominion of the Catholic Church.[81] Continuing her decades-long anti-clericalism, she assailed the Church for economically and intellectually exploiting both French men and women. At a meeting of the Society of Freethinkers in December 1880, she declared that "Yes, people, you have been fooled too much, it is you alone that can emancipate yourselves."[82] Mink called on women to abandon the Church, proclaiming that "It is you alone, *citoyenne,* who can bring the Social Revolution."[83] She held that women needed socialism for their emancipation, and socialism needed women to succeed, but the Church stood as a principal impediment to this process. Lecturing on "The Emancipation of Women" earlier that year, she had argued that in the time before Caesar, women were "free, strong, and guided the men," but then, she explained, "they became, little by little, the prey of the clergy and fell entirely under its domination." She traced the Church's oppression of women through the centuries, and concluded by exclaiming that "women's absolute emancipation can only be obtained by revolution."[84] In her analysis, Mink separated the historical Jesus from the Church itself. According to an 1883 police report, Mink called Jesus "the first socialist and the first revolutionary who preached equality, fraternity, and justice," but, she argued, his followers "had never applied the precepts that he taught."[85] She clearly attributed women's and workers' oppression to the institution and hierarchy of the Church, which she charged with abandoning the religion's core ideals. While she urged women to work toward their own liberation by leaving the Church, that solution alone would still not suffice; only socialism would free them.

Mink viewed the Church's pervasive reach as fully supported by the bourgeoisie. Although the bourgeois Republic introduced a series of measures limiting Church influence and power in the early 1880s, including the 1880 Sée law mandating secular secondary education for girls, the 1884 Naquet law legalizing divorce, and an 1884 law abolishing prayer at the opening of legislative sessions, Mink maintained that the bourgeoisie directly benefited from workers' religious domination.[86] Speaking on "Church and State" in April 1883, she argued that since the time of Clovis, the French state had relied on religion to help dominate its subjects, and that "our bourgeois Republic needs its cooperation more than ever . . . because the state and religion can not exist without each other."[87] Strongly advocating her revolutionary alternative at a meeting two weeks earlier, she had declared, "if the people no longer believe in a better afterlife . . . they will say 'You lie; I want liberty and I will take it in suppressing you . . . and I will make the revolution.'"[88] Mink's understanding of the intertwined powers of capital and the Church had remained consistent since prior to the Commune, but her political response had changed: now only socialist revolution could break the bonds.

Mink's demands for women's emancipation focused primarily on marriage and on the Church, she sought socio-economic but not political emancipation. Long adhering to a feminism of difference, she did not challenge the gender division of labor, based on her understanding of women's and men's differing "natural" roles. She did, however, advocate increased wages for women, with the intent of improving their daily existence, and as part of their larger social emancipation.[89] But in the 1880s, she would not support a fight for political rights. Rejecting the idea of women's political candidacy in 1880, Mink asserted that "For the moment, we do not desire to sit in the Chamber of Deputies. The seats there are too dirty; we must clean them before we place ourselves there. The current Republic is not a republic, it is a monarchy in disguise."[90] Mink used domestic imagery in this statement, playing on the ideology of separate spheres. As she argued, the purely male, public realm of the legislature required a feminine cleansing, to wash away masculine corruption and immorality, and to make a governmental role suitable for female participation. Beyond this rather essentialist comparison lay the political reality that despite the significant reform efforts of republicans by 1880, French citizens still lacked many democratic liberties. Thus the extant soiled republic needed purification before it could qualify as a true republic, unsullied by monarchical filth. Paradoxically, Mink asserted that women needed to step in and clean up, yet she did not support women's access through the gate.

Mink maintained this opposition for over a decade. Speaking at a public lecture on women's suffrage in 1884, she affirmed her resistance to female enfranchisement, according to a police report, because she believed women lacked sufficient education. Mink specifically responded to Hubertine Auclert, a staunch women's suffrage advocate who had earlier argued that political rights were "the keystone which will give [women] all other rights."[91] The Guesdist organization *Cercle de la bibliothèque socialiste* (Socialist Library Circle) charged Mink with combating Auclert's high-profile campaign for the vote.[92] Their debate took place concurrent to the 1884 Constitutional Assembly, which was convened to address issues including the voting laws, thus theoretically providing an opening for female enfranchisement.[93] Auclert had long clashed with feminists who either hesitated to support women's suffrage, as the bourgeois feminists Léon Richer and Maria Deraismes did in 1878 at the first international congress on women's rights, or who outright opposed it, such as Mink.[94] Auclert, a bourgeois woman of independent means, had temporarily allied with the socialists, frustrated by the republicans' refusal to act on women's emancipation. Well received at a socialist congress in 1879, Auclert spoke on the interrelated nature of gender and class oppressions; she subsequently introduced a measure supporting female suffrage, which the conference adopted.[95] But Auclert broke with organized socialism the next year, following the 1880 Le Havre conference, at which (as discussed above) she unsuccessfully attempted to include a feminist statement in the Proudhonian-influenced reformist platform. With the split between reformists and revolutionaries in the conference's wake, only the revolutionary, Marxist-influenced Guesdists presented a socialist agenda with a feminist component (one, as we have seen, bearing Mink's imprint). Auclert, living on interest from family wealth, could not breach the class divide. She returned to the republican fold, and there led the fight for women's suffrage.[96] Despite her absolute and relentless devotion to her cause, Auclert failed to establish a significant suffrage movement in France.[97]

Most republicans and socialists, and many feminists, continued to resist women's suffrage through the century's end, most frequently attributing their opposition to women's loyal adherence to the Church. The argument that women were pawns of the priests tended to mask a deeper misogyny among republicans and socialists. Additionally, republicans faced an inherent theoretical conflict. As historian Judith Stone has argued, the French women's movement and French republicanism emerged in conflict with each other during the Great Revolution. Republicanism, based on the public, rights-bearing man, and thus the private, politically excluded woman, essentially conflicted with revolutionary women's demands for political and public equality. Stone contends that this legacy established a paradox between republican claims of universal equality, and simultaneous affirmations of an ideology of separate spheres. Women could not be allowed into the republican brotherhood because they were mothers, not brothers. And republican motherhood stood opposed to the public, male individual—the enfranchised citizen.[98]

Among the socialists, the Guesdists continued to support feminism more strongly than any other faction throughout the 1880s.[99] The Guesdists formed the *Parti Ouvrier Français* (POF) in 1882, the only Marxist socialist party in *fin-de-siècle* France. Mink, certainly no Marxist, traveled and gave lectures with Jules Guesde in the mid-1880s; Louise Michel, an avowed anarchist, occasionally joined them.[100] Mink and Michel's fame and flamboyance, and their advocacy of violent revolution, made them appealing to Guesde, and so did their feminism. Before joining the POF, Mink vowed to retain her political independence and to continue working for the unity of all socialists. The POF of the early to mid-1880s, with its centralized authority and advocacy of revolution, came closest to her socialist position. And, importantly, the party maintained at least a rhetoric of, and a platform for, feminist socialism throughout the decade. Both Mink and the Guesdists supported the contention that only social revolution could emancipate women. She thus saw the POF as the best available vehicle by which to bring about her feminist socialism during these years.[101]

Mink struggled throughout the later 1880s, suffering ill health, dire financial circumstances, and increasing alienation from the Guesdists. Continuing her campaign for a unified socialism, she and her husband, Négro, unsuccessfully attempted to launch a weekly newspaper intended to bring together socialists of all factions. Intensely disappointed at their failure to establish the paper, Mink wrote of being "very ill" and "in the most frightful poverty."[102]

By the turn of the decade, her differences with the POF mounted, as the party increasingly embraced reformism and parliamentarism. In 1892, as the lone woman among 131 delegates to the POF's tenth party congress in Marseille, Mink attempted to keep the body revolutionary, and pushed them to support the general strike.[103] Originally advocated by anarchists, the general strike would involve all workers simultaneously walking off their jobs, the intended effect of which would be to destroy capitalism in one dramatic blow. Mink's push for the general strike was consistent not only with her goal of a centrally controlled, violent revolutionary event, but also with her passion for drama and spectacle. The POF, following Guesde, rejected the general strike, arguing that if a sufficient number of workers could be brought into the streets to make the strike succeed, that critical mass could just as readily vote the socialists into power. And Guesde clearly preferred the latter. Deeply dissatisfied with the POF's decision, Mink accused them of cowardice, and perceptibly retreated from the organization.

Mink had been living in Montpellier with her husband and children in the late 1880s and early 1890s, focusing her efforts on the provinces, and thus had slipped somewhat from the Parisian public eye. Dispirited and frustrated by her personal situation and by her former socialist allies' abandonment of revolutionary socialism, she took steps to alter her life and regain her public presence. Mink left her husband and moved back to Paris with her children (by this time, her oldest daughter, Wanda, was an adult). Her move was precipitated by what on the surface appeared to be a dramatic political shift: she accepted the offer of the feminist organization *Solidarité des femmes* to nominate and support her as a candidate in the Parisian municipal elections of 1893.[104]

Organized by Eugénie Potonié-Pierre and Maria Martin, former associates of Auclert, *Solidarité des femmes* attempted to bring together feminism and socialism, and to bring women into the formal political arena. In 1892 they unsuccessfully solicited socialist parties, requesting that the parties put forth a female candidate; none of the organizations, including the POF, responded. Potonié-Pierre subsequently offered to nominate four women for the Parisian municipal elections: Léonie Rouzade, a *Solidarité des femmes* member, declined; the bourgeois feminist Maria Deraismes refused, as did the journalist Séverine. Only Mink accepted their proposal.[105]

Potonié-Pierre announced Mink's consent to candidacy at a meeting on March 25, 1893.[106] Ten days later, socialist newspapers including *Germinal*, *L'Eclair*, and *Le Cri du peuple*, published the letter of acceptance that Mink sent to *Solidarité des femmes*.[107] In this statement, she provided several interrelated reasons for her decision, which can be divided into two overlapping categories: her adherence to the POF, and her potential contributions as a woman. In the first, she positioned herself firmly in the socialist party order, writing, "I agree to be your candidate in the Parisian municipal and Legislative elections because, as a disciplined soldier of the worker's party, of which I have been a member for twelve years, I believe it is my duty to put in practice the decisions of our congress, which has affirmed the economic, civil, and political equality of women."[108]

Unequivocally reaffirming her allegiance to the POF, Mink at least partially attributed her action to toeing the party line regarding female equality. She thus altered her stance to support women's civil and political rights, and not only economic and social equality. This put her in line with a socialist position held since "our workers' congress [in] . . . 1879," as Mink subsequently explained in an August interview in La Petite république.[109] By running for elected office, Mink also followed Guesde's entry into the political ring, as he (and six other socialist men) successfully ran for the Chamber of Deputies the same year. In the August interview she promoted herself "not [as] a feminine candidate . . . but a revolutionary socialist candidate. I am not running as a woman, but as a militant."[110] While wrapping herself in the socialist flag, she continued to describe herself as a "revolutionary socialist," a label that Guesde and the other party leaders in 1893 no longer embraced. As a woman, she garnered no support from the POF, nor did they take her candidacy seriously.[111] As a revolutionary socialist and advocate of the general strike, she faced marginalization by the party. And in June of that year, before her interview in La Petite république, which mentions no socialist party by name, she broke with the POF and re-affiliated with the Blanquists, joining their Comité révolutionnaire centrale.[112] Yet she continued to maintain that her loyalty rested with no particular faction, only with the workers' movement as a whole, and that her goal remained a unified socialism.

Mink's second set of reasons for running for political office, as enumerated in her acceptance letter to the Solidarité des femmes, involved her potential contributions as a woman. As she explained, "I believe that the presence of women in various elected positions . . . will render a great service . . . Women are, before everything, mothers and educators; they have a more penetrating tenderness, and a clearer understanding of economy, which they have learned from directing a household."[113] Reflective of her conceptualization of women's natural roles and abilities, Mink saw females as bringing care and financial moderation—attributes nurtured in the private sphere—into the public, political realm. Rejecting women's political candidacy in 1880, she had called the Chamber of Deputies too dirty for female occupation, and termed the republic "a monarchy in disguise"; she saw no advantage for women in this realm.[114] Thirteen years later, in a republic that would elect socialist deputies, Mink proposed that women were naturally suited to clean up and straighten out electoral politics. She continued: "the sad incidences of corruption . . . have shamefully proven that it is time to introduce a new element in the public councils."[115] To emphasize the selfless female nature, in her August La Petite république interview Mink denied being motivated by personal ambition. She concluded the interview: "For me, I know very well that I will never attain a positive personal result; I have never had any ambition other than to fulfill my duty in fighting for justice and equality for all women and men."[116] Acting for multiple reasons, including to better her and her children's lives, Mink, who was undoubtedly pleased to be back in the Parisian political limelight, nonetheless had a long history that supported her self-abnegating assertion.

Mink's embrace of women's suffrage and political rights, while obviously a notable shift, contained more continuity than dramatic changes. In a piece titled "Why I Have Posed My Candidacy," published in the newspaper *L'Eclair*, she clarified her position: "Claiming women's political and civil rights will not be sufficient to emancipate them and to end their suffering. I do not believe, oh, no! not at all, that granting women the vote will annihilate all of the abuses . . . That is why . . . all the women who seek rights and justice for all . . . must become socialist."[117]

Mink never saw suffrage as the key to women's emancipation; she considered it ameliorative to women's immediate condition. Similarly, Mink had traversed France and Switzerland, lecturing on marriage, divorce, and women's work. She addressed issues including the inequity of the Napoleonic Code and capitalists' particular exploitation of women workers, yet she never believed legal and employment reform would free women. As we have seen, she saw socialism, and particularly revolutionary socialism, as the sole means to eradicate gender and class oppression, as well as to terminate the influence and power of the church. When *Solidarité des femmes* offered to nominate Mink, she seized the opportunity to regain the Parisian political stage. A woman's legislative candidacy, which was illegal, radical, and guaranteed to draw attention and controversy, appealed to Mink's flair for the theatrical and the shocking. Mink readily (and permanently) left her husband in Montpellier, hoping to escape a life of poverty and increasing obscurity. The *Solidarité des femmes*'s proposal provided her a means of personal and political escape.

However, Mink's financial problems persisted, and she spent the 1890s mired in poverty. Forced to move from place to place, asking for money from friends, she resorted to placing ads in *La Petite république* beginning in 1895. Offering services such as giving lessons, proofreading, and writing letters, she shortly was so pushed by desperation to request "any kind of work."[118] Marilyn Boxer explains that Mink, criticized for what some socialists deemed the inappropriate use of a socialist newspaper, defended herself as a loyal, devoted, sacrificing activist, listing opportunities for personal gain on which she had passed.[119] In an August 1899 letter to Louise Michel, Mink wrote that her daughter had been seriously ill, and although no longer in danger, she faced a long hospital convalescence. Mink worried about paying her daughter's bill.[120] As a woman and single mother, she faced economic and social problems apart from those of the mostly male socialist leadership.

Throughout the 1890s and until her death in 1901, Mink remained fully engaged in Parisian feminist socialist political life. Speaking regularly in a variety of forums, she continued to commemorate and exalt the Commune, and to persistently champion the general strike and violent revolution as the only means to women's and workers' freedom. On May Day in both 1895 and 1898, Mink addressed women, challenging them in 1895 to "rise up . . . you who are doubly exploited as women and as workers,"[121] and reminding them in 1898 that "women will only be truly emancipated when the capitalist order no longer exists." And therefore, she continued, they must "join and make common cause with their brother workers . . . and together on May Day cry *'Vive la révolution sociale!'* This alone will liberate us! Down with capitalism! . . . The emancipation of the workers must be the work of the workers themselves!"[122] Finally, on May Day, 1901, thirty years after the Commune, thousands of socialists and feminist socialists marched with her funeral cortege, shouting out support for revolution and the rebirth of the Commune.[123] For decades Mink had persisted in her call for a unified socialism, which to her meant a unified feminist socialism, and she had urged women to bring their emancipatory cause together with male workers, and to take it to the streets.

Mink remained committed to her vision of social and economic justice until the end of her life. The impact of the Commune led her to abandon her grass-roots anarchism, and to embrace a more intensely focused, centrally planned revolutionary socialism. Yet she remained committed to popular agitation; she worked to incite revolt. The experience of the Commune had altered her understanding of how best to attain an egalitarian end. But her definition of that end remained constant: it was a society free of class, gender, and religious subjugation. In working toward this goal, Mink allied herself with a series of socialists and feminists, all in keeping with her ultimate aim. She proffered socialist revolution as her primary focus, but never excluded feminism and anti-clericalism from her agenda. And when she finally relinquished her opposition to women's suffrage, becoming a legislative candidate herself, she persisted in arguing that political rights constituted merely a step on the feminist socialist revolutionary road to women's emancipation. Traveling, propagandizing, agitating, writing, and living a public, radical life, Mink maintained a high-profile, flamboyant persona, brandishing the red flag as she devotedly agitated for revolutionary change.

Conclusion

In the aftermath of the Commune, Dmitrieff, Léo, and Mink each attempted to resume political activism in the wake of desperate escapes from Paris, in the shadow of intense repression, and under the ominous eye of police observation. Profoundly affected both personally and politically by their insurrectionary experiences, they faced individual sets of economic, social, political, and psychological circumstances within which they needed to function. Just as each woman had taken differing approaches to revolution, so, too, did each carve a unique path on her subsequent journey. Yet they shared a desire to continue working to alter existing hierarchies and overthrow unjust oppressions.

For Elisabeth Dmitrieff, returning to a repressive Russia whose radical milieus had changed significantly, the reimmersion into revolutionary life proved elusive. She never again found or created a political or organizational niche such as that which she developed in the International and engendered with the *Union des femmes*. The Russian political and cultural climates, combined with her personal choices, pushed Dmitrieff beyond the physical and social boundaries of radical engagement. Her use of a revolutionary pseudonym, which undoubtedly contributed to her success in eluding French, Swiss, and Russian police, ultimately denied her social and political access to her Commune-era self: she could not prove who she was. Elisabeth

Tomonovskaya Davidovskaya had no concrete, demonstrable connection to Elisabeth Dmitrieff. Time, secrecy, and her husband's status as a common, rather than political, criminal in Siberia, reconstructed her identity and removed her extraordinary experiences and accomplishments from her usable past.

André Léo shared Dmitrieff's alienation but remained engaged. Continuing her literary, intellectual approach to political activism, Léo remained committed to taking a gradualist route to a moderate, collectivist, feminist socialism. The revolutionary experience had led her to abandon women's political and legal rights as an emancipatory goal, but her underlying focus on women's and men's equal rights to liberty and equality endured through the Commune and beyond. During her decade of exile, she immersed herself in the internal politics of the International, battling within the institution for the future of socialism. Her romantic and political partner Malon, whom she married in this period, joined with her in the fight. Léo emerged from the 1870s single, both personally and politically, having subsequently separated both from Malon and from the International. She retained both forms of independence for the final twenty years of her life. Increasingly private, she continued to communicate her feminist and socialist ideas on the page, publishing articles and novels. Her earlier renown as a writer had waned, and her socialist politics appeared less radical in the context of a French republic in which socialists held elected positions. Léo faded from public life but remained known within the European socialist community. She made no alliances with particular socialists or feminists during these decades. Her intense opposition to centrally planned socialism would certainly have alienated her from Guesde and the POF, the only socialist party with at least a theoretically feminist agenda, and with whom Mink had allied in the party's earlier, radical years. Léo advocated neither parliamentarism nor women's suffrage. Disappointed with her earlier organizational experiences and alliances, she retained her feminist and socialist theoretical independence and her commitment to her ideology.

Paule Mink remained the most publicly and politically engaged of the three former communardes. Galvanized and inspired by the insurrection and her experience in the popular political clubs, then enraged and further radicalized by the Commune's brutal repression, Mink worked to reignite revolution from the moment of its defeat. She underwent the most significant ideological shift of the three women, renouncing not only her rights-based political feminism, but also her non-collectivist anarchism for the more focused and authoritarian Blanquism. She sought the most rapid and effective route to fundamental political, social, and economic change, affiliating with different socialist factions but persisting in her grass-roots agitation, refusing to toe any party line. In this quest, her alliances remained fluid. Mink joined the Guesdists during their radical revolutionary period in the 1880s, and abandoned them as they became reformist; she identified as a Blanquist, yet pursued grass-roots agitation contrary to Blanquism's centrally planned revolution from above; she subsequently dramatically altered her opposition to women's suffrage and ran for legislative office. Throughout these years, Mink remained loyal to the idea of social revolution, and her understanding that only socialism could end all three structural oppressions: class, gender, and religion. She maintained her focus on these three goals. Although socialism appeared to be the most important of her aims, it was only because she saw it as the key to unlocking other hierarchies; from her perspective, without socialism, women could not be emancipated, and the Church's exploitative power could not be terminated. Mink contested and defied France's dominant institutions and ideologies for decades. Her voluminous police dossier reflects the extent to which the forces of order considered her a threat to social stability until, and after, the end of her life. Mink exemplified and represented the ever-present specter of insurrection, as she kept the memory and hope of social revolution alive for three decades following the defeat of the Commune. Her revolutionary critique dovetailed with her radical activism. Traveling alone, speaking publicly, advocating violence, supporting regicide, crossing boundaries, flouting norms—Mink's life and words mirrored each other.

Like their biographical trajectories, Dmitrieff, Léo, and Mink's types of feminist socialisms converged in the Commune and diverged in the aftermath. The development of these ideological strands reflected the contours of each woman's experiences in the Commune and in its wake. Traversing the shifting *fin-de-siècle* political landscape, feminist socialists operated in a world of increasingly bureaucratic, parliamentarian, and reformist socialist organizations. As French socialists turned away from revolution and took an evolutionary route to socialism via the ballot box, their political organizations became increasingly narrowed and structured, allowing less space for the influence of feminists and feminisms. The socialists' electoral focus further marginalized women due to female exclusion from the franchise.

The type of feminist socialism Dmitrieff espoused never again enjoyed the size, scope, power, and influence that it held during the Commune in the form of the *Union des femmes*. While her efforts to establish a centrally controlled federation of producer-owned cooperatives could not be termed unique, the *Union des femmes* could. In an extremely short period of time, Dmitrieff had established a theoretically driven, highly ordered citywide women's labor organization, which also served as a ready defense force for Paris under siege. Influenced by Marx and by a feminist version of Russian populism, Dmitrieff had brought new ideas and forms to the Parisian context. In the Commune's repression, Dmitrieff saw not only the decimation of her comrades, but also of her feminist socialism. This type of labor-based, centrally planned democratic feminist socialism, which had taken root and spread quickly during the revolution, had no position in post-Commune republican France, particularly as socialists increasingly emphasized parliamentarism. Nor could Dmitrieff re-establish her movement in her native Russia, where she remained marginalized within radical politics. Dmitrieff had felt a sense of isolation while in Paris, disappointed that none of her London or Geneva compatriots came to join the cause, and unable or unwilling to connect with most other communarde leaders. In the insurrectionary wake, her alienation intensified when she dropped the pseudonym "Dmitrieff" and lost access her revolutionary identity and past. Just as she attained her political apex as a young woman during the Commune, so, too, did her newly conceived feminist socialism shine luminously for a brief moment, only to fade into the recesses of history.

Léo's form of feminist socialism experienced a longer-term, but less dramatic success, exemplary of her gradualist approach to social, economic, and political change. As a writer and social critic, Léo represented the theoretical and educational approach to feminist socialism, one that challenged existing inequitable ideologies of gender. Deeply opposed to any political authoritarianism, she nonetheless advocated the top-down enlightenment and guidance of workers and peasants. In this she followed and exemplified two interwoven courses: polemical fiction and political journalism. As a novelist, Léo employed personal and emotional means to critique and contest dominant gender ideologies and hierarchies of class and religion. She embraced and radicalized a tradition of female writers using male pseudonyms to express female and/or feminist perspectives. In thus appropriating the privilege and authority embodied in masculinity, Léo trespassed on male terrain, effectively broadening the boundaries of women's sphere. Léo's fiction dramatized familial and domestic issues as a microcosm of the larger society, condemning gendered power relations, dependencies, and limitations on liberty and equality. She drew clear connections between the oppressive underlying patriarchal structures of family, state, and religion. In her novels and her political journalism, Léo exposed the hypocrisy of democrats opposing autocracy in the state, but supporting it in the family.

Léo used fiction as a public and somewhat popular political tool, intended to instruct and advise, within her gradualist approach to feminist socialism. Theorizing, writing, and publishing brought her ideas to readers subtly in novels and more overtly in non-fiction. While she stayed an ideological course in terms of advocating a gradualist, non-authoritarian feminist socialism, her political writings demonstrated the Commune's clear impact on her politics: Léo, like Mink, permanently abandoned her rights-based political feminism. However, she retained her underlying goal of a society of equal individuals built on a base of liberty.

Léo's gradualist, intellectual approach to feminist socialism allowed her to take a long-term historical view. She saw the event of the Commune as the creation of an opening for fundamental change, and an opportunity to attain women's physical, social, political, and economic equality. In its wake she felt anger and frustration at the Commune government for its handling of the conflict, at bourgeois democrats for their refusal to recognize the existence and insidious nature of class conflict (which she termed the "social war"), and at the vicious brutality of the Versailles government. Léo spent the first post-insurrectionary year examining and criticizing the revolutionary event, referring to it in speeches, articles, and letters. But she then turned to the future. Her ideology enabled her to use the Commune as a learning experience; her feminist socialism was not event-driven, but rather took a long-term approach. Léo remained integrally involved in the International for seven years after the uprising, focusing on international socialism as a means to an equitable society. Although she receded from the public eye, and by 1880 also from active participation in organized politics, she never gave up. Disillusioned and disappointed, she nonetheless continued to publish, attempting to spread her vision. For Léo, the impact of her ideas held significantly greater import than personal fame. Recognizing that ideas and words live beyond a person, and demonstrating her hope for the future, Léo bequeathed a sum of money available to the first group to establish a collectivist community in France, underscoring her conviction that a feminist socialist society would be built gradually.

Mink's feminist socialism attained popular and dramatic success in *fin-de-siècle* France, presenting a grass-roots, radical alternative to the era's increasingly reformist parliamentary socialisms. Flamboyant, theatrical, and revolutionary, Mink brought together a combination of forces to create her form of feminist socialism. Championing politics from the bottom up, she attacked authority in its guises of Church, state, class, and gender, advocating socialism as the remedy, and agitating for violent class warfare as the means to such a society. She embraced this position following the Commune, the experience of which led her to abandon her grass-roots anarchist individualism as insufficiently powerful to incite insurrection. Exemplifying revolutionary feminist socialism, Mink viewed socialist revolution as the necessary prerequisite to ending not only class-based oppression, but also those of gender and religion. She privileged insurgent action over theoretical debate. Embodying a politics of personality, Mink thrived in the limelight. She lived her life publicly and radically, exemplifying a revolutionary spirit of risk, action, and sacrifice, and exposing her own gender and class-based subjugations as examples of institutional social and economic injustices.

Mink strove for the unification of socialist factions into a revolutionary party infused with feminism. Focusing variously on the International, the Guesdist POF, and the Blanquist party, she sought a forum for the integration of her feminist and socialist ideas, and a vehicle to incite rebellion—specifically the resurrection of the Commune. Mink's approach combined her grass-roots commitment to revolutionary agitation with her Blanquist embrace of centrally planned insurgency. She used both the public podium and the political party to work toward her goal.

Allied with the Guesdist *Parti Ouvrier Français* for most of the 1880s, Mink

continually pressed the organization to espouse greater feminism and revolutionism. Her influence helped shape the party platform in the early 1880s,
as it broke from its Proudhonian allies and promoted a revolutionary and
somewhat feminist socialism. But as the decade progressed, Guesde and his
male compatriots turned away from revolution, neglected their earlier feminist assertions, and moved toward electoral politics and reform. By 1892
Mink had effectively split with the organization, but her often pragmatic approach and her ongoing desire to unite factions assured that no break was
final. Increasingly alienated, she adapted her strategy while retaining her
ideals and goals.

Mink's feminist socialism rejected ideological constraints, instead emphasizing mobile strategies of radical action. Having long renounced her pre-
Commune advocacy of women's suffrage, she changed her position in 1893,
agreeing to stand as a candidate in Parisian municipal elections. Persisting
in her feminist socialist rejection of suffrage as sufficiently transformative or
as an ultimate goal, she now argued that enfranchisement could ameliorate
certain aspects of women's oppression. Her illegal candidacy also allowed
her to end an unhappy, isolated period in the provinces and return to the
Parisian glare of controversy and contention, where she would combine radical performance with party politics. Reasserting her party connections, Mink
ran as a self-identified POF adherent, but did so on terms the party refused
to recognize. She contended that her candidacy logically followed those of
Guesde and other male party members who entered parliamentary politics,
but she employed the POF's long-abandoned "revolutionary socialist" label
and presented herself as bringing a woman's particular contributions to the
electoral arena. Attempting to both utilize and shape the party, Mink entered a political forum she fundamentally opposed, from which she was
legally excluded, intending to bring support and attention to her cause. Appropriating the dominant political currency, she shifted her approach but
remained consistent in her ideology: a feminism of difference fundamentally interwoven with revolutionary socialism. The flexibility of her feminist
socialism allowed participation in an electoral process to reach ends not originally electoral in nature: inciting the new Commune. Although Mink's politics became increasingly marginalized from organized socialism, she maintained a strong popular following as she continued to travel and speak in
her final years. Her popularly based revolutionary feminist socialism presented an alternative to France's deradicalized socialist parties, sustaining a
movement refueled and inspired by the memories of the Commune, and
the potential for cataclysmic political and social rupture.

As female insurgents, all three women deeply threatened France's forces
of order. Dmitrieff crossed gender barriers in employing sophisticated organizational and leadership abilities, skills clearly gendered as male. As a foreign insurgent who appeared in Paris to command hundreds of women in
military readiness and anti-capitalist action, her revolutionary undertakings

and post-Commune disappearance confounded, frustrated, and frightened the Versailles authorities. Unable to trace her either before or after the uprising, it appeared to the police as though she had existed only in the moment—an evanescent monster wreaking havoc on the ordered society. She receded as a menace as years passed without her reappearance, ultimately vanishing from institutional memory. Léo had a long and well-known history of dangerous behavior from the perspective of the police. Widely recognized before the Commune, she had challenged gender and class hierarchies in publishing under a male pseudonym and in political journals, in the act of lecturing in political forums, and in the radicalism of her spoken and written words. Her revolutionary participation and lauding of civil war intensified Léo's status as a menace, as her journalism reached the Parisian population at large. Subsequently under surveillance for nearly a decade, police agents considered her a diminishing threat as she focused increasingly on internal socialist politics. Though the reports listed Léo's publications and her newspaper affiliations, they never included content. They viewed her writings as too rarified and narrowly received to pose a public peril. By 1880, the police deemed her so sufficiently benign as to no longer warrant surveillance. In sharp contrast, Mink's thirty-year dossier is replete with transcriptions of her lectures, as they appealed to a broad working-class audience, were frequently open to the public, and were overtly intended as propaganda. While Dmitrieff constituted a perilous specter just immediately after the Commune, Mink threatened the established order for decades. Participating in Communard political clubs, which were considered fractious even by some in the revolutionary government, her subsequent long-term efforts to incite violent revolution positioned her as a prime menace. Unlike Léo's subdued literary and intellectual approach, Mink's aggressive agitation frightened the forces of order by bringing it to the unruly masses.

All three women influenced the political and ideological landscape of the late nineteenth century in differing ways and at varied times. Léo made her mark in the years prior to the revolution, and was involved in international feminist circles and in gaining renown for her fiction and journalism. Dmitrieff's greatest impact occurred during the Commune, as she established a citywide association in which she organized and led hundreds of working women. And Mink held sway in the insurrectionary wake as a nationally known figure engaged in socialist party politics and popular agitation. The Commune stood central to their multi-faceted experiences, affecting the courses of their lives.

The rise of the Commune opened a field of opportunity, both real and imagined, for the reshaping of hierarchies and power relations, and for the potential cessation of privilege and oppression. In the years of liberalized Empire prior to the Commune, Parisians had begun to create a working-class public sphere, in which an increasing number of people participated in critiquing the social order, believing that they might be able to effect substantive change. The experience of public meetings, a free press, and the formation of popular and political organizations created an accessible forum for working-class women and men, and for female and male feminists and socialists, to engage in discussion and debate. Challenges to gender roles, class privilege, and the authority of the Catholic Church arose from this fertile milieu, presenting ideas that would find vivification in the Commune. The empowerment provided by this emerging public sphere prepared Parisians to seize the opportunity of insurgency and to work to create a new and egalitarian society. The definition of egalitarian, however, varied among Communards, as did revolutionary approaches, goals, and visions. The all-male Commune government demonstrated only peripheral concern with gender-related issues, consistent with the socialist and workers' organizations from which they emerged. Feminist socialists recognized that the attainment of what they understood as an equitable society required their own persistent planning, pressure, and action, just as was necessary in the International and other socialist contexts before the uprising. But because these feminist revolutionaries also held a range of politics, critiques, interests, and goals, they took multiple approaches and sought varied ends within their revolutionism. These manifested themselves in the plurality of feminist socialisms that emerged within the Commune.

The Commune constituted a political, ideological, and social turning point in nineteenth-century France, creating an inescapable historical fissure. Physically, the Communards took over the monuments, institutions, and churches of the city of Paris, adapting them to their radical imaginations. Working-class political clubs met in churches; socialists and workers took over the Hôtel de Ville; the Prefecture of Police was renamed the Ex-Prefecture of Police; barricades were built in the streets; buildings set ablaze; and ultimately cadavers were strewn on the boulevards: the revolutionary mark indelibly imprinted itself on Paris. In the aftermath, the visceral memory of the Commune intermingled with the legacy of past revolutions, lurking as the menace of a world turned upside down, a world in which women and workers not only took to the streets, but they *took* the streets. Feminists, socialists, anarchists, and activists of every stripe operated in a society shaped by revolutionary repercussions. Just as former Communards vowed never to let the world forget their brutal repression at the hands of Versailles, so did the forces of order strive vigilantly to prevent the resurgence of such inversions of gender and class. These concerns helped fashion political decisions and ideological movements on both the left and right for decades.

Women's participation in socialist parties, the International, and in the Commune shaped the content and contours of these movements. Feminists pressed for the inclusion of gender-related issues in party platforms and in the revolutionary milieu. These efforts combined gender-based ideologies with critiques of class, forming a range of feminist socialisms. The crucible of the Commune enabled the fusion and diffusion of these ideologies, reflecting particular foci and concerns. Whether working to alter women's economic and social dependence by revaluing and reordering female labor; theorizing and arguing for a reconceptualization of the meaning and reality of femaleness in an effort to destroy barriers to women's individual rights to socio-economic liberty and equality; or agitating from the popular public pulpit for an end to gender, class, and religious oppressions, each of these feminist socialisms emerged within the insurrectionary medium. The Commune provided the space, support, camaraderie, freedom, and excitement for these movements to begin to root and grow. Feminist socialists' visions of an equitable society all included an end to women's subjugation, but their paths, conveyances, and chosen endpoints differed substantially.

The Commune constituted a unique historical opening into which the era's radical women and men stepped, throwing open a world of seemingly limitless potential. Activist women seized the opportunity to begin constructing and shaping a range of feminist socialisms, ideas, and actions intended to reconfigure their world. Investigating the evolution of these multiple positions provides an understanding of the period's gender- and class politics and power relations, feminists' and feminisms' constitutive positions in the Commune, and the Commune's centrality to the history of feminisms and socialisms. But it also allows the contemporary reader to examine and question the efficacy and longevity of a range of political and social actions. The plurality of feminist socialisms arising in the Commune provides keys for addressing not only historical, but also contemporary problems of inequity. Studying these various movements better informs our assessments of available and viable approaches to social change, and highlights issues of work and wages, the oppressive nature of existing gender roles, and the value of party affiliation and/or public agitation. An examination of our twenty-first century world reveals injustices similar in form if not in degree to those present in the France of 1871. Patriarchy, capitalism, and theocratic influences still shape our politics, governments, economic systems, familial relations, social forms, and cultures. Greatly ameliorated in many nations, there exists, nonetheless, no place free of these forces. Perhaps the communardes' histories can inspire the courage to analyze, organize, and act against oppressive structures and power relations.

In the Commune's fourth week, when hope and optimism still reigned, André Léo wrote in *La Sociale* that future historians of Paris would "be forced to add the following paragraph to their chapters":

> There was then in Paris such a frenzy for liberty, rights, and justice, that the women fought with the men, and that they found in this city of two million souls, enough energy and moral force to balance the rest of France and vanquish the efforts of two armies.[1]

Believing in the righteousness and power of their cause, Léo declared that the Commune could successfully counter the reactionary backlash from the provinces, and fight off both the Versailles and the Prussian army, assuming that the recently hostile factions would band together in the defense of order and capital. She erred in her assessment not only of the revolution's outcome, but also of many future historians' interpretations and evaluations of the event. Léo acclaimed the passion, intensity, and power of those devoted to creating a just world, certain that their "energy and moral force" would ensure their insurgent triumph and historical recognition. Confident that the Commune would emerge as a light radiating into the future, inspiring generations to unite and challenge oppressors despite overwhelming odds, Léo and her fellow communardes fervently believed in the strength and value of a just cause.

NOTES

INTRODUCTION

1. The French word *communarde* (lower case) means a female participant in the Paris Commune (*communard* is the masculine form); the English term "Communard" (upper case) means either a male or female.

2. The book was translated as Edith Thomas, *The Women Incendiaries*, translated by James and Starr Atkinson (New York: George Braziller, 1966), xiv; Edith Thomas, *Les Pétroleuses* (Paris: Gallimard, 1963).

3. See, for example, most of the numerous Communard memoirs; also, Frank Jellinek, *The Paris Commune of 1871* (London: Victor Gallancz, 1937); and Charles Rihs, *La Commune de Paris 1871: sa structure et ses doctrines* (1955; reprint, Paris: Editions du Seuil, 1973). For exceptions to the rule of Communards excluding women, see Benoît Malon, *La Troisième défaite du prolétariat français* (Neuchâtel: G. Guillaume fils, 1871); and Prosper-Olivier Lissagaray, *Histoire de la Commune de 1871* (Paris: Maspero, 1983). Lissagaray was originally published in 1876.

4. See, for example, Jacques Rougerie, *Paris libre 1871* (Paris: Editions Seuil, 1971); Roger L. Williams, *The French Revolution of 1870–1871* (New York: W.W. Norton, 1969); Stewart Edwards, *The Paris Commune 1971* (London: Eyre and Spittiswood, 1971); William Serman, *La Commune de Paris (1871)* (Paris: Librairie Arthème Fayard, 1986).

5. Prior to Thomas, Eugene Schulkind published his germinal work, "Le Rôle des femmes dans la Commune de 1871," *1848, Revue des révolutions contemporaines* XLII, no. 185 (February 1950). Thirty-five years later he published "Socialist Women during the 1871 Paris Commune," one of the most important pieces on communarde activism to date. Eugene Schulkind, "Socialist Women during the 1871 Paris Commune," *Past and Present* 106 (February 1985): 124–63. Schulkind devoted his academic life to the Commune, bequeathing his rich collection to Sussex University, England. His other works on the Commune include "The Activity of Popular Organizations during the Paris Commune of 1871," *French Historical Studies* (Fall 1960): 394–415; "The Paris Commune of 1871: Reality or Myth?" University of Sussex lecture series, "Great Centenaries," May 20, 1971; *The Paris Commune of 1871* (London: The Historical Association, 1971); "Imagination and Revolution: Guidelines for a Historiography of the Literature of the Paris Commune," in *1871, Jalons pour une histoire de la Commune de Paris*, edited by Jacques Rougerie (Paris: Presses Universitaires de France, 1973), 539–51; Schulkind, ed., *The Paris Commune of 1871: A View From the Left* (New York: Grove Press, 1974); and, Schulkind, ed., *The Paris Commune 1871: Inventory of the Collection in the University of Sussex Library* (Brighton: University of Sus-

sex Library, 1975). Dalotel first published a collection of Paule Mink's speeches and writings in 1968, including an influential introductory analysis of Mink's life and work. Most recently, Dalotel has written important articles on communarde club women and on André Léo. The Mink, club women, and Léo pieces remain untranslated into English. Alain Dalotel, *Paule Minck: communarde et féministe* (Paris: Syros, 1968); "Socialism and Revolution," in *Voices of the People: The Social Life of "La Sociale" at the End of the Second Empire,* edited by Adrian Rifkin and Roger Thomas, translated by John Moore (New York: Routledge & Kegan Paul, 1988); "Les femmes dans les clubs rouges, 1870–1871," in *Femmes dans la cité 1815–1871,* edited by Alain Corbin, Jacqueline Lalouette, and Michèle Riot-Sarcey (Paris: Creaphis, 1997); "Benoît Malon, troisième fils d'André Léo," *Revue socialiste,* 71–91.

6. Gay L. Gullickson, *The Unruly Women of Paris: Images of the Commune* (Ithaca, N.Y.: Cornell University Press, 1996); Martin Phillip Johnson, *The Paradise of Association: Political Culture and Popular Organizations in the Paris Commune of 1871* (Ann Arbor: University of Michigan Press, 1996); Kathleen B. Jones and Françoise Vergès, "Women of the Paris Commune," *Women's Studies International Forum* 14, no. 5 (1991): 491–503; Jones and Vergès, "'Aux Citoyennes!' Women, Politics, and the Paris Commune of 1871," *History of European Ideas* 13, no. 6 (1991): 711–32.

7. Moses, Claire Goldberg, *French Feminism in the Nineteenth Century* (Albany: State University of New York, 1984), 189–96; Maïté Albistur and Daniel Armogathe, *Histoire du féminisme français du moyen âge à nos jours* (Paris: Editions des femmes, 1977), 326–35; Karen Offen, *European Feminisms: 1700–1950* (Stanford, Calif.: Stanford University Press, 2000), 145–48.

8. Laurence Klejman and Florence Rochefort, *L'Egalité en marche: le féminisme sous la Troisième République* (Paris: Editions des femmes, 1989), 49.

9. Marisa Linton, "Les femmes et la Commune de Paris de 1891," *Revue historique* 298, no. 1 (1997): 23–47.

10. Karen Offen, "Defining Feminism: A Comparative Historical Approach," *Signs* 14, no. 1 (1988): 126; Offen, *European Feminisms* 20–21.

11. Marie-Helene Zylberberg-Hocquard, *Féminisme et syndicalisme en France* (Paris: Editions anthropos, 1978), 85.

12. This is Sowerwine's implication, as he writes that "Only in the last third of the nineteenth century did there appear a feminist movement as we understand it today: the movement which culminated in women's obtaining the suffrage." Charles Sowerwine, *Sisters or Citizens? Women and Socialism in France since 1876* (Cambridge: Cambridge University Press, 1982), 4–5.

13. Sowerwine, *Sisters or Citizens?,* 34. In a more recent work, Sowerwine addresses women's Commune participation more fully, but not as feminism. Sowerwine, *France since 1870: Culture, Politics and Society* (New York: Palgrave, 2001), 18–24. Marilyn J. Boxer, in her unpublished dissertation, "Socialism Faces Feminism in France: 1879–1913" (Ph.D. dissertation, University of California, Riverside, 1975), provides a fascinating analysis of Mink as a socialist and feminist, as well as of the interrelation of feminisms and socialisms in the Commune's aftermath.

14. The organization's title translates as "The Union of Women for the Defense of Paris and Aid to the Wounded."

15. Jo Burr Margadant, ed., *The New Biography: Performing Femininity in Nineteenth-Century France* (Berkeley: University of California Press, 2000), 1–25.

16. *The Times* (London), May 6, 1871, in *The Communards of Paris, 1871,* edited

by Stewart Edwards (Ithaca, N.Y.: Cornell University Press, 1973), 109–10; Albert Soboul has called 1793 the most passionate and involved year of the Revolution, both in terms of Parisian women's activism and the popular movement as a whole. The Society of Revolutionary Republican Women, the most visible women of 1793, worked to organize women of the popular classes to support radical democracy and social revolution: they demanded economic and social justice for women and men, and the right of all to political participation. Albert Soboul, *Understanding the French Revolution* (New York: International Publishers, 1988), 158. For the Society of Revolutionary Women, see Margaret George, "The 'World Historical Defeat' of the Républicaines-Révolutionnaires," *Science and Society* 40, no. 4 (Winter 1976–77): 410–37; Darline Gay Levy and Harriet B. Applewhite, "Women and Militant Citizenship in Revolutionary Paris," in *Rebel Daughters: Women and the French Revolution*, ed. Sara E. Melzer and Leslie W. Rabine (New York: Oxford University Press, 1992), 79–101; and Darline Gay Levy, Harriet Branson Applewhite, and Mary Durham Johnson, eds., *Women in Revolutionary Paris* (Urbana: University of Illinois Press, 1979), 143–220.

17. Joan Scott, *Only Paradoxes to Offer: French Feminists and the Rights of Man* (Cambridge, Mass: Harvard University Press, 1996), 1–18.

18. Sandra Kemp and Judith Squires, "Introduction," in *Feminisms* (New York: Oxford University Press, 1997), 3–12.

19. For the relationships between feminism and socialism in the post-Commune years, see Boxer, *Socialism Faces Feminism*.

1. THE ACTORS AND THE ACTION

1. Elisabeth Dmitrieff, "Appel aux citoyennes de Paris," *Journal officiel*, April 11, 1871.

2. As Gay Gullickson has deftly demonstrated in *Unruly Women*.

3. André Léo, "La Déclaration de guerre," *Mémoires*, 44, Descaves Collection, IISH.

4. Sources used in reconstructing the narrative of the Commune include Edwards, *The Paris Commune of 1871;* Jellinek, *The Paris Commune of 1871;* Serman, *La Commune de Paris;* Jean Bruhat, Jean Dautry, and Emile Tersen, *La Commune de 1871* (Paris: Editions Sociales, 1970); Prosper-Olivier Lissagaray, *Histoire de la Commune de 1871.* (Brussels: Henri Kistemaeckers, 1876).

5. Edwards, *The Paris Commune*, 48–50; Serman, *La Commune*, 110.

6. The Hôtel de Ville is Paris's city hall. André Léo, "Le Quatre septembre," La Siège, p. 1, *Mémoires*, Descaves Collection, IISH.

7. Ibid.

8. Louise Michel, *La Commune*, 3rd ed. (Paris: P.-V. Stock, 1898), 66.

9. For details of the Empire's fall, see Serman, *La Commune*, 110–13; and Edwards, *Paris Commune*, 49–53.

10. Brocher was the granddaughter of a bourgeois, and daughter of a socialist freemason who became an artisan, a shoemaker, by choice. She worked stitching women's high button shoes. Victorine Brocher, *Victorine B . . . Souvenirs d'une morte vivante* (Paris: François Maspero, 1977), 96; Maïté Albistur and Daniel Armogathe, *Histoire du féminisme français du moyen âge à nos jours* (Paris: Editions des femmes, 1977), 322–23.

11. Léo, "Le Quatre septembre," 2.

12. Ibid., 2–3.

13. Pamela Pilbeam, *Republicanism in Nineteenth-Century France, 1814–1871* (New York: St. Martin's Press, 1995), 15.

14. Arthur Arnould, *Histoire populaire et parlementaire de la Commune de Paris* (Lyon: Editions Jacques-Marie Laffont et Associés, 1981), 16.

15. Michel, *Memoirs*, 56.

16. Robert Wolfe, "The Parisian Club de la Revolution of the 18th Arrondissement 1870–1871," *Past and Present* (April 1968): 88–89.

17. Jules Trochu, *La Politique et le Siège de Paris*, quoted in Henri Guillemin, *Nationalistes et "nationaux" (1870–1940)* (Paris: Gallimard, 1974), 13–14. Edwards, *Paris Commune*, 390. According to Edwards, the dramatic collapse of the Empire and proclamation of the Republic brought an illusory sense of unity and accomplishment to Parisian socialists and workers. The new governmental deputies exploited this sentiment to protect their own authority and avoid significant social change. Edwards, *Paris Commune*, 54–55.

18. Karl Marx, "Second Address of the General Council of the International Working Men's Association on the Franco-Prussian War," in Marx and Engels, *On the Paris Commune* (Moscow: Progress Publishers, 1971), 46.

19. Léo, "Le Quatre septembre," 3.

20. Brocher, *Victorine B.*, 104.

21. Dalotel writes that Wanda was killed, but three pages later Wanda is with her mother in exile. I assume this is an editing error rather than a revolutionary resurrection. Alain Dalotel, *Paule Minck: communarde et féministe*, 8, 21; Roger Magraw, *The Age of Artisan Revolution, 1815–1871* (Oxford: Blackwell, 1992), 259.

22. Dossier Paule Mink, BMD.

23. Rupert Christiansen, *Paris Babylon: The Story of the Paris Commune* (New York: Viking, 1994), 231, 232, and 245; Serman, *La Commune de Paris*, 145.

24. Léo, *La Siège*, 76–77.

25. Paule Mink, "Les Canons du 18 mars," *La Petite république* (Paris), March 18, 1895.

26. Edwards, *Paris Commune*, 115–34; Charles Sowerwine, *France since 1879*, 14–17.

27. Mink, "Les Canons," March 18, 1895.

28. Edwards, *The Paris Commune 1871*, 124–34.

29. Léo, *La Province, Memoires*, IISH.

30. Mink, "Les Canons," March 18, 1895.

31. Michel, *La Commune*, 139–40.

32. Ibid.

33. Mink, "Les Canons, " March 18, 1895.

34. Brocher, *Souvenirs*, 156–57.

35. Partitioned three times by Russia, Prussia, and Austria during the later eighteenth century, the final division terminated what had been the Commonwealth of Poland-Lithuania, erasing Poland from the political map. A number of nationalist Polish independence movements flourished in the nineteenth century, ranging from the conservative faction headed by Adam Czartoryski, who sought the reimposition of the Polish monarchy and traditional social structures, to multiple radical revolutionary groups, many with conflicting specific goals. I have no direct evidence of Jean Mekarski's particular affiliation, but based upon his subsequent Saint-Simonianism, and Mink's positive association and identification with the ideas and traditions of

Polish revolutionaries, one can reasonably assume her father's adherence to a relatively radical program. Alain Dalotel also labels him a progressive. Dalotel, *Paule Minck*, 12; Federal Research Division of the Library of Congress, *Poland: A Country Study* (Washington D.C.: Library of Congress, 1992); Jean Maitron, "Paule Mink," in *Dictionnaire biographique du mouvement ouvrier français*, 10 vols. (Paris: Les Editions Ouvrières, 1968).

36. Dalotel places both brothers fighting for Poland in 1863, but Maitron includes only Louis. Dalotel, *Paule Minck*, 12; Maitron, "Paule Mink."

37. Paule Mink, quoted in Albert Goullé, *L'Aurore*, May 1, 1901.

38. Edwards, *Paris Commune*, 115–34; Charles Sowerwine, *France since 1879*, 14–17.

39. Paule Mink, "Aux citoyennes de la Fédération socialiste de femmes à Paris," *Le Cri du peuple*, August 18, 1889.

40. *L'Aurore*, June 7, 1898; Boxer, "Socialism Faces Feminism in France: 1879–1913," 86.

41. Boxer, "Socialism Faces Feminism," 86.

42. The oxymoronic nature of this society's name, "The Brotherhood of Working Women," escaped perception in this context where the idea of the universal man stood completely normative.

43. "La Société du droit des femmes," 1866, Descaves Collection, IISH.

44. Little information exists regarding Mink's marriage to Bohdanowicz (or Boganowicz). "Rapport," Paris, May 7, 1872; Paule Mink, BA 1178, APP; Dalotel, *Paule Minck*, 13.

45. For Mink, Dmitrieff, and Léo during the final years of Empire, see Chapter 2, "Politics and Ideas: Staging the Struggle."

46. Gustave Lefrançais, *Souvenirs d'un révolutionnaire* (Brussels, 1902), 322–23.

47. Michel, *La Commune*, 163.

48. The author Marforio's identity is unclear. On the title page of the book in the University of Sussex's Schulkind Collection, beneath the printed author's pseudonym, someone has hand-written "Guénot-Lecomte." However, in the IISH's Descaves Collection, "Louise Lecroix" is listed as Marforio's given name. The text focuses extensively, but not primarily, on women's revolutionary participation. The author clearly opposed the Commune, yet positively portrayed certain acts and actors. The author, who remained in Paris throughout the Prussian siege and the Commune, hoped to have "the power to recount without passion, without enthusiasm, and especially without prejudice" all that he or she had seen. Marforio, *Les Echarpes rouges: souvenirs de la Commune* (Paris: Librairie Centrale Des Lettres, des Sciences et des Arts, 1872), 8.

49. As Joan Landes argues regarding the use of the allegorical female to represent France during the Great Revolution, "the female representation of the nation works best because it effaces the identifiable features of any known female person . . . Even before the revolution artists and writers depicted France, as well as justice, liberty, force, truth, and science as female allegories, but their aim was to personify abstract principles or virtues, not to depict real, living subjects." Joan Landes, "Representing the Body Politic: The Paradox of Gender in the Graphic Politics of the French Revolution," in *Rebel Daughters: Women and the French Revolution*, ed. Sara E. Melzer and Leslie W. Rabine (New York: Oxford University Press, 1992), 29.

50. André Léo, "La Révolution sans la femmes," *La Sociale* (Paris), May 8, 1871.

51. "Adresse des citoyennes à La Commission exécutive de la Commune de Paris," *Revue de France (Supplement)* (April 15, 1871), 31.

52. Louise Michel, *The Red Virgin: Memoirs of Louise Michel*, edited and translated by Bullitt Lowry and Elizabeth Ellington Gunter (University: University of Alabama Press, 1981), 59.

53. Troskéivich, a German-born Protestant, changed her name from her given "Carolina" to the Russian "Natalia Iégorovna" upon her conversion to Russian Orthodoxy, a prerequisite to marrying Kouchelev. Sylvie Braibant, *Elisabeth Dmitrieff: aristocrate et pétroleuse* (Paris: Belfond, 1993), 22–26.

54. Woodford McClellan, *Revolutionary Exiles: The Russians in the First International and the Paris Commune* (London: Frank Cass, 1979), 98–99; Braibant, *Elisabeth Dmitrieff*, 22–34; Vassili Soukholmine, "Deux femmes russes combattantes de la Commune," *Cahiers internationaux* 16 (May 1950), 53–56. The primary sources on Dmitrieff are notably sparse for the pre-Commune years. The French-language secondary scholarship is also slim and its quality varies substantially, from the hagiographic P. Tcherednitchenko's "La Vie genereuse et mouvementée d'Elisa Tomanovskaia. . . ," *Etudes Sovietiques* 82 (June 1955): 59–64, to Singer-Lecocq's overly ideological work, peppered with imagined details (e.g., Dmitrieff's thoughts at a given moment), to Braibant's more academic account, and Vassili Soukhomline's brief but scholarly article "Deux femmes russes combattantes de la Commune." The sources tend to differ on particular details, such as the specific dates of Dmitrieff's arrival in Geneva, London, and Paris. In selected translation from the original Russian, both the Knizhnik-Vetrov and the Eframova and Ivanov works provide detailed, well-documented information. My thanks to Victor and Vikka Peppard for their translation work. N. Efremova and N. Ivanov, *Russkaia soratnitsa Marksa* (Moscow: Moskovskii rabochii, 1982); Ivan Sergeevich Knizhnik-Vetrov, *Russkie deiatel'nitsy Pervogo Internatsionala i Parizhskoi Kommuny* (Moscow and Leningrad: Izdatel'stvo "Nauka," 1964); Sylvie Braibant, *Elisabeth Dmitrieff*, 52–85; Yvonne Singer-Lecocq, *Rouge Elisabeth* (Paris: Editions Stock, 1977), 93–108; McClellan, *Revolutionary Exiles*, 83–101, 154–55.

55. Dmitrieff, the pseudonym she took during the Commune, was the masculine form of Dmitrieva, her paternal grandmother's maiden name.

56. Moussorgsky may have been a distant cousin. Braibant, *Elisabeth Dmitrieff*, 30–34; Vassili Soukholmine, "Deux femmes russes combattantes de la Commune."

57. See Chapter 2, "Politics and Ideas: Staging the Struggle."

58. He died several years later. Soukholmine, "Deux femmes russes," 55–56; McClellan, *Revolutionary Exiles*, 98–99; Braibant, *Elisabeth Dmitrieff*, 58–59.

59. Michel, *La Commune*, 10.

60. "La Liberté de la presse," *La Sociale*, April 7, 1871.

61. André Léo, *La Sociale*, April 22, 1871.

62. André Léo, "Citoyens rédacteurs," *La Sociale*, May 14, 1871.

63. Lucien Descaves, *Sur A. Léo et B. Malon*, André Léo Papers, Descaves Collection, IISH; Fernanda Gastaldello, *André Léo: Quel Socialisme?* (unpublished dissertation, University of Padua, Italy, 1978–79), 12–24.

64. André Léo, *La Grande Illusion des petits bourgeois* (Paris: Siècle, 1876).

65. André Léo, *L'Enfant des Rudère* (Paris: S.E. Monillot, 1881), 280–81, quoted in Gastaldello, *André Léo*, 25–26.

66. André Léo, *Un Mariage scandaleux* (Paris: Hachette, 1862), 159.

67. Ibid.

68. This is a particularly strong theme in *Les Deux Filles de M. Plichon* (Paris: A. Faure, 1865).

69. According to Gastaldello, the Lausanne municipality only registered marriage authorization dates, not actual marriage dates. Gastaldello, *André Léo*, 29–31.

70. He also edited the journal *l'Eclaireur*. Descaves, *Sur A. Léo*, 2–4; George Sheridan, "Pierre Leroux," *Encyclopedia of 1848 Revolutions* (http://www.ohiou.edu/~Chastain/index.htm; accessed February 5, 2004).

71. Gastaldello, *André Léo*, 28–31, 372.

72. Her novels will be more closely examined in Chapter 2. André Léo, *Une Vieille Fille* (Brussels: Alphonse Lebègue, 1851). It would be eleven years until her second novel, the celebrated *Un Mariage scandaleux*, was published. A second edition of *Une Vieille Fille* was published by in Paris by A. Faure in 1864.

73. André Léo, *Un Divorce* (Paris: Librairie Internationale, 1866); Léo, *Un Mariage*. Her *Un Mariage scandaleux* was subsequently published in second and third editions by A. Faure in 1863 and 1866, respectively, and in a fourth edition by C. Marpon et E. Flammarion in 1883. For further discussion of these, and Léo's other novels, see chapter 6, "Dmitrieff and Léo in the Aftermath: Radical Denouement."

74. C. B. Derosne, *Le Constitutionnel*, July 28, 1863, quoted in Gastaldello, *André Léo*, 36–37.

75. Léo, *Les Deux Filles de M. Plichon*.

76. For her political activities and development in the 1860s, see chapter 2, "Politics and Ideas: Staging the Struggle."

77. Augustine-Malvine Blanchecotte, *Tablettes d'une femme pendant la Commune* (Paris: Didier et Cie, 1872), 211.

78. Michel, *La Commune*, 261.

79. Edwards, *Paris Commune*, 314.

80. Thomas, *Women Incendiaries*, 151–53.

81. Michel, *La Commune*, 266–67.

82. Roger Gould, "Multiple Networks and Mobilization in the Paris Commune, 1871," *American Sociological Review* 56 (December 1991): 720.

83. Rapport sur l'affaire Dmitrieff, Carton LY 22, AHG.

84. *Bulletin communale* (Paris), May 23, 1871.

85. Michel, *La Commune*, 272.

86. Brocher, *Souvenirs d'une morte vivante*, 213.

87. Gullickson, *Unruly Women*, 172–73.

88. Alexandre Dumas *fils*, *Lettres sur les choses de ce jour*, quoted in Thomas, *Women Incendiaries*, xi.

89. Estimates vary from 17,000 to 35,000 people killed, as Versailles troops buried many unidentified bodies in mass graves. The City of Paris paid for 17,000 burials, establishing that number as the fewest possible. Edwards, *Paris Commune*, 346.

2. POLITICS AND IDEAS

1. These articles were subsequently collected and published as a book under the same title. André Léo, *La Femme et les mœurs: liberté ou monarchie* (Paris: Le Droit des femmes, 1869), 171–72.

2. These labels generally describe each woman's brand of feminist socialism during the pre-Commune years, and they will be discussed and explained more thoroughly throughout this chapter. Because all three of the women developed their in-

dividual ideological positions based upon a range of intellectual and activist influences, the terms must be seen as descriptive and somewhat fluid.

3. Article 1er, "Statuts," in *Le Livre noir de la Commune de Paris: L'Internationale dévoilée* (Brussels: Office de Publicité, 1871), 31.

4. André Léo, "Signes précurseurs," *Notes et impressions, 1870–1871,* 3, *Mémoires,* Descaves Collection, IISH.

5. "The Socialism of the International," *Le Socialiste,* June 11, 1870, quoted and trans. in Eugene Schulkind, ed. and trans., *The Paris Commune of 1871: The View From the Left,* 68.

6. James Guillaume, *L'Internationale: documents et souvenirs (1864–1878),* vol. II (Paris: Société nouvelle de librairie et d'edition, 1907), 61–64; Roger Magraw, *A History of the French Working Class,* vol. I: *The Age of Artisan Revolution, 1815–1871* (Oxford: Blackwell, 1992), 264–65; Steven K. Vincent, *Between Marxism and Anarchism: Benoît Malon and French Reformist Socialism* (Berkeley: University of California Press, 1992), 24–25.

7. André Léo, *L'Egalité* (Geneva), March 2, 1869.

8. Gastaldello, *André Léo,* 99–106. Léo and Bakunin continued to have a contentious relationship over the next decade. See Chapter 4, "André Léo and the Subversion of Gender: The Battle over Women's Place."

9. E. E. Fribourg, *L'Association internationale des travailleurs* (Paris: Armand le Chevalier, 1871), 63.

10. Ibid., 65.

11. "Procès-verbaux du Congrès de l'Association internationale des travailleurs," in Jacques Freymond, ed., *La Première Internationale* (Genève: Librairie E. Droz, 1962), 211–12.

12. Ibid.

13. Léo, *La Femme et les mœurs,* 125–40.

14. Reclus refers to Tolain's action at the 1868 public meetings, held at the Vauxhall, on the *Travail des femmes.* Elisée Reclus to André Léo, n.d., André Léo, Descaves Collection, IISH.

15. Alain Dalotel, Alain Faure, and Jean-Claude Freiermuth, *Aux Origines de la Commune* (Paris: François Maspero, 1980), 172–73.

16. Quoted in Dalotel, Faure, and Freiermuth, *Aux Origines de la Commune,* 173.

17. Joan Landes, *Women and the Public Sphere in the Age of the French Revolution* (Ithaca, N.Y.: Cornell University Press, 1988), 21–38, 67–88, 138; Karen Offen, "Feminism, Antifeminism, and National Family Politics in Early Third Republic France," in Marilyn J. Boxer and Jean H. Quataert, eds., *Connecting Spheres: Women in the Western World, 1500 to the Present* (New York: Oxford University Press, 1987), 178; Edward Berenson, *The Trial of Madame Caillaux* (Berkeley: University of California Press, 1992), 104–105.

18. Proudhon is often known as the "Father of Anarchism." Charles Rihs, *La Commune de Paris,* 263–70; G. D. H. Cole, *Socialist Thought: The Forerunners, 1789–1850* (London: Macmillan and Co., 1953), 204–205, 212–13.

19. Steven K. Vincent, *Pierre-Joseph Proudhon and the Rise of French Republican Socialism* (New York: Oxford University Press, 1984), 192–94.

20. Pierre-Joseph Proudhon, "Notes et eclaircissements," quoted in ibid., 193.

21. Proudhon, "Idée générale de la révolution," quoted in ibid., 193.

22. Vincent, *Pierre-Joseph Proudhon,* 192–94.

23. Léo, *La Femme et les mœurs*.

24. Ibid., 15–16; Jenny d'Héricourt, *La Femme affranchie* (Brussels: F. van Meenen, 1860); Juliette Lambert Adam, *Idées anti-proudhonniennes sur l'amour, la femme et le mariage* (Paris, A. Taride, 1858).

25. Léo, *La Femme et les mœurs*, 126–27.

26. Ibid., 128.

27. Ibid., 137.

28. William H. Sewell, Jr., "Artisans, Factory Workers, and the Formation of the French Working Class, 1789–1848," in *Working Class Formation: Nineteenth-Century Patterns in Western Europe and the United States*, ed. Ira Katznelson and Aristide R. Zolberg (Princeton, N.J.: Princeton University Press, 1986), 51–52.

29. Mechanization eliminated the need for apprenticeship to learn the craft; previously, admission to apprenticeship had served to limit entrance to the trade—thereby regulating both quality and competition. Mechanization also sped up the production process, pressuring the "human component" to work more rapidly and less carefully. The loss of production and quality control, and the alienation of the workers from their products, demoralized workers. Jacques Rancière and Patrick Vauday, "Going to the Expo: The Worker, His Wife and Machines," in *Voices of the People: The Social Life of "La Sociale" at the End of the Second Empire*, translated by John Moore, edited by Adrian Rifkin and Roger Thomas (New York: Routledge & Kegan Paul, 1988), 23–33; Tessie P. Liu, "What Price a Weaver's Dignity? Gender Inequality and the Survival of Home-Based Production in Industrial France," in *Gender and Class in Modern Europe*, ed. Laura L. Frader and Sonya O. Rose (Ithaca, N.Y.: Cornell University Press, 1996), 57–76.

30. Fribourg, *L'Association internationale*, 122.

31. Madeleine Guilbert, *Les Fonctions de femmes dans l'industrie* (Paris: Mouton & Co., 1965), 42–45; Laura Levine Frader, "Women in the Industrial Capitalist Economy," in *Becoming Visible: Women in European History*, 2nd ed., ed. Renate Bridenthal, Claudia Koonz, and Susan Stuard (Boston: Houghton Mifflin Company, 1987), 321–23; Dalotel, Faure, and Freiermuth, *Aux Origines de la Commune*, 170.

32. Mink, quoted in Dalotel, Faure, and Freiermuth, *Aux Origines de la Commune*, 173.

33. Eugene Tataret, ed. *Commission ouvrière de 1867: recueil des procès-verbaux* (Paris: Imprimerie Augros, 1868), 1.

34. LePlay advocated an absolute division of gendered spheres, with female domesticity and a male breadwinner. Offen, *European Feminisms*, 131. For the 1867 Exposition, see *Le Livre des expositions universelles 1851–1989* (Paris: Union Central des Arts Décoratifs, 1983), 48–49; Matthew Truesdell, *Spectacular Politics: Louis-Napoléon Bonaparte and the Fête Impérial, 1849–1870* (New York: Oxford University Press, 1997), 106–12; and P. Chuard and G. Roux, *Exposition de 1867* (http://tecfa.unige.ch/~grob/1867/pres67.html; accessed February 6, 2004).

35. Tataret, *Commission ouvrière*. For the section on women's work, 213–39.

36. Ibid., 232–34.

37. Ibid., 214.

38. Ibid., 221.

39. The vast majority of delegates were men. Arnould Desvernay, *Rapports des delegations ouvrières: contenant l'origine et l'histoire des diverses professions, l'appréciation des objets exposés, la comparaison des arts et des industries en France et a l'étranger, l'exposé des*

vœux et besoins de la classe laborieuse, et l'ensemble des considérations sociales intéressant les ouvriers . . . , 3 vols. (Paris: A. Morel, 1869).

40. Pierre-Joseph Proudhon, *De la justice dans la révolution et dans l'église* (1858), in *Œuvres complètes de P.-J. Proudhon*, ed. Célestin Bouglé and Henri Moysset, XII (Paris: M. Rivière, 1923), 179–213.

41. Tataret, *Commission ouvrière*, 228.

42. Charles Sowerwine, "The Socialist Women's Movement from 1850 to 1940," in *Becoming Visible*, 2nd ed., 404; Samuel Bernstein, *The Beginnings of Marxian Socialism in France* (New York: Russell & Russell, 1965), 28–34; Bernard H. Moss, *The Origins of the French Labor Movement 1830–1914: The Socialism of Skilled Workers* (Berkeley: University of California Press, 1976), 52–56.

43. For Malon and Léo, see their correspondence in André Léo, Descaves Collection, IISH; for Varlin and Lemel, see Thomas, *Women Incendiaries*, 9–10, 39, 207–208, and Eugène Kerbaul, *Une Bretonne révolutionnaire et féministe: Nathalie Le Mel* (Paris: Ader, n.d.), 28–42, and for Varlin, see Tartaret, ed., *Commission ouvrière*, 233; for Frankel and Dmitrieff, see the *Union des femmes* documents in LY22 and LY23, AHR, and sections on the Commune and its immediate aftermath in Sylvie Braibant, *Elisabeth Dmitrieff: aristocrate et pétroleuse.*

44. André Léo, *L'Opinion nationale* (Paris), July–September 1868; Paule Mink, "Le Travail des femmes," quoted in Alain Dalotel, ed., *Paule Minck: communarde et féministe*, 114–39; Dalotel, preface to *Paule Minck*, 14–18; and Alain Dalotel, Alain Faure, and Jean-Claude Freiermuth, *Aux Origines de la Commune*, 168–78.

45. I want to thank Karen Offen for her generosity in sharing with me both her research on women's activism in the late 1860s and this unpublished work. Karen Offen, "Introduction" to "Part II: Taking Stock: The Woman Question on the Eve of the Third Republic," in "The Woman Question" (unpublished manuscript).

46. Pilbeam, *Republicanism in Nineteenth-Century France*, 251–52; Roger Magraw, *France 1815–1914: The Bourgeois Century* (New York: Oxford University Press, 1986), 180–86.

47. Theodore Zeldin, *The Political System of Napoleon III* (New York: W.W. Norton, 1971).

48. The restructuring of Paris, under the Baron Hausmann, included an extensive new sewage system; small parks throughout the city, and larger parks in the wealthier areas; central markets; and the expansion of the city and its reorganization into the current twenty-*arrondissement* system. See David Pinkney, *Napoleon III and the Rebuilding of Paris* (Princeton, N.J.: Princeton University Press, 1958).

49. Ibid., 164–65.

50. As a result, "suburb" or *"banlieue"* today has the same socio-geographical connotation in France as "inner-city" in the United States.

51. Alain Faure, "The Public Meeting Movement in Paris From 1868 to 1870," in *Voices of the People: The Social Life of "La Sociale" at the End of the Second Empire*, translated by John Moore (New York: Routledge & Kegan Paul, 1988), 207–23; James F. McMillan, *Napoleon III* (New York: Longman, 1991), 139–43; Pinkney, *Napoleon III*, 1–18 and 164–73; Magraw, *France 1815–1914*, 180–84.

52. André Léo, *L'Opinion nationale* (Paris), July–September 1868; Jacques Rougerie, "1871: la Commune de Paris," in *Encyclopédie politique et historique des femmes*, Christine Faure, ed. (Paris: Presses Universitaires de France, 1997), 415; Dalotel, Faure, and Freiermuth, *Aux Origines*, 123–26.

53. Dalotel, Faure, and Freiermuth, *Aux Origines*, 124, 176.

54. *Le Rappel*, Paris, January 2, 1869, in ibid., 127.

55. Léo, *L'Opinion nationale*, July 18, 1868.

56. Gustave Lefrançais, quoted in Rougerie, "1871: la Commune," 415. Deraismes, a bourgeois feminist, participated with Mink and Léo in *La Société du droit des femmes*, formed in 1866 to address issues including girls' education and marriage reform. Neither socialist nor revolutionary, she did not participate in the Commune. Maxime Breuil spoke frequently at the public meetings. Patrick Kay Bidelman, *Pariahs Stand Up! The Founding of the Liberal Feminist Movement in France, 1858–1889* (Westport, Conn.: Greenwood Press, 1982), 78–79.

57. Dalotel, Faure, and Freiermuth, *Aux Origines*, 168–69.

58. Maxime Breuil, *Deux discours sur le travail des femmes* (Paris: Armand le Chevalier, 1868), 7.

59. Ibid., 15.

60. Mink, "La Liberté: condition du socialisme," in Dalotel, ed., *Paule Minck*, 80–81.

61. The two sides, the minority, moderate "Proudhonians," and the majority, radical "Blanquists" or "Jacobins," are both broadly and imprecisely labeled groups. The terms *Blanquist* and *Jacobin* frequently appeared interchangeable. By 1871 the term *Jacobin* had expanded beyond specific reference to its namesake club and members. This broadly defined Jacobinism, or neo-Jacobinism, encompassed most socialisms advocating military insurgency, or class warfare, undertaken and enforced by a centralized revolutionary authority. Essentially, this included any of the non-associationist, non-federalist socialisms. On the opposing side, terming the moderate faction *Proudhonian* is ultimately contradictory. Proudhon opposed associations, strikes, and political action, considering them violations of individual liberty. Paradoxically, he pronounced that "property is theft," while supporting private ownership. The majority of Proudhon's adherents espoused a gradualist socialism and opposition to strong or centralized rule, yet they embraced differing perspectives about property and association. In terms of gender equity, Pierre-Joseph Proudhon vehemently argued for women's absolute restriction to the private sphere. Yet a number of feminist Communarde women allied themselves with the moderate faction, clearly appropriating aspects of his socialism while rejecting his misogyny. For the Proudhonian faction, see Benoît Malon to André Léo, St. Péloque, July 16, 1868, Descaves Collection, IISH; Malon, *La Troisième défaite du prolétariat français*, 272–80; "Appel aux ouvrières," *Commune de Paris*, quoted in *La Commune*, vol. 2 of *Les Murailles politiques françaises* (Paris: L. Le Chevalier, 1874), 522; Vincent, *Between Marxism and Anarchism*, 15; Moss, *French Labor Movement*, 2–7; Bernstein, *The Beginnings of Marxian Socialism in France*, 19. For the Jacobin faction, see Patrick H. Hutton, *The Cult of Revolutionary Tradition: The Blanquists in French Politics, 1864–1893* (Berkeley: University of California Press, 1981), 1–8; Cole, *Socialist Thought*, 6–7, 162–65; Bernstein, *Marxian Socialism*, 12–16; Edwards, *Paris Commune 1871*, 210, 214–15; Vincent, *Between Marxism and Anarchism*, 37–38.

62. Mink, "La Liberté," quoted in Dalotel, ed., *Paule Minck*, 82.

63. Gertrude Himmelfarb, "Introduction," in John Stuart Mill, *On Liberty* (1859; reprint, Middlesex: Penguin Books, 1985), 7–10.

64. Tartaret, *Procès-verbaux de la commission ouvrière de 1867*, quoted and translated in Rancière and Vauday, "Going to the Expo," 37.

65. Mink, "Le Travail des femmes," July 13, 1868, in Dalotel, ed., *Paule Minck*, 113–14, 135.

66. Ibid., 123.

67. Ibid., 129.

68. Ibid.

69. Ibid., 116.

70. Ibid., 135.

71. Mink, "Le Travail des femmes," in Dalotel, ed., *Paule Minck*, 135.

72. Ibid., 131–32.

73. Ibid., 132.

74. Mink, "Les Mouches et les araignées," in *Etudes Sociales* (Marseilles: Imprimerie Générale J. Doucet, 1880), 4–5.

75. Ibid.

76. Mink, "Le Mariage et le divorce," November 3, 1868, in Dalotel, ed. *Paule Minck*, 142–43.

77. Her only pre-Commune novel not to go into multiple printings was André Léo, *L'Idéal au village* (Paris: Hachette, 1867).

78. Offen, *The Woman Question*, Introduction to Part II.

79. André Léo to Léon Richer, June 8, 1869, carton 4247, Fonds Bouglé, BHVP.

80. Léo, *L'Opinion nationale*, July 20, 1868.

81. The following are Léo's novels prior to the Commune (in order of the year of their first publication): *Une Vieille Fille* (Brussels: Alphonse Lebègue, 1851); *Un Mariage scandaleux* (Paris: Hachette, 1862); *Un Divorce* (Paris, bureaux de *Siècle*, 1862); *Les Deux Filles de M. Plichon* (Paris: A. Faure, 1865); *Jacques Galéron* (Paris: A. Faure, 1865); *L'Idéal au village* (Paris: Hachette, 1867); *Aline-Ali* (Paris: *L'Opinion nationale*, 1868). She did not publish a novel again until *La Grande illusion des petits bourgeois* (Paris: Bureau du Siècle, 1876).

82. Léo, *La Femme et les mœurs*, 128.

83. Léo, *Un Mariage scandaleux*, quoted in Gastaldello, *André Léo*, 294–95.

84. The writer referred to Léo as "he," but because he compared her to two female writers, he most likely knew she was a woman. Reviews of *Un Mariage scandaleux* were reprinted in the second editions of *Une Vieille Fille* and *Jacques Galeron*. Thegel, *L'Independence Belge*, August 20, 1864, in André Léo, *Une Vieille Fille* (Paris: Librairie de Achille Faure, 1864), 211.

85. M. Duriez, *Le Siècle*, September 4, 1863, in Léo, *Une Vieille Fille* (2nd ed.), 207.

86. *Journal des Débats*, January 20, 1865, in André Léo, *Jacques Galéron*, 167; Charles-Bernard Derosne, *Le Constitutionnel*, July 28, 1863, in Léo, *Une Vieille Fille* (2nd ed.), 211.

87. "Romanciers modernes," *La Liberté* (Brussels), March 9, 1873.

88. Gastaldello, *André Léo*, 250. For an insightful analysis of many of Léo's novels, see Gastaldello's unpublished thesis, *André Léo*, 250–54.

89. Léo, *Une Vieille Fille*. It would be eleven years until her second novel, the celebrated *Un Mariage scandaleux*, was published. A second edition of *Une Vieille Fille* was published by in Paris by A. Faure in 1864.

90. Ibid., 29.

91. Ibid., 117–18.

92. Ibid., 118–19.

93. Léo, "Aline-Ali," *L'Opinion nationale*, September 6, 1868.

94. Léo, "Aline-Ali," September 12, 1868.

95. Ibid.

96. Léo, *L'Opinion nationale*, July 7, 1868; July 20, 1868; and August 9 and 23, and September 3, 1868.

97. Léo, *L'Opinion nationale*, July 20, 1868. All subsequent quotations from Léo's "Manifesto" are from this page.

98. Ibid.

99. André Léo to Léon Richer, 1869, carton 4247, Fonds Marie-Louise Bouglé, BHVP.

100. Offen, *The Woman Question*, "Introduction," Part II.

101. *Le Progrès* (Lyon), July 22 and September 4, 1868, quoted in Claire Auzias and Annik Houel, *La Grève des ovalistes: Lyon, juin-juillet 1869* (Paris: Payot, 1982), 168–73.

102. Léo, *L'Opinion nationale*, August 9 and 12, September 3, 1868.

103. Léo, "Les Theories: I," *L'Opinion nationale*, August 9, 1868.

104. Ibid.

105. Ibid.

106. Ibid.

107. Ibid.

108. Léo, *L'Opinion nationale*, August 26, 1868.

109. Ibid.

110. Truth's speech was printed on July 21, 1851 in the *Anti-Slavery Bugle*, and then again, in slightly different form, in an article by the feminist activist Frances Dana Gage, in the *New York Independent*, April 23, 1863. The speech appears not to have been translated into French by 1868, but Truth had gained significant renown among abolitionists and suffragists. Léo clearly followed this literature. She may also have known Harriet Beecher Stowe's article "Sojourner Truth, the Libyan Sibyl," published in *The Atlantic Monthly* 11, no. 66 (April 1863): 473–82. Stowe distorted and weakened Truth's image; it was as a corrective to this that Gage published her piece in the *New York Independent*. Elizabeth Fox Genovese, "Moved By the Spirit," *The Washington Post*, September 15, 1996.

111. Léo, *L'Opinion nationale*, September 3, 1868.

112. Léo, *L'Opinion nationale*, July 7, 1868.

113. Ibid.; Léo, *The American Colony in Paris in 1867*, trans. unknown (Boston: A. K. Loring, 1868).

114. Léo, *La Femme et les mœurs*, 160.

115. Ibid., 161.

116. André Léo, *Communisme et propriété* (Paris: Imprimerie D. Jouaust, 1868), 8.

117. Ibid.

118. Léo, *L'Opinion nationale*, July 7, 1868.

119. At this same historical moment, Stanton and Anthony were bitterly embattled as they opposed the Fourteenth Amendment to the U.S. Constitution which granted black men, and not white or black women, the vote. This issue caused a split in the American women's suffrage movement that would last twenty years. Léo's position on this is unknown. Sara M. Evans, *Born for Liberty: A History of Women in America* (New York: Free Press Paperbacks, 1997), 122–25.

120. Léo, *L'Opinion nationale*, July 7, 1868.

121. Offen, *The Woman Question*, Introduction to Part II.

122. Léo, *La Femme et les mœurs*, 88.

123. Léo, *The American Colony*, 7.

124. Ibid.

125. Ibid.

126. Ibid.

127. I want to thank Tom Mertes for his insights into the American context. A counter example based on similar relations of gender and power existed in Eastern European Jewish life, where women conducted business while men studied. Here scholarship was valued over commerce.

128. Léo, *La femme et les mœurs*, 88.

129. André Léo, *Observations d'une mère de famille* (Paris: Achille Faure, 1865), 11.

130. Ibid., 12–13.

131. Ibid., 30.

132. Léo, *Les Deux Filles*, 347.

133. Léo, *Jacques Galéron*, 71–73.

134. Ibid.

135. Ibid., 73–78.

136. André Léo, *La Cooperation*, February 10, 1867, quoted in Gastaldello, *André Léo*, 81–83.

137. While Michel, Léo, and Mink subsequently played significant roles in the Commune, Maria Deraismes, a republican bourgeois woman with Saint-Simonian leanings, did not participate. Jones and Vergès, "Women of the Paris Commune," 492; Sowerwine, *Sisters or Citizens?*, 6–7; Moses, *French Feminism in the Nineteenth Century*, 185. Only Jones and Vergès discuss the organizations goals.

138. Jones and Vergès, "Women of the Paris Commune," 492.

139. Alain Dalotel, "Benoît Malon, troisième fils d'André Léo," *Revue socialiste*, 78.

140. For feminisms before the Commune, see Offen, *European Feminisms;* Moses, *French Feminism in the Nineteenth Century;* Bidelman, *Pariahs Stand Up!*

141. Two future Communards, Elie Reclus and Marthe-Noémi Reclus, the brother and the wife of the anarchist Elisée Reclus, one of Léo's co-editors on *L'Agriculteur,* also participated in this organization. "Société de la revendication des droits de la femme," André Léo, Descaves Collection, IISH.

142. André Léo to Maria Verdure, LY23, AHG, Paris. Under the Commune, Maria Verdure served as a delegate of the society *l'Éducation nouvelle. Journal officiel (Commune),* April 2, 1871.

143. Léo, *L'Opinion nationale,* July 23, 1868; Léo to Richer, carton 4247, Fonds Bouglé, BHVP.

144. Léo to Verdure, AHG.

145. "Société de la revindication," IISH.

146. Ibid.

147. McClellan, *Revolutionary Exiles*, 98–99; Braibant, *Elisabeth Dmitrieff,* 58–59; Richard Stites, *The Women's Liberation Movement in Russia: Feminism, Nihilism, and Bolshevism, 1860–1930* (Princeton, N.J.: Princeton University Press, 1978), 29–49.

148. Knizhnik-Vetrov, *Russkie deiatel'nitsy,* 52; McClellan, *Revolutionary Exiles,* 87–93; Singer-Lecocq, *Rouge Elisabeth,* 102–107.

149. Jane McDermid and Anna Hillyar, *Midwives of the Revolution: Female Bolsheviks and Women Workers in 1917* (Athens, Ohio: Ohio University Press, 1999), 19–21; Stites, *The Women's Liberation Movement in Russia,* 89–99; McClellan, *Revolutionary Exiles,* 98–99.

150. Jacques Rougerie contends that Auguste Serrallier and Dmitrieff were the Commune's only true Marxists. Rougerie, *Paris libre 1871*, 189–90. For Marx's influence in France during this period, see Michelle Perrot, "Les Guesdistes: controverse sur l'introduction de Marxisme en France," *Annales: economies, sociétés, civilisations* 22 (May–June 1967): 701–710.

151. J. M. Meijer, *Knowledge and Revolution: The Russian Colony in Zuerich (1870–1873)* (Assen, Netherlands: Internationaal Instittuut Voor Sociale Geschiedenis, 1955), 73–77.

152. McClellan, *Revolutionary Exiles*, 21, 99.

153. See Chapter 3, "Elisabeth Dmitrieff and the *Union des femmes:* Revolutionizing Women's Labor."

154. Efremova and Ivanov, *Russkaia soratnitsa*, 71.

155. Comité de la section Russe to Karl Marx, December 9, 1870, quoted in Singer-Lecocq, *Rouge Elisabeth*, 115.

156. Efranova and Ivanov, *Russkaia soratnitsa*, 73–87; Knizhnik-Vetrov, *Russkie deiatel'nitsy*, 57–63.

157. Elisabeth Dmitrieff to Karl Marx, January 7, 1871, quoted in Braibant, *Elisabeth Dmitrieff*, 99–100.

158. Ibid.

159. Ibid.

160. Ibid., 102.

161. The Orléanists supported the Orléans dynasty's claim to the throne; the legitimists supported the Bourbons. Léo, *Signes et précurseurs*, 2.

162. Paule Mink, quoted in Alain Dalotel and Jean-Claude Freiermuth, "Socialism and Revolution," in *Voices of the People*, 235.

3. ELISABETH DMITRIEFF AND THE *UNION DES FEMMES*

1. Elisabeth Dmitrieff, "Appel aux citoyennes de Paris," *Journal officiel*, April 11, 1871.

2. Ibid.; "The Appeal" appeared on April 12 in Parisian newspapers including *La Sociale, L'Egalité, L'Opinion nationale, Paris libre*, and *Le Cri du peuple*.

3. Ibid.

4. Ibid.

5. The late Eugene Schulkind, one of the earliest historians to consider the Union des femmes, convincingly argued that "the Union . . . appears to have been the largest and most influential organization among the population of Paris during the Commune." *Socialist Women During the 1871 Paris Commune*, in *Past and Present* 106 (February 1985): 124–63; Schulkind first wrote on the subject in 1950. Eugene Schulkind, *Le Role des femmes dans la Commune de 1871*, in *1848, Revue des révolutions contemporaines* 42 (February 1950): 15–29.

6. The following *Union des femmes* documents are all held in the AHG, Paris. Statuts, Union des femmes pour la défense de Paris et les soins aux blessés, LY 22; Adresse du Comité Central, LY22; Statuts généraux des associations productives fédérés des travailleuses, LY 22; Projet d'organisation pour le travail des femmes, LY 22; Annexe au projet de création d'ateliers pour les femmes, LY 22.

7. *L'Opinion nationale*, April 12, 1871.

8. Adresse des citoyennes à la Commission Exécutive de la Commune de Paris, *Journal officiel,* April 14, 1871.

9. Of the provisional committee members, only Marquant, a sewing machine operator from the 3rd *arrondissement,* was elected to the Central Committee. Curiously, none of the other women appear on the final committee lists of any *arrondissement.* They may have continued their involvement as rank and file members, but membership rosters for most *arrondissements* have been lost.

10. Both Knizhnik-Vetrov and A. Nepomniachtichi give her arrival date as March 29, the day after the Commune's ceremonial declaration. Efremova and Ivanov place her in Paris on March 28, describing her participation in the day's ceremony. Braibant suggests either the March 28 or 29, but she cites a letter from Hermann Jung to Marx, dated March 29, informing him that he has "this instant received a letter from Mme. Tomanovsky [her married name] who has just arrived in Paris." Therefore it is likely that Dmitrieff did reach Paris on March 28. There is no other evidence regarding her participation in the ceremonial declaration. A. Nepomniachtchi, "Elisabeth Dmitrieva sur les barricades de la Commune," *Etudes Sovietiques* 204 (March 1965): 66; Ivan Sergeevich Knizhnik-Vetrov, *Russkie deiatel'nitsy Pervogo Internatsionala i Parizhskoi Kommuny* (Moscow and Leningrad: Izdatel'stvo "Nauka," 1964), 72–74; N. Efremova and N. Ivanov, *Russkaia soratnitsa Marksa* (Moscow: Moskovskii rabochii, 1982), 95–96, 100–102; Braibant, *Elisabeth Dmitrieff,* 108–11.

11. In the revolution's aftermath, she returned to using Tomonovskaya, and the police and military authorities could find no trace of Elisabeth Dmitrieff. See Chapter 6, "Dmitrieff and Léo in the Aftermath: Radical Denouement."

12. Singer-Lecocq, *Rouge Elisabeth,* 128.

13. Appel aux citoyennes de Paris, *Journal officiel,* April 11, 1871; Braibant, *Elisabeth Dmitrieff,* 111–12; Efremova and Ivanov, *Russkaia soratnitsa,* 108.

14. Johnson, *The Paradise of Association,* 243–48.

15. The *Union des femmes* documents are held in cartons LY 22 and LY 23 at the AHG.

16. Women would serve as military nurses (in ambulances), field cooks (for cooking stoves), and ultimately, fighters (on barricades). Union des femmes pour la défense de Paris et les soins aux blessés, statuts: administration des comités d'arrondissements, LY22, AHG.

17. The Union of Women for the Defense of Paris and Aid to the Wounded.

18. Léo also strongly advocated women's military participation; see Chapter 4. Adresse des citoyennes, *Journal officiel,* April 14, 1871.

19. Quoted in Braibant, *Elisabeth Dmitrieff,* 114.

20. Frankel and the Commission of Labor and Exchange would form the primary link between the *Union des femmes* and the Commune government, providing the organization with financial and operational assistance.

21. Adresse des citoyennes, *Journal officiel,* April 14, 1871.

22. Ibid.

23. Kathleen Jones and Françoise Vergès, "'Aux Citoyennes!': Women, Politics, and the Paris Commune of 1871," *History of European Ideas* 13 (1991): 716–19.

24. Adresse des citoyennes, *Journal officiel,* April 14, 1871.

25. Adresse du Comité Central, LY 22, AHG.

26. Michelle Barrett and Mary McIntosh, "The 'Family Wage': Some Problems for Socialists and Feminists," *Capital and Class* 11 (Summer 1980): 53–58; Jane Lewis,

"The Debate on Sex and Class," *New Left Review* 149 (Janurary–February 1985); Laura Levine Frader, "Women in the Industrial Capitalist Economy," in Bridenthal, Koonz, and Stuard, eds., *Becoming Visible*, 321–23.

27. Madeleine Guilbert, *Les Fonctions de femmes dans l'industrie*, 42–45; Tony Judt, *Marxism and the French Left: Studies in Labour and Politics in France, 1830–1981* (Oxford: Clarendon Press, 1986), 90–92.

28. Bosquet's first name is unknown. Quoted in Dalotel, Faure, and Freiermuth, *Aux Origines de la Commune*, 170.

29. Barbara Taylor, *Eve and the New Jerusalem: Socialism and Feminism in the 19th Century* (New York: Pantheon, 1983), 93–107; Carole Pateman, *The Sexual Contract* (Stanford, Calif.: Stanford University Press, 1988), 137–39; Alice Kessler-Harris, *Out to Work: A History of Wage-Earning Women in the United States* (Oxford: Oxford University Press, 1982), 69.

30. Adresse du Comité Central, LY22, AHG.

31. Alice Kessler-Harris, *A Woman's Wage: Historical Meanings and Social Consequences* (Lexington: University Press of Kentucky, 1990), 1–19; Barrett and McIntosh, *The Family Wage*, 56–68.

32. Annexe au projet de création d'ateliers pour les femmes, Union des Femmes, LY22, AHG.

33. Adresse du Comité Central, LY22, AHG.

34. Quoted in Vincent, *Between Marxism and Anarchism*, 15.

35. Quoted in Dalotel, Faure, and Freiermuth, *Aux Origines*, 172–73. The General Council of the International later expelled Tolain, on April 25, 1871, for refusing to resign his seat in France's National Assembly. The expulsion, written by Friedrich Engels, stated that "Tolain . . . after having been elected to the National Assembly as a representative of the working classes . . . has deserted their cause in the most disgraceful manner . . . the place of every French member of the I.W.M.A. (International Working Men's Association) is undoubtedly on the side of the Commune of Paris and not in the usurpatory and counter-revolutionary Assembly of Versailles." This reflected the reality that many of the first workers elected as representatives tended to be neither socialist nor labor activists, but rather democrats supportive of bourgeois parties. Quoted in Marx and Engels, *On the Paris Commune*, 235.

36. The First International Workingmen's Association, Lausanne Congress 1867, "Rapports lu au Congrès ouvrier réuni du 2 au 8 septembre 1867 à Lausanne," trans. in *Women, the Family, and Freedom: The Debate in Documents*, vol. I, edited by Susan Groag Bell and Karen M. Offen (Stanford, Calif.: Stanford University Press, 1983), 466–67, 70.

37. *The Trial of Madame Caillaux*, 11 and 100–101.

38. Pierre-Joseph Proudhon, "De la création de l'ordre dans l'humanité ou principes d'organisation politique," quoted in Moses, *French Feminism*, 153–54. For Henri Tolain, see M. Egrot and J. Maitron, *Dictionnaire biographique de mouvement ouvrier français; deuxième partie: 1864–1871*, vol. IX (Paris: Les Editions Ouvrières, 1971), 218–21.

39. Pierre-Joseph Proudhon, *Qu'est-ce que la propriété?* (Paris: Garnier Flammarion, 1966), 274–75.

40. By the end of the nineteenth century, women's "homework" became a subject of enormous study and concern. For a fascinating analysis, see Judith Coffin, *The Politics of Women's Work.* (Princeton, N.J.: Princeton University Press, 1996), 46–73.

41. Jules Simon, *L'Ouvrière* (Paris: Librarie Hachette, 1871), 61. The work was first published in 1860.

42. Ibid., 81.

43. Coffin, *Politics of Women's Work*, 66–69.

44. Simon, *L'Ouvrière*, iv–v.

45. Madeleine Guilbert and Viviane Isambert-Jamati, *Travail féminin et travail à domicile. Enquête sur le travail à domicile de la confection féminin dans la région parisienne* (Paris: Centre Nationale de la Recherche Scientifique, 1956), 11–19, and 24–26.

46. Julie-Victoire Daubié, *La Femme pauvre au XIX siècle*, quoted and trans. in *Women, the Family, and Freedom*, 457 and 58.

47. Ibid., 170; James Guillaume, 15. These are the same public meetings as those discussed in Chapter 2.

48. Paule Mink, "'Le travail des femmes,' discours prononcé par Madame Paule Mink à la réunion publique de Vauxhall le 13 juillet 1868," in *Paule Minck: communarde et féministe*, 120–22.

49. Ibid.

50. Adresse du Comité Central, LY 22, AHG.

51. Ibid.

52. Ibid.

53. Le Comité du 10e Arrondissement de l'Union des femmes, Ly 22, AHG; Le Comité du 3e Arrondissement de l'Union des femmes, LY 22, AHG.

54. Léo, La Siège, *Mémoires*, 72, Descaves Collection, IISH.

55. Mink, "Le Travail des femmes," trans. in *Women, the Family, and Freedom*, 471.

56. Briot à Ministre de la Guerre, LY 7, AHG; Louise Tilley, "Paths of Proletarianization: Organization of Production, Sexual Division of Labor, and Women's Collective Action," *Signs: Journal of Women in Culture and Society* 7 (1981): 402–405.

57. G. D. H. Cole, *Socialist Thought: The Forerunners, 1789–1850* (London: Macmillan, 1953), 61, 79, 164–65, and 178–79; Vincent, *Between Marxism and Anarchism*, 10.

58. Moss, *French Labor Movement*, 2–5.

59. Both Malon, Léo's partner, and Jaclard, husband of the Russian feminist socialist Anna Korvine-Krukovskaya Jaclard, also belonged to the International. Jaclard had voted in the minority against the 1867 Lausanne statement condemning women's labor; Malon was in St. Peloque prison on political charges in 1867, and thus did not attend the meeting. Vincent, *Between Marxism and Anarchism*, 9–10; and Serman, *La Commune de Paris*, 59–65.

60. Avis, *Les Murailles politiques française* (Paris: L. Le Chevalier, 1874), 305.

61. Comité Central, Union des femmes, LY 22, AHG.

62. Membres des Comités, Union des femmes, LY 23, AHG; Mairie du IVe Arrondissement, *Murailles politiques*, 546.

63. At least one public notice, the May 17 Appel aux Ouvrières, listed a woman, Collin (first name and arrondissement unknown) as an Executive Commission member, in place of Adèle Gauvin. Appel aux Ouvrières, *Murailles politiques*, 522; Membres des Comités, AHG.

64. This number represents an extrapolation and approximation from existing fragmentary evidence, including Membres des Comités, AHG; Commune Sociale de Paris: Union des femmes, AHG; Comité du 7e arrondissement: Organisation du Travail, AHG; Comité du 10e, AHG; Onzième arrondissement, Union des femmes, AHG; Oc-

tavie Tardif à la commission de Travail et de l'Echange, AHG; Bureau de Renseignements du Travail et de l'Echange, AHG; Thomas, *Women Incendiaries*, 74–75, and 86.

65. Appel aux Citoyennes (4 mai), reprinted in Bruhat, Dautry, and Tersen, *La Commune de 1871*, 189.

66. Quoted in Braibant, *Elisabeth Dmitrieff*, 136.

67. Henri Rochefort, quoted in Marie-Thérèse Eyquem, "Les femmes au service de la Commune," in *Voici l'aube l'Immortelle Commune de Paris* (Paris: Editions Sociales, 1972), 327.

68. Eugène Kerbaul, *Nathalie Lemel: une Bretonne révolutionnaire et féministe* (Paris: Imprimerie Ader, n.d.), 57–64.

69. Duval (Perrine Nathalie) *femme* Lemel, Rapport à la Commission de Grâce, Ministère de la Justice, August 21, 1873, BB/24/792, AN.

70. Ibid.

71. Paul Fontoulieu, *Les Eglises des Paris sous la Commune* (Paris: E. Dentu, 1873), 181–87.

72. Lemel, *Rapport à la Commission de Grâce*, BB/24/792, AN.

73. Nathalie Lemel, in Fontoulieu, *Les Eglises*, 274–75.

74. "Tribunaux: juridiction militaire, 4e Conseil de guerre," *Le Corsaire*, Paris, September 19, 1872, dossier Nathalie Lemel, BMD.

75. Her trial was postponed to September 1872 because she was hospitalized for a year following a suicide attempt. Ibid.

76. Ibid.

77. Annie Thomas, *Louise Michel: une femme libertaire* (Paris: Les Lettres Libres, 1984), 157; Edith Thomas, *Women Incendiaries*, 9.

78. Thomas, *Women Incendiaries*, 9.

79. Lucien Descaves, "Une amie de Varlin," *La Lanterne*, May 18, 1921, André Léo, *Imprimès*, 2, Descaves Collection, IISH.

80. The following announcements are published in *Les Murailles politiques français* (Paris: L. Le Chevalier, 1874): "Manifeste du Comité central de l'Union des femmes," *La Commission exécutive du Comité central*, 440; "Appel aux ouvrières," *La Commission exécutive du Comité central, Murailles politiques*, 522; "Mairie du Ive arrondissement," *La Commission exécutive du Comité central, Murailles politiques*, 546.

81. Quoted in Marguerite Thibert, "Portraits des femmes de la Commune," in *Voici l'aube. L'immortelle Commune de Paris*, 337.

82. Thomas, *Louise Michel*, 158.

83. *Rapport*, August 21, 1873, BB/24/792, AN.

84. Michel, *La Commune*, 131.

85. Descaves, "Une amie de Varlin," Descaves Collection, IISH.

86. The Central Committee consisted of five seamstresses, a sewing-machine operator, a milliner, a linen draper, a dressmaker, a vest-maker, a bookstitcher, a cardboard maker, an embroiderer of military ornaments, a gold-polisher, a bookbinder, and three women without trades. Membres des Comités, AHG.

87. Travail des femmes: Plan d'organisation, Union des femmes, LY 22, AHG.
88. Ibid.
89. Ibid.
90. Ibid.; Notes: Travail des femmes, Union des femmes, LY 22, AHG.
91. Travail des femmes: Plan d'organisation, AHG.

92. Notes: Travail des femmes, AHG.

93. Notes: Travail des femmes, AHG.

94. Ibid.

95. Ibid.

96. Notes: Travail des femmes, AHG.

97. Ibid.

98. Elisabeth Dmitrieff to Hermann Jung, quoted in Singer-Lecocq, *Rouge Elisabeth,* 143–46; and in McClellan, *Revolutionary Exiles,* 156.

99. Statutes généraux, AHG.

100. Travail des femmes: Plan d'organisation, AHG.

101. Ibid.

102. Projet d'organisation pour le travail des femmes, Union des femmes, LY 23, AHG.

103. Contemporary editors and authors attribute the authorship of this document to different sources, although none have raised this as a point of contention. I argue that the "Projet d'organisation pour le travail des femmes" is a *Union des femmes* work. It is clearly a draft, and it is unsigned. Several scholars attribute the four-page work to a male member of the Commission of Labor and Exchange, primarily due to a note on the first page that reads, "good for printing 200 copies, B. Malon." Malon, a member of Labor and Echange, signed this printing authorization, but the document is written in another hand. His note indicates that the Commune paid for the printing costs of the *Union des femmes,* as they had requested in the "Address from the *Citoyennes* to the Executive Commission of the Commune." In his memoirs, Malon indicates nothing of his, or his commission's, contribution of any specific plans or objectives to the organization. Malon, *La Troisième défaite du prolétariat français,* 272–81; Projet d'organisation, AHG; Adresse des citoyennes, *Journal officiel,* April 14, 1871; Maitron, ed., *Dictionnaire Biographique,* 230–34. The works quoting, or excerpting, the Projet d'organisation, include Jacques Rougerie, ed., *Procès des Communards* (Paris: René Julliard, 1964) 228–29; Edwards, ed., *The Communards of Paris, 1871,* 124–25; Thomas, *Women Incendiaries,* 81; Schulkind, "Socialist Women," 150; and Braibant, *Elisabeth Dmitrieff,* 146–48. Only Thomas and Braibant credit the Union des femmes with authorship.

104. Projet d'organisation pour le travail des femmes, AHG.

105. Benoît Malon to André Léo, July 16, 1868; André Léo, Descaves Collection, IISH; Benoît Malon to André Léo, n.d., André Léo, Descaves Collection, IISH; Malon, Troisième défait, 272–81; Léo Frankel, quoted in: *Journal officiel,* May 6, 1871; Appel aux ouvrières, *Murailles politiques,* 522; Léo Frankel, *L'Emancipation,* January 1, 1872, Toulouse, quoted in Schulkind, "Socialist Women during the 1871 Paris Commune," in *Past and Present* 106 (February 1985): 137; Eugéne Varlin, *Commission ouvrière de 1867,* ed. Tartaret, quoted in Schulkind, "Socialist Women," 144.

106. Assemblée Nationale, *Enquête Parlementaire sur l'insurrection du 18 mars* (Paris: Librairie Législative—A. Wittersheim, 1872), 533–35; *Dictionnaire biographique,* 91–94.

107. Annexe au projet de création d'ateliers pour les femmes, Union des femmes, LY 23, AHG.

108. Travail des femmes: Plan d'organisation, AHG.

109. Comité du 7e arrondissement, AHG; Le Comité du 10e arrondissement, AHG.

110. Travail des femmes: Plan d'organisation, AHG.

111. Travail des femmes: Projet d'organisation sous diverses formes, AHG. This document states nothing specifically about the *Union des femmes,* but I attribute it to the group based on its contents, style, and the structure of its title.

112. Communarde anti-clericalism extended well beyond resentment towards convents and their labor practices. See Chapter 5.

113. Magraw, *A History of the French Working Class,* vol. I, 253–58; Persis Hunt, "Feminism and Anti-Clericalism under the Commune," *Massachusetts Review* 12 (Summer 1971): 420; Laura Strumingher, *Women and the Making of the Working Class: Lyon 1830–1870* (St. Alban's: Eden Press, 1979), 57–61.

114. Travail des femmes: Plan d'organisation, AHG.

115. Paule Mink, "La Lutte des femmes," *Paule Minck,* 133; Léo, *La Cooperation,* February 10, 1867, quoted in Gastaldello, *André Léo,* 81–83.

116. Strumingher, *Women and Working Class,* 8–9, and 55–63; Frader, "Women in Industrial," 322.

117. Simon, *L'Ouvrière,* 58–59.

118. Fontoulieu, *Les Eglises,* 64.

119. Travail des femmes: Plan d'organisation, AHG.

120. I am grateful to Louise Tilly for this information.

121. Notes: Travail des femmes, AHG.

122. Travail des femmes: Plan d'organisation, AHG.

123. Ibid.

124. Ibid.

125. Ibid.

126. Déposition de M. de Ploeuc, *Enquête parlementaire,* 390–99; Georges Bourgin and Gabriel Henriot, eds., *Procès-Verbaux de la Commune de 1871,* vol. I. (Paris: E. Leroux, 1924), 241.

127. Une citoyenne à Commission de travail et echange, Paris, May 9, 1871, LY 23, AHG.

128. Une citoyenne de Montmartre à Commission de travail et echange, May 12, 1871, LY 22, AHG.

129. Bourgin and Henriot, eds., *Procès-Verbaux de la Commune de 1871,* vol. II, 367.

130. Ibid., 354–55.

131. Travail des femmes: Plan d'organisation, AHG.

132. Ibid.

133. Rapport des citoyennes du Comité du 10e arrondissement deleguées pour la requisition des locaux au Comité Central, Union des femmes, LY 22, AHG.

134. Ibid.

135. *Journal officiel,* April 17, 1871.

136. Appel aux ouvriers, *Murailles politiques,* 522.

137. Ibid.

138. Mairie du IVe arrondissement, *Murailles politiques,* 543.

139. Travail des femmes: Plan d'organisation, AHG.

140. Elisabeth Dmitrieff to *Union des femmes* members, reprinted in Braibant, *Elisabeth Dmitrieff,* 156.

141. Alain Dalotel, "Les Femmes dans les clubs rouges, 1870–1871," in *Femmes dans la cité, 1815–1871,* ed. Alain Corbin, Jacqueline Lalouette, and Michèle Riot-Sarcey (Paris: Creaphis, 1997), 300–301.

142. Elisabeth Dmitrieva-Tomanovsky to Hermann Jung, April 24, 1871, in Jules Rocher, ed. *Lettres de communards et de militants de la 1re Internationale à Marx, Engels et autres dans les journées de la Commune de Paris en 1871* (Paris: Bureau d'Editions, 1934), 36.

4. ANDRÉ LÉO AND THE SUBVERSION OF GENDER

1. "La Province," *Mémoires*, dossier André Léo, Descaves Collection, IISH.

2. Ibid. It is unclear why she waited to return to Paris until two weeks after the uprising began.

3. Ibid.

4. André Léo, "Signes précurseurs," *Notes et impressions, 1870–1871*, 10–11, *Mémoires*, Descaves Collection, IISH.

5. Léo, "Signes précurseurs," *Mémoires*, 9–10.

6. "La Guerre civile," *Mémoires*, dossier André Léo, Descaves Collection, IISH.

7. Ibid.

8. Ibid.

9. She founded the newspaper with the Russian-born feminist socialist Anna Korvine-Krukovskaya Jaclard, the wife of Communard Victor Jaclard. Krukovskaya Jaclard played a much smaller role than Léo in editing and writing for the newspaper. Léo also wrote for *La Commune* and *Le Cri du peuple*. All three of the papers began and ended with the Commune.

10. "Toutes avec tous," *La Sociale* (Paris), April 12, 1871.

11. Léo spoke at least once at a political club, the *Club de la révolution*, in the *Eglise Saint-Michel*, at which, according to Fontoulieu, her "success was enormous." Fontoulieu, *Les Eglises*, 224. "Appel aux citoyennes de Paris," *Journal officiel*, April 11, 1871. The "Appel" subsequently appeared on April 12, the same day as Léo's "Toutes avec tous," in Parisian newspapers including *La Sociale*, *L'Egalité*, *L'Opinion nationale*, *Paris libre*, and *Le Cri du peuple*.

12. "La Révolution sans la femme," *La Sociale*, May 8, 1871.

13. Ibid. In this same article, Léo specifically threatened alienated revolutionary women's return to the Church. See below.

14. Léo, "Signes précurseurs," *Mémoires*, 11–12.

15. Gastaldello, "André Léo, 167–68.

16. André Léo, "Les conciliateurs," *La Sociale*, April 10, 1871.

17. Léo, "Toutes avec tous," April 12, 1871.

18. André Léo, "La Marseillaise des femmes," *La Petite presse*, September 10, 1870. I want to thank Margaret Darrow for alerting me to this article.

19. Léo, "Toutes avec tous," April 12, 1871.

20. Léo, "La Marseillaise des femmes," September 10, 1870.

21. Léo, "Toutes avec tous," April 12, 1871.

22. "Les Citoyennes aux remparts," *Paris libre*, May 14, 1871.

23. For women's battalions during the Commune, see Johnson, *The Paradise of Association*, 242–54. Johnson, however, misinterprets the origins of the *Union des femmes*, and overstates the organization's connections with other revolutionary women's groups. See my chapter 3, "Elisabeth Dmitrieff and the *Union des femmes*: Revolutionizing Women's Labor."

24. There are no clear numbers on women's battlefield participation.

25. For detailed examples of women's street battling, see David Barry, *Women and Political Insurgency: France in the Mid-Nineteenth Century* (New York: St. Martin's Press, 1996), 123–31.

26. *La Sociale*, April 8 and 17, 1871.

27. Johnson, *Paradise of Association*, 249–73.

28. Marforio, *Les Echarpes rouges*, 89–92.

29. Quoted in Alain Dalotel, "Les femmes dans les clubs rouges," unpublished and undated paper, Bibliothèque Marguerite Durand, Paris, 16, 21. A later version of this paper was published as "Les femmes dans les clubs rouges, 1870–1871," in *Femmes dans la cité*, ed. Corbin, Lalouette, and Riot-Sarcey.

30. See chapter 3 for the *Union des femmes.*

31. Louise Michel, *Memoires* (Arles: Editions Sulliver, 1998).

32. *Le Cri du peuple*, April 26, 1871.

33. *Le Cri du peuple*, May 2, 1871. Léo's status as a widely recognized journalist and novelist undoubtedly aided these groups' appeals. In an April 30 *La Sociale* piece entitled "*Les Neutres,*" Léo savagely criticized those who did not act on their beliefs: the Parisians who condemned the Commune, but remained in the city, and the declared Commune supporters who remain uninvolved. The article's title, "Les Neutres," carries a potentially double meaning as both "the neutrals" and "the neutered." "Les Neutres," *La Sociale*, April 30, 1871. See also Gastaldello, *André Léo*, 181–84.

34. The creation of the Committee of Public Safety was intensely opposed by the moderate, gradualist socialist faction. The May 1 vote establishing the Committee created the majority–minority split in the Commune government between those in favor, the Blanquists–Jacobins, now the majority, and those against, the Proudhonians–gradualists, now the minority. The Committee of Public Safety took its name from Robespierre's eponymously named governmental commission. Stewart Edwards points out the irony that the original Committee under Robespierre had, at the National Assembly's behest, crushed the 1793 Paris Commune, the city's independent municipal government. Edwards, *The Paris Commune 1871*, 227–30; Philip G. Nord, "The Party of Conciliation and the Paris Commune," *French Historical Studies* 15, no. 1 (Spring 1987): 8.

35. Léo, *La Sociale*, May 5, 1871.

36. Ibid.

37. Ibid.

38. Ibid.; Gastaldello, *André Léo*, 172–73.

39. *La Sociale*, May 5, 1871.

40. Ibid.

41. Louis Rossel, *La Sociale*, May 7, 1871. A week later, Léo would defend Rossel when the Commune government accused him of treason. André Léo, "Citoyens rédacteurs," *La Sociale*, May 14, 1871.

42. Léo, *La Sociale*, May 9, 1871.

43. Linda Grant De Pauw, *Battle Cries and Lullabies: Women in War from Prehistory to the Present* (Norman: University of Oklahoma Press, 1998).

44. D. J. Joulin, *Les Caravances d'un chirurgien d'ambulances* (Paris: E. Dentu, 1871), 86, quoted in Bertrand Taithe, *Defeated Flesh: Welfare, Warfare and the Making of Modern France* (Manchester: Manchester University Press, 1999), 138.

45. Taithe, *Defeated Flesh*, 140–44.

46. Gullickson, *Unruly Women*, 89–96.

47. Jean-Paul Milliet, *Une Famille de Républicains Fouriéristes, Les Milliet*, vol. II (Paris: Chez l'Auteur, 1916), 96.

48. Ibid., 97.

49. Chanoine worked as a jewelry maker in Milliet's husband's factory. Ibid., 97, 99.

50. André Léo, *La Femme et les mœurs*, 35–36.

51. Milliet, *Une Famille de Republicains*, 96.

52. Ibid.

53. Ibid., 109.

54. "Toutes avec tous," *La Sociale*, April 12, 1871.

55. Ibid.

56. See chapter 3 for the *Union des femmes*. Manifeste de comité Central de l'Union des femmes pour la défense de Paris et les soins aux blessés, LY22, AHG.

57. Ibid.

58. *La Sociale*, May 9, 1871.

59. Léo, "Signes précurseurs," *Mémoires*, 15.

60. Gay Gullickson provides a fascinating analysis of representations of communardes, particularly of the *pétroleuse*, in *Unruly Women of Paris*.

61. Marie Vrecq, femme Bedier à Ministère de la Justice, 12 fevrier 1878, BB/24/822, AN; Marie Audrain, femme Vincent, "Notice individuelle," BB/24/773, AN.

62. Marie Madrut, femme Ehret, "Rapport à la Commission des grâces," BB/24/773, AN.

63. Nathalie Lemel, née Duval, "Rapport à la Commission des grâces," BB/24/792, AN.

64. Fille Marie Cailleux, Séries Ba, carton 375, APP.

65. Briot à Ministère de la Guerre, Ly 7, AHG.

66. Briot à Ministère de la Guerre, AHG. The Second Empire, for most of its duration, imposed authoritarian strictures on speech, the press, association, and the judiciary. While limited liberalization measures began in 1860, not until 1868 did Louis Napoleon, fearing social upheaval or revolution, introduce expanded freedoms in these areas. The relaxation of these liberties allowed an opposition press, as well as reformist and radical organizations, to develop. Zeldin, *The Political System of Napoleon III*, 101; Christiansen, *Paris Babylon*, 118.

67. Leonard Berlanstein described *unions libres*, termed "concubinage" by governmental authorities, as "solidly a part of working-class life." Bruhat, Dautry, and Tersen, *La Commune de 1871*, 182–83; Leonard Berlanstein, *The Working People of Paris, 1871–1914* (Baltimore: Johns Hopkins University Press, 1984), 33–34; Alain Corbin, *Women for Hire: Prostitution and Sexuality in France After 1850*, translated by Alan Sheridan (Cambridge, Mass.: Harvard University Press, 1990), 190–91; James F. McMillan, *Housewife or Harlot: The Place of Women in French Society, 1870–1940* (New York: St. Martin's Press, 1981), 41–44.

68. Fontoulieu, *Les Eglises*, 127–28.

69. Léo, "Signes précurseurs," *Memoires*, 15.

70. Léo, *La Femme et les mœurs*, 21–22.

71. For popular anti-clericalism, see Chapter 5.

72. Women described as "living in concubinage" included Marguerite Guinder, femme Prévost, BB/24/759, AN; Marie Catherine Rogissart, BB/24/781, AN; Laure Adéle Desfossés, femme Bonlant, BB/24/773, AN; Sophie Doctrinal, femme Poirier, BB/24/781, AN; Elisabeth Rétiffe and Eulalie Papavoine, in "Le Procès de la Commune. compte rendu des débats du Conseil de Guerre, paraissant tous les jours par livraison de huit pages, avec illustrations," in *Procès des Communards,* ed. Jacques Rougerie (Paris: René Julliard, 1964), 116–17; and 302 single women, 117 married, and 76 widows, in Briot à Ministère de la Guerre, LY 7, AHG.

73. Sophie Doctrinal, femme Lamarchand, "Rapport a la Commission des grâces," BB/24/781, AN, Paris; Jean Maitron, *Dictionnaire biographique du mouvement ouvrier français, deuxième partie: 1864–1871, La Première Internationale et la Commune,* vol. V (Paris: Les Editions Ouvrières, 1968), 356.

74. Doctrinal, "Rapport," BB/24/781, AN.

75. Ibid.; Corbin, "Intimate Relations," in *A History of Private Life: From the Fires of Revolution to the Great War,* vol. IV, ed. Michelle Perrot, translated by Arthur Gold-hammer (Cambridge, Mass.: Harvard University Press, 1990), 591.

76. Doctrinal, "Rapport," BB/24/781, AN.

77. Ibid.

78. Ibid.

79. Ibid.

80. Ibid.

81. Ibid.

82. Briot à Ministère de la Guerre, AHG.

83. Ibid.

84. Ibid.

85. Regarding the extent of *union libre* relationships, see Berlanstein, *Working People of Paris,* 33–34.

86. Alain Corbin, "Intimate Relations," in *Private Life,* 567–69, 591; McMillan, *Housewife or Harlot,* 9–10.

87. Corbin, "Intimate Relations," 591.

88. Jeffrey Weeks, *Sex, Politics and Society: The Regulation of Sexuality since 1800* (London: Longman, 1989), 29–30; McMillan, *Housewife or Harlot,* 17; Michelle Perrot, "The Family Triumphant," in *A History of Private Life,* 150.

89. Frederick Brown, *Zola: A Life* (New York: Farrar Straus Giroux, 1995), 425–27; Corbin, "Intimate Relations," in *Private Life,* 591.

90. Vrecq, femme Bediet, BB/24/822, AN.

91. Rapport, October 12, 1871, Dossier Louise Michel, Ba 1183, APP.

92. Fontoulieu, *Les Eglises,* 105.

93. Robert Tombs, in an article where he denies much of women's political intent and agency in their militant insurrectionism, rather condescendingly describes communarde leaders as "female celebrities who liked splendid uniforms with pistols and daggers" as "an eccentric few." Tombs suggests that the excessive attention paid to women's dress and appearance by observers in violent contexts "might suggest awareness of the iconic function of the women." He does not consider that judgments and descriptions of women's dress and appearance frequently play a role in assessing their behavior, intentions, and morality. Robert Tombs, "Warriors and Killers: Women and Violence During the Paris Commune, 1871," in *The Sphinx in the Tui-*

leries and Other Essays in Modern French History, ed. Robert Aldrich and Martyn Lyons (Sydney: University of Sydney, 1999), 175–78.

94. Fontoulieu, *Les Eglises,* 105.

95. Ibid., 182–83.

96. John D'Emilio and Estelle Freedman, *Intimate Matters: A History of Sexuality in America* (New York: Harper and Row, 1988); Corbin, "Intimate Relations," in *Private Life,* 567–69, 591; McMillan, *Housewife or Harlot,* 9–10.

97. Weeks, *Sex, Politics and Society,* 30.

98. Gullickson, *Unruly Women,* 159–90.

99. Fontoulieu, *Les Eglises,* 105, 182–83.

100. Ibid.

101. Thomas wrote that Caweska (whose name she spelled Lodoyska Kawecka) "contributed to *Le Journal des citoyennes de la Commune.*" However, Thomas made no other specific reference to this newspaper, nor did she list it in her bibliography. Regarding the spelling of Caweska, Eugene Schulkind wrote "Lodoïska Caweska," while Jean Maitron chose "Ladojska Kawecka," and for her husband, "Wladyslawa Konstantego Kaweckiego." Eugene Schulkind, "Le Role des femmes dans la Commune de 1871," *1848, Revue des revolutions contemporaines XLII* 185 (February 1950): 4–5, 7; Thomas, *Women Incendiaries,* 96, 99–100; Maitron, ed., *Dictionnaire biographique,* vol. 6, 416. For Marie Wolf, femme Guyard, see Ba 375, APP, and BB/24/759, AN.

102. Fontoulieu, *Les Eglises,* 182–83.

103. Ibid.

104. Corbin, *Women for Hire,* 132–33.

105. *Nana* first appeared in book form in February 1880, but had been serialized over the previous months in the newspaper *Le Voltaire.* According to Frederick Brown, Zola first conceived of *Nana* in 1869; he quotes Zola's plan for "a novel whose setting is the boudoir world and whose heroine is . . . the daughter of my working-class family. [She] is a creature noxious to society." Emile Zola, quoted in Brown, *Zola: A Life,* 414–15, 431–34; Emile Zola, *Nana,* translated by George Holden (1880; reprint, London: Penguin Books, 1972), 311.

106. Hollis Clayson, *Painted Love: Prostitution in French Art of the Impressionist Era* (New Haven, Conn.: Yale University Press, 1991), 64.

107. Brown, *Zola,* 427.

108. Maitron, *Dictionnaire biographique,* vol. 6, 424.

109. Fontoulieu, *Les Eglises,* 77.

110. Ibid.

111. Ibid., 182–83.

112. Ibid., 105.

113. André Léo, *Marianne,* Descaves Collection, IISH; Zola, *Nana;* Perrot, "Roles and Characters," 246–49; Weeks, *Sex, Politics, and Society,* 30–32; McMillan, *Housewife or Harlot,* 9–10.

114. Léo, *Marianne,* Descaves Collection.

115. Marguerite Guinder Prévost, "Rapport à la Commission des grâces," BB/24/759, AN.

116. Prévost, "Rapport," BB/24/759, AN.

117. Rapport sur l'affaire de la nommée Dmitrieff Elisabeth, Division Militaire, LY 7, AHG.

118. For a fascinating short history of the term *amazon*, see Gullickson, *Unruly Women*, 86–89.

119. Léo, *La Femme et les mœurs*, 26.

120. Fernanda Gastaldello discusses the centrality of education in Léo's work. Gastaldello, *André Léo*, 324, 330–54.

121. Edwards, *The Paris Commune 1871*, 267.

122. André Léo, "La Revolution sans la femme," *La Sociale*, May 8, 1871.

123. See Chapter 5 for working-class women's political clubs during the Commune.

124. Comité republican de vigilance des citoyennes à Citoyens membres de la Commune, 13 Germinal year 79, LY22, AHG.

125. Michel, *Memoirs*, 59.

126. "Société de la revendication des droits de la femme," dossier André Léo, Descaves Collection, IISH.

127. Quoted in Hunt, "Feminism and Anti-Clericalism," 419–20.

128. Edwards, *Paris Commune*, 267.

129. Laura Strumingher, *Women and the Making of the Working Class*, 65.

130. Hunt, "Feminism and Anti-Clericalism," 419.

131. *Le Père Duchêne* (Paris), 20 Germinal year 79.

132. In May 1871, *Le Père Duchêne* printed 50,000 copies, reaching the level of *Le Figaro* and *La Marseillaise*. Edwards, *Paris Commune*, 279.

133. Historian Linda Kerber coined the term "Republican Motherhood." Linda Kerber, *Women of the Republic: Intellect and Ideology in Revolutionary America* (Chapel Hill: University of North Carolina Press, 1980; reprint, New York: W. W. Norton, 1986), v–vi, 235.

134. *Le Père Duchêne*, 20 Germinal year 79.

135. Thomas, *Women Incendiaries*, 112–13.

136. The three male members of *l'Education nouvelle* were J. Manier, J. Rama, and Rheims. *Journal officiel*, April 2, 1871.

137. Ibid.

138. Ibid.

139. Isabelle Bricard, *Saintes ou pouliches: l'éducation des jeunes filles au XIXe siècle* (Paris: Albin Michel, 1985), 157–58.

140. *Le Cri du peuple*, May 21, 1871, quoted in Thomas, *Women Incendiaries*, 118.

141. Tinayre, who, under the late Second Empire, established a consumer cooperative, the *Société des équitables de Paris*, and spoke at Parisian political meetings, published novels under the male pseudonym Jules Paty. Thomas, *Women Incendiaries*, 10–14; Bruhat, Dautry, and Tersen, eds., *La Commune de 1871*, 182.

142. Fontoulieu, *Les Eglises*, 49–50.

143. "Comité des femmes de la rue d'Arras," Carton LY22, AHG.

144. *Journal officiel*, May 15 and 17, 1871.

145. *Le Vengeur*, April 3, 1871, quoted in *The Communards of Paris, 1871*, edited by Stewart Edwards (Ithaca, N.Y.: Cornell University Press, 1973), 115–16.

146. *Journal officiel*, May 22, 1871.

147. Léo, *Le Siècle* (Paris), July 16, 1870.

148. *Journal officiel*, April 2, 1871.

5. PAULE MINK AND THE *CLUBISTES*

1. François Bournand, *Le Clergé pendant la Commune* (Paris: Tolra, 1871), 138–39.
2. Ibid.
3. Edwards, *The Paris Commune 1871*, 277–79; Alain Dalotel, "Les femmes dans les clubs rouges, 1870–1871," in *Femmes dans la cité*, 300–301.
4. Bournand, *Le Clergé*, 140.
5. By rejecting all links between state and religion, Dmitrieff and Léo also abandoned the traditional French revolutionary anti-clerical stance.
6. Paule Mink, "Le Mariage et le divorce," in Dalotel, ed., *Paule Minck*, 143.
7. Marforio, *Les Echarpes rouges*, 15–16; Fontoulieu, *Les Eglises*, 49–50, 113, 271–72; Boxer, "Socialism Faces Feminism," 87; Dalotel, ed., *Paule Minck*, 18–19.
8. Dalotel, *Paule Minck*, 19. Her post-Commune activism is quite well documented in her extensive police file and in newspaper articles and accounts. See Chapter 6.
9. *Union des femmes*, organizational documents, LY 22, AHG; Dalotel, "Les Femmes dans les clubs rouges," 300–301.
10. Of particular value and interest is the deeply anti-Communard, pro-clerical Abbé Paul Fontoulieu's *Les Eglises de Paris sous la Commune*, a highly detailed, and rather reliable, compendium of political club meetings held in churches. The Abbé Fontoulieu occasionally wrote for *Le Figaro*, and he journalistically investigated the clubs and their members' words and actions within their church meeting places. As Martin Johnson has pointed out, Fontoulieu has been used as a primary source by historians ranging from William Serman to Jean Maitron and Jacques Rougerie. Other specific sources will be discussed as they appear in the subsequent notes. Fontoulieu, *Les Eglises;* Johnson, *The Paradise of Association*, 290.
11. Fontoulieu, *Les Eglises*, 195.
12. Jones and Vergès, "'Aux Citoyennes!,'" 23–25.
13. Quoted in Baron Marc de Villiers, *Histoire de femmes et des légions d'amazones, 1793–1848–1871* (Paris: Plon-Nourrit, 1910), 397–98.
14. M.G. de Molinari, *Les Clubs rouges péndant le siège de Paris* (Paris: Garnier Frères, 1871); Dalotel, "Les Femmes dans les clubs rouges," 293–95.
15. Malon, *La Troisième défaite*, 270.
16. Quoted in Jacques Rougerie, "1871: La Commune de Paris," in Christine Faure, ed. *Encyclopédie politique et historique des femmes* (Paris: Presses Universitaires de France, 1997), 427. Rougerie does not note the source of this quotation. Alain Dalotel notes that Marc de Villiers, Fontoulieu, and Edith Thomas each placed Léo speaking in a club one time, but each suggested a different club: de Villiers's was the itinerant *Club de délivrance;* Fontoulieu's was the *Club de la révolution* at *Saint-Michel des Batignolles,* and Thomas's was *la Trinité*. Dalotel reasonably doubts the verity of Marc de Villiers's contention, arguing that the discourse was unlike Léo's. Fontoulieu merely noted her presence, and Thomas wrote that Léo "set forth the tenets of socialism," thus making it difficult to discern the certainty of these claims. Alain Dalotel, "Les Femmes dans les clubs rouges," unpublished manuscript, note 43, BMD. This is an earlier version of Dalotel's article of the same name in *Femmes dans la cité*.
17. Malon, *La Troisième défaite*, 269.
18. Moss, *French Labor Movement*, 3.

19. Ibid., 271–72.

20. Paule Mink, "Ni dieu, ni maître," 1881, in *Paule Minck*, 104; "Extrait d'un Rapport de Genève, 18 Mars 1872," Paule Mink, BA 1178, APP.

21. Club Saint-Ambroise, LY 22, AHG, Paris.

22. Quoted in Fontoulieu, *Les Eglises*, 255–56.

23. Marforio, *Les Echarpes rouges*, 10–11, 22–25.

24. Ralph Gibson, "Why Republicans and Catholics Couldn't Stand Each Other in the Nineteenth Century," in *Religion, Society and Politics in France since 1789*, edited by Frank Tallett and Nicholas Atkin (London: Hambledon Press, 1991), 113–16.

25. Ibid.; Theodore Zeldin, *France: 1848–1945*, vol. II: *Intellect, Taste and Anxiety* (Oxford: Oxford University Press, 1977), 124–27.

26. Paule Mink, "Le Mariage et le divorce," November 3, 1868, in *Paule Minck*, 142–43.

27. Ibid.

28. The *Union des femmes* faced this competition during the Commune. "Travail des femmes: Projet d'organisation sous diverses formes," *Union des femmes*, LY 23, AHG; Paule Mink, " La Lutte des femmes," *Paule Minck*, 133; Strumingher, *Women and the Making of the Working Class*, 8–9, 13, 58–61; Hunt, "Feminism and Anti-Clericalism," 420; Roger Magraw, *The Age of Artisan Revolution, 1815–1871*, vol. I of *A History of the French Working Class* (Oxford: Blackwell, 1992), 253–58.

29. Dalotel, Faure, and Freiermuth, *Aux origines*, 200–205.

30. Quoted in ibid., 201.

31. Ibid.

32. In an 1883 speech, Paule Mink would refer to Jesus Christ as the first socialist. She blamed his followers for misinterpreting and misapplying his teachings. "Rapport," Paris, 17 April 1883, PM, APP.

33. Edward Berenson, "A New Religion of the Left: Christianity and Social Radicalism in France, 1815–1848," in *The Transformation of Political Culture 1789–1848*, vol. 3 of *The French Revolution and the Creation of Modern Political Culture*, ed. François Furet and Mona Ozouf (New York: Pergamon Press, 1989), 543–45; Magraw, *The Age of Artisan Revolution*, 253–54.

34. The population of parish clergy democratized significantly in the nineteenth century, shifting from the *Ancien Regime* dominance by elites, to a peasant and artisan class majority in the post-Revolutionary era. Ralph Gibson, *A Social History of French Catholicism 1789–1914* (New York: Routledge, 1989), 68–69, 141; Magraw, *Artisan Revolution*, 253–54.

35. The number of women's religious orders also grew enormously over the century. Judith F. Stone, "Anticlericals and *Bonnes Soeurs:* The Rhetoric of the 1901 Law of Associations," *French Historical Studies* 23, no. 1 (Winter 2000): 108–109; James F. McMillan, "Religion and Gender in Modern France: Some Reflections," in *Religion, Society and Politics*, 55–58; Gibson, *French Catholicism*, 152–53.

36. Hazel Mills, "Negotiating the Divide: Women, Philanthropy and the 'Public Sphere' in Nineteenth-Century France," in *Religion, Society and Politics*, 37–39; Stone, "Anticlericals," 109; McMillan, "Religion and Gender," 58.

37. McMillan, "Religion and Gender," 63.

38. René Redmond, *L'Anticléricalism en France de 1815 à nos jours* (Paris: Fayard, 1999), 26–27; Stone, "Anticlericals," 105–106.

39. Theodore Zeldin, "The Conflict of Moralities: Confession, Sin and Pleasure in the Nineteenth Century," in *Conflicts in French Society: Anticlericalism, Education, and Morals in the Nineteenth Century*, edited by Theodore Zeldin (London: George Allen and Unwin, 1970), 32–35; Stone, "Anticlericals," 105–106.

40. Fontoulieu, *Les Eglises*, 255.

41. According to l'abbé Delmas, twenty-four priests were killed during the Commune. The Sixth Council of War military tribunal, however, established under marshall law after the Commune, counted fifty-three executed priests. L'abbé Delmas, *La Terreur et l'église en 1871* (Paris: E. Dentu, Librairie-Editeur, 1871): 175–76; L.-P. Guénin, *Massacre de la rue Haxo, Sixième Conseil de Guerre, compte rendu in extenso des débats* (Paris: Librairie de "l'Echo de la Sorbonne," 1872), 3.

42. "Deposition de Mme. Pouisier," in L.-P. Guénin, *Massacre de la rue Haxo*, 147.

43. Rémond, *L'Anticléricalism en France*, 26–27.

44. "Prêtraille" is a derogatory term for priests. This speaker is the same unnamed *Montrouge clubiste* who termed priests "a monstrosity" and called for their deaths. See note 23. Marforio, *Les Echarpes rouges*, 24.

45. Ibid.

46. *Le Cri du peuple*, May 12, 1871.

47. Ibid.

48. Investigations later determined that the bones were approximately 150 years old. Christiansen, *Paris Babylon*, 334; Rémond, *L'Anticléricalism en France*, 169–70.

49. Fontoulieu, *Les Eglises*, 298.

50. Briot à Ministère de la Guerre, LY 7, AHG, Paris.

51. Fontoulieu, *Les Eglises*, 198.

52. Ehret had denounced the *curé*'s nephew, of the same name, for smuggling sensitive Commune government documents to the Versailles government. She therefore played no intentional role in the priest's arrest, and was subsequently acquitted. Marie Madrut, femme Ehret, BB/24/773, AN.

53. See note 41.

54. Marie Cailleux, Séries Ba, carton 375, APP; Marie Cailleux, BB/24/759, AN.

55. Cailleux, Séries Ba, carton 375, APP.

56. Marie Wolf, femme Guyard, Séries Ba, carton 375, APP.

57. Berenson, *Madame Caillaux*, 11, 243–44.

58. Marie Wolf, femme Guyard, BB/24/759, A.N.

59. Fontoulieu, *Les Eglises*, 105.

60. Quoted in Thomas, *Women Incendiaries*, 195.

61. Wolf, BB/24/759, AN.

62. Bournand, *Le Clergé*, 143–47. *Saint Sulpice* had a long revolutionary history, dating to its transformation in 1793 to the *Temple de la Raison*, and subsequently the *Temple de la Victoire*. On 15 Brumaire, three days before the coup d'etat, it was the site of a banquet honoring Napoleon on his return from Egypt. Fontoulieu, *Les Eglises*, 247.

63. Bournand, *Le Clergé*, 147–48.

64. Ibid., 148–49. Fontoulieu explained that women, including Louise Michel, only began to frequent the club *Saint Sulpice* in its final days, at which point they came to dominate it. Fontoulieu, *Les Eglises*, 254–55.

65. Fontoulieu, *Les Eglises*, 248–50.

66. Fontoulieu, *Les Eglises*, 11–12. The author rejected the use of the democratic revolutionary title *"citoyenne,"* as these women would most likely have also. Reminiscent of 1793, market women opposed the revolution, with its inherent disruption of normal buying and selling, the tendency of suppliers to hoard, and the difficulty of obtaining goods.

67. Ibid., 337.

68. Ibid., 220–29.

69. Ibid., 228.

70. Ibid.

71. Léo, *La Sociale*, May 8, 1871.

72. Delmas, *La Terreur et l'église*, 99.

73. Ibid.

74. Lynn Hunt, *Politics, Culture, and Class in the French Revolution* (Berkeley: University of California Press, 1984), 28, 32, 63–65, 98; Roger Chartier, *The Cultural Origins of the French Revolution,* translated by Lydia G. Cochrane (Durham, N.C.: Duke University Press, 1991), 93–110.

75. Edward Berenson, *Populist Religion and Left-Wing Politics in France, 1830–1852* (Princeton, N.J.: Princeton University Press, 1984), 36–37.

76. Fontoulieu, *Les Eglises*, 128.

77. Ibid., 175.

78. Magraw, *Artisan Revolution*, 257–58.

79. I am grateful to Edward Berenson for this point.

80. As Martin Johnson explains, communarde anti-clericalism was clearly not solely an effort to resurrect the revolutionary past, but a product of their lived experiences. Martin Johnson, "Memory and the Cult of Revolution in the 1871 Paris Commune," *Journal of Women's History* 9, no. 1 (Spring 1997): 39–57.

81. de Villiers, *Histoire des clubs*, 399.

82. Fontoulieu, *Les Eglises*, 78.

83. Quoted in de Villiers, *Histoire des clubs*, 402.

84. Ibid.

85. Fontoulieu, *Les Eglises*, 272.

86. Ibid.

87. Ibid.

88. Marforio, *Les Echarpes rouges*, 15–16.

89. Ibid., 20–21.

90. Fontoulieu, *Les Eglises*, 184.

91. Quoted in John Leighton, *Paris Under the Commune* (London: Bradbury Evans, 1871), 282–83.

92. Quoted in Fontoulieu, *Les Eglises*, 256.

93. Rapport de Commissaire de police, 18e arrondissement, Louise Michel, LY 23, AHG.

94. "Affaire Louise Michel, 6e Conseil de guerre de Versailles, Présidence du colonel Delaporte," *Gazette des Tribunaux*, December 16, 1871, Ba 1183, APP.

95. Louise Michel, BB/24/822, AN.

96. "Affaire Louise Michel," *Gazette des Tribunaux*, APP.

97. "Affaire Louise Michel," in Michel, *The Red Virgin*, 85.

98. Michel reiterated her confessions of sole responsibility in a series of letters

to government authorities. Louise Michel à Messieurs les colonels présidents des 3e et 4e conseils de guerre, August 21, 1871; Louise Michel à Monsieur le président et Messieurs les membres de la commission des grâce, n.d. [written in 1871, around the anniversary of the September 4 fall of the Empire]; Louise Michel à Monsieur le président de la commission des grâce, September 9, 1871; Louise Michel à Général Appert, November 17, 1871. These letters are held in carton LY 23, AHG.

99. Leo Frankel headed the Commune government's Commission of Labor and Exchange, which supported and cooperated with Dmitrieff and the *Union des femmes*. Edith Thomas, *Louise Michel, ou La Velléda de l'anarchie* (Paris: Gallimard, 1971), 87–88.

100. Michel, *Memoirs*, 201.

101. Ibid., 66.

102. Fontoulieu, *Les Eglises*, 256.

103. Thomas, *Women Incendiaries*, 45 and 101.

104. Michel, *Memoirs*, 86 and 148.

105. Michel also belonged to the Montmartre Men's Vigilance Committee. Thomas, *Louise Michel*, 73.

106. Béatrix Excoffon, "Récit de Béatrix Excoffon," in Michel, *La Commune*, 407.

107. During the Prussian Siege, vigilance committees had elected a representative Central Committee of the Twenty Arrondisements on September 13, 1870. Vincent, *Between Marxism and Anarchism*, 24; Excoffon, "Récit," in Michel, *La Commune*, 407; Thomas, *Women Incendiaries*, 92.

108. Dalotel, "Les femmes," 294–97.

109. Michel, *Mémoires*, 126.

110. Quoted in Jean Maitron, ed., *Dictionnaire biographique du mouvement ouvrier français* (Paris: Les Editions Ouvrières, 1968), vol. 8, 471.

111. Ibid., vol. 5, 356; Thomas, *Women Incendiaries*, 40.

112. Soukhomline, "Deux femmes russes," 60–61; Barbara Alpern Engel, *Mothers and Daughters: Women of the Intelligentsia in Nineteenth-Century Russia* (Cambridge: Cambridge University Press, 1983), 66–67.

113. Rapport, "Au Sujet de la femme Jaclard," Préfecture de Police, January 31, 1872, BA 1123, APP.

114. Membres des comités, *Union des femmes*, LY 23, AHG.

115. Paris 11 décembre 1880, Dossier Mink, APP.

6. DMITRIEFF AND LÉO IN THE AFTERMATH

1. Guillaume, *L'Internationale*, vol. I, 167; Singer-Lecocq, *Rouge Elisabeth*, 170–71.

2. Hélène Gosset, "Les Polonais dans la Commune de Paris," *Europe* 64–65 (April–May 1951), 156.

3. Efremova and Ivanov, *Russkaia soratnitsa*, 165–67; Singer-Lecocq, *Rouge Elisabeth*, 170–71.

4. André Léo to Mathilde Roederer, August 2, 1871, Descaves Collection, IISH; Fernanda Gastaldello, ed., *André Léo, une journaliste de la Commune* (Paris: Editions du lérot, 1987), 61–63; Guillaume, *L'Internationale*, 167.

5. In the immediate post-Commune years, bourgeois feminism re-emerged prior to socialist feminism, because the majority of socialist feminists remained in prison or exile before the General Amnesty of 1880. See, for example, Moses, *French Feminism*, 193–96; Steven Hause, *Women's Suffrage and Social Politics in the French Third Re-*

public (Princeton, N.J.: Princeton University Press, 1984), 8; Barry, *Women and Political Insurgency*, 152–54. See also Roger Magraw, *Workers and the Bourgeois Republic* (Cambridge: Blackwell Publishers, 1992), 21; Johnson, *The Paradise of Association*, 284–85; Edwards, *The Paris Commune*, 351–52; and Michelle Perrot, *Workers on Strike: France, 1871–1890* (New Haven, Conn.: Yale University Press, 1987), 33.

6. Vuilleumier estimates that over 250 exiles were in Switzerland at the end of 1871. Marc Vuilleumier, "Les Proscrits de la Commune en Suisse (1871)," *Revue Suisse d'Histoire* (1962): 501.

7. Michel was the only Commune deportee to support the indigenous Kanak's 1878 uprising against colonial rule in New Caledonia, where she had been exiled to a prison colony. The other former Communards sided with the French imperial authorities, their jailers, based on their shared European-ness. Michel returned to France in 1879; Lemel in 1878. Matt K. Matsuda, *The Memory of the Modern* (New York: Oxford University Press, 1996); Michel, *Mémoires*, 218–54; Kerbaul, *Nathalie Le Mel*, 84.

8. Rapport sur l'affaire Dmitrieff, May 23, 1872, LY22, AHG.

9. Ibid.

10. Dmitrieff: demande de renseignements à Monsieur le Prefet de police à Paris, LY22, AHG.

11. Réponse, Le Chef du Cabinet du Préfet de Police, October 1, 1872, LY22, AHG.

12. Ibid.

13. Demande en grâce, BB 24/856, dossier 2382, AN.

14. Quoted in Singer-Lecocq, *Rouge Elisabeth*, 170–71.

15. Ibid., 173; Elisabeth Dmitrieva-Tomanovsky to Hermann Jung, April 24, 1871, in Jules Rocher, ed. *Lettres de communards et de militants de la 1re Internationale à Marx, Engels et autres dans les journées de la Commune de Paris en 1871* (Paris: Bureau d'Editions, 1934), 36.

16. Dmitrieva-Tomanovsky to Jung, in Rocher, ed., *Lettres de communards*, 36.

17. Singer-Lecocq suggests that Frankel had a strong romantic interest in Dmitrieff, which she did not return. Singer-Lecocq, *Rouge Elisabeth*, 173–74.

18. Ibid., 171.

19. Quoted in Martin R. Waldman, "The Revolutionary as Criminal in 19th-Century France: A Study of the Communards and Deportées," *Science and Society* XXXVII, no. 1 (September 1973): 40.

20. Ibid; Vuilleumier, "Les Proscrits," 500–503.

21. McClellan, *Revolutionary Exiles*, 181.

22. Singer-Lecocq, *Rouge Elisabeth*, 172–90.

23. Ibid., 188–89; Richard Stites, *The Women's Liberation Movement in Russia: Feminism, Nihilism, and Bolshevism, 1860–1930* (Princeton, N.J.: Princeton University Press, 1978), 116–28.

24. Efremova and Ivanov, *Russkaia soratnitsa Marksa*, 198–205.

25. Braibant, *Elisabeth Dmitrieff*, 184.

26. Ibid.; Efremova and Ivanov, *Russkaia soratnitsa Marksa*, 208; Singer-Lecocq, *Rouge Elisabeth*, 190–92.

27. Quoted in Singer-Lecocq, *Rouge Elisabeth*, 192–93.

28. Ibid.; Efremova and Ivanov, *Russkaia soratnitsa Marksa*, 205–207.

29. Singer-Lecocq, *Rouge Elisabeth*, 190.

30. Ibid., 197–200; Knizhnik-Vetrov, *Russkie deiatel'nitsy*, 119.

31. Nicholas Outine to Karl Marx, quoted in Singer-Lecocq, *Rouge Elisabeth*, 202–203.

32. Ibid.

33. The trip took several weeks. The train did not yet go far east beyond Moscow, and much of the trip was made by wagon and boat. Ibid., 211–16; Efremova and Ivanov, *Russkaia soratnitsa Marksa*, 208.

34. Stites, *Women's Liberation Movement*, 122–23.

35. Knizhnik-Vetrov, *Russkie deiatel'nitsy*, 125–30.

36. Braibant, *Elisabeth Dmitrieff*, 208–209; Singer-Lecocq, *Rouge Elisabeth*, 220–24.

37. Between the pastry shop and the mining, they had tried farming, with little success. Dmitrieff also had full responsibility for her daughters' educations, as there was no local school. Singer-Lecocq, *Rouge Elisabeth*, 221, 226–27.

38. Braibant, *Elisabeth Dmitrieff*, 219–23; Singer-Lecocq, *Rouge Elisabeth*, 220–24.

39. Adresse du Comité Central de l'Union des femmes à la Commission de travail et d'échange, LY22, AHG.

40. Guillaume, *L'Internationale*, vol. II, 167–71.

41. Ibid., 171.

42. André Léo to Mathilde Roederer, September 1, 1871, Descaves Collection, IISH.

43. Dossier Champseix (André Léo), Ba 1008, APP.; Gastaldello, *André Léo*, 61–76; Vuilleumier, "Les Proscrits."

44. The *Ligue* originated as a secret republican society under the Second Empire. Theresa McBride, "Divorce and the Republican Family," in *Gender and the Politics of Social Reform in France, 1870–1914*, edited by Elinor A. Accampo, Rachel G. Fuchs, and Mary Lynn Stewart (Baltimore: Johns Hopkins University Press, 1995), 61; Marc Vuilleumier, "Les Proscrits," 510–14.

45. Guillaume, *L'Internationale*, vol. II, 218.

46. André Léo, *La Guerre sociale: discours prononcé au Congrès de la Paix à Lausanne (1871)* (Neuchâtel: G. Guillaume Fils, 1871), 14–15.

47. Ibid., 12.

48. Ibid., 4.

49. Ibid., 28.

50. Gastaldello, *André Léo*, 212. Léo returns here to a theme both she and Mink addressed prior to the Commune (see my Chapter 2). She, in writings including *La Femme et les mœurs: liberté ou monarchie*, questioned whether anyone has liberty in a society in which it is denied to women, and argued that liberty is merely a prerequisite to justice; Mink, in "Liberty: the Condition of Socialism," asserted the essential role and balancing of both liberty and equality for true socialism to exist. Léo, *La Femme et les mœurs*, 52; Mink, "La Liberté: condition du socialisme," in Dalotel, ed., *Paule Minck*, 80–81.

51. Léo, *La Guerre sociale*, 25–26.

52. Ibid., 5.

53. Ibid., 7.

54. Ibid.

55. Ibid., 14–15.

56. Ibid.

57. Leo Gershoy, *The French Revolution, 1789–1799* (New York: Holt, Rinehart and Winston, 1932), 63; Edwards, *Paris Commune*, 346.

58. Léo, *La Guerre sociale*, 33.

59. Ibid., 35.

60. Gastaldello, *André Léo*, 215–16.

61. Vuilleumier, "Les Proscrits," 511–12.

62. The italics are in the original. Léo, *La Guerre sociale*, 37.

63. Ibid., 38.

64. Ibid.

65. "Le Congrès de la paix," *Liberté Belge*, October 4, 1871.

66. Ibid. Louis Blanc, a republican journalist and member of the Provisional Government of 1848, went into exile in London post-1848, and returned to Paris following the September 1870 declaration of the republic. Elected to the National Assembly in February 1871, Blanc opposed the Commune but, as a republican, he decried the extent of the subsequent repression. Edgar Quinet, a liberal historian, was also a republican member of the 1871 National Assembly. Edwards, *The Paris Commune*, 116, 380; Magraw, *France 1815–1914*, 88, 100, 125–26, 196.

67. Ibid.

68. *La Révolution sociale* appeared weekly between October 26, 1871, and January 4, 1872. Guillaume, *L'Internationale*, 219.

69. Vincent, *Between Marxism and Anarchism*, 45; Vuilluemier, "Les Proscrits," 520–22; Gastaldello, 64–65, 216–17. The London General Council was, as we have seen, the faction with which Elisabeth Dmitrieff had allied.

70. André Léo to Mathilde Roederer, October 21, 1871, quoted in Guillaume, *L'Internationale*, vol. II, 219.

71. Léo to Roederer, November 12, 1871, quoted in ibid., vol. II, 222.

72. *La Révolution sociale* (Geneva), November 2, 1871, quoted in ibid., vol. II, 220.

73. Guillaume, her political ally, wrote: "This phrase is regrettable. It offends us, and I have made it known to the author." *La Révolution sociale*, November 9, 1871, quoted in ibid., vol. II, 221–22.

74. Ibid.

75. Léo, "Signes précurseurs," 14.

76. Ibid.,13.

77. Ibid., 4.

78. Ibid., 9–10.

79. Her first husband, Grégoire Champseix, died in 1863. Lucien Descaves, "Sur Benoît Malon et André Léo," n.d., Dossier André Léo, Descaves Collection, IISH.

80. André Léo to Mathilde Roederer, June 1873, Descaves Collection, IISH.

81. Ibid.

82. Ibid.

83. Léo, *La Femme et les mœurs*, 21–22. Léo supported herself via her writing and her family wealth.

84. Léo, *Un Divorce*, 475.

85. Gastaldello, *André Léo*, 326–28.

86. Léo, *Les Deux Filles de M. Plichon*, 349.

87. John Stuart Mill, *The Subjection of Women* (1869; Cambridge, Mass.: MIT Press, 1977), 95.

88. Moses, *French Feminism*, 68, 84, 110–13, 148–49, 167; Dominique Desanti, "Flora Tristan: Rebel Daughter of the Revolution," in *Rebel Daughters: Women and the*

French Revolution, ed. Sara E. Melzer and Leslie W. Rabine (New York: Oxford University Press, 1992), 277–78; Offen, *European Feminisms,* 91, 113–15.

89. M. Duriez, "Eloge de *Un Mariage scandaleux,*" *Le Siècle,* September 4, 1863, reprinted in the appendix to Gastadello, *André Léo,* 364; Léo, *Un Mariage scandaleux.*

90. Léo, *Une Vieille Fille,* 148.

91. Léo, *Une Vieille Fille,* 191.

92. André Léo to Elise Grimm, March 13, 1878, Descaves Collection, IISH.

93. André Léo to Mathilde Roederer, April 6 (or 7), 1878, Descaves Collection, IISH.

94. Léo to Grimm, March 13, 1878.

95. Ibid.

96. Léo to Roederer, April 6 (or 7), 1878.

97. Gastaldello, following Guillaume, asserts that another reason for the marriage's failure was Malon's persistent infidelities. Steven Vincent argues that this is unclear, as Léo did not mention it in her letters, and Guillaume had accused Malon in the context of a larger negative portrayal. Nonetheless, Guillaume reprinted a rather damning letter from a Mme. A. Bauler regarding Malon's behavior. Gastaldello reprints this along with a letter from Léo warning a young friend not to romantically trust a man just because he is a "democrat." Malon's infidelity thus seems likely. The extent to which this contributed to the marriage's failure, however, remains unclear. Guillaume, *L'Internationale,* vol. III, 321–22; Gastaldello, *André Léo,* 68–69; Vincent, *Between Marxism and Anarchism,* 44.

98. Bruxelles le 2 avril, and Genève le 3 août 1872, Dossier Champseix (André Léo), Ba 1008, APP; Jean Maitron, ed., *La Première International et La Commune,* vol. 5 of *Dictionnaire biographique de mouvement ouvrier français, 1864–1871* (Paris: Les Editions Ouvrières, 1968), 52; Gastaldello, *André Léo,* 65–73.

99. André Léo, *En chemin de fer,* quoted in Gastaldello, *André Léo,* 71–72.

100. André Léo, *La Commune de Malenpis: conte* (Paris: Librairie de la Bibliothèque Democratique, 1874), 15.

101. Ibid., 191.

102. Sowerwine, *France since 1870,* 34–35.

103. Quoted in Georges-André Euloge, *Histoire de la police et de la gendarmerie: des origines à 1940* (Paris: Plon, 1985), 13.

104. Genève 3 août 1872, and Summaire: Leonie Béra Vve. Champseix, Dossier Champseix (André Léo), Ba 1008, APP.

105. Paris, 9 octobre 1873, Ba 1008, APP.

106. Genève, 2 avril 1872, Ba 1008, APP.

107. Paris, 31 mai 1878, Ba 1008, APP.

108. Londres, 20 novembre 1878, Ba 1008, APP.

109. André Léo to unknown, quoted in Lucien Descaves, "Cahier Noir," Descaves Collection, IISH. The "Cahier Noir" is a notebook of Descaves's notes on Léo, as well as letters he copied.

110. Lucien Descaves, "Une socialiste d'autrefois," *Le Petit Procençal* (Marseille), March 25, 1935, Descaves Collection, IISH; Gastaldello, *André Léo,* 372–79.

111. Lucien Descaves, "Sur Benoît Malon et André Léo," Descaves Collection, IISH.

112. It is unclear whether or not they had remained in contact. Vincent, *Beyond Marxism and Anarchism,* 135.

113. J. Engell-Gunther to André Léo, December 1886, Descaves Collection, IISH; Augusto Mazzuchetti to André Léo, December 1891, Descaves Collection, IISH; P. Bonnaud to André Léo, n.d., Descaves Collection, IISH.

114. Descaves, "Sur Benoît Malon," Dossier André Léo, IISH; Dombasle, "Une expérience collectiviste," *Le Siècle* (Paris), October 27, 1900.

115. In 1991, Alain Dalotel and members of the Association André Léo erected a stone on her grave reading "Mme. Champseix, Née Leodile Béra, Dite André Léo, Romancière Journaliste Feministe, Communarde, 1824–1900." (Madame Champseix, Born Leodile Béra, Known as André Léo, Novelist Journalist Feminist, Communarde, 1824–1900) Fernanda Gastaldello, *André Léo (1824–1900), femme écrivain au XIXe siècle* (Chauvigny: Association des publications chauvinoises, 2001), 38; Gastaldello, ed., preface to *André Léo, une journaliste de la Commune,* 3.

7. MINK IN THE AFTERMATH

1. "Obseques de Paule Mink," May 2, 1901, Dossier Paule Mink (Mekarska), Ba 1178, APP, Paris.

2. Guillaume, *L'Internationale,* 167.

3. "Nouvelles de Suisse," *Belge,* October 1, 1871, Ba 1178, APP.

4. Ibid.; Vuilleumier, "Les Proscrits," 513.

5. Extrait d'un Rapport de Genève, March 18, 1872, Paule Mink (PM), BA 1178, APP.

6. Mink, Discours prononcé le 27 septembre 1871 au Congrès de la Paix et de la Liberté, in Dalotel, ed., *Paule Minck,* 83.

7. Paule Mink, *L'Egalité,* Geneva.

8. Ibid.

9. Ibid.

10. Prior to the September 1870 fall of the Empire, most Blanquists boycotted the Parisian sections of the International, considering their heavily trade unionist membership "co-opted" for accepting Napoleon III's limited toleration of unions. The organization's new, post-1870 openness to Blanquists may have contributed to Mink's desire to not only remain affiliated with the association following her ideological shift, but also to see in it the potential for what she would have considered further positive change. Ibid.; Mink, "Congrès de la Paix," in Dalotel, ed., *Paule Minck,* 82–86; McClellan, *Revolutionary Exiles,* 48–51; Serman, *La Commune de Paris,* 62–65; Guillaume, *L'Internationale,* 6–24.

11. Versailles, June 20, 1872, Ba 431, APP; Dalotel, *Paule Minck,* 20–21; Vuilleumier, "Les proscrits," 503.

12. Mink later had two sons with her second husband, the worker Maxime Négro. See below.

13. Paris, February 5, 1872, Ba 1178, APP; May 7, 1872, Ba 1178 APP; *Versailles,* 20 June 1872, Ba 431, APP; Maitron, ed. *Dictionnaire biographique;* Marilyn J. Boxer, "Socialism Faces Feminism: The Failure of Synthesis in France, 1879–1914," in *Socialist Women: European Socialist Feminism in the Nineteenth and Early Twentieth Centuries,* eds. Marilyn J. Boxer and Jean H. Quataert (New York: Elsevier, 1978), 91; Dalotel, *Paule Minck,* 21.

14. Genève, March 30, 1872, Ba 431, APP.

15. They provide no explanation for her defeat, but one could assume that the members of the organization had an attitude similar to the informant's regarding a woman directing their group.

16. A Monsieur le Ministre du l'Intérior, Paris, May 20, 1872, Ba 1178; See also Genève, March 16, 1872, Ba 1178; Genève, March 21, 1872, Ba 1178; Genève, August 9, 1872, Ba 1178, APP.

17. Genève, May 11, 1872, Ba 1178, APP.

18. March 16, 1872, Ba 1178, APP.

19. Genève, August 9, 1872, Ba 1178, APP.

20. Vevey, March 1, 1872, Ba 1178, APP.

21. Genève, February 9, 1872, Ba 1178, APP; See the dossier Mink, Ba 431 and Ba 1178, APP.

22. June 1872, Ba 1178, APP.

23. Signalement de Paule Mink, Dossier Mink (Mekarska), Ba 1178, APP.

24. Summaire, Ba 1008, APP.

25. Versailles, June 20, 1872, Ba 431, APP.

26. Ibid.

27. Paris, January 22, 1880, Ba 1178, APP.

28. Chaux de fonds, March 21, 1880, Ba 1178, APP; *Petit-Lyonnais*, May 12, 1880, Ba 1178, APP; *Lyon-Republicain*, August 26, 1880, Ba 1178, APP; Boxer, "Socialism Faces Feminism," 94.

29. Paris, October 2, 1880, Ba 1178, APP.

30. Ibid.; Boxer, "Socialism Faces Feminism," 94–97.

31. Paris, le . . . 188 . . . , PM, APP. This undated document has "188_" printed at the top. Its content indicates that it was written in the mid-1880s.

32. Paris, November 25, 1880, Ba 1178, APP.

33. Paule Mink to Louise Michel, December 14, 1880, in *Je vous écris da ma nuit: correspondance générale de Louise Michel, 1850–1904* (Paris: Les Editions de Paris, 1999), 266–67.

34. Ibid.

35. Edith Thomas, *Louise Michel*, translated by Penelope Williams (Montreal: Black Rose Books, 1980), 168–69.

36. Quoted in Anne Sizaire, *Louise Michel: l'absolu de la générosité* (Paris: Desclée de Brouwer, 1995), 96–97.

37. Ibid., 97–99; Bullitt Lowry and Elizabeth Ellinton Gunter, introduction to *The Red Virgin: Memoirs of Louise Michel* (Tuscaloosa: The University of Alabama Press, 1981), xi.

38. Thomas, *Louise Michel*, 279–82.

39. Gullickson, *Unruly Women*, 147–57.

40. Edith Thomas asserts that "unlike the other women of the Commune, [Michel] wrote a great deal." Thomas clearly had not discovered Léo's substantial oeuvre, which rivaled Michel's. Thomas, *Louise Michel*, 12.

41. Hutton, *The Cult of Revolutionary Tradition*. For examples of Mink's use of revolutionary references, see, among many other documents and clippings Mink's Ba 1178 file in the APP, Paris, October 2, 1880, Ba 1178; *Lyon-Republicain*, May 1, 1880, Ba 1178; *L'Intransigeant*, April 7, 1884.

42. Paris, April 15, 1883, Ba 1178, APP.

43. Paris, April 17, 1883, PM, APP.

44. Montpellier, 18 Mars—télégramme, PM, APP.

45. *Bataille,* March 4, 1883.

46. Lyon, November 7, 1880, Ba 1178, APP.

47. Boxer, "Socialism Faces Feminism," 103–12.

48. *L'Intransigeant,* November 25 and 27, 1880, quoted in ibid., 109, 112.

49. Boxer, "Socialism Faces Feminism," 109–12.

50. Ibid., 107, 113.

51. Toulon, March 23, 1881, Ba 1178, APP.

52. *Révolution Sociale,* April 3, 1881.

53. Hutton, *Cult of the Revolutionary,* 60, 88, 111–13.

54. Mink spoke at Blanqui's funeral. See below.

55. Paule Mink to Louise Michel, copy, Toulon, April 9, 1881, Ba 1178, APP.

56. Jessa Helfmann's name, transliterated from the Russian, occasionally appears as Gesya Helfman (Boxer), Guessia Helfman (Dalotel), or Gessa Gelfman (Stites). *L'Intransigeant* (Paris), May 10, 1881.

57. Stites, *Women's Liberation,* 148.

58. Lyon, May 23, 1881, Ba 1178, APP; Jean-Marie Mayeur and Madeleine Rebérioux, *The Third Republic from its Origins to the Great War, 1871–1914* (Cambridge: Cambridge University Press, 1984), 41, 71–81; Boxer, "Socialism Faces Feminism," 118.

59. Paris, May 29, 1881, Ba 1178, APP.

60. Lyon, May 23, 1881, Ba 1178, APP.

61. *Le Citoyen,* May 26, 1881, Ba 1178, APP.

62. Ibid.

63. Ibid.; *Le procès de Marseille,* June 20, 1881. Marilyn Boxer cites Charles Vérecque's recollection that Mink was the first woman to brandish the revolutionary red flag in France after the Commune. Boxer, "Socialism Faces Feminism," 118.

64. Paule Mink to M. Cazot, June 3, 1881, copy, Ba 1178, APP.

65. Ruth Harris, *Murders and Madness: Medicine, Law, and Society in the Fin de Siècle* (Oxford: Clarendon Press, 1989), 19.

66. Paule Mink to M. Cazot, June 3, 1881, copy, Ba 1178, APP.

67. Ibid.

68. Paule Mink to Louise Michel, copy, Marseilles, June 5, 1881, Ba 1178, APP.

69. *L'Excommunié* (Grenoble), July 3, 1881, Ba 1178, APP.

70. *Le Citoyen,* June 23, 1881.

71. In 1890, a judge attempted to institutionalize Michel when she protested a judicial decision that she felt privileged her, because of her renown, over her fellow protestors and co-defendants. Pierre Durand, *Louise Michel: la passion* (Paris: Messidor, 1987), 170–71; *Paris,* June 27, 1881, Ba 1178, APP; *Paris,* June 3, 1881, Ba 1178, APP; *L'Excommunié,* July 3, 1881.

72. Mink's supporters also held a demonstration in Paris, protesting the conditions of her imprisonment, and publicly reading two letters she had addressed to the president of the republic and to his son regarding her treatment while incarcerated. Paris, June 20, 1881, Ba 1178, APP. The Marseilles authorities subsequently released Mink from prison a day before her sentence was complete, specifically to avoid the demonstration her supporters had planned for her official discharge. *Nouvelliste* (Marseilles), July 2, 1881, Ba 1178, APP; *Siècle,* July 2, 1881, Ba 1178, APP; *Courrier de Lyon,* July 3, 1881, Ba 1178, APP.

73. *Le Moniteur,* July 10, 1881.

74. Mink had been awarded the Legion of Honor for her efforts, but she refused to accept the accolade from a government she disdained. Ibid.

75. "Un Mariage obligatoire," *Le Petit Provençal,* July 19, 1881.

76. Her first husband, Bohdanowicz, had died at some time before this. Boxer, "Socialism Faces Feminism," 343–44, n. 43.

77. *Le Pays,* July 19, 1881.

78. *Henri IV,* July 21, 1881.

79. *France Nouvelle,* September 4, 1881.

80. She was referring to the *loi du 11 germinal an XI* (Law of April 1, 1803), which stated "Only those names found on different calendars and those of people renowned in ancient history will be accepted as given names in *état civil* registers for recording the birth of children, and it is forbidden for public officers to admit any other name." Anne Lefebvre-Teillard, *Le Nom: droit et histoire* (Paris: Presses Universitaires de France, 1990); Marie-Louise Néron, "Les Morts d'hier," *La Fronde,* April 29, 1901, Dossier Paule Mink, BMD, Paris; *Bataille,* March 1, 1884.

81. Mayeur and Reberioux, *The Third Republic,* 81–90.

82. Paris, December 7, 1880, Ba 1178, APP.

83. Paris, December 7, 1880, Ba 1178, APP.

84. Paris, October 11, 1880, Ba 1178, APP.

85. Paris, April 17, 1883, Ba 1178, APP.

86. Mayeur and Reberioux, *The Third Republic,* 83–90.

87. Paris, April 17, 1883, Ba 1178, APP.

88. Paris, April 8, 1883, Ba 1178, APP.

89. June 1884, Ba 1178, APP.

90. Paris, October 2, 1880, Ba 1178, APP.

91. Paris, April 20, 1884, Ba 1178, APP; Hubertine Auclert, *La Citoyenne,* February 13, 1881, quoted in James H. McMillan, *France and Women 1789–1914: Gender, Society, and Politics* (New York: Routledge, 2000), 188. Auclert published the newspaper *La Citoyenne* from 1881 to 1891.

92. Dalotel, *Paule Minck,* 25–26.

93. I thank Karen Offen for pointing out this simultaneity. Mayeur and Reberioux, *The Third Republic,* 83.

94. *European Feminisms,* 51–52.

95. Hubertine Auclert, "Egalité sociale et politique de la femme et de l'homme," quoted and translated in Offen and Bell, *Women, the Family, and Freedom: The Debate in Documents,* vol. I (Stanford, Calif.: Stanford University Press, 1983), 511, 515–17; Klejman and Rochefort, *L'Egalité en marche,* 209–10.

96. Offen and Bell, *Women, the Family* vol. I, 511; *Lyon,* November 7, 1880, Ba 1178, APP; Boxer, "Socialism Faces Feminism," 103–13.

97. Marilyn Boxer, "'First Wave' Feminism in Nineteenth-Century France: Class, Family, and Religion," *Women's Studies International Forum* 5, no. 6 (1982): 553; McMillan, *France and Women,* 188–91. Auclert also wrote about and critiqued the condition of women under imperialism and colonialism, particularly in Algeria where she lived for four years. See articles in her newspaper *La Citoyenne* (1881–1891), and Hubertine Auclert, *Les Femmes arabes en Algérie.* Paris: Société d'Editions Littéraires, 1900.

98. Judith Stone, "The Republican Brotherhood: Gender and Ideology," in *Gender*

and the Politics of Social Reform in France, 1870–1914 (Baltimore: Johns Hopkins University Press, 1995), 55–58.

99. For feminism, gender, Guesde, and the POF, see Robert Stuart's articles: "'Calm, with a Grave and Serious Temperament, Rather Male': French Marxism, Gender and Feminism, 1882–1905," *International Review of Social History* 41 (1996): 57–82; "Whores and Angels: Women and the Family in the Discourse of French Marxism 1882–1905," *European History Quarterly* 27, no. 3 (1997): 339–69; "Gendered Labour in the Ideological Discourse of French Marxism: The Parti Ouvrier Français, 1882–1905," *Gender and History* (1997): 107–29.

100. See police documents for these years in Mink's dossier Ba 1178, APP.

101. Dalotel, *Paule Minck*, 25–29; Stuart, "Calm," 61–66, 69–70.

102. Quoted in Dalotel, *Paule Minck*, 29.

103. Maitron, *Dictionnaire biographique.*

104. Sowerwine, *Sisters or Citizens?*, 70–71; Dalotel, *Paule Minck*, 29–30.

105. Hause and Kenney, *Women's Suffrage and Social Politics*, 48; Sowerwine, *Sisters or Citizens?*, 70–71.

106. March 1893, Ba 1178, APP.

107. *Germinal*, April 7, 1893; *L'Eclair*, April 7,1893; *Le Cri du peuple*, April 7, 1893.

108. *Germinal*, April 7, 1893.

109. *La Petite république*, August 19, 1893.

110. Ibid.

111. Boxer, "Socialism Faces Feminism," in *Socialist Women*, 85–86.

112. Dalotel, *Paule Minck*, 32; Maitron, *Dictionnaire biographique.*

113. *Germinal*, April 7, 1893.

114. Paris, October 2, 1880, Ba 1178, APP.

115. *Germinal*, April 7, 1893. This is a similar argument to that used by suffragists in the United States.

116. *La Petite république*, August 19, 1893.

117. *L'Eclair*, May 1, 1893.

118. *La Petite république*, April 4, July 2, August 22, 1895, and August 28, 1897, quoted in Boxer, "Socialism Faces Feminism," 172–74.

119. Boxer, "Socialism Faces Feminism," 172–74.

120. Paule Mink to Louise Michel, August 21, 1899, carton 4248, Fonds Marie-Louise Bouglé, BHVP.

121. *La Petite république*, May 2, 1895.

122. *Les Trois huit*, May 2, 1898.

123. "Obseques de Paule Mink," May 2, 1901, Ba 1178, APP.

CONCLUSION

1. Léo, "Toutes avec tous," April 12, 1871.

BIBLIOGRAPHY

ARCHIVES

Archives de la Préfecture de la Police (APP), Paris.
Archives Historiques de la Guerre (AHG), Vincennes, Paris.
Archives Nationale (AN), Paris.
Bibliothèque Historique de la Ville de Paris (BHVP), Paris.
Bibliothèque Marguerite Durand (BMD), Paris.
Bibliothèque Nationale (BN), Paris.
International Institute for Social History (IISH), Descaves Collection, Amsterdam.
University of Sussex Library, Schulkind Collection, Sussex, England.

PRIMARY SOURCES

Adam, Juliette Lamber. *Mes angoisses et nos luttes, 1871–1873.* Paris: Alphonse Lemerre, 1907.
———. *Idées anti-proudhonniennes sur l'amour, la femme et le mariage.* Paris: A. Taride, 1858.
———. *Mes illusions et nos souffrances pendant le Siège de Paris.* Paris: Alphonse Lemerre, 1906.
L'Agriculteur. Paris, 1870.
Arnould, Arthur. *Histoire populaire et parlementaire de la Commune de Paris.* Reprint, Lyon: Editions Jacques-Marie Laffont, 1981.
Assemblée Nationale. *Enquête parlementaire sur l'insurrection du 18 mars.* 3 vols. Paris: Librairie Législative—A. Wittersheim, 1872.
Auclert, Hubertine. *La Citoyenne.* February 13, 1881.
———. "Egalité sociale et politique de la femme et de l'homme." Translated and quoted in *Women, the Family, and Freedom: The Debate in Documents,* vol. 1, edited by Karen Offen and Susan Groag Bell. Stanford, Calif.: Stanford University Press, 1983.
———. *Les Femmes arabes en Algérie.* Paris: Société d'Editions Litteraires, 1900.
Audebrand, Philibert. *Histoire intime de la révolution du 18 mars.* Paris: E. Dentu, 1871.
Bakunin, Mikhail. "Revolutionary Catechism." In *Bakunin on Anarchy,* edited and translated by Sam Dolgoff. New York: Alfred A. Knopf, 1972.
Barberet, J. *Le Mouvement ouvrier à Paris de 1870–1874.* Paris: Librairie de la Bibliothèque Ouvrière, 1874.
Bargès, J.-J.-L. *Notre-Dame des Victoires pendant la Commune.* Paris: Lecoffre, 1889.
Belge. October 1871.
Blanchecotte, Augustine-Malvine. *Tablettes d'une femme pendant la Commune.* Paris: Didier et Cie, 1872.

Bournand, François. *Le Clergé pendant la Commune*. Paris: Tolra, 1871.

Bowen, W. E. *Edward Bowen: A Memoir*. London: Longmans, Green, and Co., 1902.

Breuil, Maxime. *Deux discours sur le travail des femmes*. Paris: Armand le Chevalier, 1868.

Brocher, Victorine. *Victorine B . . . Souvenirs d'une morte vivante*. Reprint, Paris: François Maspero, 1977.

Le Citoyen. May 1881.

Commission ouvrière de 1867: recueil des procès-verbaux. Paris: Imprimerie Augros, 1868.

La Commune. Paris, March–May 1871.

Le Corsaire. Paris, September 1872.

Coullié, L'Abbé Pierre-Hector. *Saint-Eustache pendant la Commune*. 4th edition. Paris: Imprimerie et Librairie Administratives, 1872.

Le Cri du peuple. Paris, March–May 1871.

Dauban, C.A., ed. *La Fond de la société sous la Commune*. Paris: E. Plon, 1873.

Daubié, Julie-Victoire. *La Femme pauvre au XIX siècle*. Translated and quoted in Karen Offen and Susan Groag Bell, eds., *Women, the Family, and Freedom*, vol. I. Stanford, Calif.: Stanford University Press, 1983.

de Villiers, Baron Marc. *Histoire des clubs de femmes et des légions d'amazones 1793–1848–1871*. Paris: Plon-Nourrit, 1910.

Delmas, l'Abbé. *La Terreur et l'église en 1871*. Paris: E. Dentu, 1871.

Delpit, M. Martial. *Le Dix-huit mars: récit des faits et recherche des causes de l'insurrection*. Paris: Chez Léon Techener, 1872.

Descaves Collection, IISH, Amsterdam.

Desvernay, Arnould. *Rapports des delegations ouvrières: contenant l'origine et l'histoire des diverses professions, l'appréciation des objets exposés, la comparaison des arts et des industries en France et a l'étranger, l'exposé des vœux et besoins de la classe laborieuse, et l'ensemble des considérations sociales intéressant les ouvriers . . . 3 vols*. Paris: A. Morel, 1869.

Dossier de la Commune devant les Conseils de Guerre. Paris: Librairie des Bibliophiles, 1871.

L'Egalité. Paris, March–May 1871.

L'Emancipation. Toulouse, January 1872.

Etudes sociales. Marseilles: Imprimerie Générale J. Doucet, 1880.

Excoffon, Béatrix. "Récit de Béatrix Excoffon." In *La Commune*. Louise Michel. 3rd ed. Paris: P. V. Stock, 1898.

Fonds Marie-Louise Bouglé, BHVP.

Fontoulieu, Paul. *Les Eglises des Paris sous la Commune*. Paris: E. Dentu, 1873.

Fribourg, E. E. *L'Association internationale des travailleurs*. Paris: Armand le Chevalier, 1871.

Gazette des tribunaux. Paris, 1871.

Goncourt, Edmond, and Jules Goncourt. *Paris Under Siege, 1870–1871*. Edited and translated by George J. Becker. Ithaca, N.Y.: Cornell University Press, 1969.

Guénin, L.-P. *Massacre da la rue Haxo*. Paris: Librarie de "l'Echo de la Sorbonne," 1872.

Guesde, Jules. *Le Livre rouge de la justice rurale*. Geneva: V. Blanchard, 1871.

Guillaume, James. *L'Internationale: documents et souvenirs (1864–1878)*. 2 vols. Paris: Société Nouvelle de Librairie et d'Edition, 1905.

Héricourt, Jenny P. d'. *La Femme affranchie*. Brussels: F. van Meenen, 1860.

L'Intransigeant. April 1884.

Journal officiel. Paris, March–May 1871.

Lefrançais, Gustave. *Souvenirs d'un révolutionnaire*. Brussels, 1902.

Leighton, John. *Paris under the Commune.* London: Bradbury Evans, 1871.

Léo, André. *Aline-Ali.* Paris: L'Opinion nationale, 1868.

———. *The American Colony in Paris in 1867.* Translator unknown. Boston: A. K. Loring, 1868.

———. *La Commune de Malenpis: conte.* Paris: Librarie de la Bibliothèque Democratique, 1874.

———. *Communisme et propriété.* Paris: D. Jouaust, 1868.

———. *Les Deux Filles de M. Plichon.* Paris: Achille Faure, 1865.

———. *Un Divorce.* Paris: bureaux de Siècle, 1862.

———. *La Femme et les mœurs: liberté ou monarchie.* Paris: Librarie Internationale, 1866.

———. *La Guerre sociale.* Neuchâtel: G.Guillaume fils, 1871.

———. *L'Idéal au village.* Paris: Hachette, 1867.

———. *Jacques Galéron.* Paris: A. Faure, 1866, 2nd edition.

———. *Un Mariage scandaleux.* Paris: Hachette, 1862.

———. *Observations d'une mère de famille.* Paris: Achille Faure, 1865.

———. *Une Vieille Fille.* Brussels: Alphonse Lebègue, 1851.

Lettres de Communards et de militants de la 1re Internationale à Marx, Engels et autres dans les journées de la Commune de Paris en 1871. Edited by Jules Rocher. Paris: Bureau d'Editions, 1934.

Levy, Darline Gay, Harriet Branson Applewhite, and Mary Durham Johnson, ed. and trans. *Women in Revolutionary Paris 1789–1795.* Urbana: University of Illinois Press, 1979.

Le Livre noir de la Commune de Paris: l'International dévoilée. Brussels: Office de Publicité, 1871.

Lissagaray, Prosper O. *Histoire de la Commune de 1871.* Brussels: Henri Kistemaeckers, 1876.

L'Opinion nationale. Paris, July–September 1868; March–May, 1871.

Lyon-Republicain. Lyon, May 1880–May, 1881.

Malon, Benoît. *La Troisième défaite du prolétariat français.* Neuchâtel: G. Guillaume fils, 1871.

Marforio [pseud.]. *Les Echarpes rouges.* Paris: Librairie Centrale des Lettres, des Sciences et des Arts, 1872.

Marx, Karl, and Friedrich Engels. *On the Paris Commune.* Moscow: Progress Publishers, 1971.

———. *Writings on the Paris Commune.* Edited by Hal Draper. New York: Monthly Review Press, 1971

Marx, Karl, and V. I. Lenin. *Civil War in France: The Paris Commune.* New York: International Publishers, 1940.

Michel, Louise. *La Commune.* 3rd ed. Paris: P. V. Stock, 1898.

———. *Mémoires.* Arles: Editions Sulliver, 1998.

———. *The Red Virgin: Memoirs of Louise Michel.* 1886. Translated and edited by Bullitt Lowry and Elizabeth Ellington Gunter. University: University of Alabama Press, 1981.

Mill, John Stuart. *On Liberty.* Introduction by Gertrude Himmelfarb. 1859. Reprint, Middlesex: Penguin Books, 1985.

———. *The Subjection of Women.* 1869. Reprint, Cambridge, Mass.: MIT Press, 1977.

Milliet, Jean Paul. *Une famille de républicains Fouriériste, Les Milliet.* 2 vols. Paris: Chez l'Auteur, 1916.

Mink, Paule. "La Liberté: condition du socialisme." 1869. In *Paule Minck: communarde et féministe 1839–1901*, edited by Alain Dalotel. Paris: Syros, 1968.

———. "Le Mariage et le divorce (séance du 3 novembre 1868)." In *Paule Minck: communarde et féministe 1839–1901*, edited by Alain Dalotel. Paris: Syros, 1968.

———. "Les Mouches et les araignées." 1869. In *Paule Minck: communarde et féministe 1839–1901*, edited by Alain Dalotel. Paris: Syros, 1968.

———. "Ni Dieu, ni maître." 1881. In *Paule Minck: communarde et féministe 1839–1901*, edited by Alain Dalotel. Paris: Syros, 1968.

———. "Le Travail des femmes." 1868. In *Paule Minck: communarde et féministe 1839–1901*, edited by Alain Dalotel. Paris: Syros, 1968.

Molinari, M. G. *Les Clubs rouges pendant le siége de Paris.* Paris: Garnier Frères, 1871.

Murailles politiques français. 2 vols. Paris: L. Le Chevalier, 1874.

Néron, Marie Louise. "Les Morts d'hier." *La Fronde*, April 29, 1901.

Paris libre. Paris, March–May 1871.

Paris under Siege: A Journal of the Events of 1870–1871. Translated and edited by Joanna Richardson. London: The Folio Society, 1982.

Paule Minck: communarde et féministe 1839–1901. Edited by Alain Dalotel. Paris: Editions Syros, 1968.

Le Père Duchêne. Paris, March–May 1871.

La Petite presse. Paris, September 1870.

Le Petit Provençal. July 1881.

La Petite République. Paris, March 1895.

Procès-Verbaux de la Commune de 1871. 2 vols. Edited by Georges Bourgin and Gabriel Henriot. Paris: Imprimerie A. Lahure, 1945.

Le Progrès, Lyon, July 20 and September 4, 1868. In Claire Auzias and Annik Houel, *La Grève des ovalistes: Lyon, juin–juillet 1869.* Paris: Payot, 1982.

Proudhon, Pierre-Joseph. *Œuvres complètes de P.-J. Proudhon.* Edited by Célestin Bouglé and Henri Moysset. Paris: M. Rivière, 1923.

———. *Qu'est-ce que la propriété?* 1840. Reprint, Paris: Garnier Flammarion, 1966.

Le Rappel. Paris, January 1869.

La République des travailleurs. Paris, 1871.

Le Réveil du peuple. Paris, March–May 1871.

Revue de France. Paris, 1871.

Ritchie, Charlotte. *A Memoir.* London: Spottiswoode & Co., 1879.

Simon, Jules. *L'Ouvrière.* Paris: Librarie Hachette, 1871.

La Sociale. Paris, March–May 1871.

Tataret, Eugene, ed. *Commission ouvrière de 1867: Recueil des procès-verbaux.* Paris: Imprimerie Augros, 1868.

Tristan, Flora. "Promenades dans Londres." In *Flora Tristan (1803–1844).* Edited by Stéphane Michaud. Paris: Les Editions Ouvrières, 1984.

Le Vengeur. Paris, April 1871.

Voilquin, Suzanne. *Souvenirs d'une fille du peuple, ou La Saint-Simonienne en Egypte.* Introduction by Lydia Elhadad. Paris: François Maspero, 1978.

La Voix des femmes. Paris, 1848.

Wollstonecraft, Mary. *Vindication of the Rights of Woman.* 1792. Reprint, New York: Penguin Books, 1986.

Zola, Emile. *Nana.* Translated by George Holden. London: Penguin Books, 1972.

SECONDARY SOURCES

Accampo, Elinor. "Gender, Social Policy and the Formation of the Third Republic: An Introduction." In *Gender and the Politics of Social Reform in France, 1870–1914,* edited by Elinor Accampo, Rachel Fuchs, and Mary Lynn Stewart. Baltimore: Johns Hopkins University Press, 1995.

———, Rachel Fuchs, and Mary Lynn Stewart, eds. *Gender and the Politics of Social Reform in France, 1870–1914.* Baltimore: Johns Hopkins University Press, 1995.

Agulhon, Maurice. *Marianne into Battle.* Translated by Janet Lloyd. Cambridge: Cambridge University Press, 1981.

———. *The Republican Experiment, 1848–1852.* New York: Cambridge University Press, 1983.

Albistur, Maïté, and Armogathe, Daniel. *Histoire du feminisme français, du moyen âge à nos jours.* Paris: Editions des Femmes, 1977.

Aminzade, Ronald. *Ballots and Barricades: Class Formation and Republican Politics in France, 1830–1871.* Princeton, N.J.: Princeton University Press, 1993.

Anderson, Benedict. *Imagined Communities: Reflections on the Origin and Spread of Nationalism.* London: Verso, 1991.

Arnould, Arthur. *Histoire populaire et parlementaire de la Commune de Paris.* Lyon: Editions Jacques-Marie Laffont et Associès, 1981.

Aron, Jean Paul, ed. *Misérable et glorieuse, la femme du XIXe siècle.* Paris: Fayard, 1980.

l'Association André Léo. *André Léo: une journaliste de la Commune.* Paris: Editions Lérot, 1987.

Auzias, Claire, and Annik Houel. *La Grève des ovalistes: Lyon, juin-juillet 1869.* Paris: Payot, 1982.

Barrett, Michelle, and Mary McIntosh. "The 'Family Wage': Some Problems for Socialists and Feminists." *Capital and Class* 11 (Summer 1980).

Barry, David. *Women and Political Insurgency: France in the Mid-Nineteenth Century.* New York: St. Martin's Press, 1996.

Beecher, Jonathan. *Charles Fourier: the Visionary and His World.* Berkeley: University of California Press, 1986.

Bellet, Roger. "André Léo, écrivain-idéologue." *Romantisme: revue de dix-neuvième siècle* 77 (1992): 61–66.

Berenson, Edward. "A New Religion of the Left: Christianity and Social Radicalism in France, 1815–1848." In *The Transformation of Political Culture, 1789–1848,* vol. 3 of *The French Revolution and the Creation of Modern Political Culture,* edited by François Furet and Mona Ozouf. New York: Pergamon Press, 1989.

———. *Populist Religion and Left-Wing Politics in France, 1830–1852.* Berkeley: University of California Press, 1984.

———. *The Trial of Madame Caillaux.* Berkeley: University of California Press, 1992.

Berlanstein, Leonard. *The Working People of Paris, 1871–1914.* Baltimore: Johns Hopkins University Press, 1984.

Bernstein, Samuel. *The Beginnings of Marxian Socialism in France.* New York: Russell and Russell, 1965.

Bertocchi, Philip A. *Jules Simon: Republican Anticlericalism and Cultural Politics in France, 1848–1886.* Columbia: University of Missouri Press, 1978.

Bidelman, Patrick Kay. *Pariahs Stand Up! The Founding of the Liberal Feminist Movement in France, 1858–1889*. Westport, Conn.: Greenwood Press, 1982.

Boxer, Marilyn J. "'First Wave' Feminism in Nineteenth-Century France: Class, Family and Religion." *Women's Studies International Forum* 5, no. 6 (1982): 553.

———. "Socialism Faces Feminism in France: 1879–1913." Ph.D. dissertation, University of California, Riverside, 1975.

———. "Socialism Faces Feminism: The Failure of Synthesis in France, 1879–1914." In *Socialist Women: European Socialist Feminism in the Nineteenth and Early Twentieth Century*, edited by Marilyn Boxer and Jean H. Quataert. New York: Elsevier, 1978.

Boxer, Marilyn J., and Jean H. Quataert. "Women in Industrializing and Liberalizing Europe." In *Connecting Spheres: Women in the Western World, 1500 to the Present*, edited by Marilyn J. Boxer and Jean H. Quataert, 95–135. New York: Oxford University Press, 1987.

Braibant, Sylvie. *Elisabeth Dmitrieff: aristocrate et pétroleuse*. Paris: Belfond, 1993.

Brenner, Robert. "Agrarian Class Structure and Economic Development in Pre-Industrial Europe." In *The Brenner Debate: Agrarian Class Structure and Economic Development in Pre-Industrial Europe*, ed. T. H. Aston and C. H. E. Philpin, 10–78. Cambridge: Cambridge University Press, 1985.

Bricard, Isabelle. *Saintes ou pouliches: l'éducation des jeunes filles au XIXe siècle*. Paris: Albin Bichel, 1985.

Brown, Frederick. *Zola: A Life*. New York: Farrar Straus Giroux, 1995.

Brown, Irene Coltman. "Mary Wollstonecraft and the French Revolution or Feminism and the Rights of Men." In *Women, State and Revolution: Essays on Power and Gender in Europe since 1789*, edited by Siân Reynolds. Sussex: Wheatsheaf Books, 1986.

Bruhat, Jean, Jean Dautry, and Emile Tersen. *La Commune de 1871*. Paris: Editions Sociales, 1970.

Bullard, Alice. *Exile to Paradise: Savagery and Civilization in Paris and the South Pacific, 1790–1900*. Stanford: Stanford University Press, 2000.

Cahm, Eric. "French Socialist Theories of the Nation to 1889." In *Socialism and Nationalism in Contemporary Europe (1848–1945)*, vol. II, edited by Eric Cahm and Vladimir Claude Fisera. Nottingham: Spokesman, 1979.

Chartier, Roger. *The Cultural Origins of the French Revolution*. Translated by Lydia G. Cochrane. Durham, N.C.: Duke University Press, 1991

Christiansen, Rupert. *Paris Babylon: The Story of the Paris Commune*. New York: Viking, 1994.

Chuard, P., and G. Roux. *Exposition de 1867*. http://tecfa.unige.ch/~grob/1867/pres67.html. Accessed February 6, 2004.

Clayson, Hollis. *Painted Love: Prostitution in French Art of the Impressionist Era*. New Haven, Conn.: Yale University Press, 1991.

Coffin, Judith. *The Politics of Women's Work*. Princeton, N.J.: Princeton University Press, 1996.

———. "Social Science Meets Sweated Labor: Reinterpreting Women's Work in Late Nineteenth-Century France." *Journal of Modern History* 63 (June 1991): 230–70.

Cole, G. D. H. *Socialist Thought: The Forerunners, 1789–1850*. London: Macmillan, 1953.

Corbin, Alain. "Backstage." In *A History of Private Life: From the Fires of Revolution to the Great War*, vol. IV, 451–688. Edited by Michelle Perrot and translated by Arthur Goldhammer. Cambridge, Mass.: Harvard University Press, 1990.

———. "Intimate Relations." In *A History of Private Life: From the Fires of Revolution to the Great War,* vol. IV, 591. Edited by Michelle Perrot and translated by Arthur Goldhammer. Cambridge, Mass.: Harvard University Press, 1990.

———. "Le 'Sexe en deuil' et l'histoire des femmes au XIX siècle." In *Une Histoire des femmes est-elle possible?* Paris: Editions Rivages, 1984.

———. *Women For Hire: Prostitution and Sexuality in France after 1850.* Translated by Alan Sheridan. Cambridge, Mass.: Harvard University Press, 1990.

Cott, Nancy F. *The Bonds of Womanhood: "Woman's Sphere" in New England, 1780–1835.* New Haven, Conn.: Yale University Press, 1977.

Crafts, N. F. R. "Economic Growth in France and Britain, 1830–1910: A Review of the Evidence." *The Journal of Economic History* XLIV, no. 1 (March 1984): 49–67.

Cross, Máire, and Tim Gray. *The Feminism of Flora Tristan (1803–1844).* Paris: Les Editions Ouvrières, 1984.

Dalotel, Alain. "Benoît Malon, troisième fils d'André Léo." *Revue Socialiste,* 71–91.

———. "Les Femmes dans les clubs rouges, 1870–1871." In *Femmes dans la cité 1815–1871,* edited by Alain Corbin, Jacqueline Lalouette, and Michèle Riot-Sarcey. Paris: Creaphis, 1997.

———. *Paule Minck: communarde et féministe.* Paris: Syros, 1968.

———. "Socialism and Revolution." In *Voices of the People: The Social Life of "La Sociale" at the End of the Second Empire,* edited by Adrian Rifkin and Roger Thomas, translated by John Moore. New York: Routledge & Kegan Paul, 1988.

Dalotel, Alain, Alain Faure, and Jean-Claude Freiermuth. *Aux Origines de la Commune: le mouvement des réunions publiques à Paris 1868–1870.* Paris: François Maspero, 1980.

D'Eaubonne, Françoise. *Louise Michel la Canaque, 1873–1880.* Paris: Nouvelle Société des Editions ENCRE, 1985.

de Gaudemar, Martine. "Louise Michel, martyre? ou 'artiste revolutionnaire.'" In *Colloque Louise Michel.* Centre d'Etudes Féminines de l'Université de Provence. Aix-en-Provence: Université de Provence, 1982.

D'Emilio, John, and Estelle Freedman. *Intimate Matters: A History of Sexuality in America.* New York: Harper and Row, 1988.

DePauw, Linda Grant. *Battlecries and Lullabies: Women in War from Prehistory to the Present.* Norman: University of Oklahoma Press, 1998.

Desanti, Dominique. *Flora Tristan.* In *Rebel Daughters: Women and the French Revolution,* edited by Sara E. Melzer and Leslie W. Rabine. New York: Oxford University Press, 1992.

Descaves, Lucien. "Une amie de Varlin." *La Lanterne,* Paris, May 18, 1921.

Dommanget, Maurice. *L'Enseignement, l'enfance et la culture sous la Commune.* Paris: Editions-Librairie de l'Etoile, 1964.

Dubois, Jean. *Le Vocabulaire politique et social en France de 1869 à 1872.* Paris: Librairie Larousse, 1962.

Ducatel, Paul. *Histoire de la Commune et du siège de Paris, vue à travers l'imagerie populaire.* Paris: Jean Grassin, 1973.

Durand, Pierre. *Louise Michel: La Passion.* Paris: Messidor, 1987.

Edwards, Stewart. *The Paris Commune 1871.* London: Eyre and Spottiswood, 1971.

———, ed. *The Communards of Paris, 1871.* Ithaca, N.Y.: Cornell University Press, 1973.

Efremova, N., and N. Ivanov. *Russkaia Soratnitsa Marksa.* Moscow: Moskovskii Rabochii, 1982.

Eichner, Carolyn J. "'To Assure the Reign of Work and Justice': The *Union des femmes* and the Paris Commune of 1871." *Osterreichische Zeitschrift für Geschichtweissenschaften* 9, no. 4 (1998): 525–55.

———. "'Vive la Commune!' Feminism, Socialism, and Revolutionary Revival in the Aftermath of the 1871 Paris Commune." *Journal of Women's History* 15, no. 2 (Summer 2003): 68–98.

Ellis, Jack D. *The Physician-Legislators of France: Medicine and Politics in the Early Third Republic, 1870–1914.* Cambridge: Cambridge University Press, 1990.

Elwitt, Sanford. *The Making of the Third Republic: Class and Politics in France, 1868–1884.* Baton Rouge: Louisiana State University Press, 1975.

Engel, Barbara Alpern. *Mothers and Daughters: Women of the Intelligentsia in Nineteenth-Century Russia.* Cambridge: Cambridge University Press, 1983.

Euloge, George-André. *Histoire de la police et de la gendarmerie: des origines à 1940.* Paris: Plon, 1985.

Evans, Sara M. *Born for Liberty: A History of Women in America.* New York: Free Press Paperbacks, 1997.

Eyquem, Marie-Thérèse. "Les Femmes au service de la Commune." In *Voici l'aube; l'immortelle Commune de Paris.* Colloque de l'Institut Maurice Thorez (6–9 May 1971). Paris: Editions Sociales, 1972.

Faderman, Lillian. *Surpassing the Love of Men.* New York: Morrow, 1981.

Faure, Alain. "The Public Meeting Movement in Paris from 1868 to 1870." In *Voices of the People: The Social Life of "La Sociale" at the End of the Second Empire,* edited by Adrian Rifkin and Roger Thomas, translated by John Moore. New York: Routledge & Kegan Paul, 1988.

Fauré, Christine. *Democracy Without Women: Feminism and the Rise of Liberal Individualism in France.* Translated by Claudia Gorbman and John Berks. Bloomington: Indiana University Press, 1991.

Fleming, Marie. *The Anarchist Way to Socialism: Elisée Reclus and Nineteenth-Century European Anarchism.* London: Croom Helm, 1979.

Fowlie, Wallace. "Rimbaud and the Commune." In *Revolution and Reaction: The Paris Commune 1871,* edited by John Hicks and Robert Tucker. Boston: University of Massachusetts Press, 1973.

Frader, Laura Levine. "Bringing Political Economy Back In: Gender, Culture, Race, and Class in Labor History." *Social Science History* 22, no. 1 (1998): 7–18.

———. "Women in the Industrial Capitalist Economy." In *Becoming Visible: Women in European History,* 2nd ed., edited by Renate Bridenthal, Claudia Koonz, and Susan Stuard, 310–30. Boston: Houghton Mifflin, 1987.

———, and Sonya Rose, eds. *Gender and Class in Modern Europe.* Ithaca, N.Y.: Cornell University Press, 1996.

Fuchs, Rachel G. *Poor and Pregnant in Paris: Strategies for Survival in the Nineteenth Century.* New Brunswick, N.J.: Rutgers University Press, 1992.

———, and Leslie Moch Page. "Getting Along: Poor Women's Networks in Nineteenth Century Paris." *French Historical Studies* 18, no. 1 (Spring 1993): 34–49.

Gastaldello, Fernanda. *André Léo (1824–1900), femme écrivain au XIXe siècle.* Chauvigny, France: Association des publications Chauvinoises, 2001.

———. *André Léo: Quel Socialisme?* Unpublished dissertation, University of Padua. Italy, 1979.

————, ed. Preface to *André Léo, une journaliste de la Commune*. Paris: Editions du Lérot, 1987.

Gauthier, Xavière. *Je vous écris de ma nuit: correspondance générale de Louise Michel, 1850–1904*. Paris: Les Editions de Paris, 1999.

Genovese, Elizabeth Fox. "Moved by the Spirit." *The Washington Post*, 15 September 1996.

George, Margaret. "The 'World Historical Defeat' of the Républicaines-Révolutionnaires." *Science and Society* 40, no. 4 (Winter 1976–77): 410–37.

Gershoy, Leo. *The French Revolution, 1789–1799*. New York: Holt, Rinehart and Winston, 1932.

Gibson, Ralph. *A Social History of French Catholicism, 1789–1914*. New York: Routledge, 1989.

————. "Why Republicans and Catholics Couldn't Stand Each Other in the Nineteenth Century." In *Religion, Society and Politics in France since 1789*, edited by Frank Tallett and Nicholas Atkin. London: The Hambleton Press, 1991.

Girardet, Raoul. *Le Nationalisme français 1871–1914*. Paris: Armand Colin, 1966.

Gosset, Hélène. "Les Polonais dans la Commune de Paris." *Europe* 64–65 (April–May 1951): 156.

Gould, Roger V. "Multiple Networks and Mobilization in the Paris Commune, 1871." *American Sociological Review* 56 (December 1991): 716–29.

Grant, Richard B. "Edmond de Goncourt and the Paris Commune." In *Revolution and Reaction: The Paris Commune 1871*, edited by John Hicks and Robert Tucker. Boston: University of Massachusetts Press, 1973.

Guilbert, Madeleine. *Les Fonctions de femmes dans l'industrie*. Paris: Mouton & Co., 1965.

————, and Viviane Isambert-Jamati. *Travail féminin et travail à domicile de la confection féminin dans la région parisienne*. Paris: Centre Nationale de la Recherche Scientifique, 1956.

Guillemin, Henri. *Nationalistes et "nationaux" (1870–1940)*. Paris: Gallimard, 1974.

Gullickson, Gay. "La Pétroleuse: Representing Revolution." *Feminist Studies* 17, no. 2 (Summer 1991): 241–65.

————. *Unruly Women of Paris*. Ithaca, N.Y.: Cornell University Press, 1996.

Hall, Catherine. "The Sweet Delights of Home." In *A History of Private Life: From the Fires of Revolution to the Great War*, vol. IV, 47–93. Edited by Michelle Perrot and translated by Arthur Goldhammer. Cambridge, Mass.: Harvard University Press, 1990.

Harrington, Michael. "The Misfortune of 'Great Memories." *Dissent* 18, no. 5 (1971): 472–77.

Harris, Ruth. *Murders and Madness: Medicine, Law and Society in the Fin de Siècle*. Oxford: Clarendon Press, 1989.

Harsin, Jill. *Policing Prostitution in Nineteenth Century France*. Princeton, N.J.: Princeton University Press, 1985.

Hause, Steven. *Women's Suffrage and Social Politics in French Third Republic*. Princeton, N.J.: Princeton University Press, 1984.

Himmelfarb, Gertrude. "Introduction." In John Stuart Mill, *On Liberty*. 1859. Reprint, Middlesex: Penguin Books, 1985.

Hobsbawm, Eric J. *Nations and Nationalism since 1780: Programme, Myth, Reality*. Cambridge: Cambridge University Press, 1990.

Horne, Allistair. *The Terrible Year: The Paris Commune, 1871.* New York: The Viking Press, 1971.

Hunt, Lynn. *Politics, Culture, and Class in the French Revolution.* Berkeley: University of California Press, 1984.

Hunt, Persis. "Feminism and Anti-Clericalism under the Commune." *Massachusetts Review* 12 (Summer 1971): 418–31.

Hutton, Patrick H. *The Cult of Revolutionary Tradition: The Blanquists in French Politics, 1864–1893.* Berkeley: University of California Press, 1981.

Jacquemet, Gérard. *Belleville au XIXe siècle: du faubourg à la ville.* Paris: Editions de l'Ecole des Hautes Etudes en Sciences Sociales, 1984.

Jagger, Alison. *Feminist Politics and Human Nature.* Sussex: The Harvester Press, 1983.

Jellinek, Frank. *The Paris Commune of 1871.* 1937. Reprint, New York: Grosset and Dunlap, 1965.

Jenkins, Brian. *Nationalism in France: Class and Nation since 1789.* London: Routledge, 1990.

Johnson, Christopher. *Utopian Communism in France: Cabet and the Icarians, 1839–1851.* Ithaca, N.Y.: Cornell University Press, 1974.

Johnson, Martin Phillip. "Citizenship and Gender: The Légion des fédérées in the Paris Commune of 1871." *French History* 8, no. 3 (September 1994): 276–95.

———. "Memory and the Cult of Revolution in the 1871 Paris Commune." *Journal of Women's History* 9, no. 1 (Spring 1997): 39–57.

———. *The Paradise of Association: Political Culture and Popular Organizations in the Paris Commune of 1871.* Ann Arbor: University of Michigan Press, 1996.

Jones, Kathleen, and Françoise Vergès. "'Aux Citoyennes!' Women, Politics, and the Paris Commune of 1871." *History of European Ideas* 13, no. 6 (1991): 711–32.

———. "Women of the Paris Commune." *Women's Studies International Forum* 14, no. 5 (1991): 491–503.

Joulin, D. J. *Les Caravances d'un chirurgien d'ambulances.* E. Dentu, 1871, 86, quoted in Bertrand Taithe, *Defeated Flesh: Welfare, Warfare and the Making of Modern France.* Manchester: Manchester University Press, 1999.

Judt, Tony. *Marxism and the French Left: Studies in Labour and Politics in France, 1830–1981.* Oxford: Clarendon Press, 1986.

Kemp, Sandra, and Judith Squires, eds. "Introduction." In *Feminisms.* New York: Oxford University Press, 1997.

Kerbaul, Eugène. *Nathalie Lemel: une Bretonne révolutionnaire et féministe.* Paris: Imprimerie Ader, 1997.

Kerber, Linda. *Women of the Republic: Intellect and Ideology in Revolutionary America.* New York: W. W. Norton, 1986.

Kessler-Harris, Alice. *Out to Work: A History of Wage-Earning Women in the United States.* Oxford: Oxford University Press, 1982.

———. *A Woman's Wage: Historical Meanings and Social Consequences.* Lexington: University Press of Kentucky, 1990.

Klejman, Laurence, and Florence Rochefort. *L'Egalité en marche: le féminisme sous la Troisième République.* Paris: Editions des femmes, 1989.

Knizhnik-Vetrov, Ivan Sergeevich. *Russkie deiatel'nitsy Pervogo Internatsionala i Parizhskoi Kommuny.* Moscow and Leningrad: Izdatel'stvo Nauka, 1964.

Kulstein, David. *Napoleon III and the Working Class: A Study of Government Propaganda Under the Second Empire.* Sacramento: California State Colleges, 1969.

Landes, Joan. "Representing the Body Politic: The Paradox of Gender in the Graphic Politics of the French Revolution." In *Rebel Daughters: Women and the French Revolution,* edited by Sara E. Melzer and Leslie W. Rabine. New York: Oxford University Press, 1992.

———. *Woman and the Public Sphere in the Age of the French Revolution.* Ithaca, N.Y.: Cornell University Press, 1988.

Lefebvre-Teillard, Anne. *Le Nom: droit et histoire.* Paris: Presses Universitaires de France, 1990.

Lejeune, Paule. *Louise Michel l'indomptable.* Paris: Editions des Femmes, 1978.

Le Livre des expositions universelles 1851–1989. Paris: Union Central des Arts Décoratifs, 1983.

Le Quillec, Robert. *La Commune de Paris bibliographie critique, 1871–1997.* Paris: La Boutique de l'Histoire, 1997.

Levy, Darline Gay, and Harriet B. Applewhite. "Women and Militant Citizenship in Revolutionary Paris." In *Rebel Daughters: Women and the French Revolution,* edited by Sara E. Melzer and Leslie W. Rabine, 79–101. New York: Oxford University Press, 1992.

Lewis, Jane. "The Debate on Sex and Class." *New Left Review* 149 (January–February 1985).

Liu, Tessie P. "What Price a Weaver's Dignity? Gender Inequality and the Survival of Home-Based Production in Industrial France." In *Gender and Class in Modern Europe,* edited by Laura Frader and Sonya O. Rose. Ithaca, N.Y.: Cornell University Press, 1996.

Magraw, Roger. *The Age of Artisan Revolutions, 1815–1871.* Oxford: Blackwell, 1992.

———. *France 1815–1914: The Bourgeois Century.* New York: Oxford University Press, 1986.

———. *A History of the French Working Class.* Vol. I: *The Age of Artisan Revolution, 1815–1871.* Oxford: Blackwell, 1992.

Maitron, Jean, ed. *Dictionnaire biographique du mouvement ouvrier français.* 10 vols. Paris: Les Editions Ouvrières, 1968.

Margadant, Jo Burr, ed. *The New Biography: Performing Femininity in Nineteenth-Century France.* Berkeley: University of California Press, 2000.

Matsuda, Matt K. *The Memory of the Modern.* New York: Oxford University Press, 1996.

Mayeur, Jean Marie, and Madeline Reberioux. *The Third Republic from Its Origins to the Great War, 1871–1914.* Cambridge: Cambridge University Press, 1984.

McBride, Theresa. "Divorce and the Republican Family." In *Gender and the Politics of Social Reform France 1870–1914,* edited by Elinor A. Accampo, Rachel G. Fuchs, and Mary Lynn Stewart. Baltimore: Johns Hopkins University Press, 1995.

McClellan, Woodford. *Revolutionary Exiles: The Russians in the First International and the Paris Commune.* London: Frank Cass, 1979.

McDermid, Jane, and Anna Hillyar. *Midwives of the Revolution: Female Bolsheviks and Women Workers in 1917.* Athens: Ohio University Press, 1999.

McLaren, Angus. *Sexuality and Social Order: The Debate over the Fertility of Women and Workers in France, 1770–1920.* New York: Holmes and Meier, 1983.

McManners, John. *Church and State in France, 1878–1914.* New York: Harper & Row, 1972.

McMillan, James F. *France and Women 1789–1914: Gender, Society and Politics.* New York: Routledge, 2000.

————. *Housewife or Harlot: The Place of Women in French Society, 1870–1940*. New York: St. Martin's Press, 1981.

————. *Napoleon III*. New York: Longman, 1991.

————. "Religion and Gender in Modern France: Some Reflections." In *Religion, Society and Politics in France since 1789*, edited by Frank Tallett and Nicholas Atkin. London: The Hambleton Press, 1991.

Meijer, J. M. *Knowledge and Revolution: The Russian Colony in Zurich (1870–1873)*. Assen, Netherlands: Internatonaal Instituut Voor Sociale Geschiedenes, 1955.

Melzer, Sara E., and Leslie W. Rabine, eds. *Rebel Daughters: Women and the French Revolution*. New York: Oxford University Press, 1992

Mills, Hazel. "Negotiating the Divide: Women, Philanthropy and the 'Public Sphere' in Nineteenth-Century France." In *Religion, Society and Politics in France since 1789*, edited by Frank Tallett and Nicholas Atkin. London: The Hambleton Press, 1991.

Moon, Joan. "Feminism and Socialism: The Utopian Synthesis of Flora Tristan." In *Socialist Women: European Socialist Feminism in the Nineteenth and Early Twentieth Centuries*, edited by Marilyn J. Boxer and Jean H. Quataert, 19–50. New York: Elsevier, 1978.

Moses, Claire Goldberg. "Debating the Present Writing the Past: 'Feminism' in French History and Historiography." *Radical History Review* 52 (1992): 78–94.

————. "'Equality' and 'Difference' in Historical Perspective: A Comparative Examination of the Feminisms of French Revolutionaries and Utopian Socialists." In *Rebel Daughters: Women and the French Revolution*, edited by Sara E. Melzer and Leslie W. Rabine. New York: Oxford University Press, 1992.

————. *French Feminism in the Nineteenth Century*. Albany: State University of New York Press, 1984.

————, and Leslie Rabine. *Feminism, Socialism, and French Romanticism*. Bloomington: Indiana University Press, 1993.

Moss, Bernard. *The Origins of the French Labor Movement 1830–1914: The Socialism of Skilled Workers*. Berkeley: University of California Press, 1976.

Mullaney, Marie Marmo. *Revolutionary Women: Gender and the Socialist Revolutionary Role*. New York: Praeger, 1983.

————. "Sexual Politics in the Career and Legend of Louise Michel." *Signs* 15, no. 2 (Winter 1990): 300–22.

Musée d'art et d'histoire de Saint-Denis. *La Commune de Paris: 1871–1971, Exposition de Centenaire*. Paris: Corbière & Jugain, 1971.

Nardinelli, Clark. "Productivity in Nineteenth-Century France and Britain: A Note on the Comparisons." *The Journal of European Economic History* 17, no. 2 (Fall 1988): 427–34.

Nepomniachtchi, A. "Elisabeth Dmitrieva sur les barricades de la Commune." *Etudes Sovietiques* 204 (March 1965): 65–67.

Nord, Philip G. "The Party of Conciliation and of the Paris Commune." *French Historical Studies* 15, no. 1 (Spring 1987): 8.

Nye, Robert. *Masculinity and Male Codes of Honor in Modern France*. Berkeley: University of California Press, 1993.

Offen, Karen. "Defining Feminism: A Comparative Historical Approach." *Signs: Journal of Women in Culture and Society* 14, no. 1 (1988): 119–57.

————. *European Feminisms, 1700–1950*. Stanford, Calif.: Stanford University Press, 2000.

———. "Feminism, Antifeminism, and National Family Politics in Early Third Republic France." In *Connecting Spheres: Women in the Western World, 1500 to the Present,* edited by Marilyn J. Boxer and Jean H. Quataert. New York: Oxford University Press, 1987.

———. "What! Such Things Have Happened and No Women Were Taught about Them": A Nineteenth-Century French Woman's View of the Importance of Women's History." *Journal of Women's History* 9, no. 2 (Summer 1997): 147–53.

———. "Women's History as French History." *Journal of Women's History* 8, no. 1 (Spring 1996): 147–54.

———, and Susan Groag Bell, eds. *Women, the Family, and Freedom: The Debate in Documents.* Vols. I and II. Stanford, Calif.: Stanford University Press, 1983.

Pateman, Carole. *The Sexual Contract.* Stanford, Calif.: Stanford University Press, 1988.

———. "Equality, Difference, Subordination: The Politics of Motherhood and Women's Citizenship." In *Beyond Equality and Difference: Citizenship, Feminist Politics, and Female Subjectivity,* edited by Gisela Bock and Susan James. New York: Routledge, 1992.

Pérennès, Roger. *Déportés et forçats de la Commune: de Belleville à Nouméa.* Nantes: Ouest Editions, Université Inter-Ages de Nantes, 1991.

Perrot, Michelle. "The Family Triumphant." In *A History of Private Life: From the Fires of Revolution to the Great War,* vol. IV, 99–166. Edited by Michelle Perrot. Translated by Arthur Goldhammer. Cambridge, Mass.: The Belknap Press of Harvard University Press, 1990.

———. "'Les Guesdistes' controverse sur l'introduction du Marxisme en France." *Annales E.S.C.* 22, no. 3 (May–June 1967): 701–10.

———. "Roles and Characters." In *A History of Private Life: From the Fires of Revolution to the Great War,* vol. IV, 167–260. Edited by Michelle Perrot. Translated by Arthur Goldhammer. Cambridge, Mass.: The Belknap Press of Harvard University Press, 1990.

———. "Women, Power and History: the Case of Nineteenth-Century France." In *Women, State and Revolution: Essays on Power and Gender in Europe since 1789,* edited by Siân Reynolds. Sussex: Wheatsheaf Books, 1986.

———. *Workers on Strike: France, 1871–1890.* New Haven, Conn.: Yale University Press, 1987.

Pick, Daniel. *Faces of Degeneration: A European Disorder c. 1848–c. 1918.* Cambridge: Cambridge University Press, 1989.

Pilbeam, Pamela. *French Socialists Before Marx: Workers, Women, and the Social Question in France.* Montreal: McGill-Queens University Press, 2000.

———. *Republicanism in Nineteenth Century France, 1814–1871.* New York: St. Martin's Press, 1995.

Pinkney, David. *Napoleon III and the Rebuilding of Paris.* Princeton, N.J.: Princeton University Press, 1958.

Planche, Fernand. *La Vie ardente et intrépide de Louise Michel.* Paris: Chez l'Auteur, 1946.

Planté, Christine. "Le Récit impossible: Malvina Blanchecotte, Tablettes d'une femme pendant la Commune." In *Ecrire la Commune: témoignages, récots et romans (1871–1931),* edited by Roger Bellet and Philippe Régnier. Tusson, Charente: Du Lérot, 1994.

Price, R. D. "Ideology and Motivation in the Paris Commune of 1871." *Historical Journal* 15 (January 1972): 75–86.

Price, Roger. *An Economic History of Modern France.* New York: St. Martin's Press, 1975.

Rabaut, Jean. *Histoire des féminismes français.* Paris: Editions Stock, 1978.

Rancière, Jacques, and Patrick Vauday. "Going to the Expo: The Worker, His Wife and Machines." In *Voices of the People: The Social Life of "La Sociale" at the End of the Second Empire,* edited by Adrian Rifkin and Roger Thomas, translated by John Moore. New York: Routledge & Kegan Paul, 1988.

Redmond, René. *L'Anticléricalism en France de 1815 à nos jours.* Paris: Fayard, 1999.

Rihs, Charles. *La Commune de Paris: sa structure et ses doctrines (1871).* Geneva: Librairie E. Droz, 1955.

Riot-Sarcey, Michèle. "Lecture de la révolution par des femmes de 1848." In *Le XIXe siècle et la Révolution française.* Paris: Editions Créaphis, 1992.

Roberts, J. M. "La Mémoire des vaincus: l'example de Victorine B., Souvenirs d'une morte vivante." In *Ecrire la Commune: témoignages, récits et romans (1871–1931),* edited by Roger Bellet and Philippe Régnier. Tusson, Charente: Du Lérot, 1994.

———. "The Paris Commune from the Right." *The English Historical Review,* Supplement 6. London: Longman, 1973.

Rocher, Jules, ed. *Lettres de Communards et de militants de la 1re Internationale à Marx, Engels et autres dans les journées de la Commune de Paris en 1871.* Paris: Bureau D'Editions, 1934.

Rosa, Annette. *Citoyennes: Les Femmes et la révolution française.* Paris: Messidor, 1988.

Rose, R. B. "The Paris Commune: The Last Episode of the French Revolution or the First Dictatorship of the Proletariat?" In *Paradigm for Revolution? The Paris Commune 1871–1971,* edited by Eugene Kamenka. Canberra: Australian National University Press, 1972.

Rougerie, Jacques. "1871: la Commune de Paris." In *Encyclopédie politique et historique des femmes,* edited by Christine Faure. Paris: Presses Universitaires de France, 1997.

———. "L'A.I.T. et le mouvement ouvrier à Paris pendant les événements de 1870–1871." In *1871, Jalons pour une histoire de la Commune de Paris,* edited by Jacques Rougerie. Paris: Presses Universitaires de France, 1973.

———. "Composition d'une population insurgée: l'example de la Commune." *Le Mouvement Social* (July–September 1964): 31–47.

———. *Paris libre, 1871.* Paris: Editions du Seuil, 1971.

———, ed. *1871, Jalons pour une histoire de la Commune de Paris.* Paris: Presses Universitaires de France, 1973.

———, ed. *Procès des Communards.* Paris: René Julliard, 1964.

Rowbotham, Sheila. *Women, Resistance, and Revolution.* New York: Vintage Books, 1972.

Sargent, Lydia, ed. *The Unhappy Marriage of Marxism and Feminism: A Debate of Class and Patriarchy.* London: Pluto Press, 1981.

Schulkind, Eugene. "The Activity of Popular Organizations During the Paris Commune of 1871." *French Historical Studies* (Fall 1960): 394–415.

———. *The Paris Commune of 1871.* London: The Historical Association, 1971.

———. "The Paris Commune of 1871: Reality or Myth?" University of Sussex lecture series, "Great Centenaries," May 20, 1971.

———. "Le Rôle des femmes dans la Commune de 1848." *Revue des revolutions contemporaines XLII* 185 (February 1950).

———. "Socialist Women during the 1871 Paris Commune." *Past and Present* 106 (February 1985): 124–63.

————, ed. *The Paris Commune of 1871: A View from the Left.* New York: Grove Press, 1974.

————, ed. *The Paris Commune 1871: Inventory of the Collection in the University of Sussex Library.* Brighton: University of Sussex Library, 1975.

Scott, Joan Wallach. *Gender and the Politics of History.* New York: Columbia University Press, 1989.

————. *Only Paradoxes to Offer: French Feminists and the Rights of Man.* Cambridge, Mass.: Harvard University Press, 1996.

Serman, William. *La Commune de Paris.* Paris: Fayard, 1986.

Sewell, William H., Jr. "Artisans, Factory Workers, and the Formation of the French Working Class, 1789–1848." In *Working Class Formation: Nineteenth-Century Patterns in Western Europe and the United States,* edited by Ira Katznelson and Aristide R. Zolberg. Princeton, N.J.: Princeton University Press, 1986.

Shafer, David. "Plus que des ambulancières: Women in Articulation and Defence of the Ideals during the Paris Commune (1871)." *French History* 7, no. 1 (1993): 85–101.

Sizaire, Anne. *Louise Michel: l'absolu de la générosité.* Paris: Desclée de Brouwer, 1995.

Singer-Lecocq, Yvonne. *Rouge Elisabeth.* Paris: Editions Stock, 1977.

Soboul, Albert. *The Sans-Culottes: The Popular Movement and Revolutionary Government 1793–1794.* Translated by Helene Zahler. Princeton, N.J.: Princeton University Press, 1980.

————. *A Short History of the French Revolution, 1789–1799.* Translated by Geoffrey Symcox. Berkeley: University of California Press, 1977.

————. *Understanding the French Revolution.* New York: International Publishers, 1988.

Soprani, Anne. *La Révolution et les femmes de 1789 à 1796.* Paris: MA Editions, 1988.

Soukholmine, Vassili. "Deux femmes russes combattantes de la Commune." *Cahiers Internationaux* XVI (May 1950): 53–62.

Southerland, D. M. G. *France 1789–1815: Revolution and Counterrevolution.* New York: Oxford University Press, 1986.

Sowerwine, Charles. *France since 1879: Culture, Politics and Society.* New York: Palgrave, 2001.

———— *Sisters or Citizens? Women and Socialism in France since 1876.* Cambridge: Cambridge University Press, 1982.

————. "The Socialist Women's Movement from 1850 to 1940." In *Becoming Visible: Women in European History,* 2nd ed., edited by Renate Bridenthal, Claudia Koonz, and Susan Stuard. Boston: Houghton Mifflin, 1987.

Stansell, Christine. *City of Women: Sex and Class in New York, 1789–1860.* New York: Knopf, 1986.

Stites, Richard. *The Women's Liberation Movement in Russia: Feminism, Nihilism, and Bolshevism, 1860–1930.* Princeton, N.J.: Princeton University Press, 1978.

Stone, Judith F. "Anticlericals and Bonne Soeurs: The Rhetoric of the 1901 Law of Associations." *French Historical Studies* 23, no. 1 (Winter 2000): 103–128.

————. "The Republican Brotherhood: Gender and Ideology." In *Gender and Politics of Social Reform in France, 1870–1914.* Baltimore: Johns Hopkins University Press, 1995.

————. *Sons of Revolution: Radical Democrats in France, 1862–1914.* Baton Rouge: Louisiana State University Press, 1996.

Stuart, Robert. "'Calm, with a Grave and Serious Temperament, Rather Male':

French Marxism, Gender and Feminism, 1882–1905." *International Review of Social History* 41 (1996): 57–82.

———. "Gendered Labour in the Ideological Discourse of French Marxism: The Parti Ouvrier Français, 1882–1905." *Gender and History* (1997): 107–29.

———. *Marxism At Work: Ideology, Class and French Socialism during the Third Republic.* Cambridge: Cambridge, 1992.

———. "Whores and Angels: Women and the Family in the Discourse of French Marxism 1882–1905." *European History Quarterly* 27, no. 3 (1997): 339–69.

Struminger, Laura. *Women and the Making of the Working Class: Lyon 1830–1870.* St. Alban's, Vt.: Eden Press, 1979.

Taithe, Bertrand. *Defeated Flesh: Welfare, Warfare and the Making of Modern France.* Manchester: Manchester University Press, 1999.

Talbot, Margaret. "An Emancipated Voice: Flora Tristan and Utopian Allegory." *Feminist Studies* 17, no. 2 (Summer 1991): 219–39.

Taylor, Barbara. *Eve and the New Jerusalem: Socialism and Feminism in the 19th Century.* New York: Pantheon, 1983.

Tcherednitchenko, P. "La Vie genereuse et mouvementée d'Elisa Tomanovskaia." *Etudes Sovietiques* LXXXVII (June 1955): 59–64.

Thibert, Marguerite. "Portraits des femmes de la Commune." In *Voici l'aube: l'immortelle Commune de Paris.* Colloque de l'Institut Maurice Thorez (May 6–9, 1971). Paris: Editions Sociales, 1972.

Thomas, Annie. *Louise Michel: une femme libertaire.* Paris: Les Lettres Libres, 1984.

Thomas, Edith. *Les Femmes de 1848.* Paris: Presses Universitaires de France, 1948.

———. *Louise Michel.* Montreal: Black Rose Books, 1990.

———. *Louise Michel, ou La Velléda de l'anarchie.* Paris: Gallimard, 1971.

———. *The Women Incendiaries.* Translated by James and Starr Atkinson. New York: George Braziller, 1966.

Tilly, Louise. "Paths of Proletarianization: Organization of Production, Sexual Division of Labor, and Women's Collective Action." *Signs: Journal of Women in Culture and Society* 7, no. 2 (1981): 400–17.

———. "Women and Work, Plus Gender." *Gender and History* 4, no. 1 (1992): 90–95.

———, and Joan W. Scott. *Women, Work, and Family.* New York: Holt, Reinhart, and Winston, 1978.

Tombs, Robert. "Harbingers or Entrepreneurs? A Workers' Cooperative during the Paris Commune." *The Historical Journal* 27, no. 4 (1984): 969–97.

———. "Warriors and Killers: Women and Violence during the Paris Commune, 1871." In *The Sphinx in the Tuilleries and Other Essays in Modern French History,* edited by Robert Aldrich and Martyn Lyons. Sydney: University of Sydney, 1999.

Travis, Karen. "Unveiling Virtue: The Unity of Virtuous Practice in Wollstonecraft's *A Vindication of the Rights of Woman.*" Unpublished paper, UCLA, 1994.

Trotsky, Leon. *Leon Trotsky on the Paris Commune.* New York: Pathfinder Press, 1970.

Truesdell, Matthew. *Spectacular Politics: Louis Napoleon Bonaparte and the Fête Impérial, 1849–1870.* New York: Oxford University Press, 1997.

Varias, Alexander. *Paris and the Anarchists: Aesthetes and Subversives during the Fin de Siècle.* New York: St. Martin's Press, 1996.

Vincent, Steven K. *Between Marxism and Anarchism: Benoît Malon and French Reformist Socialism.* Berkeley: University of California Press, 1992.

————. *Pierre-Joseph Proudhon and the Rise of French Republican Socialism*. New York: Oxford University Press, 1984.

Vuilleumier, Marc. "Les Proscrits da la Commune en Suisse (1871)." In *Revue Suisse d'Histoire* 12, no. 4 (1962), edited by Paul Kläui and Jean-Charles Biaudet: 498–537.

Waldman, Martin R. "The Revolutionary as Criminal in 19th Century France: A Study of the Communards and Deportées." *Science and Society* XXXVII, no. 1 (September 1973): 31–55.

Walkowitz, Judith. *Prostitution and Victorian Society: Women, Class and the State*. Cambridge: Cambridge University Pres, 1980.

Weeks, Jeffrey. *Sex, Politics and Society: The Regulation of Sexuality since 1800*. London: Longman, 1989.

Williams, Roger L. *The French Revolution of 1870–1871*. New York: W. W. Norton, 1969.

Wolfe, Robert. "The Parisian Club de la Revolution of the 18th Arrondissement 1870–1871." *Past and Present* (April 1968): 81–119.

Zeldin, Theodore. "The Conflict of Moralities: Confession, Sin and Pleasure in the Nineteenth Century." In *Conflicts in French Society: Anticlericalism, Education, and Morals in the Nineteenth Century*, edited by Theodore Zeldin. London: George Allen and Unwin, 1970.

————. *The Political System of Napoleon III*. New York: W.W. Norton, 1971.

————. *France: 1848–1945*. Vol. II: *Intellect, Taste and Anxiety*. Oxford: Oxford University Press, 1977.

Zola, Emile. *Nana*. New York: Harper, 1957.

Zylberberg-Hocquard, Marie-Helene. *Féminisme et syndicalisme en France*. Paris: Editions anthropos, 1978.

INDEX

Page numbers in italics refer to illustrations.

CAROLYN J. EICHNER is a historian and Associate Professor of Women's Studies at the University of South Florida.